THE
COMPLETE
POEMS
OF
C. DAY LEWIS

THE
COMPLETE
POEMS
OF
C. DAY LEWIS

SINCLAIR-STEVENSON

First published in Great Britain by
Sinclair-Stevenson Limited
7/8 Kendrick Mews
London SW7 3HG, England

British Library Cataloguing in Publication Data
A CIP catalogue record for this book is available from the British Library.
Hardback: ISBN: 1 85619 130 3
Paperback: ISBN: 1 85619 144 3

Photoset by Rowland Phototypesetting Limited
Printed and bound in Great Britain by
Biddles Ltd, Guildford and King's Lynn

DEDICATION

This collection is dedicated with love to our children, Tamasin and Daniel Day Lewis, whose achievements would have made their father proud if he had lived to see them.

ACKNOWLEDGEMENTS

My warmest thanks go to Christopher Sinclair-Stevenson for making this book possible, with his trust in me sight unseen, and to these friends: Freda Berkeley, 'the midwife'; Elizabeth Dove, who types the indecipherable with enthusiasm and grace; Iona Opie, Quentin Stevenson and Adolf Wood, who have given me their invaluable help.

Contents

ix

Introduction

I T IS TWENTY years since C. Day Lewis died. It is thirty-eight years since his *Collected Poems* were published to celebrate his fiftieth birthday in 1954, though there followed five more publications . . . In that collection he withheld the Juvenilia, and made cuts in *A Time to Dance* and *Noah and the Waters*. Christopher Sinclair-Stevenson and I have decided that the Complete Works must offer everything, so that the development of the poems from 1925 to 1972 can be seen at last.

I shall now call him Cecil, though at his insistence his Christian name, which he disliked, was never printed after 1927, except in ignorance.

In his preface to the *Collected Poems 1954* he wrote, after re-reading them:

> I have felt both surprise and regret: regret, that so much energy should so often have run to waste; surprise to hear a buried self speaking, now and then, with such urgency. Some poets can rewrite and improve their early work, years later. I wish I could do so; but the selves who wrote those poems are strangers to me, and I cannot resume their identities or go back into the world where they lived. There are certain themes, no doubt, linking these dead selves together. Perhaps these constant themes compose the personal tradition of a poet – his one continuity, defining and preserving, through every change of language, every change of heart, what is essential to him . . .

It might be helpful to remind today's readers of some of the facts comprehensively documented elsewhere. The 'Macspaunday'* poets who flowered in the 'thirties were friends, but never a group. They had shared the same privileged background, public school and Oxford – in Cecil's case through scholarships and exhibitions, as his father was a parson of no means. However, adolescent life in his father's Nottinghamshire mining parish also included tennis parties in 'the Dukeries' and he

---

* C. Day Lewis, W. H. Auden, Louis MacNeice, Stephen Spender.

became acutely aware of the contrast between the lowest and highest strata of society. In his poem *Sketches for a Portrait* (*Poems 1943–1947*) he

> looked for a lost ball
> In the laurels, they smirched with pit-grime . . .

He had seen his father sitting by the bedsides of miners coughing themselves to death. His outrage at social injustice stemmed from that time. Then, with the onset of fascism and the Spanish Civil War, came the urgent wish to prevent war. For the time being he turned to communism along with many other artists and intellectuals of this period.

The late Clifford Dyment, in his booklet *C. Day Lewis*, 1955,* thought that the poetic powers of the author of the so-called 'Political' poems could carry the reader over the rough places and sometimes didactic tone 'by the beauty and momentum of the verse itself'. Cecil was a man with music in his bones (he had a ravishing light tenor singing voice, and was one of the finest speakers of verse of his generation – accomplishments not universal among poets). Stanzas from these love poems of the 'Political' period show his lyricism.

> . . . Desire is a witch
> And runs against the clock.
> It can unstitch
> The decent hem
> Where space tacks on to time:
> It can unlock
> Pandora's privacies . . .
>
> *Transitional Poem*

> . . . With me, my lover makes
> The clock assert its chime:
> But when she goes, she takes
> The mainspring out of time . . .
>
> *Transitional Poem*

* Published by the British Council and the National Book League.

> Beauty's end is in sight,
> Terminus where all feather joys alight.
> Wings that flew lightly
> Fold and are iron. We see
> The thin end of mortality . . .
>
> *From Feathers to Iron*

> . . . Do not expect again a phoenix hour,
> The triple-towered sky, the dove complaining,
> Sudden the rain of gold and heart's first ease
> Tranced under trees by the eldritch light of sundown . . .
>
> *From Feathers to Iron*

Those early love lyrics nearly cost him his job at Cheltenham Junior School. In his autobiography *The Buried Day* he tells how the headmaster had seen *Transitional Poem* in the local bookshop and summoned Cecil to his study. H.M. was clearly deeply embarrassed, and asked C. if he thought he was fit to teach little boys, because the poems were . . . (he couldn't bring himself to say it) 'extremely . . . excessively . . . er . . . SEXUAL'. 'But they're love poems,' blurted out Cecil, 'addressed to my wife.'

As a schoolmaster, and later as a professor, Cecil insisted that one must respond to a poem directly, spontaneously, positively – 'to be able to enjoy before we can learn to discriminate'. He also said: 'Modern poetry is every poem, whether written last year or five centuries ago, that has meaning for us still.' The reader will find some themes prevailing throughout his work: hero-worship, fear, compassion, transience, very often the conflict of a divided heart and mind, and always the relentless compulsion to know himself.

Cecil was a modest man; I wish to make no extravagant claims on his behalf. He himself thought that only his sonnet sequence *O Dreams, O Destinations* (*Word Over All*) might, possibly, endure. At the end of his life, when asked to contribute to James Gibson's anthology *Let The Poet Choose*, he submitted the last of those nine sonnets, and *On Not Saying Everything* (*The Room*) which he wrote during a fruitful time at Harvard in 1964–5, when he held the Charles Eliot Norton Chair. This is

xiii

what he said: 'May I suggest . . . the sonnet because, though I wrote it 30 years ago, it still stands up and says something I feel to be truthful about the human condition: 'On not saying everything' because I believe so strongly in the doctrine of limitations it speaks for – that everything, a tree, a poem, a human relationship, lives and thrives by the limits imposed on it.'

Of course poets are not always their own best judges. However, in their solitude, they cannot realise how much and where they touch other people's lives. I am touched myself when friends, and often strangers, quote passages of Cecil's which move them and, moreover, sustain them. *Walking Away* (*The Gate*) usually brings many reactions whenever it is broadcast or read in public.

> . . . I have had worse partings, but none that so
> Gnaws at my mind still. Perhaps it is roughly
> Saying what God alone could perfectly show –
> How selfhood begins with a walking away,
> And love is proved in the letting go.

Anyone who has lost a child, or simply left one at the new school gate, can identify with the parting. *My Mother's Sister* (*The Room*) is a poignant poem about the beloved aunt who brought him up from the age of four when his mother died. In both these poems he avoids sentimentality – a real achievement. It is interesting that religious images appear often in Cecil's poems, even though he became a rather 'churchy' agnostic after the years of living in a parsonage. The title poem in *The Gate* was dedicated to Trekkie Parsons. One week-end in her house, he couldn't take his eyes off a picture she had painted. I could see it was saying something to him, and thanks to her generosity I bought it for him in instalments.

> . . . We expect nothing (the flower might add), we only
> Await: this pure awaiting –
> It is the kind of worship we are taught.

It was greatly encouraging to Cecil that Henry Moore, after reading a typescript of *The Expulsion* (*Posthumous Poems*), told him he had learned something new about the fresco by Masaccio which had inspired the poem. Only recently – I wish I could tell the author – that superb pianist and scholar Graham Johnson said to me that *Cornet Solo* (*Word Over All*) was 'the most evocative poem I know about the power of music in childhood's memory'.

> . . . Strange how those yearning airs could sweeten
> And still enlighten
> The hours when solitude gave me her breast.
> Strange they could tell a mere child how hearts may beat
> in
> The self-same tune for the once-possessed
> And the unpossessed . . .

Adverse academic criticism could not demolish these statements of faith by other artists.

Some of those who declared that CDL 'had no voice of his own' had not, perhaps, listened or looked carefully enough. This is what he said himself about influences: 'I myself have been technically influenced, and enabled to clarify my thoughts, by such diverse poets as Yeats, Wordsworth, Robert Frost, Virgil, Valéry, Auden and Hardy. They suggested to me ways of saying what I had to say. Any given poem thus influenced is not necessarily secondhand. I think it possible that a reader with a sensitive ear, a dispassionate point of view, and a thorough knowledge of the poetry of Hardy, say, would find as much difference as similarity between a poem of mine, influenced by him, and one of Hardy's own.'

In one case, until I pointed this out, a scholar actually failed to observes the initials under the titles of each pastiche in the *Florence: Works of Art* section of *An Italian Visit*. Earlier I wrote of hero-worship as a recurrent theme. I think it is one of the constituents of these pastiches. There are certainly many examples of this in music. Cecil matched the subjects of some of the Florentine pictures and sculpture he most loved, with poems in the style of poets he deeply admired: Yeats, Hardy, Robert Frost, W. H. Auden and Dylan Thomas. He wrote 'in the style of' and was admonished for being merely imitative . . .

At his best, he was a formidable craftsman. He was a story-teller in verse. This mastery of the narrative – a rare gift today – was shown first in *A Time to Dance*. Part of it is a gripping tale of a flight to Australia by two men in a decrepit aircraft after the First World War. Cecil had a tremendous reverence for brave men of action, and he had a passion for flying. The poem is an extraordinary feat of technique: long, rhythmic, 'airborne' lines, containing rhymes, half rhymes and internal rhymes (very much part of his 'voice'). He was to demonstrate this narrative skill again in *The Nabara* (*Overtures to Death*).

They preferred, because of the rudeness of their heart, to die rather than to surrender.

Phase One

Freedom is more than a word, more than the base coinage
Of statesmen, the tyrant's dishonoured cheque, or the
                              dreamer's mad
Inflated currency. She is mortal, we know, and made
In the image of simple men who have no taste for carnage
But sooner kill and are killed than see that image
                              betrayed.
Mortal she is, yet rising always refreshed from her ashes:
She is bound to earth, yet she flies as high as a passage
                              bird
To home wherever man's heart with seasonal warmth is
                              stirred:
Innocent is her touch as the dawn's, but still it unleashes
The ravisher shades of envy. Freedom is more than a
                              word . . .

He was over forty when, after the war, he was able to afford his first holiday abroad and immediately he fell in love with

Italy, like so many poets before him. Later, we did the journeys all over again together. *Flight to Italy* was exactly as he told it in *An Italian Visit*. (It was before the days of jet aircraft, and I did not share his wild elation at take-off or when 'the atrocious Alps' were, literally, upon us, not below, and we eventually landed in Milan in a turmoil of forked lightning.) In the middle of the narrative is a contemplative passage I often quote to people who are recovering from illness and finding – as we all do – that convalescence can be the hardest part:

> . . . After a hard winter, on the first warm day
> The invalid venturing out into the rock-garden,
> Pale as a shaft of December sunshine, pauses,
> All at sea among the aubretia, the alyssum
> And arabis – halts and moves on how warily,
> As if to take soundings where the blossom foams and
> tumbles:
> But what he does sound is the depth of his own weakness
> At last, as never when pain-storms lashed him.
> So we, convalescent from routine's long fever,
> Plummeting our gaze down to river and plain,
> Question if indeed that dazzling world beneath us
> Be truth or delirium; and finding still so tentative
> The answer, can gauge how nearly we were ghosts,
> How far we must travel yet to flesh and blood . . .

In *Pegasus*, the narrative poems are new workings of Greek legends. The title poem is a powerful allegory about the creative process; a large number of his poems were about writing. The allegories *A Failure* and *The Unwanted* (*Poems 1943–1947*), *Final Instructions* (*Pegasus*) and *Circus Lion* (*The Gate*) say a great deal about the discipline, devotion and pain of being a poet. In a lighter mood is a charming poem with an intricate, elegant stanza form dedicated to Robert Frost, called *Sheepdog Trials in Hyde Park* (*The Gate*). Cecil challenged Frost to write one too, when, in 1957, they spent an afternoon together at this unlikely entertainment for a New England farmer.

xvii

. . . What's needfully done in the solitude of sheep-runs –
Those tough, real tasks – becomes this stylized game,
A demonstration of intuitive wit
Kept natural by the saving grace of error.
To lift, to fetch, to drive, to shed, to pen
Are acts I recognize, with all they mean
Of shepherding the unruly, for a kind of
Controlled woolgathering is my work too.

At this time he wrote his first Dramatic Monologue for me: *Ariadne on Naxos*. He never succeeded in writing a play, but had a great gift for dialogue in poetry (and in the detective novels written by his alter ego Nicholas Blake). Later, in *The Gate*, he wrote two more Dramatic Monologues *The Disabused* (which he performed brilliantly and chillingly) and *Not Proven*, which he dedicated to our friend, George Rylands, the distinguished scholar, with whom we gave many recitals, and who was a co-founder of the Apollo Society.

In 1940 Cecil published his translation of Virgil's *Georgics*.* He had been a classical scholar at Wadham College, Oxford, and all his translations were exact, as well as being poems in their own right. He set out to steer the course between 'the twin vulgarities of flashy colloquialism and perfunctory grandiloquence'. He was a countryman for preference and was always minutely observant and accurate in his study of nature and the land. This is evident in all the poems. He felt intensely patriotic about his roots in the countryside on the Dorset/Devon border, and the threat of invasion intensified these feelings. Through them he was linked to Virgil, who had written of the land and husbandry with such tenderness all those centuries before.

In *Poems 1943–1947* there is his fine translation of Paul Valéry's *Le Cimetière Marin*. It is faithful, and it is a poem of his own. I felt impelled to go there after his death, when the Spenders were giving me refuge in Provence. Natasha and I started out very early before the blistering heat of a July day. She drove me to Sète; we arrived at noon. It was extraordinary – we

* Not included in this Collection.

had walked into the poem (Cecil himself had never seen the graveyard).

> This quiet roof, where dove-sails saunter by,
> Between the pines, the tombs, throbs visibly.
> Impartial noon patterns the sea in flame –
> That sea for ever starting and re-starting.
> When thought has had its hour, oh how
>   rewarding
> Are the long vistas of celestial calm!
>
> What grace of light, what pure toil goes to form
> The manifold diamond of the elusive foam!
> What peace I feel begotten at that source!
> When sunlight rests upon a profound sea,
> Time's air is sparkling, dream is certainty –
> Pure artifice both of an eternal Cause . . .

The last volume to be published in his lifetime was *The Whispering Roots*, in 1970, when his health had been failing for many years. More than half the poems spring from his Anglo-Irish provenance: the childhood memories; his Goldsmith ancestry; our 1966 visit to Dublin to commemorate the Easter Rising of 1916 (there were many other Dublin visits); the glorious summers we spent yearly with our children in Connemara and County Mayo – 'a source held near and dear'. In this book there are thirty-seven different stanza forms in thirty-four poems, and only one is repeated. Of a particular anonymous review of the poems Professor Samuel Hynes said, five years after C's death: 'It was not so much a review, I thought, as a literary mugging.' The reviewer, Geoffrey Grigson, had not had one good word to say about a single poem, and it was the last piece that Cecil ever read about his work before he died. It was a cruel blow to one who was always magnanimous, and had spent years of his life helping other writers. It was in character that he behaved stoically. I discovered we were each hiding the review from the other. We were not subscribers to the periodical, but 'well wishers' had posted it.

The *vers d'occasion* are collected for the first time. These *are* verses with no pretension to being poetry, and they bring me back to his craftsmanship. First of all he made it clear on becoming Poet Laureate that he would try to involve himself in public issues that attracted him and needed support, not just Royal events. The variety of subjects speaks for itself, and I have no doubt that he would feel passionately about any number of the world's problems that concern us all today. As it was, I like to recollect his enchanting, challenging smile (grin, really) when he said to me: 'If I can write some verses on the amalgamation of six Teesside boroughs I shall feel I've really achieved something.' The many admirers of our friend Ronald Searle will look with affection (I hope) on *A Short Dirge for St. Trinian's* written when the artist wished to bury the girls formally and finally.

When I edited *Posthumous Poems* I did not include *At Lemmons*, the last poem he wrote on his deathbed (called by Professor Hynes 'a small masterpiece – reticent and calm, and very moving'). The reason for this is that it had already been included in a selection of *Poems 1925–1972*, many of them very much abridged without my fore-knowledge. If I had been consulted, I would not have given permission for the wildly random cuts. 'Either the whole poem or not at all,' I would have said. I wish I had re-published *At Lemmons* at the end of *Posthumous Poems*. However, the last poem in that volume, *Children Leaving Home*, was his moving valedictory to Tamasin and Daniel. They must have thought he was detached, which is not uncommon with artists who are preoccupied. In his case it was also a conscious effort 'to ride them on a loose rein' (his phrase). He was an affectionate, reassuring and sage parent who had much to teach me, and here again 'the love is proved in the letting go'. All too soon they had to go forth. They were eighteen and just fifteen.

Cecil is buried in Stinsford churchyard, very near Thomas Hardy. Samuel Hynes said: 'His burial there seems to me entirely appropriate, not because he was of the stature of Hardy, who seems more and more clearly to be the greatest of modern English poets, but because he was of Hardy's company, a decent minor poet in the same tradition. By writing in the English lyric

xx

tradition, he helped to keep that tradition alive, and earned his place with Hardy in Stinsford churchyard.' I can picture again that special, gratified smile were he to read such a compliment, and happy incredulity at the knowledge that he was buried there in his beloved Dorset. 'The writing of poetry,' Cecil once wrote, 'is a vocation, a game, a habit, and a search for truth.' His life's work was all of these, and much more.

> . . . *Shall I be gone long?*
> For ever and a day.
> *To whom there belong?*
> Ask the stone to say,
> Ask my song. . . .
>
> *Is It Far To Go? Poems 1943–1947*

JILL BALCON

BEECHEN VIGIL

and other poems

For the Lady Dream-Maker

'It is a little star-dust caught, a segment
of the rainbow which I have clutched.'
THOREAU

The Net

Poet, sink the shining net
   In ebb and flow.
Only there thy spoil is met
   Where all tides go.

Bend above the wavering net.
   Those silvery hordes
Often shall o'erleap the cords,
   And thou shalt fret

For so much beauty unharvested.
   Some hour will bless,
And thou one lasting gleam shalt add
   To loveliness.

Beechen Vigil

I

Come, dust, spread thine oblivion above
   My heart and all the words it wove
For her. Now in these branches cannot die
   Remembrance of the hour when I
Kept vigil with the lady that I love.

II

We watched, while day sank down to sleep
Among the beeches in green tranquillity.
   The west ran gold, and every tree
     Put on a stronger magic.
   We saw the solemn shadows creep
Like acolytes of that hushed mystery.

5

And when your eager head was bent
Seerwise above the fire, I suddenly knew
　　How from dim time this chapel grew
　　　　But to enshrine our vigil,
　　And felt a glory imminent
That should o'erleap its source – build heaven anew.

III

Beeches, how fortunate a mood
Brought us mazed children beneath the benison
　　Of your unaging motherhood!

Shadow and sunset, leaf and fire
Have sung together a rune miraculous
　　To heal our doubt and blind desire.

What though beyond a thousand years
Stands the full pattern? It is enough that now
　　Our purpose strides amid the stars.

A Creation

From the unerring chisel at fall of shadow
　　Beautiful stood forth Adam.

Then God upon lawns of that young, unwalled garden
　　Set singing a thousand thrushes.
Whatever joyance of dew and early hedgerows,
　　What brave, new thing soever
Their voices' wondering ecstasy betokened
　　He hid in a flame-wrought casket.

Thereafter beside the waters He took a shell,
  Sighed faintly against its lip.
And all its virginal austerity
  Grew tremulant with such sorrow
As Beauty alone may know, mourning for lovers
  Long dust, and forsaken cities.

This song likewise He hid. And the flame-wrought casket,
  Unimaginably brimming
With essence of all tears and laughter, ordained
  To Man for a soul inviolate.

Rose-Pruner

Meanders around the rose-beds, gnarled, clay-brown,
Old Tom the pruner, snic-snac up and down.

'Look, Tom, you've snipped a young shoot from the tree!'

'Aye, so I have; but I bean't ashamed,' says he,
'The Lord Hisself has made mistakes ere now.
  Come Lammastide 'twere twenty year ago
He said, 'Old Tom's turn now,' and upped His shears –
My son He took, the young green sprig o' the tree,
The garden's pride.
  Mebbee He'm gettin' old and tired; mebbe
His eyes be smudged like mine awhiles with tears
For a strong son as died.'

In a Wood

I met an old man in a wood.
He had a coat of bracken brown,
And boughs hung round him like a hood.

The winter sun was a red pomegranate
To weigh the branches down.
Pale lemon was the winter moon.

Pointing gnarled finger and gnarled stick
He said, 'You think that is the moon?'
 He said,
'Long time ago the moon fell sick –

'Twas all along o' my white cheeses –
   And now the moon is dead.
Yon is her ghost. She died of envy.'

He pulled apart the branchy hood,
And went a'bumbling through the wood –
''Twas all along o' my white cheeses.'

Songs of Sirens

Look not too long upon the golden hours,
Look not too long!
Those sirens will unstring thy powers
That made a minstrelsy of suns and showers,
Of every stone a song.
See how the wind's bleak trumpet stuns each hill
To colder immobility!

Fool!
And canst thou quick and wakeful be
When all thy frail heart is one Philomel
With music sweetly chill –
Voices of siren echoing silverly?

Look not again on that too golden land
Or else delight
Will curdle up thy soul; and thee, unmanned
By beauty that is thy bane,
Those barren nymphs will leave on the brink of night
Forlorn, a pulseless stalactite.

O, look not back upon the golden land,
Look not again.

Words

Were I this forest pool
And you the birch tree bending over,
Your thoughts in shaken leaves could drop
Upon my heart. And we would never
So fret our happiness taming
Rebellious words that sulk, run crazy
And gibber like caged monkeys,
Mocking their tamers.

A Rune for Anthony John

May the splendid earth renew
Her first loveliness for you.

May the flowers, red and blue,
At your coming blithely strew

Poecil carpets, and the dew
Brightlier shine beneath your shoe.

May the sad, sinister yew
Smile again because of you.

May each cow benignly moo
When you run the meadows through.

All outlandish creatures, too, –
Quagga, chimpanzee and gnu,

Platypus and kangaroo,
Kneel and say a prayer for you.

Leprechaun and fairy brew
Spells to make you think and do.

So will your life be every hue
Of paroqueet and cockatoo.

Fairy to Children

It is I who touch with wonder
  Wrinkled brows and solemn eyes;
I can make with powerful magic
  Sleeping loveliness to rise;
Mistletoe bear pearls for berries,
Rubies hang instead of cherries,
  Dust to build a diamond house.

I can summon all adventure
  From a footstep in the snow.
To the sound of one toy trumpet
  Unseen armies come and go.
Children, when I pipe my ditties,
March away to sack great cities
  With your wooden sword and bow!

Stay quite still! Now can you hear me
  Pipe the dances from a strand
Delicate as winter sunshine?
  Run and take the fairy's hand!
Just beyond the garden-paling
There's a sea, and ships are sailing
  Every hour for fairyland.

Song of Fairies

We have known no sorrow from time's beginning,
  And therefore we dance the centuries through;
Twilight ebbs on the tide of our singing,
  Our singing flows with the dawn's first blue.

11

Our white arms curve like waves of the ocean,
  Our white feet flutter like vanishing foam;
Unwearied we of tempestuous motion
  Under the echoing forest dome.
The fairy meadows were made for our pleasure,
  The meadows of earth for a hiding-place.
The flowers spring up where we weave a measure,
  The flowers crouch down when we cover our face.
All the children of beauty know us;
  Violets strew us a purple bed;
Spiders are spinning their nets below us;
  Great clouds bend down to shelter our head.
We are the light, the joy and the laughter;
  The hands that beckon and vanish away;
The sweet content of a smoky rafter;
  The bird-like cries of children at play.
To paint your dreams we have dipped our brushes
  In pools where the feet of the rainbow stand:
They mingle and change like wavering rushes
  Caressed by the wind's impetuous hand.
Wherever a heart is brimming with beauty,
  And washed in the starry water of dreams;
Wherever dim eyes are strained after beauty
  And fevered lips bend over her streams;
There we frolic and dance together,
  Spinning a delicate, powerful spell
With threads the moonlight hangs on the heather,
  And threads of mist from the fairy well.
We have known no sorrow from time's beginning,
  And therefore we dance the centuries through;
Twilight ebbs on the tide of our singing,
  Our singing flows with the dawn's first blue.

Tapestries

I lingered in that unfriended room
Where wind in the keyhole croons forlornly
As a woman barren of womb
Over a dusty cradle.
   I lingered. Nothing was there
   But tapestries cobwebbed and threadbare,
   Stirred by the uneasy air.

And, as I watched them, on the wall
Hound and hunter and quarry, lake and garden
And young girls playing at ball
Shook off their trance: grew dimly aware,
Remembering the delightful fingers
That wove them into life.
      And soon to me
   Those figures, ghostly and fantastical,
   Seemed a forgotten madrigal
   Sung by dead lips at midnight merrily.

Lost

Whither is now that city vanished
Where once I walked with innocence hand in hand?
   O, an insidious tide hath drowned
     Deeper than regret
     Cupola, minaret,
   And all the streets are sand.

Surely the streets were emerald-paven
When I walked there with innocence. Alas!
Vainly, vainly I peer into
 The water's riddling face,
 There is left no trace
Of my lost Lyonesse.

Lines from the French

Give me your eyes, give me your hands,
Give me your hands so fairy-fine.
To lead me past the lonely lands
Give me your eyes, give me your hands,
 Your childish hands in mine.

Give me your eyes, give me your hands,
Give me your hands stretched through the Veil.
To lead where Life grown lovely stands
Give me your eyes, give me your hands,
 Your hands rose-petal-frail.

No Meaner Quest

Had she lived in perilous days
There had been many courtyards bright
With lances pennoned for her praise.
Now a solitary knight
Rides upon no meaner quest.

The sword her beauty made of fire
Shall strike at many a fear unguessed;
The sword that fighting may not tire
Shall shine through many an unthought field.
Should I tremble while her trust
Is a flame upon my shield?

Friends, when you see the impatient West
Engulf me, say – 'He was a knight
In joy and fortitude not less
Than they, the troubadour's delight,
Who sought a lady's happiness.'

Late Summer

Sleepy the earth lies still at Edwinstowe;
   That brown and green slashed coverlet,
Meadow and ploughland, hides the faces I knew
   When every primrose bent eyes wet
With happiness, so graciously Spring did go.

How many ages of winter have burdened me
   Since last I saw the buttercups
Sprinkling their golden laughter over the lea,
   And poppies shaken like wine-drops
On the corn's hair in summer revelry!

Dream-Maker

A chance word, and you sat there at the table,
    Candlelight sharp against your hair's rich cloud,
And that voice speaking, like a queen of fable
    In rose-lamped gardens, passionate and proud.

I marvelled to have forgotten how your throat
Would curve so eagerly, and with what wonder
Seeing your eyes I had seen lilies under
    Mysterious bridges slumbrously afloat.

I had forgotten all, forgetting this –
That all my dreams have flowed beneath those bridges,
That my soul heard your voice from heaven's ridges,
    Was shaken by its stormy loveliness.

No one is there. Only the coals grow livid,
    Night-breath, and through the window starlight spills.
But still your voice is echoing, cool and vivid,
    Like a horn blown at morning beyond the hills.

Once in Arcady

TO V. C. C.-B.

Sometime we two have sat together,
   Brown, crisp-limbed shepherd boys,
In meadows under the golden weather.
   Air would be shaking with noise
Of bees and honey-sweet sheep bells,
   Dully, as from a gong
Once smitten. Over there the hills
   Seaward would troop along
Like white fawns to their drinking-pool.
   The cave – I see it all –
Stagnant with green silence, and cool;
   Grapes sunnily on the wall
Asleep; and we two sprawling outside,
   Slim pipes a-trill, or gazing
Where shadows fall and hide
   The slow flock grazing.

There, when night hushed the whispering poplars,
   Silence would blossom into a green tree:
Beauty would lean her whiteness against the branches
   And sing for us most marvellously
   Those songs for which all poets have wept,
Waking to find them dream. But we should awaken,
   Dawn fragrant still with Beauty's footfall
Lingering by the cave where we had slept.

A Forest Piece

Only in the forest
    Walks Silence for men to see.

At one breathless moment
Tree huddles closer to tree,
Mosses more greenly burn,
Curls up in an ecstasy
Each delicate-fingered fern.
No rabbit stirs. The jay
Has left her querulous chatter,
Subdued by death of day.
Perching among the branches
Wind pauses upon tip-toe.

Now from blue mist-pavilion
You may see King Silence go
Royally through the forest –

Slips on a bough wind's foot;
Sudden a berry patters.
    Look! Silence shivers, is not.

Only in the forest
    Walks Silence for men to see.

Lines from Catullus

I

My lady said that she could love no other,
Though God should come from heaven to be her suitor.
She said – but woman's words to eager lover
Are writ on wind and the unstable water.

II

O heart distraught by her so splendid shame,
Thus hath love mazed thee. Now, if she became
Without a flaw thou could'st not wish her well,
Not cease to love, if she were queen in Hell.

III

I hate and love.
How may this be,
You ask. I do not know.
I only feel 'tis so,
And it is agony.

Sanctuary

Swung in this hammock between hills
we have dreamed a nobler quietude
than the breathless after-hush when bells
tire of their silver tumbling.
Our mood
is crystal, bright as primrose laughter
rippling beneath the bracken, clear
as rain's metallic plash from a rafter.

19

How are we grown into this hour!
   Drunk with the strong sun-vintage
   we have seen the larchwood spire –
   emerald sparks for leafage –
     upwards in urgent fire . . .

Time lolls here, a laburnum slanting
   its languid tongues.
               Now do you seem
   all pagan loveliness, enchanting
     to witch Time's eyelids into dream.

Lie so. Be beautiful.
            Once Time rested,
   kept for such beauty long eclipse;
   so Deidre lay and Naisi tasted
     an age of morning upon her lips.

An April Mood

Now you have gone, I remember only your smile,
Flame-like and vivid as first green in March hedgerows,
Telling the wayfarers that every mile
Is bringing them nearer to sunshine and the dog-rose.

I only remember now a beauty alien
Hanging on chair and table, cypresses
Hung with a night's snowfall. Never Pygmalion
So quickened delight from dead stone with kisses.

Beneath your hands, so magical to sain
Fevered unreason, I found cool certitude.
Deep in my being flowers an April mood;
Strangely the sunlit hedgerows blossom again.

Eve

Dancing and revelling shouted the earth
   Delirious with morning
And the turbulent splendour of birth.
   Under the singing leaf
   Laid her white innocence
      Eve.
Lion and butterfly – all of her naming
   Went from their gaming
To gaze at the beauty of Princess Eve.

Cooing-ly, mellow-ly, like honeyed lute
   In a moon-rich garden,
The delightsome and terrible fruit
   Called her and called . . . Elate
   Up to the Tree she crept;
      Ate.
Snapped every lute string with cackle of laughter;
   Panic thereafter
Came agate-eyed, gibbering, past the gate.

Guiltily, craftily, slunk to his lair
   The lion, and dreamed of
Torn bodies, and out of the air
   Storm hurled the butterfly.
   Faint hear the falling leaves
      Cry,
'We whose life shaded Eve from the sun's gladness
   Perish. Our deadness
Dumbly shall cover her cold body.'

He Thanks Earth for his Beloved

I

All day the spirit have we breathed
Of ferny hills and valleys and clouds hill-steep,
   Knowing not how nor whence bequeathed
     Joy was arisen
Lovelier than fountains seen in sleep.

   Whence should have come this strange rebirth,
This rose in abandoned gardens blossoming,
   Had we not long ago made Earth
     Our secret altar
Garlanded with our worshipping?

II

   When she was young, Earth, loving thee,
Blessed us with halcyon noontide, tranquil night.
   And now in eye and mouth I see
     Beauty resurgent
That could not perish, being so bright.

   Surely my song had fashioned first
Some alchemy for thy body's quickening,
   Before its splendour was dispersed
     A few dumb ashes
Into the cool of evening.

The Fisher

When at last I am abiding
  Where I would be,
Think gently of the wind-snatched rumour
  That was once me.

  Can you forget
How, dreaming I should find one beauty,
One silver-perfect thing to give her,
  I cast the net?

How in those dark, unquiet waters
  I found defeat;
And how I laid the meshes, empty,
  Before her feet?

1925

COUNTRY COMETS

'Ye country comets, that portend
No war nor prince's funeral,
Shining unto no higher end
Than to presage the grass's fall.'
ANDREW MARVELL

TO HER WHOSE MIND AND BODY
ARE A POETRY I HAVE NOT ACHIEVED
I GIVE THESE POEMS

28

Prelude

Let up the curtain.
  The conjuror
Spangled and certain
  Of hand will appear.
He recks not your 'bravo,'
  Nor counts your pence:
He plays to a shadow
  Audience.
Cheers or hisses –
  Whichever you will:
Nor for this is
  Rehearsed his skill;
But for remembrance
  Of dreams untrue,
Lest their loved semblance
  Should vanish too.
A girl's young beauty
  That was not his –
These are his only
  Properties.
Though he tricks your vision
  By wizard stealth,
Alas, the magician
  Can't trick himself.
And if he is slow in
  Sleight of hand,
It is through knowing
  He may not command –
For all his patter
  And ivory wand –
The love that a greater
  Wizard has banned.

Autumn of the Mood

On the heart's hidden verge
To mark where love is buried
　　Mourner lilies spring
Out of the stunted spurge.
And a small wind sings dirge
　　Under the last leaves fluttering.

This autumn of the mood
Lives not beyond the rustle
　　Of its own leaves falling;
And soon, where lilies stood,
Brittle stalks in the wood
　　Shiver, like spectres at cock-calling.

Sun and Waterfall

Sun and waterfall conspire
To shape a thing of airy grace
Apt as Helen's breast to baffle
And shame and haunt the very desire
To which it yields in hot embrace.
Now stands the poet with his bottle
Of cut glass by the waterfall,
To trap the rainbow glittering there;
Gloating he comes to his dark study –
O, the rainbow he would enthrall
Is a few waterdrops, its rare
Essence eludes him.
　　　　　　　But somebody
Passing the window at high noon

Looks in the bottle, and climbs upon
Some peak, and cries across the valleys: –
'Each petty husk of life shall soon
Mix with the dust of Ilion –
Fleas, churches, men and factory-chimneys:
But who shall keep alive the spark
That clamps together Life's whole frame
Rotting to dissolution?' Giddy,
He falls. The seer finds no bulwark
From his own vision. And the same
Inertia of field and city
Hails one more martyr.
                                    Yet maybe
Some ears still heed a challenging,
A trumpet-call that drowns the little
Gossiping tongues: Some eyes can see
A flash in the air, as though the King-
Eagle swooped ominous of battle.
Then there are cannonades, alarms,
And hearts are stung to nobleness;
Smashing of eikons, bursting of fetters
That rusted on complaisant arms.
While by the waterfall no less
Intangibly a rainbow glitters.

Cyprian! Cyprian!

I

Here is green lacquer
Spread by the willows
On glossy water
Where the ballet of minnows
Moving together
In lithe sarabande
Suddenly waver
When they have seen your hand
Ruffle the water –
Stare and are hesitant,
So gracious a dancer
That ivory visitant.

II

Here, as I lay and watched the sunlight playing
A visual music in your eyes,
I thought, 'This grand surprise
We have of beauty's disarraying
Alone is real: without it we are less
Than ghosts, as the musician's even
Poised hands are meaningless
But for the fire they bring from heaven!'

III

How little the love that cramps similitude
Of the beloved within this transient mirage,
Earth's beauty! For you there is no image
In wave and tree:
No branch has motion or quietude

To match your fingers' wizardry
That do but touch, and Reason
Is futile as a creaking skeleton.
I hear your voice make of each trivial thought
Aria so lovely that all philosophies seem
An ocean of greybeard waves
Chattering the same old, outworn theme.
Save in your body Poetry is naught
But a painted bawd who lives
On another's graces at any crossroad bought.
And so will I throw off this flaunting
Motley of wisdom: it only would obscure
In my heart's clouded air
That bright and birdlike haunting
When you and Love are moving there.

Naked Woman with Kotyle

She moved to the slow
Dance of supplication;
Her body's flow
Was a moon in motion.

Like the moon that swims
In a cold river
And eddies at its whims
She seemed to her lover.

She danced alone,
Whiter than a column
Of the Parthenon,
Virginal and solemn.

So he prayed to the stars,
Took enamel and graver,
And toiling on this vase
Timeless grace gave her.

He looked with heartbreak
On the vase, so petty
So frail a thing to take
All her live beauty.

Now are they gone –
Trancèd and entrancer.
Dust dancing in the sun
Is that forgotten dancer.

Haven in Ithaca

When my heart's Odyssey
Finds the despaired-of Ithaca on your lips,
And in that moment dies the misery
Of storm and calm and the sick ship's
Seafaring over an endless sea;

This haven of delight
Will happier be because it holds a swell
Sea-borne, an after thrill of the long fight –
The mountainous swoop from heaven to hell,
The blind masts reeling against the night.

Magicians in Dorset

No one, I thought, shall invade
This faery fastness that holds us; the battlement
    Of fern with a rare enchantment
    Impregnable we have made.

No one, 'tis sure, can invade . . .
And then; 'Have ye seen a stray calf anywhere?'
    In the quiet Dorsetshire
    Accents; and a horse neighed.

Like a puckish Abraham
The rider seemed, or a bearded Oberon:
    So wizardly his face shone
    That our spells grew empty and sham.

For his was the simpleness
Born of earth-magic, finer than fantasy;
    The unconscious dignity
    Of hills and wind-laden grass.

Certainly we were the least
Of magicians; or else, when they turned away through
    the green
    Battlement, we would have seen
    The man and his elfin beast –

Wings asprout from their shoulders –
Climb up to the sun, sedately fantastical
    As spray from the waves that fall
    Upon distant Atlantic boulders.

From the Waters of Loch Linnhe

Rest now in your places, you calm hills,
Priestesses of quiet!
Rest now! You have kept the secret
of your repose that fills
My heart only with sharp unrestfulness.
No storm thrusting across the sky
Black menacing antlers, nothing distemperate
Has power to violate
You, cloistered up in your own serenity
From every storm and stress.

Lament, you winds! Skirl, skirl
Over the hills and the deep-rooted loch
Love's desperate coronach!
Their heart stirs not. Unheeding as this proud girl,
Unheeding they must be ever.
O she is cold, she is lovely and ruinous
As a spear flung into the sunset
Never to find a target:
She was born to spend her impetuous
Spring-time upon no lover.

II

The hills reply

Do not cry out. When truth's whole firmament quakes
It will be time to scream and scold:
Love that is cast in the heroic mould
Covers his countenance, but makes
No vain lamenting.

Will you be never satisfied to feel
    Her beauty beating through your eyes?
Are they dim with search for brighter ardencies,
    To those the present times reveal
    Still unconsenting?

Do not cry out. Think rather how the days
    Because she lived them at your side
Swung in an epic rhythm; each beautified,
    A flower, a summer, each, to praise
    Her April brow.
With her you watched the gorgeous stars along
    Cool skies ride out the night, until
Her face grew rapt and fervent as the trill
    Of a blackbird startled into song
    By one green bough.

And since of hurrying wind, anchorless wave,
    Of mist and curlew-call and star
She seemed thus essence and interpreter,
    Why do you envy us our grave
    Cerement of quiet?
Cling then to these, folding away despair;
    In them there's better than heart's ease,
Lovelier than tranquillity, for these
    Stamped you at the core of her, to share
    The young blood's riot.

The Shadow-Pimp

I thought, 'Had I this body of my Hope
Coffined, earthed up, and out of ken;
This false friend whispering at the elbow,
Pointing horizonward, stunting the scope
Of here and now; this pimp of shadow,
Dream and futility: – then might I win
A mellow, chimney-corner ease.
No more my thought would go with the high branches
Fingering at the moon. I would have release
From the not quite desperate despair that clutches
Hope's hem like a starving child.
My clock would be a register
Of minutes each sucked dry, of hours beguiled
To glow upon me placidly
As evening light in the stillroom on pewter.
Time would not lag, thus, pregnant with a burden
Of clogged expectancy.'

    So I rose up one night and strangled Hope,
    Buried him twelve foot deep at the end of the garden.

I might have known one cannot cope
With such. Next day the grim persistent spark
Came bodied out anew in windier boast
And promise, whispering at my elbow;
Pointing my heart towards the fruitless dark . . .
I suppose I must take this too substantial ghost
For undivorceable bed fellow.

It is the True Star

I will remember this night. So long as mind
Endures to captain against the vandal Doom
Her forlorn hopes – nerve, blood and bone designed
After death's image, let me remember this night.
    There were daffodils at one corner of my room
Poised in a golden trance, and the four white-
Panelled walls made cosmos in miniature
Serene as a dewdrop or a Chinese poem,
And I its essence and demiurge. So pure
A oneness (I thought) is every man. No stir
From the street breaks on his Self, a play without proem
Or epilogue, dreamed in the theatre
He calls his life: being actor and audience,
To the last posture of decay he claps,
Hisses, yawns at himself.
                                    But then, what sense
Have they the pioneer-minded, the rebel-hearted,
If man's fulfilment rest on no 'perhaps'
Outside him? They are bell-buoys adrift from their charted
Safe shallows, sagging inanely through a sea
That yerks them up to meaningless stars, clanging,
Clanging for Eldorado, dementedly.
Monad or Nomad? What difference, since either state
Binds us with a law, each soul from each estranging,
To be thus terribly masters of our fate.
    And I was sickened by this philosophy
That would benight each man in a six-foot cell,
Proud Playboy of his own complacency.
So I opened the window and put out my head,
Thought's fog, portentous pachyderm, to dispel.
('The monad has no windows,' Leibnitz said.)
    Firm stood the moon, and all the sky marched on
Rank after rank of cloud in ragged battalions

Before its face: as though Napoleon,
The squat dynamic man, straddling the snow
Watched while his glorious tatterdemalions
Trailed home and left his hope-blood at Moscow.
Then, lapped in that magnificence, I knew
Suddenly how all creatures from one source
Take breath and purpose, and again renew
It with their greatness. How the very star
That held Columbus to his homeric course
Waned on the waters around St. Helena.

  'This star that constant is for our possession,
Find we its gleam amid whatever skies –
In valour's dayspring, or the dry noontide passion
To probe beneath life's semblances, or drowned
In the deep-sea midnight of a woman's eyes:
This star, whose mere reflection will astound
Us out of false content, by its possessing
Mates every true possessor; and so fills
Each creature with Creation, itself amassing
From men the stuff of Godhead.' . . .

         As I spoke
Quietly like a clump of daffodils
Out of the night grew dawn, and sparrows awoke.

Between Hush and Hush

  Dear, do not think that I
  Will praise your beauty the less,
  Believing death for ever
  Snows up its fair impress.

  Nor slight my love because
  It claims no magic re-birth,

But deems all kissing over
When lips are laid to earth.

I'll praise your beauty as
A dewdrop fast on its prime –
A still perfection lasting
But for one blink of time.

So short its hour, your love
To mine should bravelier rush,
Bird-note to bird-note thrusting
Out between hush and hush.

A Second Narcissus

Stoop, stoop, Narcissus,
Over the shadowed pool
That is her heart; no flaw there
Lurks to befool
Thy gaze with mirrored
Grimace. Yet not as he,
The Grecian, crazed by his new-
Found symmetry:
Seek the spring rather
Whence thy true image well'd,
Plumbing the heart from shallow
Glances withheld.

Stoop, stoop thou over
Thy pool, a constant sun
In pearls of dew updrawing
Its benison:
And like a sun so

Let down the beams of thine
Own love to stab the pool with
Their leonine
Radiance. O surely
Of fire and water blent
There'll leap to lovely birth a
New element.

Retrospect: From a Street in Chelsea

Here are the houses: this is the house. No smile
Lingers on the staid countenance to mark
It from its fellows, though beauty breathless and stark
As a rout of maenads kept carnival here awhile.

House, are the ghosts of our felicity
Haunting together still in you, as linger
Hands when the dance is done, finger to finger,
Loth to forsake their strange complicity?

Surely you harbour one poor frustrate ghost,
The child of fancy erring unreproved,
Conceived in the hour when she and I almost
Forgot we were not lovers, and almost loved.

(Her breath comes on the twilight here and brushes
My face with music elfin and remote:
I marvel once again that only the thrushes
And she should have sweet April in their throat.)

House, you are thridded with spectres. See, they press
Around me – ghosts of her mouth, her breasts, her
                                        eyes,

Her body's lilt. Yet would I exorcise
Them all, though it left us companionless.

If the heart could, if the mind knew how, then I
Would curse and scatter these lovely ghosts at random;
For wheresoever they go follows the phantom
Of love that died before its epiphany.

The only Pretty Ring-Time

See now, where Spring has put young leaves
Fluttering like an emerald snow
Round the beech-trunks, and lovers enacting
Earth's quaint mythologies below.

Another Venus, another Mars,
Before the Vulcan-net of crude
Fact mews them up, believe Creation
Was only built to frame their mood.

And now the green goes out of the Spring:
The lovers quarrel: one mind jolts
Upon its mate. But still, it is Hera
And Zeus playing at thunderbolts.

Disgruntled fools, you would think yourselves
Fortunate, did you guess how soon
Love, its Olympian discords vanished,
Becomes a barrel-organ tune.

Under the Willow

I

The willows by the waterside
Gather their green above their feet
Like lissom, finicky ladies
Before they cross over a wet street.

We will anchor our boat under this willow,
And under the willow ask of To-day
No dearer thing than thus to be cradled
With the stream's indolent lullay.

Dear, for one day let us yield to Fate,
And so forget him; and so forget
That our halcyon time is a dalliance
Under the brow of Olivet.

Come, let us turn our backs on the sword-flash
Sentinelling a Paradise
We have never known. Is your heart cold? – Then
We'll hew an Eden out of ice.

II

And now each common sight
Assumes a diadem
Of crystalline delight,
And trails a purple hem.
The meadows all are paven
With gold the stream along;
Dangles a lark from heaven
On silver threads of song.

Delight floats over us
Awhile, ethereally
As floats the nautilus –
That rare wild-rose of the sea.
Sure, we have found a glass
To focus mind with matter
In a microcosm of bliss
The tiniest mote will shatter.

Yet Beauty, that can bring
Sense to this razor-edge,
Is arrogant as a king
Guarding his privilege:
He lends your loveliness,
So I but contemplate;
'Tis yearning to possess
Hurls me from his estate.

III

It is late. The thrush drops few of his hoarded notes –
Pinpricks through a pall of silence, epitome
Of those rare times when from the desert we
Sniff Love's banquet, and know we are scapegoats.

O that the noisy day was here again!
For now, Earth's minor keys predominant,
Ripple on leaf and water, gnat's whine and scant
Starlight all come to orchestrate our pain.

I'd brook no comfort watering down desire,
Yet I cannot think my love a document
That one handclasp will, when the paper is spent,
Scrawl 'finis' to and toss upon the fire.

Your throat bent back upon the cool half-light
Is white as a moonbeam frozen into flesh:
Small comfort, for lips throbbing with one wild wish,
That kisses could not make it more lovely white.

We must divine some cosmic cruelty
When there's no article of beauty but
Renders the heart more vulnerable to regret
With hints of a Beauty that can never be.

Even prisoners on Pisgah may share some
Austere delights; but O, how brief their span,
When yearns the heart toward its Canaan!
Come, dear, your hand in mine. We'd best go home.

Photograph of a Bacchante

When for long weeks this mind,
This bladder of ambition and inhibition,
Had sulked, swollen, bravadoed, whined
After its pigmy fashion;
One day I took up the photograph of you
Dancing the dance Bacchante
With all your body, from eager head to toe,
Vibrant and beautiful as a line from Dante.

And I felt the pangs of one distressed
In mortal sickness who, starting from his pillow,
Sees trenchant upon the West
The mountains, and a halo
Of saffron empassioned light behind –
The mountains he will never now be treading,
Nor take one waft of their myrtle-scented wind
Where he is speeding.

At Greenlanes

(An Epistle)

Do you remember, Margaret, how we came
Out on the heath our first evening
Together? How the pines rose like a name
Cried once by a dying man; and whirriting
Nearby the nightjar's bell
Rang down reluctant curtain on the day?
Do you remember the brute smell
Of bracken that heaved at the darkness where we lay?
    I could hear my heart like a lupin pod
Rattle its wizened dreams. (What now could rally
Hope grown dead pale feeding on its own blood?)
And then I heard your voice say 'Tell me!'
It was the dew that falls on the castaway –
Honest and small as the dew but far more tender –
A sweetness drugging his dismay,
Though yet no rescuer sail flares up from under
The parched horizon.
                        So I was happier
Than I had been since loneliness began,
Secure with you, my wise and witty dear,
And Douglas the rabelaisian keen man.
Honeysuckle tuned our world
To roundelays that made the stiff sun nod;
All the summers of Arcady were revealed
In a blackbird's period.
This hollow, where noon lay down to drowse and blink,
Every night became a bowl
Brimmed by the moon with nectar for me to drink
Rapt in the clear refectory of your soul.
    I felt your thought reach out sure fingers
For mine, that had groped so long, so emptily,

Finding no flame but a touch turned it to cinders.
Your hands on mine, we worked the key
(How rustily it stammered!) of this dark mind,
This cupboard crammed with sour forgotten
Live skeletons yammering underground –
Fantastic fears in strait-jackets, all sodden
With solitude.
                    We turned the key. We let
The brave, bird-echoing sunlight in.
No monster showed: there was only Margaret,
And love, and a dead most laughable mannequin.

My Love came to Me

I

In a windless garden
At the time of plum-gathering
When the hedge is plumy
With Traveller's Joy,
Beautiful gay candid
My love came to me.

Autumn closed around her,
But her breath was all daffodils
And her face all springtime:
And now she has laid
On my heart perennial
Spring to renew me.

In a windless garden
At the time of plum-gathering
My love came to me.

So long Love cramped in the chrysalis
And hopeless of the sun had lain,
He could not dream there how one kiss
Cancels a century of pain.
How could he guess, then, that the first
Encounter of the flesh but quells
One thirst with another thirst
And builds, beneath new heavens, new hells.

Love's eye is grown too clear, too clear:
He sees in play of mouth or wrist
Enough to split a hemisphere;
And then, turning anatomist,
Pins happiness upon the table
With scalpels to lay bare its law: –
He'd better try to stick a label
On the flash of a meteor.

They are all gone into the past,
The sands we lay and laughed upon,
The heathery mountains where we kissed,
And the stars round your head are gone.
From their ebb I have saved but this –
How on the stroke of love you drew
Breath swift and sweet and laborious
As the sweeps of a racing crew.
Yet if Love's spring-tide left no more
Than this brief flurry of pulses, thrown
Like driftwood high upon the shore,
Residue of one hurricane;
I think it would take root, and where
Was wrack a tree would be upspringing,
Surprising all the vacuous air
With salvoes of green and with bird-singing.

My love, she is gone.
But this low whitewashed house,
Ringed round with fuchsia and the drone
Of bees continually,
Bears witness that in each one
Of all our dumb tremendous kisses
The dayspring was, the sun
That rides above eclipse.
My love is a fine house
Wherein are flowers and kettles,
Buccaneers holding carouse,
Cradles, and persons of quality
Dancing a minuet sedately:
I will so ring her round
With coloured love, singing love,
She will not notice even the sound
Death makes upon the casement.

Wreck near Ballinacarig

Your voyaging past,
Lie you forsaken,
Repining like an
Ariadne cast
Away on the dune
By a false sea-lover,
All but the fervour
Of freedom gone.

Two buccaneering
Children laugh
On your deck, far off

To a Blessed Isle steering:
Their first fond breath
Wrecked them on life, no less
Than you the apprentices
Of Master Death.

Now your rudder
Is ruled by the sand
Whose fluent hand
Very soon will smother
The last spar, standing
Lorn as a prayer
That whimpers on air,
And no God heeding.

Time silting over
The brave, the merry,
Dune-deep doth bury
Every sweet rover –
Keel, cabin, spars;
Leaving but shore and sea
To keep stern colloquy
Under the stars.

Arcadian

We will buy an old house
When we are richer;
One to arouse
The pen of an etcher:
Seeming – so mellow –
To have grown from the ground,
Sown in a hollow

With birches around.
Under an oaken
Quiet of beams
By the years unshaken
We'll dream our dreams.
Beyond the lintel
We'll see a mere
Keeping its crystal
Silences near;
Whence for our drink
Will flow a freshet
With primrosed brink,
And coo like a cushat.
And since at ten-forty
Each clock will be set,
Time must report by
The twinkling bat,
By thrushes' orison,
Birch-leaf's fall,
And the plumpening of cherries on
Lichened wall.
Not that we'd bother
With seasons or clocks,
While our hearts shone together
In love's equinox.
Our youth, poised finely
Thus, would believe
That age can be only
Midsummer eve.

To his Mistress

(With a ring of jade and silver)

Winter oak with boughs akimbo,
Beech of autumn, summer willow,
Star-light, dew-light gave this stone:
Tell her, ring, that while our seasons
Fit each to each – mirths, dreams and passions –
Love at heyday will remain.

Glutton Time, be not so greedy
For my slim and subtle lady,
Forget your appetite until
I have learnt with mouth and finger
Each mortal inch of her my hunger
Made heroic as the Grail.

The Perverse

Love being denied, he turned in his despair
And couched with the Absolute a summer through;
He got small joy of the skimpy bedfellow –
Formulas gave no body to lay bare.

His pretty came among the primroses
With open breast for him. No more denied
Seemed no more ideal. He was unsatisfied
Till he strained her flesh to thin philosophies.

Love being remote, dreams at the midnight gave
A chill enchanted image of her flesh;
Such phantoms but inflamed his waking wish
For the quick beauty no dream-chisels grave.

Now she was won. But our Pygmalion –
If so he could have graven like a kiss
On Time's blank shoulder that hour of loveliness
– He would have changed her body into stone.

Apologue

Here is nothing singular.
Night has Orion –
Needs she the lesser star?
Ravish divinity
If you can, Actaeon:
Never just play the spy.

Here are no estimable riches:
A mind, now hot now cold,
Turning all it touches
Into quicksilver;
The heart that looked for gold
Has found a garden of myrrh.

On Artemis pondering,
That inaccessible sprite,
I gazed at a slumbering
World from the lattice of my despairs:
The night was large enough, the night
Pastured a million stars.

'Galeotto fu il libro, e chi lo scrisse;
  quel giorno più non vi leggemmo avante.'
                                    DANTE: *Inferno.*

1928

TRANSITIONAL POEM

TO
R. E. WARNER

Part 1

'Ira brevis, longa est pietas, recidiva voluptas;
Et cum posse perit, mens tamen una manet.'

MAXIMIAN.

1

Now I have come to reason
And cast my schoolboy clout,
Disorder I see is without,
And the mind must sweat a poison
Keener than Thessaly's brew;
A pus that, discharged not thence,
Gangrenes the vital sense
And makes disorder true.
It is certain we shall attain
No life till we stamp on all
Life the tetragonal
Pure symmetry of brain.

I felt, in my scorning
Of common poet's talk,
As arrogant as the hawk
When he mounts above the morning.
'Behold man's droll appearance,
Faith wriggling upon his hooks,
Chin-deep in Eternal Flux
Angling for reassurance!'
I care not if he retorts –
'Of all that labour and wive
And worship, who would give
A fiddlestick for these thoughts
That sluggishly yaw and bend,
Fat strings of barges drawn

59

By a tug they have never seen
And never will comprehend?'

   I sit in a wood and stare
Up at untroubled branches
Locked together and staunch as
Though girders of the air:
And think, the first wind rising
Will crack that intricate crown
And let the daylight down.
But there is naught surprising
Can explode the single mind: –
Let figs from thistles fall
Or stars from their pedestal,
This architecture will stand.

2

Come, soul, let us not fight
Like cynical Chinee
Beneath umbrella, nor wish to trade
Upon neutrality.
For the mind must cope with
All elements or none –
Bask in dust along with weevils,
Or criticise the sun.

   Look, where cloud squadrons are
Stampeded by the wind,
A boy's kite sits as calm as Minos
If the string be sound:
But if there are no hands
To keep the cable tense
And no eyes to mark a flaw in it,
What use the difference
Between a gust that twitters

Along the wainscot at dawn
And a burly wind playing the zany
In fields of barleycorn?

The time has gone when we
Could sprawl at ease between
Light and darkness, and deduce
Omnipotence from our Mean.
For us the gregorian
Example of those eyes
That risked hell's blight and heaven's blinding
But dared not compromise.

3

That afternoon we lay on Lillington Common
The land wallowed around us in the sunlight;
But finding all things my strenuous sense included
Ciphers new-copied by the indefinite sunlight,
I fell once more under the shadow of my Sphinx.
The aimlessness of buttercup and beetle
So pestered me, I would have cried surrender
To the fossil certitudes of Tom, Dick, and Harry,
Had I known how or believed that such a surrender
Could fashion aught but a dead Sphinx from the live Sphinx.
    Later we lit a fire, and the hedge of darkness –
Garnished with not a nightingale nor a glow-worm –
Sprang up like the beanstalk by which our Jack aspired
    once.
Then, though each star seemed little as a glow-worm
Perched on Leviathan's flank, and equally terrible
My tenure of this plateau that sloped on all sides
Into annihilation – yet was I lord of
Something: for, seeing the fall of a burnt-out faggot
Make all the night sag down, I became lord of
Light's interplay – stoker of an old parable.

4

Come up, Methuselah,
You doddering superman!
Give me an instant realized
And I'll outdo your span.

In that one moment of evening
When roses are most red
I can fold back the firmament,
I can put time to bed.

Abraham, stint your tally
Of concubines and cattle!
Give place to me – capitalist
In more intrinsic metal.

I have a lover of flesh
And a lover that is a sprite:
To-day I lie down with finite,
To-morrow with infinite.

That one is a constant
And suffers no eclipse,
Though I feel sun and moon burning
Together on her lips.

This one is a constant,
But she's not kind at all;
She raddles her gown with my despairs
And paints her lip with gall.

My lover of flesh is wild,
And willing to kiss again;
She is the potency of earth
When woods exhale the rain.

My lover of air, like Artemis
Spectrally embraced,
Shuns the daylight that twists her smile
To mineral distaste.

Twin poles energic, they
Stand fast and generate
This spark that crackles in the void
As between fate and fate.

5

My love is a tower.
Standing up in her
I parley with planets
And the casual wind.
Arcturus may grind
Against our wall: – he whets
A tropic appetite,
And decorates our night.
'What happier place
For Johnny Head-in-Air,
Who never would hear
Time mumbling at the base?'

I will not hear, for she's
My real Antipodes,
And our ingrowing loves
Shall meet below earth's spine
And there shall intertwine,
Though Babel falls above.
Time, we allow, destroys
All aërial toys:
But to assail love's heart
He has no strategy,
Unless he suck up the sea
And pull the earth apart.

6

Dismayed by the monstrous credibility
Of all antinomies, I climbed the fells
To Easedale Tarn. Could I be child again
And grip those skirts of cloud the matriarch sky
Draggled on mere and hillside? . . . ('So the dog
Returns to his vomit,' you protest. Well only
The dog can tell what virtue lies in his vomit.)
    Sleep on, you fells and profound dales: there's no
Material wind or rain can insulate
The mind against its own forked speculation,
When once that storm sets in: and then the flash
That bleakly enlightens a few sour acres leaves but
A more Egyptian darkness whence it came.
    Mountains are the musicians; they despise
Their audience: but the wind is a popular preacher
And takes more from his audience than he gives them.
How can I wear the clouds, who feel each mountain
Yearn from its flinty marrow to abdicate
Sublimity and globe-trot with the wind?
    By Easedale Tarn, where I sought a comforter,
I found a gospel sterner than repentance.
Prophetic earth, you need no lumber of logic
Who point your arguments alike with a primrose
And a sick sheep coughing among the stones:
And I have only words; yet must they both
Outsoar the mountain and lap up the wind.

7

Few things can more inflame
This far too combative heart
Than the intellectual Quixotes of the age
Prattling of abstract art.

No one would deny it –
But for a blind man's passion
Cassandra had been no more than a draggle-skirt,
Helen a ten-year fashion.
Yet had there not been one hostess
Ever whose arms waylaid
Like the tough bramble a princeling's journey, or
At the least no peasant maid
Redressing with rude heat
Nature's primeval wrong,
Epic had slumbered on beneath his blindness
And Helen lacked her song.

(So the antique balloon
Wobbles with no defence
Against the void but a grapnel that hops and ploughs
Through the landscape of sense.)

Phrase-making, dress-making –
Distinction's hard to find;
For thought must play the mannequin, strut in phrase,
Or gape with the ruck: and mind,
Like body, from covering gets
Most adequate display.
Yet time trundles this one to the rag-and-bone man,
While that other may
Reverberate all along
Man's craggy circumstance –
Naked enough to keep its dignity
Though it eye God askance.

Part II

8

It is becoming now to declare my allegiance,
To dig some reservoir for my springtime's pain,
Bewilderment and pride, before their insurgence
Is all sopped up in this dry regimen.

Laughable dwarfs, you may twirl and tweak my heart, –
Have I not fought with Anakim at the crossways?
Once I was Cicero, though pedant fate
Now bids me learn the grammar of my days.

These, then, have my allegiance; they whose shining
Convicted my false dawn of flagrant night,
Yet ushered up the sun, as poets leaning
Upon a straw surmise the infinite.

You, first, who ground my lust to love upon
Your gritty humorous virginity,
Then yielding to its temper suddenly
Proved what a Danube can be struck from stone:
With you I ran the gauntlet for my prime,
Then living in the moment lived for all time.

Next the hawk-faced man, who could praise an apple
In terms of peach and win the argument. Quick
Was he to trip the shambling rhetoric
Of laws and lions: yet abstract turned the tables

And his mind, almost, with a whiff of air
Clothed first in a woman and after in a nightmare.

She next, sorrow's familiar, who turned
Her darkness to our light; that 'brazen leech'
Alleviating the vain cosmic itch
With fact coated in formulæ lest it burned
Our tongue. She shall have portion in my praise,
And live in me, not memory, for always.

Last the tow-haired poet, never done
With cutting and planing some new gnomic prop
To jack his all too stable universe up: –
Conduct's Old Dobbin, thought's chameleon.
Single mind copes with split intelligence,
Breeding a piebald strain of truth and nonsense.

   These have I loved and chosen, once being sure
Some spacious vision waved upon their eyes
That troubles not the common register;
And love them still, knowing it otherwise.

Knowing they held no mastership in wisdom
Or wit save by certificate of my love,
I have found out a better way to praise them –
Nestor shall die and let Patroclus live.

So I declare it. These are they who built
My house and never a stone of it laid agley.
So cheat I memory that works in gilt
And stucco to restore a fallen day.

9

I thought to have had some fame
As the village idiot

Condemned at birth to sit
Oracle of blind alleys:
Shanghaied aboard the galleys
I got reprieve and shame.

Tugging at his oar
This idiot who, for lack
Of the striped Zodiac,
Swore that every planet
Was truck, soon found some merit
In his own abject star.

Then there came disgust
Of the former loon who could
Elbow a bridge and brood
From Chaos to last Trump
Over the imbecile pomp
Of waters dribbling past.

For what can water be
But so much less or more
Gravamen to the oar? –
(Reasons our reformed dunce)
It is high time to renounce
This village idiocy.

10

How they would jeer at us –
Ulysses, Herodotus,
The hard-headed Phœnicians
Or, of later nations,
Columbus, the Pilgrim Fathers
And a thousand others
Who laboured only to find
Some pittance of new ground,

Merchandise or women.
Those rude and bourgeois seamen
Got glory thrown in
As it were with every ton
Of wave that swept their boat,
And would have preferred a coat
For keeping off the spray.

Since the heroes lie
Entombed with the recipe
Of epic in their heart,
And have buried – it seems – that art
Of minding one's own business
Magnanimously, for us
There's nothing but to recant
Ambition, and be content
Like the poor child at play
To find a holiday
In the sticks and mud
Of a familiar road.

11

If I bricked up ambition and gave no air
To the ancestral curse that gabbles there,
I could leave wonder on the latch
And with a whole heart watch
The calm declension of an English year.

I would be pædagogue – hear poplar, lime
And oak recite the seasons' paradigm.
Each year a dynasty would fall
Within my orchard wall –
I'd be their Tacitus, and they my time.

Among those pippin princes I could ease
A heart long sick for some Hesperides:
    Plainsong of thrushes in the soul
    Would drown that rigmarole
Of Eldorados, Auks, and Perilous Seas.

(The God they cannot see sages define
In a slow-motion. If I discipline
    My flux into a background still
    And sure as a waterfall
Will not a rainbow come of that routine?)

So circumscribe the vampire and he'll die soon –
Lunacy and anæmia take their own.
    Grounded in temperate soil I'll stay,
    An orchard god, and say
My glow-worms hold a candle to the moon.

12

Enough. There is no magic
Circle nor prophylactic
Sorcery of garlic
Will keep the vampire in.
See! – that authentic
Original of sin
Slides from his cabin
Up to my sober trees
And spits disease.
Thus infected, they
Start a sylvan rivalry,
Poplar and oak surpass
Their natural green, and race
Each other to the stars.

Since my material
Has chosen to rebel,
It were most politic –
Ere I also fall sick –
To escape this Eden.
Indeed there has been no peace
For any garden
Or for any trees
Since Priapus died,
And lust can no more ride
Over self-love and pride.

Leave Eden to the brutes:
For he who lets his sap
Run downward to the roots
Will wither at the top
And wear fool's-cap.
I am no English lawn
To build a smooth tradition
Out of Time's recession
And centuries of dew . . .
Adam must subdue
The indestructible serpent,
Outstaring it: content
If he can transplant
One slip from paradise
Into his own eyes.

13

Can the mole take
A census of the stars?
Our firmament will never
Give him headache.

The man who nuzzles
In a woman's lap
Burrows toward a night
Too deep for puzzles:

While he, whose prayer
Holds up the starry system
In a God's train, sees nothing
Difficult there.

So I, perhaps,
Am neither mole nor mantis;
I see the constellations,
But by their gaps.

14

In heaven, I suppose, lie down together
Agonised Pilate and the boa-constrictor
That swallows anything: but we must seize
One horn or the other of our antitheses.
When I consider each independent star
Wearing its world of darkness like a fur
And rubbing shoulders with infinity,
I am content experience should be
More discontinuous than the points pricked
Out by the mazy course of a derelict,
Iceberg, or Flying Dutchman, and the heart
Stationary and passive as a chart.
In such star-frenzy I could boast, betwixt
My yester and my morrow self are fixed
All the birds carolling and all the seas
Groaning from Greenwich to the Antipodes.

But an eccentric hour may come, when systems
Not stars divide the dark; and then life's pistons

Pounding into their secret cylinder
Begin to tickle the most anchorite ear
With hints of mechanisms that include
The man. And once that rhythm arrests the blood,
Who would be satisfied his mind is no
Continent but an archipelago?
They are preposterous paladins and prance
From myth to myth, who take an Agag stance
Upon the needle points of here and now,
Where only angels ought to tread. Allow
One jointure feasible to man, one state
Squared with another – then he can integrate
A million selves and where disorder ruled
Straddle a chaos and beget a world.

Peals of the New Year once for me came tumbling
Out of the narrow night like clusters of humming-
Birds loosed from a black bag, and rose again
Irresponsibly to silence: but now I strain
To follow them and see for miles around
Men square or shrug their shoulders at the sound.
Then I remember the pure and granite hills
Where first I caught an ideal tone that stills,
Like the beloved's breath asleep, all din
Of earth at traffic: silence's first-born,
Carrying over each sensual ravine
To inform the seer and uniform the seen.
So from this ark, this closet of the brain,
The dove emerges and flies back again
With a Messiah sprig of certitude –
Promise of ground below the sprawling flood.

15

Desire is a witch
And runs against the clock.

73

It can unstitch
The decent hem
Where space tacks on 'to time:
It can unlock
Pandora's privacies.

It puffs in these
Top-gallants of the mind,
And away I stand
On the elemental gale
Into an ocean
That the liar Lucian
Had never dared retail.

When my love leans with all
Her shining breast and shoulder,
I know she is older
Than Ararat the hill,
And yet more young
Than the first daffodil
That ever shews a spring.

When her eyes delay
On me, so deep are they
Tunnelled by love, although
You poured Atlantic
In this one and Pacific
In the other, I know
They would not overflow.

Desire clicks back
Like cuckoo into clock;
Leaves me to explain
Eyes that a tear will drown
And a body where youth
Nor age will long remain
To implicate the truth.

It seems that we must call
Anything truth whose well
Is deep enough;
For the essential
Philosopher-stone, desire,
Needs no other proof
Than its own fire.

16

Remembering how between
Embrace and ultimate bone
Always have interposed
Strata undiagnosed
In Love's geology;
And even memory
Is bullied by the flesh
Out of its usual dish;
I railed upon desire,
The silly self-betrayer
Whose Cronic appetite
Gobbles up all his brood;
And I found, in body's despite,
A moral to clinch the mood.

They say that a mathematician
Once fell to such a passion
For x and y, he locked
His door to keep outside
Whatever might distract
Him from his heavenly bride:
And presently died
In the keenest of blisses
With a dozen untasted dishes
Outside his door.

O man,
Feed Cronos with a stone.
He's easily decoyed
Who, perched on any throne,
Happily gnaws the void.

From this theoric tower
Corn-land and city seem
A lovely skiagram:
You could not guess what sour
Contagion has outworn
Those streets of men and corn.
Let body doubt: the pure
Shadow will reassure,
For shadow gives a free
Licence to lunacy. –
And yet fools say it is
The heart that's credulous . . .
For once, O sceptic heart,
Will you not play your part?

17

When nature plays hedge-schoolmaster,
Shakes out the gaudy map of summer
And shows me charabanc, rose, barley-ear
And every bright-winged hummer,

He only would require of me
To be the sponge of natural laws
And learn no more of that cosmography
Than passes through the pores.

Why must I then unleash my brain
To sweat after some revelation

76

Behind the rose, heedless if truth maintain
On the rose-bloom her station?

When bullying April bruised mine eyes
With sleet-bound appetites and crude
Experiments of green, I still was wise
And kissed the blossoming rod.

Now summer brings what April took,
Riding with fanfares from the south,
And I should be no Solomon to look
My Sheba in the mouth.

Charabancs shout along the lane
And summer gales bay in the wood
No less superbly because I can't explain
What I have understood.

Let logic analyse the hive,
Wisdom's content to have the honey:
So I'll go bite the crust of things and thrive
While hedgerows still are sunny.

Part III

'But even so, amid the tornadoed Atlantic
of my being, do I myself still centrally dis-
port in mute calm.'

HERMAN MELVILLE.

18

On my right are trees and a lank stream sliding
Impervious as Anaconda to the suns
Of autumn; and the boughs are vipers writhing
To slough the summer from their brittle bones.
Here is the Trojan meadow, here Scamander;
And I, the counterfeit Achilles, feel
A river-god surge up to tear me asunder,
A serpent melancholy bruise my heel.

On my left is the city famed for talk
And tolerance. Its old men run about
Chasing reality, chasing the Auk
With butterfly-nets. Its young men swell the rout
Gaping at Helen in the restaurant,
Mocking at Helen from monastic towers.
Boy Achilles, who has known Helen too long
To scold or worship, stands outside and glowers.

Between the stream and city a rubbish heap
Proclaims the pleasant norm with smouldering stenches.
See! the pathetic pyre where Trojans keep
Well out of sight the prey of time's revenges;
Old butterfly-nets, couches where lovers lay –
All furniture out of fashion. So the fire
Guts the proud champions of the real: so Troy
Cremates her dead selves and ascends to higher.

Grecians awake, salute the happy norm!
Now may Achilles find employment still;
And once again the blood-lust will grow warm,
Gloating on champions he could never kill.
And if Scamander rears up and pursues,
This ring of rubbish fire will baffle all
His rage. Hero, you're safe, in the purlieus
Of God's infernal acre king and thrall.

19

When April comes alive
Out of the small bird's throat,
Achilles in the sunshine
Kept on his overcoat.
Trojan and Greek at battle,
Helen wantoning –
None but heroic metal
Could ignore the spring.

When honeysuckle and summer
Suffocate the lane,
That sulky boil was broken
And I at last a man.
I'd have stripped off my skin to
The impacts of hate and love –
Rebel alone because I
Could not be slave enough.

Bodies now, not shadows,
Intercept the sun:
It takes no rod to tell me
That discipline's begun.
Seeking the fabled fusion
From love's last chemical,
I found the experiment
Makes monads of us all;

For love still keeps apart,
And all its vanities
But emphasise higher heaven,
As February trees
When rooks begin their noisy
Coronation of the wood
Are turreted with folly
Yet grow toward some good.

I thought, since love can harness
Pole with contrary pole,
It must be earthed in darkness
Deeper than mine or mole.
Now that I have loved
A while and not gone blind,
I think love's terminals
Are fixed in fire and wind.

20

How often, watching the windy boughs
Juggle with the moon, or leaning
My body against a wind
That sets all earth careening;
Or when I have seen flames browsing
On the prairie of night and tossing
Their muzzles up at Orion;
Or the sun's hot arsenal spent
On a cloud salient
Till the air explodes with light;
How often have I perceived a delight
Which parallels the racing mind,
But never rides it off the course.

Another fire, another wind
Now take the air, and I
Am matched with a stricter ecstasy.
For he whom love and fear enlist
To comb his universe
For what Protagoras missed,
Needs be reborn hermaphrodite
And put himself out to nurse
With a syren and a sybil.
So the spider gradually,
Drawing fine systems from his belly,
Includes creation with a thread
And squats on the navel of his world.
Yet even that arch-fakir must feed
Austerity on warm blood.

The tracks of love and fear
Lead back till I disappear
Into that ample terminus
From which all trains draw out
Snorting towards an Ultima Thule.
Nothing is altered about
The place, except its gloom is newly
Lacquered by an unaccustomed eye,
Yet cannot blunt mine eyes now
To the clear finality
Of all beginnings.
                    Outside
In the diamond air of day
The engines simmer with delay,
Desiring a steely discipline
No less, though now quite satisfied
They travel a loop-line.

My lover is so happy, you well might say
One of the Hellene summers had lost its way
And taken shelter underneath her breast.
None but its proper fear can now arrest
Our meteoric love: but still we grieve
That curves of mind and body should outlive
All expectation, and the heart become
A blunt habitual arc, a pendulum
Wagged by the ghost of its first impetus.
Love keeps the bogey slave to admonish us
Of vanity, yet through this fear we scrawl
Our sky with love's vain comets ere it fall.

And then, up on High Stoy standing alone,
We saw the excellence of the serious down
That shakes the seasons from its back, and bears
No obligation but to wind and stars.
What paroxysm of green can crack those huge
Ribs grown from Chaos, stamped by the Deluge?

Later, within the wood sweetly reclining
On bluebell and primrose, we loved; whose shining
Made a poor fiction of the royal skies,
But were to love alone repositories
Of what by-product wonder it could spare
From lips and eyes. Yet nothing had such power
As prattle of small flowers within the brake
To mount the panic heart and rein it back
From the world's edge. For they, whose virtue lies
In a brief act of beauty, summarize
Earth's annual passion and leave the naked earth
Still dearer by their death than by their birth.
So we, who are love's hemispheres hiding
Beneath the coloured ordeal of our spring,

Shall be disclosed, and I shall see your face
An autumn evening certain of its peace.

22

It is an easier thing
To give up great possessions
Than to forego one farthing
Of the rare unpossessed.

But I've been satellite
Long enough to this moon,
The pharisee of night
Shining by tradition

There's no star in the sky
But gazing makes it double
And the infatuate eye
Can breed dilemmas on it.

Wiser it were to sheath
My burning heart in clay
Than by this double breath
To magnify the tomb.

I'd live like grass and trees,
Familiar of the earth,
Proving its basalt peace
Till I was unperturbed

By synod of the suns
Or a moon's insolence
As the ant when he runs
Beneath sky-scraping grass.

You've trafficked with no beast but unicorn
Who dare hold me in scorn
For my dilemmas. Nor have you perceived
The compass-point suggest
An east by pointing to the west,
Or you'd not call me thus deceived
For fixing my desire
On this magnetic north to gyre
Under the sheer authority of ice.

I have seen what impertinence
Stokes up the dingy rhetoric of sense:
I've seen your subaltern ambitions rise
Yellow and parallel
As smoke from garden cities that soon fades
In air it cannot even defile. Poor shades,
Not black enough for hell,
Learn of this poplar which beyond its height
Aspires not, and will bend beneath the thumb
Of every wind; yet when the stars come
It is an omen darker than the night.

The rest may go. No satisfaction lies
In such. And you alone shall hear
My pride, whose love's the accurate frontier
Of all my enterprise.
While your beauties' succession
Holds my adventure in a flowery chain
As the spring hedgerows hold the lane,
How can I care whether it ends upon
Marsh or metropolis?

But look within my heart, see there
The tough stoic ghost of a pride was too severe
To risk an armistice

With lesser powers than death; but rather died
Welcoming that iron in the soul
Which keeps the spirit whole,
Since none but ghosts are satisfied
To see a glory passing and let it pass.

   For I had been a modern moth and hurled
Myself on many a flaming world,
To find its globe was glass.
In you alone
I met the naked light, by you became
Veteran of a flame
That burns away all but the warrior bone.
And I shall know, if time should falsify
This star the company of my night,
Mine is the heron's flight
Which makes a solitude of any sky.

24

Farewell again to this adolescent moon;
   I say it is a bottle
For papless poets to feed their fancy on.
   Once mine sucked there, and I dreamed
The heart a record for the gramophone –
   One scratch upon the surface,
And the best music of that sphere is gone.
   So I put passion away
In a cold storage and took its tune on trust,
   While proper men with church-bells
Signal a practised or a dreamt-of lust . . .
   No fear could sublimate
The ennui of a tomb where music slept
   In artificial frost,
Nor could it long persuade me to accept
   Rigidity for peace,

Moon-stricken I worked out a solitude
    Of sand and sun, believing
No other soil could bear the genuine rood.
    But nothing grew except
The shadow at my heels. Now I confess
    There's no virtue in sand:
It is the rose that makes the wilderness.
    I thought integrity
Needed a desert air; I saw it plain,
    A chimney of stone at evening,
A monolith on the skyline after rain.
    Instead, the witless sun
Fertilised that old succubus and bred
    A skeleton in a shadow.
Let cactus spring where hermits go to bed
    With those they come to kill.
Three-legged I ran with that importunate curse,
    Till I guessed (in the sexual trance
Or playing darts with drunken schoolmasters)
    The integrity that's laid bare
Upon the edge of common furniture.
    Now to the town returning
I accept the blind collisions that ensure
    Soul's ektogenesis.

25

Where is the true, the central stone
That clay and vapour zone,
That earthquakes budge nor vinegar bites away,
That rivets man against Doomsday?

You will not find it there, although
You sink a shaft below
Despair and see the roots of death close-curled
About the kernel of your world.

Where is the invaluable star
Whose beams enlacèd are
The scaffolding of truth, whose stages drawn
Aside unshutter an ideal dawn?

It is well hid. You would not find
It there, though far you mined
Up through the golden seams that cram the night
And walked those galleries of light.

Above, below, the Flux tight-packed
Stages its sexual act –
An ignominious scuffling in the dark
Where brute encounters brute baresark.

Keep to the pithead, then, nor pry
Beyond what meets the eye,
Since household stuff, stone walls, mountains and trees
Placard the day with certainties.

For individual truth must lie
Within diversity;
Under the skin all creatures are one race,
Proved integers but by their face.

So he, who learns to comprehend
The form of things, will find
They in his eye that purest star have sown
And changed his mind to singular stone.

26

Chiefly to mind appears
That hour on Silverhowe
When evening's lid hung low
And the sky was about our ears.

Buoyed between fear and love
We watched in eastward form
The armadas of the storm
And sail superbly above;
So near, they'd split and founder
On the least jag of sense,
One false spark fire the immense
Broadside the confounding thunder.
They pass, give not a salvo,
And in their rainy wash
We hear the horizons crash
With monitors of woe.

Only at highest power
Can love and fear become
Their equilibrium,
And in that eminent hour
A virtue is made plain
Of passionate cleavage
Like the hills' cutting edge
When the sun sets to rain.
This is the single mind,
This the star-solved equation
Of life with life's negation.
A deathless cell designed
To demonstrate death's act,
Which, the more surely it moves
To earth's influence, but proves
Itself the more intact.

27

With me, my lover makes
    The clock assert its chime:
But when she goes, she takes
    The mainspring out of time.

Yet this time-wrecking charm
  Were better than love dead
And its hollow alarum
  Hammered out on lead.

Why should I fear that Time
  Will superannuate
These workmen of my rhyme –
  Love, despair and hate?

Fleeing the herd, I came
  To a graveyard on a hill,
And felt its mould proclaim
  The bone gregarious still.

Boredoms and agonies
  Work out the rhythm of bone: –
No peace till creature his
  Creator has outgrown.

Passion dies from the heart
  But to infect the marrow;
Holds dream and act apart
  Till the man discard his narrow

Sapience and folly
  Here, where the graves slumber
In a green melancholy
  Of overblown summer.

Part IV

'The hatches are let down
And the night meets the day
The spirit comes to its own
The beast to its play.'
                    W. H. AUDEN.

28

In the beginning was the Word.
   Under different skies now, I recall
   The childhood of the Word.
                   Before the Fall,
   Was dancing on the green with sun and moon:
And the Word was with God.
   Years pass, relaxed in a faun's afternoon.
And the Word was God.
   For him rise up the litanies of leaves
   From the tormented wood, and semi-breves
   Of birds accompany the simple dawn.
   Obsequious to his mood the valleys yawn,
   Nymphs scamper or succumb, waterfalls part
   The hill-face with vivacious smiles. The heart,
   Propped up against its paradise, records
   Each wave of godhead in a sea of words.
   He grows a wall of sunflower and moonflower blent
   To protest his solitude and to prevent
   Wolf or worm from trespassing on his rule.
   Observe how paradise can make a fool:
   They can't get in; but he – for a god no doubt
   Is bound by his own laws – cannot get out.
And the Word was made flesh,
   Under different skies now,
   Wrenching a stony song from a scant acre,

The Word still justifies its Maker.
   Green fields were my slippers,
      Sky was my hat,
   But curiosity
      Killed the cat.
   For this did I burst
      My daisy band –
   To be clapped in irons
      By a strange hand?
Nevertheless, you are well out of Eden:
For there's no wonder where all things are new;
No dream where all is sleep; no vision where
Seer and seen are one; nor prophecy
Where only echo waits upon the tongue.
   Now he has come to a country of stone walls,
Breathes a precarious air.
Frontiers of adamant declare
A cold autonomy. There echo starves;
And the mountain ash bleeds stoically there
Above the muscular stream.
What cairn will show the way he went?
A harrow rusting on defeated bones?
Or will he leave a luckier testament –
Rock deeply rent,
Fountains of spring playing upon the air?

29

   Those Himalayas of the mind
   Are not so easily possessed:
   There's more than precipice and storm
   Between you and your Everest.

   You who declare the peak of peaks
   Alone will satisfy your want,

Can you distil a grain of snow?
Can you digest an adamant?

Better by far the household cock
Scratching the common yard for corn,
Whose rainy voice all night at will
Can signify a private dawn.

Another bird, sagacious too,
Circles in plain bewilderment
Where shoulder to shoulder long waves march
Towards a magnetic continent.

'What are these rocks impede our pomp?'
Gesticulating to the sun
The waves part ranks, sidle and fume,
Then close behind them and march on.

The waves advance, the Absolute Cliffs
Unaccountably repel:
They linger grovelling; where assault
Has failed, attrition may tell.

The bird sees nothing to the point;
Shrugs an indifferent wing; proceeds
From rock to rock in the mid-ocean
Peering for barnacles and weeds.

30

In the chaotic age
  This was enough for me –
Her beauty walked the page
  And it was poetry.

Now that the crust has cooled,
　　The floods are kept in pen,
Mountains have got their mould
　　And air its regimen.

Nothing of heat remains
　　But where the sacred hill
Conserves within her veins
　　The fiery principle.

Fire can no longer shake
　　Stars from their sockets down;
It burns now but to make
　　Vain motions above the town.

This glum canal, has lain
　　Opaque night after night,
One hour will entertain
　　A jubilee of light,

And show that beauty is
　　A motion of the mind
By its own dark caprice
　　Directed or confined.

31

Where is the fool would want those days again
　　Whose light was globed in pain
　　And danced upon a point of wire?
　　When the charged batteries of desire
　　　Had licence but to pass
Into a narrow room of frosted glass?

The globe was broken and the light made free
　　Of a king's territory.

Artemis then, the huntress pale,
Flung her black dogs upon the trail:
　　So with one glance around
The hunted lightning ran and went to ground.

Safer perhaps within that cell to stay
　　Which qualified its ray
And gave it place and period,
Than be at liberty where God
　　Has put no firmament
Of glass to prove dark and light different.

But Artemis leaps down. At her thin back
　　Wheel the shades in a pack.
At once that old habit of fire
Jumps out, not stopping to inquire
　　Whether it follows or flies,
Content to use the night for exercise.

And I, when at the sporting queen's halloo
　　The light obedient flew
Blazing its trail across the wild –
Resigned now but not reconciled,
　　That ancient Sphinx I saw
Put moon and shades like mice beneath its paw.

32

The red nor-easter is out:
Trees in the covert strain
Like dogs upon a leash
And snuff the hurricane.
Another wind and tree now
Are constant to their west:
The breath that scours the midday
Unseen, is manifest

94

In this embittered thorn –
Forcing the stubborn frame
To grow one way and point
His constancy and aim.

This wind that fills the hollow
Sky, of a vacuum
Was purely bred. The thorn once
In modest seed lay mum
That squats above the Atlantic
Promontoried on pride.
For my tenacious tree
Requires not, to decide
That he has roots somewhere,
A tropic foliage;
Since that the leaf recurs
Is a sufficient gauge.

Again, what of this glass
Whereby the formulæ
Of sense should all be solved?
It cannot enlarge a flea
Nor accurately define
The features of a star.
Gazing through it I saw
Nothing particular
Distant or close. A summer
Accident it was
Explained its property.
It is a burning-glass
Which interrupts the sun
To make him more intense,
And touch to a single flame
The various heap of sense.

33

Seventeen months ago
We came to the mine on the moor. A crow
Sees more than meets the eye –
What marrow in fleshless bones may lie.
And now I passed by a forbidding coast
Where ironworks rust
On each headland: goats crop the salted grass:
Steam oozes out of the mud. Earth has
No promise for proprietors. I from far
Came, and passing saw something oracular.
Put down the tripod here.

I stretched a line from pole to pole
To hang my paper lanterns on. Poor soul,
By such a metaphysical conceit
Thinking to make ends meet!
This line, spun from the blind heart –
What could it do but prove the poles apart?
More expert now, I twist the dials, catch
Electric hints, curt omens such
As may be heard by one tapping the air
That belts an ambiguous sphere.
Put down the tripod here.

This is the interregnum of my year;
All spring except the leaf is here,
All winter but the cold.
Bandage of snow for the first time unrolled
Lays bare the wounds given when any fate
And most men's company could humiliate:
Sterilized now; yet still they prick
And pulse beneath the skin, moving me like
An engine driven on

By sparks of its own combustion.
There are going to be some changes made to-day.

Then add to this that I
Have known, and shall again, the greedy thigh;
Browned by that sun, but not betrayed,
Which puts the Dog-Star in the shade:
For though my world at one Equator meet,
These Arctic zones are still complete.
Baring my skin to every bruise
Love gives, I'll love the more; since they're but dues
That flesh must pay to bone
Till each is overthrown.
There are going to be some changes made to-day.

34

The hawk comes down from the air.
Sharpening his eye upon
A wheeling horizon
Turned scrutiny to prayer.

He guessed the prey that cowers
Below, and learnt to keep
The distance which can strip
Earth to its blank contours.

Then trod the air, content
With contemplation till
The truth of valley and hill
Should be self-evident.

Or as the little lark
Who veins the sky with song,
Asking from dawn to dark
No revenues of spring:

But with the night descends
Into his chosen tree,
And the famed singer ends
In anonymity.

So from a summer's height
I come into my peace;
The wings have earned their night,
And the song may cease.

NOTES

The central theme of this poem is the single mind. The poem is divided into four parts, which essentially represent four phases of personal experience in the pursuit of single-mindedness: it will be seen that a transition is intended from one part to the next such as implies a certain spiritual progress and a consequent shifting of aspect. As far as any definitions can be attached to these aspects, they may be termed (1) metaphysical, (2) ethical, (3) psychological; while (4) is an attempt to relate the poetic impulse with the experience as a whole. Formally, the parts fall with fair accuracy into the divisions of a theorem in geometry, *i.e.* general enunciation, particular enunciation, proof, corollaries. The following notes may be of assistance to the diligent; they are intended simply for the elucidation of the text, and do not necessarily imply assent to any proposition that may be advanced in them.   C. D. L.

January 1929.

Page 59, lines 3–8, *cf.* Spinoza, *Letters*. 'I would warn you that I do not attribute to nature either beauty or deformity, order or confusion. Only in relation to our imagination can things be called beautiful or ugly, well-ordered or confused.'

Page 59, line 4, *cf.* Spinoza, *De intell. emend.* 'But above all a method must be thought out of healing the understanding and purifying it at the beginning. . . .'

Page 64, line 13, *cf.* Exodus x, 21 and 27.

Page 66, line 6, *cf.* Deuteronomy ix, 2; also i, 28.

Page 71, line 3 *sqq.*, *cf.* page 91, line 10.

Page 75, line 18, Cronos is here used as a symbol for desire.

Page 76, line 6 *sqq.*, contrast Donne:

> 'But up into the watch-tower get,
> And see all things despoiled of fallacies.'

Page 76, line 8, 'skiagram' – a drawing in shadow, not strictly the Greek sense.

Page 84, line 15, *cf.* Dante, *Inferno*:

> 'Ed egli a me: Questo misero modo
> Tengon l'anime triste di coloro,
> Che visser senza infamia e senza lodo.'

Page 86, line 5, *cf.* Isaiah xxxv, 1.

Page 87, lines 17–24, *cf.* Wyndham Lewis, *Art of Being Ruled*, Part 12, Chapter VII.

Page 88, line 1, 'Fear and love' throughout this poem represent the general principles of attraction and repulsion.

Page 90, line 1, 'the Word' in this poem stands for the individual poetic impulse, as a part of the Logos in the theologian's sense of 'mind expressing God in the world.'

Page 90, line 4, *cf.* 'The Ballad of the Twa Brothers':

> "'O when will you come hame again?
>   Dear Willie, tell to me!'
> 'When the sun and moon dance on yon green;
>   And that will never be.''

Page 93, line 12, *cf.* Henry James, *The Ambassadors*: 'Whether or no he had a grand idea of the lucid, he held that nothing ever was in fact – for anyone else – explained. One went through the vain motions, but it was mostly a waste of life.'

Page 93, lines 13–16, *cf.* note on page 59, lines 3–8.

Page 94, line 21, *cf.* page 61, line 16.

Page 97, line 2, the refrain of a song sung by Miss Sophie Tucker.

Page 97, line 14, *cf.* page 59, line 15.

Page 97, lines 22–25, *cf.* Spinoza, *De intell. emend.* 'Finally, perception is that wherein a thing is perceived through its essence alone. . . . A thing is said to be perceived through its essence alone when from the fact that I know something, I know what it is to know anything. . . .'

1929

FROM FEATHERS TO IRON

TO THE MOTHER

Do thoughts grow like feathers, the dead end of life?
W. H. AUDEN

We take but three steps from feathers to iron.
JOHN KEATS

1

Suppose that we, tomorrow or the next day,
Came to an end – in storm the shafting broken,
Or a mistaken signal, the flange lifting –
Would that be premature, a text for sorrow?

Say what endurance gives or death denies us.
Love's proved in its creation, not eternity:
Like leaf or linnet the true heart's affection
Is born, dies later, asks no reassurance.

Over dark wood rises one dawn felicitous,
Bright through awakened shadows fall her crystal
Cadenzas, and once for all the wood is quickened.
So our joys visit us, and it suffices.

Nor fear we now to live who in the valley
Of the shadow of life have found a causeway;
For love restores the nerve and love is under
Our feet resilient. Shall we be weary?

Some say we walk out of Time altogether
This way into a region where the primrose
Shows an immortal dew, sun at meridian
Stands up for ever and in scent the lime tree.

This is a land which later we may tell of.
Here-now we know, what death cannot diminish
Needs no replenishing; yet certain are, though
Dying were well enough, to live is better.

Passion has grown full man by his first birthday.
Running across the bean-fields in a south wind,
Fording the river mouth to feel the tide-race –
Child's play that was, though proof of our possessions.

Now our research is done, measured the shadow,
The plains mapped out, the hills a natural boundary.
Such and such is our country. There remains to
Plough up the meadowland, reclaim the marshes.

2

Let's leave this town. Mutters of loom
Nor winding gear disturb
The flat and residential air –
A city all suburb.

Go not this road, for arc-lamps cramp
The dawn; sense fears to take
A mortal step, and body obeys
An automatic brake.

Ah, leave the wall-eyed town, and come
Where heaven keeps open house;
Watch not the markets but the stars;
Get shares of gilt-edged space.

For what we have in hand is no
Business of shop and street.
This is our strait, our Little Minch
Where wind and tide meet.

You are the tides running for ever
Along their ancient groove:
Such winds am I, pause not for breath
And to fresh shores will move.

Back to the countryside
That will not lose its pride
When the green flags of summer all are taken,
Having no mind to force
The seasons from their course
And no remorse for a front line forsaken.

Look how the athletic field
His flowery vest has peeled
To wrestle another fall with rain and sleet.
The rock will not relent
Nor desperate earth consent
Till the spent winter blows his long retreat.

Come, autumn, use the spur!
Let us not still defer
To drive slow furrows in the impatient soil:
Persuade us now these last
Silk summer shreds to cast
And fasten on the harsh habit of toil.

The swallows are all gone
Into the rising sun.
You leave tonight for the Americas.
Under the dropping days
Alone the labourer stays
And says that winter will be slow to pass.

4

Come on, the wind is whirling our summer away,
And air grows dizzy with leaves.
It is time to lay up for a winter day,

Conserve earth's infant energy, water's play,
Bind the sun down in sheaves.

Contact of sun and earth loads granary;
Stream's frolic will grind flour;
Tree's none the worse for fruit. Shall we
Insulate our strong currents of ecstasy
Or breed units of power?

Bodies we have, fabric and frame designed
To take the stress of love,
Buoyant on gust, multi-engined.
Experiment's over. We must up and find
What trade-routes are above.

This is no pleasure trip. We carry freight
To a certain end; not whirled
Past earth's pull, nosing at no star's gate.
We'll have fresh air; will serve, perhaps, the state;
Surely, enlarge our world.

Or, think. Tightens the darkness, the rails thrum
For night express is due.
Glory of steam and steel strikes dumb;
Sense sucked away swirls in the vacuum.
So passion passes through.

Here is love's junction, no terminus.
He arrives at girl or boy.
Signal a clear line and let us
Give him the run of life: we shall get thus
A record of our joy.

5

Beauty's end is in sight,
Terminus where all feather joys alight.
Wings that flew lightly
Fold and are iron. We see
The thin end of mortality.

We must a little part,
And sprouting seed crack our cemented heart.
Who would get an heir
Initial loss must bear:
A part of each will be elsewhere.

What life may now decide
Is past the clutch of caution, the range of pride.
Speaking from the snow
The crocus lets me know
That there is life to come, and go.

6

Now she is like the white tree-rose
That takes a blessing from the sun:
Summer has filled her veins with light,
And her warm heart is washed with noon.

Or as a poplar, ceaselessly
Gives a soft answer to the wind:
Cool on the light her leaves lie sleeping,
Folding a column of sweet sound.

Powder the stars. Forbid the night
To wear those brilliants for a brooch
So soon, dark death, you may close down
The mines that made this beauty rich.

Her thoughts are pleiads, stooping low
O'er glades where nightingale has flown:
And like the luminous night around her
She has at heart a certain dawn.

7

Rest from loving and be living.
Fallen is fallen past retrieving
The unique flyer dawn's dove
Arrowing down feathered with fire.

Cease denying, begin knowing.
Comes peace this way here comes renewing
With dower of bird and bud knocks
Loud on winter wall on death's door.

Here's no meaning but of morning.
Naught soon of night but stars remaining,
Sink lower, fade, as dark womb
Recedes creation will step clear.

8

HE We whom a full tornado cast up high,
      Two years marooned on self-sufficiency,
      Kissing on an island out of the trade-routes
      Nor glancing at horizon, – we'll not dare
      Outstay the welcome of our tropic sun.

SHE Here is the dark Interior, noon yet high,
      Light to work by and a sufficiency
      Of timber. Build then. We may reach the
                           trade-routes.
      We'll take the winds at their word; yes, will dare
      Wave's curling lip, the hot looks of the sun.

HE Hull is finished. Now must the foraging eye
Take in provisions for a long journey:
Put by our summertime, the fruits, the sweet roots,
The virgin spring moss-shadowed near the shore,
And over idle sands the halcyon.

SHE No mark out there, no mainland meets the eye.
Horizon gapes; and yet must we journey
Beyond the bays of peace, pull up our sweet roots,
Cut the last cord links us to native shore,
Toil on waters too troubled for the halcyon.

BOTH Though we strike a new continent, it shall be
Our islet; a new world, our colony.
If we miss land, no matter. We've a stout boat
Provisioned for some years: we need endure
No further ill than to be still alone.

9

Waning is now the sensual eye
Allowed no flaw upon the skin
And burnt away wrinkle and feature,
Fed with pure spirit from within.

Nesciently that vision works.
Just so the pure night-eye, the moon,
Labours, a monumental mason,
To gloss over a world of stone.

Look how she marbled heath and terrace,
Effacing boundary and date.
She took the sky; earth was below her
A shining shell, a featherweight.

No more may pupil love bend over
A plane theorem, black and white.
The interlocking hours revolve,
The globe goes lumbering into light.

Admiral earth breaks out his colours
Bright at the forepeak of the day;
Hills in their hosts escort the sun
And valleys welcome him their way.

Shadow takes depth and shape turns solid:
Far-ranging, the creative eye
Sees arable, marsh, enclosed and common,
Assents to multiplicity.

10

Twenty weeks near past
Since the seed took to earth.
Winter has done his worst.
Let upland snow ignore;
Earth wears a smile betrays
What summer she has in store.
She feels insurgent forces
Gathering at the core,
And a spring rumour courses
Through her, till the cold extreme
Sleep of grove and grass is
Stirred, begins to dream.
So, when the violins gather
And soar to a final theme,
Broadcast on winds of ether
That golden seed extends
Beneath the sun-eye, the father,
To ear at the earth's ends.

11

There is a dark room,
The locked and shuttered womb,
Where negative's made positive.
Another dark room,
The blind, the bolted tomb,
Where positives change to negative.

We may not undo
That or escape this, who
Have birth and death coiled in our bones.
Nothing we can do
Will sweeten the real rue,
That we begin, and end, with groans.

12

As one who wanders into old workings
Dazed by the noonday, desiring coolness,
Has found retreat barred by fall of rockface;
Gropes through galleries where granite bruises
Taut palm and panic patters close at heel;
Must move forward as tide to the moon's nod,
As mouth to breast in blindness is beckoned.
Nightmare nags at his elbow and narrows
Horizon to pinpoint, hope to hand's breadth.
Slow drip the seconds, time is stalactite,
For nothing intrudes here to tell the time,
Sun marches not, nor moon with muffled step.
He wants an opening, – only to break out,
To see the dark glass cut by day's diamond,
To relax again in the lap of light.

But we seek a new world through old workings,
Whose hope lies like seed in the loins of earth,

Whose dawn draws gold from the roots of darkness.
Not shy of light nor shrinking from shadow
Like Jesuits in jungle we journey
Deliberately bearing to brutish tribes
Christ's assurance, arts of agriculture.
As a train that travels underground track
Feels current flashed from far-off dynamos,
Our wheels whirling with impetus elsewhere
Generated we run, are ruled by rails.
Train shall spring from tunnel to terminus,
Out on to plain shall the pioneer plunge,
Earth reveal what veins fed, what hill covered.
Lovely the leap, explosion into light.

13

But think of passion and pain.
Those absolute dictators will enchain
The low, exile the princely parts:
They close a door between the closest hearts:
Their verdict stands in steel,
From whose blank rigour kings may not appeal.

When in love's airs we'd lie,
Like elms we leaned together with a sigh
And sighing severed, and no rest
Had till that wind was past:
Then drooped in a green sickness over the plain
Wanting our wind again.

Now pain will come for you,
Take you into a desert without dew,
Labouring through the unshadowed day
To blast the sharp scarps, open up a way
There for the future line.
But I shall wait afar off and alone.

Small comfort may be found,
Though our embraced roots grope in the same ground;
Though on one permanent way we run,
Yes, under the same sun.
Contact the means, but travellers report
The ends are poles apart.

14

Now the full-throated daffodils,
Our trumpeters in gold,
Call resurrection from the ground
And bid the year be bold.

Today the almond tree turns pink,
The first flush of the spring;
Winds loll and gossip through the town
Her secret whispering.

Now too the bird must try his voice
Upon the morning air;
Down drowsy avenues he cries
A novel great affair.

He tells of royalty to be;
How with her train of rose
Summer to coronation comes
Through waving wild hedgerows.

Today crowds quicken in a street,
The fish leaps in the flood:
Look there, gasometer rises,
And here bough swells to bud.

For our love's luck, our stowaway,
Stretches in his cabin;

Our youngster joy barely conceived
Shows up beneath the skin.

Our joy was but a gusty thing
Without sinew or wit,
An infant flyaway; but now
We make a man of it.

15

I have come so far upon my journey.
This is the frontier, this is where I change,
And wait between two worlds to take refreshment.
 I see the mating plover at play
Blowing themselves about over the green wheat,
And in a bank I catch
The shy scent of the primrose that prevails
Strangely upon the heart. Here is
The last flutter of the wind-errant soul,
Earth's first faint tug at the earthbound soul.
 So, waiting here between winter and summer,
Conception and fruition, I
Take what refreshment may be had from skies
Uncertain as the wind, prepare
For a new route, a change of constitution.

Some change of constitution, where
Has been for years an indeterminate quarrel
Between a fevered head and a cold heart;
Rulers who cannot rule, rebels who will not
Rebel; an age divided
Between tomorrow's wink, yesterday's warning.
 And yet this self, contains
Tides continents and stars – a myriad selves,
Is small and solitary as one grass-blade
Passed over by the wind

Amongst a myriad grasses on the prairie.
    You in there, my son, my daughter,
Will you become dictator, resolve the factions?
Will you be my ambassador
And make my peace with the adjacent empires?

16

More than all else might you,
My son, my daughter,
Be metal to bore through
The impermeable clay
And rock that overlay
The living water.

Through that artesian well
Myself may out,
Finding its own level.
This way the waste land turns
To arable, and towns
Are rid of drought.

17

Down hidden causeways of the universe
Through space-time's cold
Indifferent airs I strolled,
A pointless star: till in my course
I happened on the sun
And in a spurt of fire to her did run.

That heavenly body as I neared began
To make response,
And heaved with fire at once.
One wave of gathered heat o'er-ran

Her all and came to a head,
A mountain based upon an ardent bed.

(Faith may move mountains; but love's twice as strong,
For love can raise
A mountain where none was:
Also can prove astronomers wrong
Who deem the stars too hot
For life: – here is a star that has begot.)

Soon from the mother body torn and whirled
By tidal pull
And left in space to cool
That mountain top will be a world
Treading its own orbit,
And look to her for warmth, to me for wit.

18

It is time to think of you,
Shortly will have your freedom.
As anemones that renew
Earth's innocence, be welcome.
Out of your folded sleep
Come, as the western winds come
To pasture with the sheep
On a weary of winter height.
Lie like a pool unwrinkled
That takes the sky to heart,
Where stars and shadows are mingled
And suns run gold with heat.
Return as the winds return,
Heir to an old estate
Of upland, flower and tarn.

But born to essential dark,
To an age that toes the line
And never o'ersteps the mark.
Take off your coat: grow lean:
Suffer humiliation:
Patrol the passes alone,
And eat your iron ration.
Else, wag as the world wags –
One more mechanical jane
Or gentleman in wax.
Is it here we shall regain
Championship? Here awakes
A white hope shall preserve
From flatterers, pimps and fakes
Integrity and nerve?

19

Do not expect again a phœnix hour,
The triple-towered sky, the dove complaining,
Sudden the rain of gold and heart's first ease
Tranced under trees by the eldritch light of sundown.

By a blazed trail our joy will be returning:
One burning hour throws light a thousand ways,
And hot blood stays into familiar gestures.
The best years wait, the body's plenitude.

Consider then, my lover, this is the end
Of the lark's ascending, the hawk's unearthly hover:
Spring season is over soon and first heatwave;
Grave-browed with cloud ponders the huge horizon.

Draw up the dew. Swell with pacific violence.
Take shape in silence. Grow as the clouds grew.

Beautiful brood the cornlands, and you are heavy;
Leafy the boughs – they also hide big fruit.

20

Sky-wide an estuary of light
Ebbs amid cloud-banks out of sight.
At her star-anchorage shall swing
Earth, the old freighter, till morning.

Ride above your shadow and trim
Cargo till the stars grow dim:
Weigh then from the windless river;
You've a treasure to deliver.

Behold the incalculable seas
Change face for every cloud and breeze:
But a prime mover works inside,
The constant the integral tide.

Though black-bordered fancies vex
You and veering moods perplex,
Underneath's a current knowing
Well enough what way it's going.

Stroked by their windy shadows lie
The grainlands waving at the sky.
That golden grace must all be shed
To fill granaries, to make bread.

Do not grieve for beauty gone.
Limbs that ran to meet the sun
Lend their lightness to another;
Child shall recreate the mother.

21

Your eyes are not open. You are alone.
You then, to be my first-born, this is for you.
    May know, as I, sleet from a bland sky falling,
Perfidious landmark, false dawn:
Look out through panes at a spoilt holiday,
And weep, taking eternity to bed.
    When the hair grows, perceive a world
Officered by semi-cads and second baboons,
Be stood in the far corner.
    Later, after each dream of beauty ethereal,
Bicycling against wind to see the vicar's daughter,
Be disappointed.
    And yet there is yet worse to come:
Desire worn to the bone leaves room for pride's attrition.
For they shall ride in bloody uniform,
Offering choice of a sooner death or a later;
Mark you to ground, stop the earths,
Jog home to supper under a bland sky.
    Yes, you may know, as I do, self foreshortened,
Blocked out with blackness finally all the works of days.
O you who turn the wheel and look to both sides,
Consider Phlebas, who shall be taller and handsomer than
                                                   you.

    One shall rub shoulders with the firmfoot oak
And with all shifting shade join hands:
Shall have the heels of time, shall shoot from afar
And find the loopholes of the armoured train.
    When the machine's run in, will get
Free play, better no doubt for the contracting
Of an indeterminate world.
    Day and night will make armistice for this one,
Entering the walled garden who knows the hour of spirit
Reconciled to flesh.
    Then falling leaf falls to renew

Acquaintance with old contours, with a world in outline.
Is time now to set house in order, bury
The dead and count the living, consolidate
The soul against proved enemies:
Time with the lengthening shadow to grow tall.
   Thus the free spirit emerges, in courts at ease,
Content with standing-room, pleased in a small allotment.

22

In this sector when barrage lifts and we
Are left alone with death,
There'll be no time to question strategy.
But now, midsummer offensive not begun,
We wait and draw mutinous breath,
Wondering what to gain
We stake these fallow fields and the good sun.

This has happened to other men before,
Have hung on the lip of danger
And have heard death moving about next door.
Yet I look up at the sky's billowing,
Surprised to find so little change there,
Though in that ample ring
Heaven knows what power lies coiled ready to spring.

What were we at, the moment when we kissed –
Extending the franchise
To an indifferent class, would we enlist
Fresh power who know not how to be so great?
Beget and breed a life – what's this
But to perpetuate
Man's labour, to enlarge a rank estate?

Planted out here some virtue still may flower,
But our dead follies too –

A shock of buried weeds to turn it sour.
Draw up conditions – will the heir conform?
Or thank us for the favour, who
Inherits a bankrupt firm,
Worn-out machinery, an exhausted farm?

23

This was not the mind's undertaking,
But as outrageous heat
Breaking in thunder across hills
Sweetens our aching dust.

Such is not answerable to mind,
Is random as a flake
Blindly down-dancing here or clouds
That take their windy course.

Thin from thin air reason issues;
We live on living earth
Whose trees enlarge their fruit without
Misgiving or excuse.

Reason is but a riddle of sand;
Its substance shifts in storm.
Space-spanned, God-girdled, love will keep
Its form, being planned of bone.

24

Speak then of constancy. Thin eyelids weakly thus
Batted to beauty, lips that reject her, is not this;
Nor lust of eye (Christ said it) denied the final kiss.

Rather a set response, metal-to-magnet affair;
Flows with the tidal blood, like red of rose or fire
Is a fast dye outlasts the fabric of desire.

Happy this river reach sleeps with the sun at noon,
Takes dews and rains to her wide bed, refusing none
That full-filled peace, yet constant to one sea will run.

So melt we down small toys to make each other rich,
Although no getting or spending can extend our reach
Whose poles are love, nor close who closer lie than leech.

For think – throbbing our hearts linked so by endless band,
So geared together, need not otherwise be bound.

25

And since, though young, I know
Not to expect much good,
Our dreams from first to last
Being treacherous underfoot;

Best I dare wish for you,
That once (my son, my daughter)
You may get home on rock
Feet tired of treading water.

Lucky, will have also
An outward grace to ease
The axles of your world
And keep the parts at peace:

Not the waste random stuff
That stops the gannet's wing;
I mean, such oil ensures
A turbine's smooth running.

26

Beauty breaks ground, oh, in strange places.
Seen after cloudburst down the bone-dry watercourses,
In Texas a great gusher, a grain-
Elevator in the Ukraine plain;
To a new generation turns new faces.

Here too fountains will soon be flowing.
Empty the hills where love was lying late, was playing,
Shall spring to life: we shall find there
Milk and honey for love's heir,
Shadow from sun also, deep ground for growing.

My love is a good land. The stranger
Entering here was sure he need prospect no further.
Acres that were the eyes' delight
Now feed another appetite.
What formed her first for seed, for crop must change her.

This is my land, I've overheard it
Making a promise out of clay. All is recorded –
Early green, drought, ripeness, rainfall,
Our village fears and festivals,
When the first tractor came and how we cheered it.

And as the wind whose note will deepen
In the upgrowing tree, who runs for miles to open
His throat above the wood, my song
With that increasing life grew strong,
And will have there a finished form to sleep in.

27

Dropping the few last days, are drops of lead,
Heavier hang than a lifetime on the heart.

Past the limetrees that drug the air jackdaws
Slanting across a sluggish wind go home:
On either side of the Saltway fields of clover
Cling to their sweetness under a threatening sky.
Numb with crisis all, cramped with waiting.
Shallowly breathes the wind or holds his breath,
As in ambush waiting to leap at convoy
Must pass this way – there can be no evasions.
Surly the sky up there and means mischief;
The parchment sky that hourly tightens above us,
Screwed to storm-pitch, where thunder shall roll and roll
Intolerably postponing the last movement.

Now the young challenger, too tired to sidestep,
Hunches to give or take decisive blow.
The climbers from the highest camp set out
Saying goodbye to comrades on the glacier,
A day of rock between them and the summit
That will require their record or their bones.
Now is a charge laid that will split the hill-face,
Tested the wires, the plunger ready to hand.
For time ticks nearer to a rebel hour,
Charging of barricades, bloodshed in city:
The watcher in the window looking out
At the eleventh hour on sun and shadow,
On fixed abodes and the bright air between,
Knows for the first time what he stands to lose.

Crisis afar deadens the nerve, it cools
The blood and hoods imagination's eye,
Whether we apprehend it or remember.
Is fighting on the frontier: little leaks through
Of possible disaster, but one morning
Shells begin to drop in the capital.
So I, indoors for long enough remembering
The round house on the cliff, the springy slopes,

The well in the wood, nor doubting to revisit
But if to see new sunlight on old haunts
Swallows and men come back *but if* come back
From lands *but if* beyond our view *but if*
She dies? Why then, here is a space to let,
The owner gone abroad, never returning.

28

Though bodies are apart
The dark hours so confine
And fuse our hearts, sure, death
Will find no way between.

Narrow this hour, that bed;
But room for us to explore
Pain's long-drawn equator,
The farthest ice of fear.

Storm passes east, recurs:
The beaked lightnings stoop:
The sky falls down: the clouds
Are wrung to the last drop.

Another day is born now.
Woman, your work is done.
This is the end of labour.
Come out into the sun!

29

Come out in the sun, for a man is born today!
Early this morning whistle in the cutting told
Train was arriving, hours overdue, delayed
By snow-drifts, engine-trouble, Act of God, who cares
    now? –

For here alights the distinguished passenger.
Take a whole holiday in honour of this!

Kipfer's back from heaven, Bendien to Holland,
Larwood and Voce in the Notts eleven.
Returning also the father the mother,
Chastened and cheered by underworld excursion,
Alive returning from the black country,
Take a whole holiday in honour of this.

Now shall the airman vertically banking
Out of the blue write a new sky-sign;
The nine tramp steamers rusting in the estuary
Get up full pressure for a trade revival;
The crusty landlord renew the lease, and everyone
Take a whole holiday in honour of this.

Today let director forget the deficit,
Schoolmaster his handicap, hostess her false face:
Let phantasist take charge of flesh-and-blood situation,
Petty-officer be rapt in the Seventh Symphony.
For here a champion is born and commands you
Take a whole holiday in honour of this.

Wherever radiance from ashes arises –
Willowherb glowing on abandoned slagheaps,
Dawn budding scarlet in a bed of darkness,
Life from exhausted womb outstriving –
There shall the spirit be lightened and gratefully
Take a whole holiday in honour of this.

Epilogue
LETTER TO W. H. AUDEN

A mole first, out of riddling passages
You came up for a breather into my field,
Then back to your engineering; a scheme conjectured
From evidence of earth not cast at random.
The surly vegetable said 'What's this
Butting through sand for unapparent reasons?'
The animal said 'This fellow is no runner.'
Mineral said 'Brother, you like the dark.'
What are you at down there, nosing among
Saxon skulls, roots of our genealogies?
This is the field of ghosts. There are no clues here;
But dead creators packed in close fibre.
Perhaps you are going straight to some point, straighter
And further than these furrows I drive in daylight.
Daffodils now, the pretty debutantes,
Are curtsying at the first court of the year:
Their schoolgirl smell unmans young lechers. You
Preferred, I remember, the plump boy, the crocus.
Enough of that. They only lie at your feet.
But I, who saw the sapling, prophesied
A growth superlative and branches writing
On heaven a new signature. For I
Looked at no garden shrub, chantry of thrushes;
But such a tree as, gripping its rock perch
On a northern fell within the sound of hammers,
Gives shadow to the stonechat and reminder
Of chastity to men: grown venerable
Will give its name to that part of the country.
This was the second time that you had pulled
The rusty trigger summoning the stragglers.
Once more the bird goes packing, the skeleton
Sets teeth against a further dissolution.

And what have we to hope for who are bound,
Though we strip off the last assurance of flesh
For expedition, to lay our bones somewhere?
Say that a rescue party should see fit
To do us some honour, publish our diaries,
Send home the relics – how should we thank them?
The march is what we asked for; it is ended.
Still, let us wear the flesh away and leave
Nothing for birds, anatomy to men.

1931

THE MAGNETIC MOUNTAIN

TO W. H. AUDEN

PART ONE

Come, then, companions, this is the spring of blood,
Heart's heyday, movement of masses, beginning of good.

R. E. WARNER

1

Now to be with you, elate, unshared,
My kestrel joy, O hoverer in wind,
Over the quarry furiously at rest
Chaired on shoulders of shouting wind.

Where's that unique one, wind and wing married,
Aloft in contact of earth and ether;
Feathery my comet, Oh too often
From heaven harried by carrion cares.

No searcher may hope to flush that fleet one
Not to be found by gun or glass,
In old habits, last year's hunting-ground,
Whose beat is wind-wide, whose perch a split second.

But surely will meet him, late or soon,
Who turns a corner into new territory;
Spirit mating afresh shall discern him
On the world's noon-top purely poised.

Void are the valleys, in town no trace,
And dumb the sky-dividing hills:
Swift outrider of lumbering earth
Oh hasten hither my kestrel joy!

2

But Two there are, shadow us everywhere
And will not let us be till we are dead,

Hardening the bones, keeping the spirit spare,
Original in water, earth and air,
Our bitter cordial, our daily bread.

Turning over old follies in ante-room,
For first-born waiting or for late reprieve,
Watching the safety-valve, the slackening loom,
Abed, abroad, at every turn and tomb
A shadow starts, a hand is on your sleeve.

O you, my comrade, now or tomorrow flayed
Alive, crazed by the nibbling nerve; my friend
Whom hate has cornered or whom love betrayed,
By hunger sapped, trapped by a stealthy tide,
Brave for so long but whimpering in the end:

Such are the temporal princes, fear and pain,
Whose borders march with the ice-fields of death,
And from that servitude escape there's none
Till in the grave we set up house alone
And buy our liberty with our last breath.

3

Somewhere beyond the railheads
Of reason, south or north,
Lies a magnetic mountain
Riveting sky to earth.

No line is laid so far.
Ties rusting in a stack
And sleepers – dead men's bones –
Mark a defeated track.

Kestrel who yearly changes
His tenement of space

At the last hovering
May signify that place.

Iron in the soul,
Spirit steeled in fire,
Needle trembling on truth –
These shall draw me there.

The planets keep their course,
Blindly the bee comes home,
And I shall need no sextant
To prove I'm getting warm.

Near that miraculous mountain
Compass and clock must fail,
For space stands on its head there
And time chases its tail.

There's iron for the asking
Will keep all winds at bay,
Girders to take the leaden
Strain of a sagging sky.

Oh there's a mine of metal,
Enough to make me rich
And build right over chaos
A cantilever bridge.

4

Make no mistake, this is where you get off,
Sue with her suckling, Cyril with his cough,
Bert with a blazer and a safety razor,
Old John Braddleum and Terence the toff.
And now, may I ask, have you made any plans?
You can't go further along these lines;

137

Positively this is the end of the track;
It's rather late and there's no train back.
So if you are wanting to get anywhere
You must use your feet or take to the air,
The penny-a-liner, the seven-course-diner,
Prebendary Cute and the water-diviner –
Are you sure you don't want to go somewhere?
'Is it mountain there or mirage across the sand?'
That's Terra Incognita, Bogey-Man's-Land:
Why not give it a trial? You might go further
And fare much worse. 'No, no, that's going rather
Too far; besides, the whole thing may just be a sell.'
Then book your bed-sitter at the station hotel
Or stay at the terminus till you grow verminous,
Eating chocolate creams from the slot-machines;
But don't blame me when you feel unwell.
Line was a good line, ballasted on grit,
Surveyors weren't fools, platelayers didn't quit,
Viaduct for river, embankment for marsh,
Cutting for tough rock, signal for smash.
Can you keep the system going? Can you replace
Rolling stock? Is everything all right at the base?
Supposing they cut your communications
Can you live on here without any rations?
Then don't blame me when you're up the tree,
No trains coming through and you're feeling blue,
When you're left high and dry and you want to cry,
When you're in the cart and you've got a weak heart,
When you're up the pole and you can't find your soul,
When the shops are all looted and you've run out of coal.
  So it's me for the mountain. But before I begin
I'm taking a light engine back along the line
For a last excursion, a tour of inspection,
To clear the head and to aid the digestion.
Then I'll hit the trail for that promising land;
May catch up with Wystan and Rex my friend,

Go mad in good company, find a good country,
Make a clean sweep or make a clean end.

5

Let us be off! Our steam
Is deafening the dome.
The needle in the gauge
Points to a long-banked rage,
And trembles there to show
What a pressure's below.
Valve cannot vent the strain
Nor iron ribs refrain
That furnace in the heart.
Come on, make haste and start
Coupling-rod and wheel
Welded of patient steel,
Piston that will not stir
Beyond the cylinder
To take in its stride
A teeming countryside.

A countryside that gleams
In the sun's weeping beams;
Where wind-pump, byre and barrow
Are mellowed to mild sorrow,
Agony and sweat
Grown over with regret.
What golden vesper hours
Halo the old grey towers,
What honeyed bells in valleys
Embalm our faiths and follies!
Here are young daffodils
Wind-wanton, and the hills
Have made their peace with heaven.
Oh lovely the heart's haven,

Meadows of endless May,
A spirit's holiday!

Traveller, take care,
Pick no flowers there!

PART TWO

Drive your cart and your plough over the bones of the dead.
WILLIAM BLAKE

6

Nearing again the legendary isle
Where sirens sang and mariners were skinned,
We wonder now what was there to beguile
That such stout fellows left their bones behind.

Those chorus-girls are surely past their prime,
Voices grow shrill and paint is wearing thin,
Lips that sealed up the sense from gnawing time
Now beg the favour with a graveyard grin.

We have no flesh to spare and they can't bite,
Hunger and sweat have stripped us to the bone;
A skeleton crew we toil upon the tide
And mock the theme-song meant to lure us on:

No need to stop the ears, avert the eyes
From purple rhetoric of evening skies.

7

First Defendant speaks
I that was two am one,

We that were one are two.
Warm in my walled garden the flower grew first,
Transplanted it ran wild on the estate.
Why should it ever need a new sun?
Not navel-string in the cold dawn cut,
Nor a weaned appetite, nor going to school
That autumn did it. Simply, one day
He crossed the frontier and I did not follow:
Returning, spoke another language.
Blessed are they that mourn,
That shear the spring grass from an early grave:
They are not losers, never have known the hour
When an indifferent exile
Passes through the metropolis *en route*
For Newfoundland.

    Mother earth, understand me. You send up
So many leaves to meet the light,
So many flights of birds,
That keep you all their days in shade and song;
And the blown leaf is part of you again
And the frozen blackbird falls into your breast.
Shall not the life-giver be life-receiver?
Am I alone to stand
Outside the natural economy?
Pasteurize mother's milk,
Spoon out the waters of comfort in kilogrammes,
Let love be clinic, let creation's pulse
Keep Greenwich time, guard creature
Against creator, and breed your supermen!
But not from me: for I
Must have life unconditional, or none.
So, like a willow, all its wood curtailed,
I stand by the last ditch of narrowing world,
And stir not, though I see
Pit-heads encroach or glacier crawl down.

This was your world and this I owe you,
Room for growing, a site for building,
The braced sinew, the hands agreeing,
Mind foreseeing and nerve for facing.
You were my world my breath my seasons
Where blood ran easy and springs failed not,
Kind was clover to feet exploring
A broad earth and all to discover.
Simple that world, of two dimensions,
Of stone mansions and good examples;
Each image actual, nearness was no
Fear and distance without a mirage.
Dawn like a greyhound leapt the hill-tops,
A million leaves held up the noonday,
Evening was slow with bells pealing,
And night compelling to breast and pillow.
This was my world, Oh this you gave me,
Safety for seed, petal uncurled there;
Love asked no proving nor price, a country
Sunny for play, for spring manœuvres.

Woman, ask no more of me;
Chill not the blood with jealous feud:
This is a separate country now,
Will pay respects but no tribute.
Demand no atavistic rites,
Preference in trade or tithe of grain;
Bound by the limiting matrix I
Increased you once, will not again.
My vision's patented, my plant
Set up, my constitution whole;
New fears, old tunes cannot induce
Nostalgia of the sickly soul.
Would you prolong your day, transfuse

Young blood into your veins? Beware
Lest one oppressed by autumn's weight
May thrill to feel death in the air.
Let love be like a natural day
That folds her work and takes to bed;
Ploughland and tree stand out in black,
Enough memorial for the dead.

9

Second Defendant speaks
Let us now praise famous men,
Not your earth-shakers, not the dynamiters,
But who in the Home Counties or the Khyber,
Trimming their nails to meet an ill wind,
Facing the Adversary with a clean collar,
Justified the system.
Admire the venerable pile that bred them,
Bones are its foundations,
The pinnacles are stone abstractions,
Whose halls are whispering-galleries designed
To echo voices of the past, dead tongues.
White hopes of England here
Are taught to rule by learning to obey,
Bend over before vested interests,
Kiss the rod, salute the quarter-deck;
Here is no savage discipline
Of peregrine swooping, of fire destroying,
But a civil code; no capital offender
But the cool cad, the man who goes too far.
Ours the curriculum
Neither of building birds nor wasteful waters,
Bound in book not violent in vein:
Here we inoculate with dead ideas
Against blood-epidemics, against
The infection of faith and the excess of life.

143

Our methods are up to date; we teach
Through head and not by heart,
Language with gramophones and sex with charts,
Prophecy by deduction, prayer by numbers.
For honours see prospectus: those who leave us
Will get a post and pity the poor;
Their eyes glaze at strangeness;
They are never embarrassed, have a word for everything,
Living on credit, dying when the heart stops;
Will wear black armlets and stand a moment in silence
For the passing of an era, at their own funeral.

10

You'll be leaving soon and it's up to you, boys,
Which shall it be? You must make your choice.
There's a war on, you know. Will you take your stand
In obsolete forts or in no-man's-land?
That ancestral castle, that picturesque prestige
Looks well on paper but will it stand a siege?
All modern conveniences – still, I should change
Position now the enemy knows the range.
Blockade may begin before you're much older –
Will you tighten the belt and shrug the shoulder
Or plough up the playing-fields, sow new soil,
Build a reservoir and bore for oil?
'Take a sporting chance', they tell you. But will it suffice
To wear a scrum-cap against falling skies?
'Play the game': but supposing the other chap kicks,
You'd like to have learnt some rough-house tricks.
It boils down to this – do you really want to win
Or prefer the fine gesture of giving in?
Are you going to keep or to make the rules,
Die with fighters or be dead with fools?
Men are wanted who will volunteer
To go aloft and cut away tangled gear;

Break through to blocked galleries below pit-head,
Get in touch with living and raise from the dead:
Men to catch spies, fly aeroplanes,
Harrow derelict acres and mend the drains.
There'll be work for you all if you're fain without feigning
To give up toys and go into training.
But you'll have to forget a great deal you've learnt,
The licence of Saturn, lacerations of Lent,
Self-abuse, your dignity, the Bad and the Good,
Heroism in phantasy and fainting at blood.
And you'll have to remember a great deal you've forgotten,
How to love a girl and how to sew a button,
Tiger's shock-tactics, elephant's defence,
The integral spirit and the communal sense.
Can you sing at your work? Enforce discipline
Without insignia? Then you've still a chance to win.

11

Third Defendant speaks
     I have always acted for the best.
     My business is the soul: I have given it rope,
     Coaxed it heavenward, but would not let it escape me.
     The peoples have sought a Ruler:
     I conjured one for each after his own image;
     For savage a Dark Demon, for Hebrew a Patriot,
     For Christian a Comforter, for atheist a Myth.
     The rulers have sought an Ally:
     I have called down thunders on the side of authority,
     Lightnings to galvanize the law;
     Promising the bread of heaven to the hungry of earth,
     Shunting the spirit into grassy sidings,
     I have served the temporal princes.
     There have been men ere now, disturbers of the peace,
     Leaders out of my land of milk and honey,
     Prescribing harder diet;

Whom I thrashed, outlawed, slew, or if persisting
Deified, shelving them and their dynamite doctrines
Up in the clouds out of the reach of children.
I have always acted for the best:
Hung on the skirts of progress, the tail of revolution,
Ready to drug the defeated and bless the victor.
I am a man apart
Who sits in the dark professing a revelation:
Exploiting the Word with the letter I turn
Joy into sacraments, the Holy Ghost to a formula.
But an impious generation is here,
Let in the light, melt down my mysteries,
Commission the moon to serve my altars
And make my colleagues village entertainers.
That tree of Grace, for years I have tended,
Is a slow-grower, not to be transplanted,
They'll cut it down for pit-props;
That harvest of Faith, not without blood ripened,
They have ploughed in; their dynamos chant
Canticles of a new power: my holy land is blasted,
The crust crumbles, the veins run vinegar.

12

Oh subterranean fires, break out!
Tornadoes, pity not
The petty bourgeois of the soul,
The middleman of God!

Who ruins farm and factory
To keep a private mansion
Is a bad landlord, he shall get
No honourable mention.

Who mobbed the kestrel out of the air,
Who made the tiger tame,

Who lost the blood's inheritance
And found the body's shame;

Who raised his hands to brand a Cain
And bless a submarine –
Time is up: the medicine-man
Must take his medicine.

The winter evening holds her peace
And makes a crystal pause;
Frozen are all the streams of light,
Silent about their source.

Comrade, let us look to earth,
Be stubborn, act and sleep:
Here at our feet the lasting skull
Keeps a stiff upper lip:

Feeling the weight of a long winter,
Grimaces underground;
But never again will need to ask
Why spirit was flesh-bound.

And we whom winter days oppress
May find some work to hand,
Perfect our plans, renew parts,
Break hedges down, plough land.

So when primroses pave the way
And the sun warms the stone,
We may receive the exile spirit
Coming into its own.

13

Fourth Defendant speaks
　　To sit at head of one's own table,
　　To overlook a warm familiar landscape,
　　Have large cupboards for small responsibilities –
　　Surely that does outweigh
　　The rent veil and the agonies to follow?
　　Me the Almighty fixed, from Eve fallen,
　　Heart-deep in earth, a pointer to star fields,
　　Suffering sapflow, fruitage, early barrenness;
　　Changeable reputed, but to change constant,
　　Fickle of fashion no more than the months are;
　　Daily depend on surroundings for sustenance,
　　On what my roots reach, what my leaves inhale here.
　　Grant me a rich ground, wrapped in airs temperate,
　　Not where nor'-easters threaten the flint scarps;
　　Consequence then shall I have, men's admiration
　　Now, and my bones shall be fuel for the future.
　　Yet have I always failed.
　　For he, who should have been my prime possession,
　　Was not to be possessed.
　　I leant o'er him, a firmament of shadow,
　　But he looked up through me and saw the stars.
　　I would have bound him in the earth-ways,
　　Fluid, immediate, the child of nature.
　　But he made bricks of earth, iron from fire,
　　Turned waves to power, winds to communication;
　　Setting up Art against Chaos, subjecting
　　My flux to the synthetic frost of reason.
　　I am left with a prone man,
　　Virtue gone out of him; who in the morning
　　Will rise to join Crusades or assist the Harlequins.
　　Though I persuade him that his stars are mine eyes'
　　Refraction, that wisdom's best expressed in
　　The passive mood, – here's no change for the better:

I was the body's slave, am now the spirit's.
Come, let me contemplate my own
Mysteries, a dark glass may save my face.

14

Live you by love confined,
There is no nearer nearness;
Break not his light bounds,
The stars' and seas' harness:
There is nothing beyond,
We have found the land's end.
We'll take no mortal wound
Who felt him in the furnace,
Drowned in his fierceness,
By his midsummer browned:
Nor ever lose awareness
Of nearness and farness
Who've stood at earth's heart careless
Of suns and storms around,
Who have leant on the hedge of the wind,
On the last ledge of darkness.

We are where love has come
To live: he is that river
Which flows and is the same;
He is not the famous deceiver
Nor early-flowering dream.
Content you. Be at home
In me. There's but one room
Of all the house you may never
Share, deny or enter.
There, as a candle's beam
Stands firm and will not waver
Spire-straight in a close chamber,
As though in shadowy cave a

Stalagmite of flame,
The integral spirit climbs
The dark in light for ever.

15

Consider. These are they
Who have a stake in earth
But risk no wing on air,
Walk not a planet path.

Theirs the reward of all
That live by sap alone,
Flourishing but to show
Which way the wind has gone.

While oaks of pedigree
Stand over a rich seam,
Another sinks the shaft,
Fills furnace, gets up steam.

These never would break through
The orbit of their year,
Admit no altered stress,
Decline a change of gear.

The tree grips soil, the bird
Knows how to use the wind;
But the full man must live
Rooted yet unconfined.

PART THREE

Never yield before the barren.
D. H. LAWRENCE

16

Look west, Wystan, lone flyer, birdman, my bully boy!
Plague of locusts, creeping barrage, has left earth bare:
Suckling and centenarian are up in air,
No wing-room for Wystan, no joke for kestrel joy.

Sky-scrapers put high questions that quench the wind's
                                                    breath,
Whose shadow still comes short of truth, but kills the grass:
Power-house chimneys choke sun, ascetic pylons pass
Bringing light to the dark-livers, charged to deal death.

Firework fêtes, love displays, levitation of dead,
Salvation writ in smoke will reassure the town,
While comfy in captive balloons easily brought down
Sit frail philosophers, gravity gone to the head.

Gain altitude, Auden, then let the base beware!
Migrate, chaste my kestrel, you need a change of air!

17

First Enemy speaks
Begin perhaps with jokes across the table,
Bathing before breakfast, undressing frankly,
Trials of strength, innocent invasions;
Concealing velvet hand in iron grip
Play the man, let woman wait indoors.
I do like doing things with you.

151

Shoot home the bolt, draw close the silken cordon:
Regrets for youth, malice at mutual friends,
Excluding company with a private smile,
Longer looks noting, change of tune. Ah, now
To find one's touch, anticipate the last movement!
You are so different from the others.

This is my act, who can play Cleopatra,
Can hear state secrets, see the guarded plans:
A man my empire, darling I proclaim
Through sultry eyes dominion appetites –
To be called a queen, be a subject for sonnets.
You can't really think me beautiful?

Then set the stage, lights for a final tableau –
I never shall love the dark since Maurice died –
Buzzards are wheeling above, horns blowing around;
We come to a point, circle the trembling prey
In sunny fern or many-mirrored bedroom.
I love to watch your face.

Now am I in the very lists of love,
Clutching the terminals may surely hope
To make a contact. Feel, body, Oh fail not!
Shall the harsh friction the gritted teeth of lust
Not generate a spark, bring me to life?
I've never felt like this before.

So, so again. And he that was alive
Is dead. Or sleeps. A stranger to these parts.
Nerve insulated, flesh unfused, this is
No consummation; yet a dear achievement:
Reach for the powder-puff, I have sinned greatly.
I suppose you hate me, now.

18

Not hate nor love, but say
Refreshment after rain,
A lucid hour; though this
Need not occur again.

You shall no further feast
Your pride upon my flesh.
Cry for the moon: here's but
An instantaneous flash.

My wells, my rooted good
Go deeper than you dare:
Seek not my sun and moon,
They are centred elsewhere.

I know a fairer land,
Whose furrows are of fire,
Whose hills are a pure metal
Shining for all to share.

And there all rivers run
To magnify the sea,
Whose waves recur for ever
In calm equality.

Hands off! The dykes are down.
This is no time for play.
Hammer is poised and sickle
Sharpened. I cannot stay.

19

Second Enemy speaks
Now sir, now madam, we're all plain people here,
Used to plain speaking: we know what is what,
How to stretch a point and where to draw the line.
You want to buy. I have the goods.
   Read about rector's girls
   Duke's disease synthetic pearls
   Latest sinners tasty dinners
   Plucky dogs shot Sinn Feiners
   Flood in China rape in Wales
   Murderer's tears scenes at sales
   That's the stuff aren't you thrilled
   Sit back and see the world.
Yet, though abiding by the law and the profits,
I have a solemn duty and shall not shirk it
Who stand *in loco parentis* to the British Public,
We must educate our bastards.
   Professor Jeans spills the beans
   Dean Inge tells you a thing
   A man in a gown gives you the low-down
   A man with a beard says something weird
   Famous whore anticipates war
   Woman mayor advises prayer
   A grey-haired gaga says leave it to mother
   Run off and play no more lessons today.
And third, brethren, you must be saved from yourselves,
From that secret voice, that positive contagion.
I'll have no long faces on this ship while I'm captain.
And you know what happens to mutineers.
   Is the boss unkind? Have you dropped a stitch?
   Smile! All together! You'll soon be better.
   Have you got a grouch? Do you feel an itch?
   There, there! Sit down and write uncle a letter.
   Lock the front door, here are your slippers,

Get out your toys and don't make a noise;
Don't tease the keepers, eat up your kippers,
And you'll have a treat one day if you're good boys.

20

Fireman and farmer, father and flapper,
I'm speaking to you, sir, please drop that paper;
Don't you know it's poison? Have you lost all hope?
Aren't you ashamed, ma'am, to be taking dope?
There's a nasty habit that starts in the head
And creeps through the veins till you go all dead:
Insured against accident? But that won't prove
Much use when one morning you find you can't move.

They tell you all's well with our lovely England
And God's in our capital. Isn't it grand
Where the offal of action, the rinsings of thought
From a stunted peer for a penny can be bought?
It seems a bargain, but in the long run
Will cost you your honour, your crops and your son.
They're selling you the dummy, for God's sake don't buy it!
Baby, that bottle's not clean, don't try it!

You remember that girl who turned the gas on –
They drove her to it, they couldn't let her alone.
That young inventor – you all know his name –
They used the plans and he died of their fame.
Careful, climber, they're getting at your nerve!
Leader, that's a bribe, they'd like you to serve!
Bull, I don't want to give you a nightmare,
But, keep still a moment, are you quite sure you're there?

As for you, Bimbo, take off that false face!
You've ceased to be funny, you're in disgrace.
We can see the spy through that painted grin;

You may talk patriotic but you can't take us in.
You've poisoned the reservoirs, released your germs
On firesides, on foundries, on tubes and on farms.
You've made yourself cheap with your itch for power
Infecting all comers, a hopeless whore.

Scavenger barons and your jackal vassals,
Your pimping press-gang, your unclean vessels,
We'll make you swallow your words at a gulp
And turn you back to your element, pulp.
Don't bluster, Bimbo, it won't do you any good;
We can be much ruder and we're learning to shoot.
Closet Napoleon, you'd better abdicate,
You'd better quit the country before it's too late.

21

Third Enemy speaks
God is a proposition,
And we that prove him are his priests, his chosen.
From bare hypothesis
Of strata and wind, of stars and tides, watch me
Construct his universe,
A working model of my majestic notions,
A sum done in the head.
Last week I measured the light, his little finger;
The rest is a matter of time.

God is an electrician,
And they that worship him must worship him
In ampere and in volt.
Scrap sun and moon, your twilight of false gods:
X. is not here or there;
Whose lightning scrawls brief cryptograms on sky,
Easy for us to solve;

Whose motions fit our formulae, whose temple
Is a pure apparatus.

God is a statistician:
Offer him all the data; tell him your dreams.
What is your lucky number?
How do you react to bombs? Have you a rival?
Do you really love your wife?
Get yourself taped. Put soul upon the table:
Switch on the arc-lights; watch
Heart's beat, the secret agents of the blood.
Let every cell be observed.

God is a Good Physician,
Gives fruit for hygiene, crops for calories.
Don't touch that dirty man,
Don't drink from the same cup, sleep in one bed:
You know He would not like it.
Young men, cut out those visions, they're bad for the eyes:
I'll show you face to face
Eugenics, Eupeptics and Euthanasia,
The clinic Trinity.

22

Where is he, where? How the man stares!
Do you think he is there, buttoned up in your stars?
Put by that telescope;
You can't bring him nearer, you can't, sir, you haven't a
                                                    hope.
Is he the answer to your glib equations,
The lord of light, the destroyer of nations?
To be seen on a slide, to be caught on a filter? The Cause
Limed in his own laws?
Analyst, you've missed him. Or worse and worst
You've got him inside? You must feel fit to burst.

Here, there, everywhere
Or nowhere. At least you know where. And how much do
you care?

Where then, Oh where? In earth or in air?
The master of mirth, the corrector of care?
Nightingale knows, if any,
And poplar flowing with wind; and high on the sunny
Hill you may find him, and low on the lawn
When every dew-drop is a separate dawn.
In the moment before the bombardment, poised at peace
He hides. And whoever sees
The cloud on the sky-line, the end of grief,
Dust in the distance that spells a relief,
Has found. Shall have his share
Who naked emerges on the far side of despair.

This one shall hear, though from afar,
The clear first call of new life, through fear
Piercing and padded walls:
Shall arise, shall scatter his heirlooms, shall run till he
falls.
That one is slower, shall know by growing,
Not aware of his hour, but suddenly blowing
With leaves and roses, living from springs of the blood.
These ones have found their good:
Facing the rifles in a blind alley
Or stepping through ruins to sound reveille
They feel the father here,
They have him at heart, they shake hands, they know he is
near.

23

Fourth Enemy speaks
I'm a dreamer, so are you.

See the pink sierras call,
The ever-ever land of dew,
Magic basements, fairy coal.
There the youngest son wins through,
Wee Willie can thrash the bully,
Living's cheap and dreams come true;
Lying manna tempts the belly;
Crowns are many, claims are few.

Come along then, come away
From the rush hour, from the town:
Blear and overcast today
Would put a blackcap out of tune,
Spoil the peacock's June display.
Rigid time of driving-belts
Gives no rest for grace-notes gay:
Fear and fever, cables, bolts
Pin the soul, allow no play.

You're a poet, so am I:
No man's keeper, intimate
Of breeding earth and brooding sky,
Irresponsible, remote,
A cool cloud, creation's eye.
Seek not to turn the winter tide
But to temperate deserts fly:
Close chain-mail of solitude
Must protect you or you die.

Come away then, let us go;
Lose identity and pass
Through the still blockade of snow,
Fear's frontier, an age of ice:
Pierce the crust and pass below
Towards a red volcanic core,
The warm womb where flesh can grow

Again and passion sleep secure
In creative ebb and flow.

24

Tempt me no more; for I
Have known the lightning's hour,
The poet's inward pride,
The certainty of power.

Bayonets are closing round.
I shrink; yet I must wring
A living from despair
And out of steel a song.

Though song, though breath be short,
I'll share not the disgrace
Of those that ran away
Or never left the base.

Comrades, my tongue can speak
No comfortable words,
Calls to a forlorn hope,
Gives work and not rewards.

Oh keep the sickle sharp
And follow still the plough:
Others may reap, though some
See not the winter through.

Father, who endest all,
Pity our broken sleep;
For we lie down with tears
And waken but to weep.

And if our blood alone
Will melt this iron earth,
Take it. It is well spent
Easing a saviour's birth.

25

Consider these, for we have condemned them;
Leaders to no sure land, guides their bearings lost
Or in league with robbers have reversed the signposts,
Disrespectful to ancestors, irresponsible to heirs.
Born barren, a freak growth, root in rubble,
Fruitlessly blossoming, whose foliage suffocates,
Their sap is sluggish, they reject the sun.

The man with his tongue in his cheek, the woman
With her heart in the wrong place, unhandsome,
   unwholesome;
Have exposed the new-born to worse than weather,
Exiled the honest and sacked the seer.
These drowned the farms to form a pleasure-lake,
In time of drought they drain the reservoir
Through private pipes for baths and sprinklers.

Getters not begetters; gainers not beginners;
Whiners, no winners; no triers, betrayers;
Who steer by no star, whose moon means nothing.
Daily denying, unable to dig:
At bay in villas from blood relations,
Counters of spoons and content with cushions
They pray for peace, they hand down disaster.

They that take the bribe shall perish by the bribe,
Dying of dry rot, ending in asylums,
A curse to children, a charge on the state.
But still their fears and frenzies infect us;

Drug nor isolation will cure this cancer:
It is now or never, the hour of the knife,
The break with the past, the major operation.

PART FOUR

He comes with work to do, he does not come to coo.

26

Junction or terminus – here we alight.
A myriad tracks converge on this moment,
This man where all ages and men are married,
Who shall right him? Who shall determine?

Standing astonished at the close of day
We know the worst, we may guess at good:
Geared too high our power was wasted,
Who have lost the old way to the happy ending.

A world behind us the west is in flames,
Devastated areas, works at a standstill;
No seed awakes, wary is no hunter,
The tame are ruined and the wild have fled.

Where then the saviour, the stop of illness?
Hidden the mountain was to steel our hearts.
Is healing here? An untrodden territory
Promises no coolness, invites but the brave.

But see! Not far, not fiction, a real one,
Vibrates like heat-haze full in the sun's face
Filling the heart, that chaste and fleet one,
Rarely my kestrel, my lucky star.

162

O man perplexed, here is your answer.
Alone who soars, who feeds upon earth –
Him shall you heed and learn where joy is
The dance of action, the expert eye.

Now is your moment, O hang-fire heart;
The ice is breaking, the death-grip relaxes,
Luck's turned. Submit to your star and take
Command, Oh start the attacking movement!

27

Wystan, Rex, all of you that have not fled,
This is our world, this is where we have grown
Together in flesh and live; though each alone
Shall join the enclosed order of the dead,
Enter the silent brotherhood of bone.

All you that have a cool head and safe hands
Awaken early, there is much to do;
Hedges to raze, channels to clear, a true
Reckoning to find. The other side commands
Eternity. We have an hour or two.

Let us speak first against that ancient firm
Who sell an armament to any cause,
Fear and Pain brothers: call them bullies and curs
Who take us into corners and make us squirm,
Finding the weak spot, fumbling at secret doors.

Let us tell them plainly now they haven't a chance,
We are going about together, we've mingled blood,
Taken a tonic that's set us up for good;
Their disguises are tabled, their movements known in
                                        advance,
We have found out who hides them and gives them food.

163

Lipcurl, Swiveleye, Bluster, Crock and Queer,
Mister I'll-think-it-over, Miss Not-to-day,
Young Who-the-hell-cares and old Let-us-pray,
Sir Après-moi-le-déluge. It is here.
They get their orders. These will have to pay.

Hear, the ice-wall of winter at our back,
Spring's first explosions throbbing across the plain,
Earth's diastole, flood-tide of heart and vein:
Collect your forces for a counter-attack,
New life is on the way, the relief train.

28

Though winter's barricade delays,
Another season's in the air;
We'll sow the spring in our young days,
Found a Virginia everywhere.

Look where the ranks of crocuses
Their rebel colours will display
Coming with quick fire to redress
The balance of a wintry day.

Those daffodils that from the mould
Drawing a sweet breath soon shall flower,
With a year's labour get their gold
To spend it on a sunny hour.

They from earth's centre take their time
And from the sun what love they need:
The proud flower burns away its prime,
Eternity lies in the seed.

Follow the kestrel, south or north,
Strict eye, spontaneous wing can tell

A secret. Where he comes to earth
Is the heart's treasure. Mark it well.

Here he hovers. You're on the scent;
Magnetic mountain is not far,
Across no gulf or continent,
Not where you think but where you are.

Stake out your claim. Go downwards. Bore
Through the tough crust. Oh learn to feel
A way in darkness to good ore.
You are the magnet and the steel.

Out of that dark a new world flowers.
There in the womb, in the rich veins
Are tools, dynamos, bridges, towers,
Your tractors and your travelling-cranes.

29

But winter still rides rough-shod upon us,
Summer comes not for wishing nor warmth at will:
Passes are blocked and glaciers pen us
Round the hearth huddled, hoping for a break,
Playing at patience, reporting ill.
Aware of changed temperature one shall wake
And rushing to window arouse companions
To feel frost surrender, an ice age finished;
Whose strength shall melt from the mountains and run
Riot, careering down corries and canyons.
What floods will rise then through rivers replenished,
Embankments broken, and bluffs undone,
Laid low old follies, all landmarks vanished.
Is it ready for launching, the Argo, the Ark,
Our transport, our buoyant one, our heart of oak?

Make haste, put through the emergency order
For an overtime day, for double shifts working:
Weather is breaking, tomorrow we must board her,
Cast off onto chaos and shape a course.
Many months have gone to her making,
Wood well-seasoned for watertight doors,
The old world's best in her ribs and ballast,
White-heat, high pressure, the heart of a new
In boiler, in gadget, in gauge, in screw.
Peerless on water, Oh proud our palace,
A home for heroes, the latest of her line;
A beater to windward, obedient to rudder,
A steamer into storm, a hurricane-rider,
Foam-stepper, star-steerer, freighter and fighter –
Name her, release her, anoint her with wine!

Whom shall we take with us? The true, the tested,
Floods over to find a new world and man it,
Sure-foot, Surveyor, Spark and Strong,
Those whom winter has wasted, not worsted,
Good at their jobs for a break-down gang:
Born haters will blast through debris or granite,
Willing work on the permanent ways,
And natural lovers repair the race.
As needle to north, as wheel in wheel turning,
Men shall know their masters and women their need,
Mating and submitting, not dividing and defying,
Force shall fertilize, mass shall breed.
Broad let our valleys embrace the morning
And satisfied see a good day dying,
Accepting the shadows, sure of seed.

30

You who would come with us,
Think what you stand to lose –

An assured income, the will
In your favour and the feel
Of firmness underfoot.
For travellers by this boat
Nothing to rest the eyes on
But a migrant's horizon,
No fixtures or bric-à-brac –
Wave walls without a break.
Old acquaintance on the quay
Have come to clutch your knee –
Merry-Andrew and Cassandra,
Squeamish, Sponge and Squanderer,
The Insurance Agent, the Vicar,
Hard Cheese the Confidence-Tricker,
Private Loot, General Pride,
And Lust the sultry-eyed.
Others you hate to leave
Wave with autumnal grief,
The best of what has been,
Props of an English scene;
A day we may not recover,
A camp you must quit for ever.

Now, if you will, retract.
For we are off to act
Activity of young
And cut the ravelled string.
Calm yourselves, you that seek
The flame, and whose flesh is weak
Must keep it in cold storage:
For we shall not encourage
The would-be hero, the nervous
Martyr to rule or serve us.
Stand forward for volunteers
Who have tempered their loves and fears
In the skilled process of time,

Whose spirit is blown to a flame
That leaves no mean alloys.
You who have heard a voice –
The siren in the morning
That gives the worker warning,
The whisper from the loam
Promising life to come,
Manifesto of peace
Read in an altered face –
Who have heard; and believe it true
That new life must break through.

31

In happier times
When the heart is whole and the exile king returned
We may sing shock of opposing teams
And electric storms of love again.

Our voices may be tuned
To solo flight, to record-breaking plane;
Looking down from hill
We may follow with fresh felicities
Wilful the light, the wayward motion of trees,
In happier times when the heart is whole.

In happier times
When the land is ours, these springs shall irrigate
Good growing soil until it teems,
Redeemed from mortgage, drilled to obey;
But still must flow in spate.
We'll focus stars again; though now must be
Map and binoculars
Outlining vision, bringing close
Natural features that will need no glass
In happier times, when the land is ours.

Make us a wind
To shake the world out of this sleepy sickness
Where flesh has dwindled and brightness waned!
New life multiple in seed and cell
Mounts up to brace our slackness.
Oppression's passion, a full organ swell
Through our throats welling wild
Of angers in unison arise
And hunger haunted with a million sighs,
Make us a wind to shake the world!

Make us the wind
From a new world that springs and gathers force,
Clearing the air, cleaning the wound;
Sets masses in motion and whips the blood.
Oh they shall find him fierce
Who cling to relics, dead wood shall feel his blade.
Rudely the last leaves whirled,
A storm on fire, dry ghosts, shall go in
Fear and be laid in the red of their own ruin.
Make us the wind from a new world!

32

You that love England, who have an ear for her music,
The slow movement of clouds in benediction,
Clear arias of light thrilling over her uplands,
Over the chords of summer sustained peacefully;
Ceaseless the leaves' counterpoint in a west wind lively,
Blossom and river rippling loveliest allegro,
And the storms of wood strings brass at year's finale:
Listen. Can you not hear the entrance of a new theme?

You who go out alone, on tandem or on pillion,
Down arterial roads riding in April,
Or sad beside lakes where hill-slopes are reflected

Making fires of leaves, your high hopes fallen:
Cyclists and hikers in company, day excursionists,
Refugees from cursed towns and devastated areas;
Know you seek a new world, a saviour to establish
Long-lost kinship and restore the blood's fulfilment.

You who like peace, good sorts, happy in a small way
Watching birds or playing cricket with schoolboys,
Who pay for drinks all round, whom disaster chose not;
Yet passing derelict mills and barns roof-rent
Where despair has burnt itself out – hearts at a standstill,
Who suffer loss, aware of lowered vitality;
We can tell you a secret, offer a tonic; only
Submit to the visiting angel, the strange new healer.

You above all who have come to the far end, victims
Of a run-down machine, who can bear it no longer;
Whether in easy chairs chafing at impotence
Or against hunger, bullies and spies preserving
The nerve for action, the spark of indignation –
Need fight in the dark no more, you know your enemies.
You shall be leaders when zero hour is signalled,
Wielders of power and welders of a new world.

33

Come for a walk in our pleasant land:
We must wake up early if we want to understand
The length and breadth and depth of decay
Has corrupted our vowels and clogged our bowels,
Impaired our breathing, eaten pride away.
What do they believe in – these yellow yes-men,
Pansies, politicians, prelates and pressmen,
Boneless wonders, unburstable bouncers,
Back-slappers, cheer-leaders, bribed announcers
Broadcasting All-Clear as the raiders draw near;

Would mend a burst dam with sticking-plaster
And hide with shocked hand the yawn of disaster –
What do they believe in? A god of gold,
A gilt-edged proposition; but it seems they've been sold.
All you fine ladies, once you were flowers
England was proud of, rich blooms, good growers;
But overblown now; and we can't afford you
Your missions and fashions, your synthetic passions;
We don't want to bed you and we'd rather not board you:
Weedy, greedy, unsatisfied, unsexed,
You're not living in this world, and as for the next –
You could hand white feathers on the judgement day
And give the damned a charity matinée.
Our holy intellectuals – what are they at?
Filling in hard times with literary chat,
Laying down the law where no one listens,
Finding the flaw in long-scrapped systems
And short cuts to places no more on the map:
Though off their feed now and inclined to mope.
Nasties, nudists, bedlamites, buddhists,
Too feeble to follow, unable to guide,
It's time we asked them to step aside.
Children of the sahib, the flag and the mater,
Grim on golf-courses and haggard on horses
They try to live but they've ceased to matter:
Who'll give a penny to the poor old guy?
These were the best that money could buy
And it isn't good enough. For what can they fight? –
The silver spoon, the touched hat, the expensive seat:
Marching at the orders of a mad physician
Down private roads to common perdition.
Where is the bourgeois, the backbone of our race?
Bent double with lackeying, the joints out of place;
Behind bluffs and lucky charms hiding to evade
An overdue audit, anæmic, afraid.
Trimmers and schemers, pusillanimous dreamers,

At cinemas, shop-windows and arenas we've found them
Bearing witness to a life beyond them.
They're paying for death on the instalment plan
Who hoped to go higher and failed to be men.
   We'd like to fight but we fear defeat,
   We'd like to work but we're feeling too weak,
   We'd like to be sick but we'd get the sack,
   We'd like to behave, we'd like to believe,
   We'd like to love, but we've lost the knack.

34

(FOR FRANCES WARNER)

What do we ask for, then?
Not for pity's pence nor pursy affluence,
Only to set up house again:
Neither a coward's heaven, cessation of pain,
Nor a new world of sense,
But that we may be given the chance to be men.
For what, then, do we hope?
Not longer sight at once but enlarged scope;
Miraculous no seed or growth of soul, but soil
Cleared of weed, prepared for good:
We shall expected no birth-hour without blood
Nor fire without recoil.

Publish the vision, broadcast and screen it,
Of a world where the will of all shall be raised to highest
                                        power,
Village or factory shall form the unit.
Control shall be from the centres, quick brain, warm heart,
And the bearings bathed in a pure
Fluid of sympathy. There possessions no more shall be part
Of the man, where riches and sacrifice
Are of flesh and blood, sex, muscles, limbs and eyes.

Each shall give of his best. It shall seem proper
For all to share what all produced.
Men shall be glad of company, love shall be more than a
                                                        guest
And the bond no more of paper.

Open your eyes, for vision
Is here of a world that has ceased to be bought and sold
With traitor silver and fairy gold;
But the diamond of endurance, the wrought-iron of passion
Is all their currency.
As the body that knows through action they are splendid,
Feeling head and heart agree;

Young men proud of their output, women no longer stale
With deferred crisis; the old, a full day ended,
Able to stand down and sit still.
Only the exploiter, the public nuisance, the quitter
Receive no quarter.

Here they do not need
To flee the birthplace. There's room for growing and
                                                working.
Bright of eye, champions for speed,
They sing their own songs, they are active, they play not
                                                watch:
Happy at night talking
Of the demon bowler cracked over the elm-trees,
The reverse pass that won the match.
At festivals knowing themselves normal and well-born
They remember the ancestors that gave them ease,
Harris who fought the bully at Melbourne,
What Wainwright wrote with his blood, Rosa in prison –
All who sucked out the poison.

173

35

In these our winter days
Death's iron tongue is glib
Numbing with fear all flesh upon
A fiery-hearted globe.

An age once green is buried,
Numbered the hours of light;
Blood-red across the snow our sun
Still trails his faint retreat.

Spring through death's iron guard
Her million blades shall thrust;
Love that was sleeping, not extinct,
Throw off the nightmare crust.

Eyes, though not ours, shall see
Sky-high a signal flame,
The sun returned to power above
A world, but not the same.

36

Now raise your voices for a final chorus,
Lift the glasses, drink tomorrow's health –
Success to the doctor who is going to cure us
And those who will die no more in bearing wealth.
On our magnetic mountain a beacon burning
Shall sign the peace we hoped for, soon or late,
Clear over a clean earth, and all men turning
Like infants' eyes like sunflowers to the light.

Drink to the ordered nerves, the sight restored;
A day when power for all shall radiate
From the sovereign centres, and the blood is stirred

To flow in its ancient courses of love and hate:
When the country vision is ours that like a barn
Fills the heart with slow-matured delight,
Absorbing wind and summer, till we turn
Like infants' eyes like sunflowers to the light.

For us to dream the birthday, but they shall act it –
Bells over fields, the hooters from the mine,
On New Year's Eve under the brideroom's attic
Chorus of coastguards singing Auld Lang Syne.
Now at hope's horizon that day is dawning,
We guess at glory from a mountain height,
But then in valley towns they will be turning
Like infants' eyes like sunflowers to the light.

Beckon O beacon, and O sun be soon!
Hollo, bells, over a melting earth!
Let man be many and his sons all sane,
Fearless with fellows, handsome by the hearth.
Break from your trance: start dancing now in town,
And, fences down, the ploughing match with mate.
This is your day: so turn, my comrades, turn
Like infants' eyes like sunflowers to the light.

1933

A TIME TO DANCE

Learning to Talk

See this small one, tiptoe on
The green foothills of the years,
Views a younger world than yours;
When you go down, he'll be the tall one.

Dawn's dew is on his tongue –
No word for what's behind the sky,
Naming all that meets the eye,
Pleased with sunlight over a lawn.

Hear his laughter. He can't contain
The exquisite moment overflowing.
Limbs leaping, woodpecker flying
Are for him and not hereafter.

Tongue trips, recovers, triumphs,
Turning all ways to express
What the forward eye can guess –
That time is his and earth young.

We are growing too like trees
To give the rising wind a voice:
Eagles shall build upon our verse,
Our winged seeds are tomorrow's sowing.

Yes, we learn to speak for all
Whose hearts here are not at home,
All who march to a better time
And breed the world for which they burn.

Though we fall once, though we often,
Though we fall to rise not again,
From our horizon sons begin;
When we go down, they will be tall ones.

Moving In

Is it your hope, hope's hearth, heart's home, here at the
                                    lane's end?
Deeds are signed, structure is sound though century-old;
Redecorated throughout, all modern convenience, the
                                    cable extended;
Need grope no more in corners nor cower from dark and
                                    cold.

Who between town and country dreams of contact with
                                    the two worlds
Earthquake will wake, a chasm at his feet, crack of doom
                                    overhead.
What deeds can survive, what stone can shoulder the shock
                                    of a new world?
Dark and cold, dancing no spark, when the cable is dead.

Fear you not ghosts of former tenants, a fell visitation
From them whose haunts you have sealed, whose secrets
                                    you haled to light?
Gay as grass are you? Tough as granite? But they are
                                    patient,
Waiting for you to weaken, awaiting a sleepless night.

You have cut down the yews, say you, for a broader view?
                                    No churchyard
Emblems shall bind or blind you? But see, the imperative
                                    brow
Frowns of the hills, offers no compromise, means far harder
Visions than valley steeples call to, a stricter vow.

Though your wife is chaste, though your children lustily
                                    throng, though laughing
Raise you a record crop, yet do you wrong your powers,

Flattered no longer by isolation nor satisfied loving.
Not box hedge where the birds nest, not embankments of
                                        flowers.

Guard from regret. No private good will let you forget all
Those, time's accessories, whose all is a leaden arc
Between work and sleep; who might have been men,
                                        brighter metal,
Proudly reaped the light, passed peacefully into dark.

The Conflict

I sang as one
Who on a tilting deck sings
To keep men's courage up, though the wave hangs
That shall cut off their sun.

As storm-cocks sing,
Flinging their natural answer in the wind's teeth,
And care not if it is waste of breath
Or birth-carol of spring.

As ocean-flyer clings
To height, to the last drop of spirit driving on
While yet ahead is land to be won
And work for wings.

Singing I was at peace,
Above the clouds, outside the ring:
For sorrow finds a swift release in song
And pride its poise.

Yet living here,
As one between two massing powers I live
Whom neutrality cannot save
Not occupation cheer.

None such shall be left alive:
The innocent wing is soon shot down,
And private stars fade in the blood-red dawn
Where two worlds strive.

The red advance of life
Contracts pride, calls out the common blood,
Beats song into a single blade,
Makes a depth-charge of grief.

Move then with new desires,
For where we used to build and love
Is no man's land, and only ghosts can live
Between two fires.

Losers

Those are judged losers and fortune-flouted
Whose flighted hopes fell down short of satisfaction;
The killed in action, the blasted in beauty, all choosers

Of the wrong channel for love's seasonal spate:
Cheerless some amid rock or rank forest life-long
Laboured to hew an estate, but they died childless:

Those within hail of home by blizzard o'ertaken;
Those awakening from vision with truth on tongue, struck
                                        dumb:
Are deemed yet to have been transfigured in failure.

Men mourn their beauty and promise, publish the diaries;
Medals are given; the graves are evergreen with pity:
Their fire is forwarded through the hearts of the living.

What can we say of these, from the womb wasted,
Whose nerve was never tested in act, who fell at the start,
Who had no beauty to lose, born out of season?

Early an iron frost clamped down their flowing
Desires. They were lost at once: they failed and died in the
                                                    whirling
Snow, bewildered, homeless from first to last.

Frightened we stop our ears to the truth they are telling
Who toil to remain alive, whose children start from sleep
Weeping into a world worse than nightmares.

Splendour of cities they built cannot ennoble
The barely living, ambitious for bread alone. Pity
Trails not her robe for these and their despairs.

In Me Two Worlds

In me two worlds at war
Trample the patient flesh,
This lighted ring of sense where clinch
Heir and ancestor.

This moving point of dust
Where past and future meet
Traces their battle-line and shows
Each thrust and counterthrust.

185

The armies of the dead
Are trenched within my bones,
My blood's their semaphore, their wings
Are watchers overhead.

Their captains stand at ease
As on familiar ground,
The veteran longings of the heart
Serve them for mercenaries.

Conscious of power and pride
Imperially they move
To pacify an unsettled zone –
The life for which they died.

But see, from vision's height
March down the men to come,
And in my body rebel cells
Look forward to the fight.

The insolence of the dead
Breaks on their solid front:
They tap my nerves for power, my veins
To stain their banners red.

These have the spirit's range,
The measure of the mind:
Out of the dawn their fire comes fast
To conquer and to change.

So heir and ancestor
Pursue the inveterate feud,
Making my senses' darkened fields
A theatre of war.

A Warning to those who Live on Mountains

You inhabit the mountains, half-way to heaven;
Wind carries your wishes like winged seeds
Over the valley, not sowing in vain:
Breathe rarest air, with the pure red rowan
Have graceful grown and calm as glaciers.
You are proud of the view; on plateau and peak
Rampant your telescopes rake the horizon,
Make nothing of the distance to nearest or next world.
You have made your mark on the stony-hearted massif,
Galleried granite and worked for gold
Till a solid world turned to fantastic tracery:
In snow-line receding your power we see,
Your heraldic pride hewn on the hillface.

Remember the ringed ammonite, running
Crazy, was killed for being too clever.

Impatient grow the peoples of the plain,
They wait for a word, the helio winking
As it talks of truce, the exile's return.
Labouring aloft you forget plain language,
Simple the password that disarms suspicion:
Starved are your roots, and still would you strain
The tie between brain and body to breaking-point?
Your power's by-products have poisoned their streams,
Their vision grows short as your shadow lengthens,
And your will walls them in. Beware, for a heavy
Charge is laid against you, Oh little longer
Will the hand be withheld that hesitates at the wire's end,
And your time totters like a tenement condemned.

Famous that fall, or shall they tell how in the final
Moment remaining you changed your mind?

Johnny Head-In-Air

It was an evening late in the year
When the frost stings again,
Hard-bitten was the face of the hills
And harsh breathed the plain.

Along a stony watershed
Surly and peaked with cold
I saw a company straggling over,
Over an endless wold.

The plain breathed up in smoke: its breath
Like a dying curse did freeze:
The fingers of the fog reached up
And took them by the knees.

Cruel, cruel look the stars
Fixed in a bitter frown:
Here at our feet to left and right
The silly streams run down.

We have left the ice-fields far behind,
Jungle, desert and fen;
We have passed the place of the temperate race
And the land of the one-eyed men.

The road reels back a million miles,
It is high time we came
Dropping down to the rich valleys
Where each can stake his claim.

Iron, iron rang the road,
All iron to the tread:
Heaven's face was barred with steel
Star-bolted overhead.

The well, the ill, on foot or on wheel,
The shattered, the shamed, the proud –
And limousines like painted queans
Went curving through the crowd.

What are these shapes that drive them on?
Is it the ravenous host
Of the dead? Or are they shadows of children
Not born, nipped by the frost?

The viaduct's broken down behind:
They cannot turn again.
Telegraph poles stride on before them
Pacing out their pain.

Where are you going, you wan hikers,
And why this ganglion gear?
What are those packs that on your backs
Through frost and fog you bear?

Through frost and fog, by col and crag
Leads on this thoroughfare
To kingdom-come: it is our gods
That on our backs we bear.

True they had travelled a million miles
If they had travelled one:
They walked or rode, each with his load,
A leaden automaton:

But never the sun came out to meet them
At the last lap of land,
Nor in the frore and highest heaven
Did the flint-eyed stars unbend.

Now they have come to night's massif;
Those sheer, unfissured walls
Cry halt, and still the following shadows
Rustle upon their heels.

They have come to the crisis of the road,
They have come without maps or guides:
To left and right along the night
The cryptic way divides.

I looked and I saw a stark signpost
There at the road's crest,
And its arms were the arms of a man pointing,
Pointing to east and west.

His face was pure as the winnowed light
When the wild geese fly high,
And gentle as on October evenings
The heron-feathered sky.

The mists grovelled below his feet
And the crowd looked up to pray:
From his beacon eyes a tremendous backwash
Of darkness surged away.

Speak up, speak up, you skyward man,
Speak up and tell us true;
To east or west – which is the best,
The through-way of the two?

The heaven-wind parts your hair, the sun
Is wintering in your eyes;
Johnny Head-In-Air, tell us
Which way our good luck lies.

Wirily stirred the stiffening grasses
With a chitter of migrant birds:
Wearily all that horde fell silent
Waiting for his words.

Each way the blindly spearing headlights
Were blunted on the gloom:
Only his eyes like keen X-rays
Saw into the night's womb.

I look to right, to right, comrades,
I look to right and I see
A smooth decline past rowan and pine
That leads to a low country.

Roses cling to a second summer
There, and the birds are late
To bed; the dying sun has left it
A legacy of light:

Winds browse over the unreaped corn,
Rivers flow on gems,
Shades dream in the dust of glory, and steeples
Hum with remembered chimes.

But go you now or go you then,
Those ferlies you'll not behold
Till the guardians of that valley have crossed
Your hand with fairy gold.

Who takes that gold is a ghost for ever
And none shall hear his cries,
He never shall feel or heat or hail,
He never shall see sun rise.

I look to left, to left, comrades,
I look to left, and there –
Put off those gods, put off those goods
That on your backs you bear –

For he must travel light who takes
An eagle's route, and cope
With canyons deeper than despair
And heights o'ertopping hope:

Only the lifting horizon leads him
And that is no man's friend:
Only his duty breath to whisper
All things come to an end.

But all shall be changed, all shall be friends
Upon that mountainside;
They shall awake with the sun and take
Hilltops in their stride.

Out of their crimson-hearted east
A living day shall dawn,
Out of their agonies a rare
And equal race be born.

His arms were stretched to the warring poles,
The current coursed his frame:
Over the hill-crest, niched in night,
They saw a man of flame.

Come down, come down, you suffering man,
Come down, and high or low
Choose your fancy and go with us
The way that we should go.

That cannot be till two agree
Who long have lain apart:
Traveller, know, I am here to show
Your own divided heart.

The Ecstatic

Lark, skylark, spilling your rubbed and round
Pebbles of sound in air's still lake,
Whose widening circles fill the noon; yet none
Is known so small beside the sun:

Be strong your fervent soaring, your skyward air!
Tremble there, a nerve of song!
Float up there where voice and wing are one,
A singing star, a note of light!

Buoyed, embayed in heaven's noon-wide reaches –
For soon light's tide will turn – Oh stay!
Cease not till day streams to the west, then down
That estuary drop down to peace.

Poem for an Anniversary

Admit then and be glad
Our volcanic age is over.
A molten rage shook earth from head to toe,
Seas leapt from their beds,
World's bedrock boiling up, the terrible lava.
Now it is not so.

Remember, not regret
Those cloudy dreams that trod on air
How distantly reflecting fire below:
The mating in air, the mute
Shuddering electric storms, the foul or fair
Love was used to know.

Admire, no more afraid,
Country made for peace. Earth rent,
Rocks like prayers racked from the heart, are now
Landmarks for us and shade:
Hotfoot to havoc where the lava went,
Cooler rivers flow.

Survey what most survives –
Love's best, climate and contour fine:
We have trained the giant lightning to lie low
And drive our linked lives;
Those clouds stand not in daydream but for rain,
And earth has grain to grow.

Sonnet

This man was strong, and like a seacape parted
The tides. There were not continents enough
For all his fledged ambitions. The hard-hearted
Mountains were moved by his explosive love.
Was young: yet between island and island
Laid living cable and whispered across seas:
When he sang, our feathery woods fell silent:
His smile put the fidgeting hours at ease.

194

See him now, a cliff chalk-faced and crumbling,
Eyes like craters of volcanoes dead;
A miser with the tarnished minutes fumbling,
A queasy traveller from board to bed:
The voice that charmed spirits grown insane
As the barking of dogs at the end of a dark lane.

Two Songs

I've heard them lilting at loom and belting,
Lasses lilting before dawn of day:
But now they are silent, not gamesome and gallant –
The flowers of the town are rotting away.

There was laughter and loving in the lanes at evening;
Handsome were the boys then, and girls were gay.
But lost in Flanders by medalled commanders
The lads of the village are vanished away.

Cursed be the promise that takes our men from us –
All will be champion if you choose to obey:
They fight against hunger but still it is stronger –
The prime of our land grows cold as the clay.

The women are weary, once lilted so merry,
Waiting to marry for a year and a day:
From wooing and winning, from owning or earning
The flowers of the town are all turned away.

> Come, live with me and be my love,
> And we will all the pleasures prove
> Of peace and plenty, bed and board,
> That chance employment may afford.

I'll handle dainties on the docks
And thou shalt read of summer frocks:
At evening by the sour canals
We'll hope to hear some madrigals.

Care on thy maiden brow shall put
A wreath of wrinkles, and thy foot
Be shod with pain: not silken dress
But toil shall tire thy loveliness.

Hunger shall make thy modest zone
And cheat fond death of all but bone –
If these delights thy mind may move,
Then live with me and be my love.

A Carol

Oh hush thee, my baby,
Thy cradle's in pawn:
No blankets to cover thee
Cold and forlorn.
The stars in the bright sky
Look down and are dumb
At the heir of the ages
Asleep in a slum.

The hooters are blowing,
No heed let him take;
When baby is hungry
'Tis best not to wake.
Thy mother is crying,
Thy dad's on the dole:
Two shillings a week is
The price of a soul.

A Time to Dance

IN MEMORY OF
L. P. HEDGES*

For those who had the power
    of the forest fires that burn
Leaving their source in ashes
    to flush the sky with fire:
Those whom a famous urn
    could not contain, whose passion
Brimmed over the deep grave
    and dazzled epitaphs:
For all that have won us wings
    to clear the tops of grief,
My friend who within me laughs
    bids you dance and sing.

Some set out to explore
    earth's limit, and little they recked if
Never their feet came near it
    outgrowing the need for glory:
Some aimed at a small objective
    but the fierce updraught of their spirit
Forced them to the stars.
    Are honoured in public who built
The dam that tamed a river;
    or holding the salient for hours
Against odds, cut off and killed,
    are remembered by one survivor.

All these. But most for those
    whom accident made great,

---

* A brilliant cricketer and amateur actor. CDL's colleague at Cheltenham Junior School, who died untimely.

As a radiant chance encounter
　　of cloud and sunlight grows
Immortal on the heart:
　　whose gift was the sudden bounty
Of a passing moment, enriches
　　the fulfilled eye for ever.
Their spirits float serene
　　above time's roughest reaches,
But their seed is in us and over
　　our lives they are evergreen.

＊　　　＊　　　＊

Let us sing then for my friend not a dirge, not a funeral
　　　　　　　　　　　　　　anthem,
But words to match his mirth, a theme with a happy end;
A bird's buoyancy in them, over the dark-toned earth
To hold a sustained flight, a tune sets death to dancing;
The stormcock's song, the ecstatic poise of the natural
　　　　　　　　　　　　　　fighter,
And a beat as of feet advancing to glory, a lilt emphatic.

＊　　　＊　　　＊

Sing we the two lieutenants, Parer and M'Intosh,
After the War wishing to hie them home to Australia,
Planned they would take a high way, a hazardous crazy
　　　　　　　　　　　　　　air-way:
Death their foregone conclusion, a flight headlong to
　　　　　　　　　　　　　　failure,
We said. For no silver posh
Plane was their pigeon, no dandy dancer quick-stepping
　　　　　　　　　　　　　　through heaven,
But a craft of obsolete design, a condemned D.H. nine;
Sold for a song it was, patched up though to write an
　　　　　　　　　　　　　　heroic
Line across the world as it reeled on its obstinate stoic
Course to that southern haven.

198

On January 8th, 1920, their curveting wheels kissed
England goodbye. Over Hounslow huddled in morning mist
They rose and circled like buzzards while we rubbed our
                                       sleepy eyes:
Like a bird scarce-fledged they flew, whose flying hours are
                                       few –
Still dear is the nest but deeper its desire unto the skies –
And they left us to our sleeping.
They felt earth's warning tug on their wings: vain to
                                      advance
Asking a thoroughfare through the angers of the air
On so flimsy a frame: but they pulled up her nose and the
                                  earth went sloping
Away, and they aimed for France.

Fog first, a wet blanket, a kill-joy, the primrose-of-
                              morning's blight,
Blotting out the dimpled sea, the ample welcome of land,
The gay glance from the bright
Cliff-face behind, snaring the sky with treachery, sneering
At hope's loss of height. But they charged it, flying blind;
They took a compass-bearing against that dealer of doubt,
As a saint when the field of vision is fogged gloriously
                                    steels
His spirit against the tainter of air, the elusive taunter:
They climbed to win a way out,
Then downward dared till the moody waves snarled at the
                                    wheels.

Landing at last near Conteville, who had skimmed the
                                crest of oblivion,
They could not rest, but rose and flew on to Paris, and
                                    there
Trivially were delayed – a defective petrol feed –
Three days: a time hung heavy on
Hand and heart, till they leapt again to the upper air,

Their element, their lover, their angel antagonist.
Would have taken a fall without fame, but the sinewy
                              frame-work the wrist
Of steel the panting engine wrestled well: and they went
South while the going was good, as a swallow that guide
                                        nor goad
Needs on his sunny scent.

At Lyons the petrol pump failed again, and forty-eight
                                        hours
They chafed to be off, the haughty champions whose
                              breathing-space
Was an horizon span and the four winds their fan.
Over Italy's shores
A reverse, the oil ran out and cursing they turned about
Losing a hundred miles to find a landing-place.
Not a coast for a castaway this, no even chance of
                              alighting
On sward or wind-smooth sand:
A hundred miles without pressure they flew, the engine
                              fighting
For breath, and its heart nearly burst before they dropped
                              to land.

And now the earth they had spurned rose up against them
                              in anger,
Tier upon tier it towered, the terrible Apennines:
No sanctuary there for wings, not flares nor landing-lines,
No hope of floor and hangar.
Yet those ice-tipped spears that disputed the passage set
                              spurs
To their two hundred and forty horse power; grimly they
                              gained
Altitude, though the hand of heaven was heavy upon them,
The downdraught from the mountains: though desperate
   eddies spun them

Like a coin, yet unkindly tossed their luck came uppermost
And mastery remained.

Air was all ambushes round them, was avalanche
                             earthquake
Quicksand, a funnel deep as doom, till climbing steep
They crawled like a fly up the face of perpendicular night
And levelled, finding a break
At fourteen thousand feet. Here earth is shorn from sight:
Deadweight a darkness hangs on their eyelids, and they
                                    bruise
Their eyes against a void: vindictive the cold airs close
Down like a trap of steel and numb them from head to
                                 heel;
Yet they kept an even keel,
For their spirit reached forward and took the controls while
                          their fingers froze.

They had not heard the last of death. When the mountains
                           were passed,
He raised another crest, the long crescendo of pain
Kindled to climax, the plane
Took fire. Alone in the sky with the breath of their enemy
Hot in their face they fought: from three thousand feet
                          they tilted
Over, side-slipped away – a trick for an ace, a race
And running duel with death: flame streamed out behind,
A crimson scarf of, as life-blood out of a wound, but the
                            wind
Of their downfall stanched it; death wilted,
Lagged and died out in smoke – he could not stay their
                             pace.

A lull for a while. The powers of hell rallied their legions.
On Parer now fell the stress of the flight; for the plane had
                        been bumped,

Buffeted, thrashed by the air almost beyond repair:
But he tinkered and coaxed, and they limped
Over the Adriatic on into warmer regions.
Erratic their course to Athens, to Crete: coolly they rode

          her
Like a tired horse at the water-jumps, they jockeyed her

          over seas,
Till they came at last to a land whose dynasties of sand
Had seen Alexander, Napoleon, many a straddling invader,
But never none like these.

England to Cairo, a joy-ride, a forty-hour journey at most,
Had cost them forty-four days. What centuried strata of life
Fuelled the fire that haled them to heaven, the power that

          held them
Aloft? For their plane was a laugh,
A patch, brittle as matchstick, a bubble, a lift for a ghost:
Bolts always working loose of propeller, cylinder, bearer;
Instruments faulty; filter, magneto, each strut unsound.
Yet after four days, though we swore she never could leave

          the ground,
We saw her in headstrong haste diminish towards the

          east –
That makeshift, mad sky-farer.

Aimed they now for Baghdad, unwritten in air's annals
A voyage. But theirs the fate all flights of logic to refute,
Who obeyed no average law, who buoyed the viewless

          channels
Of sky with a courage steadfast, luminous. Safe they

          crossed
Sinai's desert, and daring
The Nejd, the unneighbourly waste of Arabia, yet higher

         soaring
(Final a fall there for birds of passage, limed and lost
In shifty the sand's embrace) all day they strove to climb

Through stormy rain: but they felt her shorten her stride
and falter,
And they fell at evening time.

Slept that night beside their machine, and the next
morning
Raider Arabs appeared reckoning this stranded bird
A gift: like cobras they struck, and their gliding shadows
athwart
The sand were all their warning.
But the aeronauts, knowing iron the coinage here, had
brought
Mills bombs and revolvers, and M'Intosh held them off
While Parer fought for life –
A spark, the mechanic's right answer, and finally wrought
A miracle, for the dumb engine spoke and they rose
Convulsively out of the clutch of the desert, the clench of
their foes.

Orchestrate this theme, artificer-poet. Imagine
The roll, crackling percussion, quickening tempo of engine
For a start: the sound as they soar, an octave-upward slur
Scale of sky ascending:
Hours-held note of level flight, a beat unhurried,
Sustaining undertone of movement never-ending:
Wind shrill on the ailerons, flutes and fifes in a flurry
Devilish when they dive, plucking of tense stays.
These hardly heard it, who were the voice, the heavenly
air
That sings above always.

We have seen the extremes, the burning, the freezing, the
outward face
Of their exploit; heroic peaks, tumbling-to-zero depressions:
Little our graph can show, the line they traced through
space,

Of the heart's passionate patience.
How soft drifts of sleep piled on their senses deep
And they dug themselves out often: how the plane was a
                              weight that hung
And swung on their aching nerve; how din drilled through
                              the skull
And sight sickened – so slow earth filtered past below.
Yet nerve failed never, heart clung
To height, and the brain kept its course and the hand its skill.

Baghdad renewed a propeller damaged in desert. Arid
Baluchistan spared them that brought down and spoilt
                              with thirst
Armies of Alexander. To Karachi they were carried
On cloud-back: fragile as tinder their plane, but the winds
                              were tender
Now to their need, and nursed
Them along till teeming India made room for them to alight.
Wilting her wings, the sweltering suns had moulted her
                              bright
Plumage, rotten with rain
The fabric: but they packed her with iron washers and
                              tacked her
Together, good for an hour, and took the air again.

Feats for a hundred flights, they were prodigal of: a fairest
Now to tell – how they foiled death when the engine failed
Above the Irrawaddy, over close-woven forest.
What shoals for a pilot there, what a snarled passage and
                              dark
Shelves down to doom and grip
Of green! But look, balanced superbly, quick off the mark
Swooping like centre three-quarter whose impetus storms a
                              gap –
Defenders routed, rooted their feet, and their arms are
                              mown

Aside, that high or low aim at his overthrow –
M'Intosh touched her down.

And they picked her up out of it somehow and put her at
                                        the air, a
Sorry hack for such steeplechasing, to leap the sky.
'We'll fly this bloody crate till it falls to bits at our feet,'
Said the mechanic Parer.
And at Moulmein soon they crashed; and the plane by
                                        their spirit's high
Tension long pinned, girded and guarded from dissolution,
Fell to bits at their feet. Wrecked was the undercarriage,
Radiator cracked, in pieces, compasses crocked;
Fallen all to confusion.
Their winged hope was a heap of scrap, but unsplintered
                                        their courage.

Six weeks they worked in sun-glare and jungle damps,
                                        assembling
Fragments to make airworthy what was worth not its
                                        weight in air,
As a surgeon, grafter of skin, as a setter of bones tumbling
Apart, they had power to repair
This good for naught but the grave: they livened her engine
                                        and gave
Fuselage faith to rise rejuvenated from ruin.
Went with them stowaways, not knowing what hazard
                                        they flew in –
Bear-cubs, a baby alligator, lizards and snakes galore;
Mascots maybe, for the plane though twice she was floored
                                        again
Always came up for more.

Till they came to the pitiless mountains of Timor. Yet
                                        these, untamed,

Not timorous, against the gradient and Niagara of air they
                                              climbed
Scarce-skimming the summits; and over the shark-toothed
                                              Timor sea
Lost their bearings, but shirked not the odds, the deaths
                                              that lurked
A million to one on their trail:
They reached out to the horizon and plucked their destiny.
On for eight hours they flew blindfold against the
                              unknown,
And the oil began to fail
And their flying spirit waned – one pint of petrol remained
When the land stood up to meet them and they came into
                                              their own.

Southward still to Melbourne, the bourn of their flight,
                              they pressed
Till at last near Culcairn, like a last fretted leaf
Falling from brave autumn into earth's breast,
D.H. nine, their friend that had seen them to the end,
Gave up her airy life.
The Southern Cross was splendid above the spot where she
                                              fell,
The end of her rainbow curve over our weeping day:
And the flyers, glad to be home, unharmed by that dizzy
                                              fall,
Dazed as the dead awoken from death, stepped out of the
                                              broken
Body and went away.

              What happened then, the roar
                  and rave of waving crowds
              That fêted them, was only
                  an afterglow of glory
              Reflected on the clouds
                  where they had climbed alone,

Day's golden epilogue:
    and them, whose meteor path
Lightened our eyes, whose great
    spirit lifted the fog
That sours a doubtful earth,
    the stars commemorate.

In February, a world of hard light,
A frosty welcome, the aconites came up
Lifting their loving cups to drink the sun:
Spring they meant, mounting and more of hope.
And I thought of my friend, like these withered too soon,
Who went away in a night
Before the spring was ready, who left our town
For good. Like aconites he pledged the spring
Out of my grief-bound heart, and he made me sing
The spirit of life that nothing can keep down.

But yesterday, in May, a storm arose
Clouding the spring's festivities, and spoilt
Much would have been admired and given us shade.
We saw this year's young hopes beat down and soiled,
Blossoms not now for fruit, boughs might have made
Syringa's* wreath of snows.
A fortune gone time held for us in trust.
And I knew no bold flourish of flowers can write
Off the dead loss, when friends dissolve in night
Changing our dear-invested love to dust.

Strange ways the dead break through. Not the Last Post
Brings them, nor clanging midnight: for then is the inner
Heart reinforced against assault and sap.
On break-up day or at the cricket-club dinner
Between a word and a word they find the gap,

* See note on *Fathers to Sons (Pegasus)* p. 514.

207

And we know what we have lost.
Sorrow is natural thirst: we are not weaned
At once. Though long withdrawn the sickening blade,
Deeply we remember loss of blood
And the new skin glosses over an active wound.

Remember that winter morning – no maroon
Warned of a raid; death granted no farewell speech,
Acted without prologue, was a bell and a line
Speaking from far of one no more within reach.
Blood ran out of me. I was alone.
How suddenly, how soon,
In a moment, while I was looking the other way,
You hid yourself where I could never find you –
Too dark the shadows earth sheeted around you.
So we went home: that was the close of play.

Still I hoped for news. Often I stood
On promontories that straining towards the west
Fret their hearts away. Thence on a clear
Day one should glimpse the islands of the blest,
And he, if any, had a passport there.
But no, it was no good.
Those isles, it proved, were broken promises,
A trick of light, a way wishes delude:
Or, if he lived out there, no cable was laid
To carry his love whispering over seas.

So I returned. Perhaps he was nearer home
And I had missed him. Here he was last seen
Walking familiar as sunlight a solid road;
Round the next turn, his door. But look, there has been
Landslide: those streets end abruptly, they lead
The eye into a tomb.
Scrabble for souvenirs. Fit bone to bone;
Anatomy of buried joys you guess,

But the wind jeers through it. Assemble the shattered glass;
A mirror you have, but the face there is your own.

Was so much else we could have better spared –
Churches, museums, multiple stores: but the bomb
Fell on the power-house: total that eclipse.
He was our dynamo, our warmth, our beam
Transmitter of mirth – it is a town's collapse
Not easily repaired.
Or as a reservoir that, sharing out
Rain hoarded from heaven, springs from the valley,
Refreshment was for all: now breached and wholly
Drained, is a barren bed, a cup of drought.

Then to the hills, as one who dies for rain,
I went. All day the light makes lovely passes
There, whose hands are healing, whose smile was yours,
And eloquent winds hearten the dry grasses.
They have come to terms with death: for them the year's
Harvest, the instant pain,
Are as clouds passing indifferent over
Their heads, but certain givers in the end.
Downright these hills, hiding nothing they stand
Firm to the foot and comfort the eye for ever.

They say, 'Death is above your weight, too strong
For argument or armies, the real dictator:
He never was one to answer the question, Why?
He sends for you tomorrow, for us later:
Nor are you the Orpheus who could buy
Resurrection with a song.
Not for long will your chalk-faced bravado
Stand the erosion of eternity:
Learn from us a moment's sanity –
To be warm in the sun, to accept the following shadow.'

In my heart's mourning underworld I sang
As miners entombed singing despair to sleep –
Their earth is stopped, their eyes are reconciled
To night. Yet here, under the sad hill-slope
Where I thought one spring of my life for ever was sealed,
The friend I had lost sprang
To life again and showed me a mystery:
For I knew, at last wholly accepting death,
Though earth had taken his body and air his breath,
He was not in heaven or earth: he was in me.

Now will be cloudburst over a countryside
Where the tongues of prophets were dry and the air was
                                        aching:
Sky-long the flash, the thunder, the release,
Are fresh beginning, the hour of the weather breaking.
Sing, you watercourses, bringers of peace!
Valleys, open wide
Your cracked lips! You shall be green again
And ease with flowers what the sun has seared.
Waking tomorrow we'll find the air cleared,
Sunny with fresh eloquence after rain.

For my friend that was dead is alive. He bore transplanting
Into a common soil. Strongly he grows
Upon the heart and gives the tentative wing
Take-off for flights, surety for repose.
And he returns not in an echoing
Regret, a hollow haunting,
Not as a shadow thrown across our day;
But radiant energy, charging the mind with power
That all who are wired to receive him surely can share.
It is no flying visit: he comes to stay.

His laughter was better than birds in the morning: his smile

Turned the edge of the wind: his memory
Disarms death and charms the surly grave.
Early he went to bed, too early we
Saw his light put out: yet we could not grieve
More than a little while,
For he lives in the earth around us, laughs from the sky.
Soon he forgave – still generous to a fault –
My crippling debt of sorrow, and I felt
In grief's hard winter earth's first melting sigh.

Think. One breath of midsummer will start
A buried life – on sunday boys content
Hearing through study windows a gramophone,
Sweet peas arrested on a morning scent –
And the man sighs for what he has outgrown.
He wastes pity. The heart
Has all recorded. Each quaver of distress,
Mirth's every crotchet, love's least tremolo –
Scarce-noted notes that to full movements flow –
Have made their mark on its deep tenderness.

Much more should he, who had life and to spare,
Be here impressed, his sympathy relayed
Out of the rich-toned past. And is. For through
Desert my heart he gives a fiery lead,
Unfolding contours, lengthening the view.
He is a thoroughfare
Over all sliding sands. Each stopping-place
Wears his look of welcome. May even find,
When I come to the snow-line, the bitter end,
His hand-holds cut on death's terrific face.

Distant all that, and heaven a hearsay word –
Truth's fan-vaulting, vision carved in flight
Perhaps, or the last delirium of self-loving.
But now a word in season, a dance in spite

211

Of death: love, the affirmative in all living,
Blossom, dew or bird.
For one is dead, but his love has gone before
Us, pointing and paving a way into the future;
Has gone to form its very flesh and feature,
The air we shall breathe, the kindling for our fire.

Nothing is lost. There is a thrifty wife,
Conceives all, saves all, finds a use for all.
No waste her deserts: limited rock, lightnings
And speedwell that run riot, seas that spill
Over, grass and man – whatever springs
From her excess of life
Is active and passive, spending and receipt.
And he took after her, a favourite son
In whom she excelled, through whom were handed on
Dewy her morning and her lasting heat.

Now we have sorrow's range, no more delaying –
Let the masked batteries of spring flash out
From ridge and copse, and flowers like shrapnel burst
Along the lanes, and all her land-mines spout
Quick and hanging green. Our best, our boast,
Our mood and month of maying,
For winter's bleak blockade is broken through
And every street flies colours of renaissance.
Today the hawk goes up for reconnaissance,
The heart beats faster having earth's ends in view.

Leave to the mercies of the manifold grass,
Will cover all earth's faults, what in his clay
Were but outcrops of volcanic life.
You shall recall one open as the day,
Many-mooded as the light above
English hills where pass
Sunlight and storm to a large reconciling.

You shall recall how it was warmth to be
With him – a feast, a first of June; that he
Was generous, that he attacked the bowling.

Lay laurels here, and leave your tears to dry –
Sirs, his last wishes were that you should laugh.
For those in whom was found life's richest seam
Yet they asked no royalty, one cenotaph
Were thanks enough – a world where none may scheme
To hoard, while many die,
Life; where all lives grow from an equal chance.
Tomorrow we resume building: but this
Day he calls holiday, he says it is
A time to dance, he calls you all to dance.

Today the land that knew him shall do him honour,
Sun be a spendthrift, fields come out with gold,
Severn and Windrush be Madrigal and Flowing,
Woodlarks flash up like rockets and unfold
In showers of song, cloud-shadows pace the flying
Wind, the champion runner.
Joy has a flying start, our hopes like flames
Lengthen their stride over a kindled earth,
And noon cheers all, upstanding in the south.
Sirs, be merry: these are his funeral games.

Epilogue

For those who had the power,
Unhesitating whether to kill or cure:
Those who were not afraid
To dam the estuary or start the forest fire:
Whose hearts were filled

213

With enthusiasm as with a constant wind
That, lifting the fog, the pall of vision, unveiled
Their own memorial, the stars:
There need be neither obituary nor wreath,
Accomplices of death.
These disappeared into the darkness ahead.
Followers shall find
Them walking larger than legends in that virgin land,
Their spirit shall be blowing out of the sunrise,
Their veins our rivers, their bones our bread.

Others, too, will die hard.
Spenders of life, they dealt freely with danger:
These could not learn to hoard,
To count the cost or to examine the change.
A hungry soul
Urged them to try new air-routes, and their skill
Raftered the sky with steel:
They took the field with laughter, they attacked the
                                        bowling.
In the machine's heart, regularly breathing,
We hear their hearts still beat,
Inherit their strength and swiftness through the turbine:
Pausing between shifts or in the pub at evening
We feel their generous heat;
We remember them as the glowing fruit remembers
Sap-flow and sunshine.

1935

NOAH AND THE WATERS

TO
CHARLES FENBY

AUTHOR'S FOREWORD

This work was begun as the 'book' for a choral ballet. The author, however, soon discovered he was producing something in the tradition of the mediæval morality plays. *Noah and the Waters* is probably not, on the other hand, suitable as it stands for the modern stage: like that of the morality plays, its drama derives largely from the weight and imminence of the issue it represents and little from any conscious dramatic construction. This issue is the choice that must be made by Noah between clinging to his old life and trusting himself to the Flood.

C. D. L.

'Finally, when the class war is about to be fought to a finish, disintegration of the ruling class and the old order of society becomes so active, so acute, that a small part of the ruling class breaks away to make common cause with the revolutionary class, the class which holds the future in its hands. . . .'

The Communist Manifesto.

Prologue

This curve of ploughland, one clean stroke
Defining earth's nature constant to four seasons,
Fixes too for ever her simple relationship
With the sky and all systems imaginable there.

This clean red stroke, like a heart-beat of the earth's heart
Felt here under the sunlight's velvet hand,
Draws something simple and perfect as breath – that leaves
No more to be said,
And yet implies what wonders beyond, what breathing
    cities,
Pasture broad and untainted prairies of air.

This curve – the naked breasts of woman exalted for love,
Cradle both and summit of your superb ambition,
Move not more certainly to that far-flying
Among star-fields above even the wind's excitement,
And exhausted eddying down to peace.

Lover's eye is hawk's eye, on the whole earth
Spread for him seeing only the point of desire.

And then there is the poet's –
His gaze that like the moonlight rests on all
In level contemplation, making roof and ruin
Treachery scorn and death into silver syllables
And out of worn fragments a seamless coat.

These I must have; but more.
To see this ploughland curve as a graph of history,
The unregarded sweat that has made it fertile,
Reading between the furrows a desperate appeal
From all whose share in them was bitter as iron,

Hearing the young corn whisper
The wishes of men that had no other voice.

Only then am I able to know the difficult
Birth of our new seed and bear my part of the harvest.

CHORUS.
   Stand with us here
On the south-western cliff of the great Jurassic escarpment,
A common for rare wood-larks, a place where wind-pumps
                                  veer
Constant as your necessity, drinking that reservoir
Free to all: invisible the veins it is life to open,
The lake only your death may look on.

   Stand with us now and hear
Only the wood-lark's irrelevant song, the shepherd's
                                whistle,
And seven-league footfall of wind striding through dry
                                grasses.
For as yet the torrents to come are but a roaring in the ear
Of prophets, or the raving fancy of one delirious with
                                thirst.
Pacific the sky, a delight for shepherds and hikers; though a
                                seer
Might behold over the cities to north and north-east
                              spreading
A stain, clouds not white, the coaling-up of wrath.

   Stand with us here.
Feel underfoot the linked vertebræ of your land
Stretching north to the far fells, the head of rivers.
Prehistory sleeps below in many beds. Before
Man set a value on his thoughts or made a prison for fear,

These hills were grown up, to the sky happily married,
That now are wrinkled with the rains of more than mortal
                                        years,
Old enough to remember the first birds and the great
                                        reptiles.

    Stand with us. Far and near
See history unfolded in the scrolled hills, her secret
Indelible as hieroglyphs stamped on their stone, clear
To the eye but hard for you to interpret. The green barrows
Of Britons. The high camps where Roman eagles kept
                                        watch
On Wales unblinking. The manors, cosy in combes. Dear
The dewponds, and still black the circles of Jubilee
                                        bonfires.

    Stand with us here,
The past at your feet, your fingers nervous like the lark's
                                        wing
To be up and doing. And now, for to-day's sun goes higher,
Let your hearts grow warm as wax to take note of the
                                        future:
Let him step forward, if one there be wise to weather,
From behaviour of martens or altered tones of the smooth-
                                        voiced weir
Able to learn and to beware.

    Now look away
Into the valley and deep into the unregarded
Sweat that has made it fertile. That curve of ploughland
                                        see
As a graph of history, and hear what the young corn tries
                                        to say.
Read between those furrows a desperate appeal
Of men who had no other voice.

Now look beyond, this way.
Behold a different growth: set in ancient wood,
Grafted on to the valley stock, a new life – the Town.
Consider the uniform foliage of roofs, hiding decay
And rain-fearing pests and all the diversities of loving:
Wind-screens dazzled by the sun: strip-built roads that
stray
Out like suckers to drain the country; and routes familiar
To night-expresses, the fire-crest flyers, migrating south.

Now come away
From these self-flattering heights, and like a diver plunging
Into his own image, enter the Town. You pass
Nurseries that splash crude colour over war's pale griefs,
Nurturing seed for a soil shallow as soldiers' graves:
Huts, the butt-ends of a war, Honour's sloven retreat;
And ashamed asphalt where the naked put on indifference
– to-day
Willowherb grows in the cracks, the idiot flower of
exhaustion.

Now closer look this way.
Do not be deceived by the two-faced traffic signs, the
expensive
Flood-lit smile of civic beauties, the fountains that play
In limelight like spoilt children. See rather how the old
Their wintering ghosts creep out on gusts of warm
nostalgia:
The young, their run-ahead hope barred by Death's one-
way
Approach: and the good like madmen preaching to locked
faces.

Look not away –
Though ugly this, it is your foundation and your
predicament.

224

Behind the image of glass, the mirage of brick, you await
A judgment and a choice. But listen for that which is still
Less than the whisper of clouds assembling, of arrows
                                        falling.
But look to him we will call Noah, figure of your fate,
Him understand, him obey.

FIRST VOICE.
Call Noah!

SECOND VOICE.
Call Noah!

CHORUS.
Noah! Noah! Noah! Noah! Noah! Noah!

(*Enter* NOAH)

FIRST VOICE.
I am the One that amounts to many,
The collector of autographs, the coiner of money:
I love you all, I built this town
Because I was unhappy living alone.

SECOND VOICE.
I am the One who rents this villa,
Now a recluse, but once I was a killer:
I hate you all, I preserve my pride
Looking down on the many I have locked outside.

FIRST VOICE.
I am the One that means to be more,
I undress quickly, I leave open the door:
My kisses are questions, until I can squeeze
The whole world in my arms I'll not be at ease.

225

SECOND VOICE.
I am the One that looks to be less,
I tear up the riddles you are trying to guess:
I will undress quickly, I am ready for bed
For I'll not be myself again until I am dead.

FIRST VOICE.
I am the One that makes you grow big,
I am silver to beggars, there's gold where I dig:
I'm at home in the red cell or the cyclists' rally,
But my best friends have to admit I'm unruly.

SECOND VOICE.
I am the One that makes you feel small,
The machine-gun's mouth is the way I smile:
My friends are the spy, the bacillus and the warder,
I may be no beauty but I keep you in order.

BOTH VOICES.
We are the furnace, we are the snow,
The maze and the monolith, the yes and the no:
We are the fish and we are the bait,
We are Noah, the figure of your fate.

CHORUS.
And now behold
Burgesses, neighbours of Noah, cutting a fine figure,
Canny to cut their losses, whose imagination runs on gold
Like a hearse on rubber tyres. But something is wrong, they
are galled
By the trace of some tightening necessity, and restive their
assurance.
Why do they stand breathless as old
Men who into a doorway run from sudden rain?

(Enter three BURGESSES, *reading newspapers)*

FIRST BURGESS.
Seven and a half inches registered at Carlisle

SECOND BURGESS.
Derwent dam cracking under pressure

THIRD BURGESS.
Forty men swept to death on Merseyside

FIRST BURGESS.
Failure of Ham Hill power-station

SECOND BURGESS.
Birmingham and Coventry plunged into darkness

THIRD BURGESS.
Asparagus-crop threatened in Evesham valley

FIRST BURGESS.
Most disturbing

SECOND BURGESS.
Unprecedented

THIRD BURGESS.
Highly irregular

FIRST BURGESS.
Though of course it must stop soon

SECOND BURGESS.
We are safe here

THIRD BURGESS.
Undoubtedly

FIRST BURGESS.
At the same time, my factory in Nottingham

SECOND BURGESS.
My racing-stables, the boast of Berkshire

THIRD BURGESS.
My daughter's house-party at Tunbridge Wells

FIRST BURGESS.
We have therefore come to ask you, Noah

SECOND BURGESS.
To use your influence at this juncture

THIRD BURGESS.
Your unquestioned organizing ability

FIRST BURGESS.
Since the Government seems pledged to inaction

SECOND BURGESS.
The Church still hunting for a formula

THIRD BURGESS.
The Police unable to control the situation

FIRST BURGESS.
All right-thinking citizens

SECOND BURGESS.
Must come

THIRD BURGESS.
Exactly

(NOAH *makes no sign*)

FIRST BURGESS.
Please do not misunderstand our motives

SECOND BURGESS.
We are willing to make any reasonable sacrifice

THIRD BURGESS.
We can take our losses as well as the next man

FIRST BURGESS.
But this is no longer a personal affair

SECOND BURGESS.
It has become a matter of common humanity

THIRD BURGESS.
At such a time we sink our petty differences

FIRST BURGESS.
You cannot fail to be alarmed, Noah

SECOND BURGESS.
By the wholesale destruction of property we hear of

THIRD BURGESS.
To say nothing of the loss of valuable lives

(NOAH *moves uneasily*)

FIRST BURGESS.
Ah, I knew you would not fail us

SECOND BURGESS.
It is terrible to think of one's own children

THIRD BURGESS.
My point about valuable lives it was that moved him

FIRST BURGESS.
Of course within limits this flood might prove a blessing

SECOND BURGESS.
There's much in our country that needs cleansing

THIRD BURGESS.
Conditions in the North I am told are scandalous

FIRST BURGESS.
But now these waters have got out of hand

SECOND BURGESS.
Lives and landmarks they remove they cannot restore

THIRD BURGESS.
In a word – destruction for the sake of destruction

FIRST BURGESS.
One asks, is it worth it

SECOND BURGESS.
Just so

THIRD BURGESS.
Hear, Hear

FIRST VOICE.
I hear a great army deploy on a plain,
Distant the footfalls irregular as rain:

Does it spell destruction, does it signal relief?
A menace to mine or a message to live?

SECOND VOICE.
I hear a great car lapping fast overland,
It is racing towards me, will it stop where I stand?
Will they climb out and hand me the master-keys,
The signed death-warrant, unconditional release?

FIRST VOICE.
Hang your head down, Noah, hark to the wind!
The willows are trembling, the gulls have been warned:
Someone is walking to you out of the sea,
Love is looking for you and me.

SECOND VOICE.
Hang your head down, Noah, hark to the rain!
The weathercock is waiting, the life-guards have run:
Something is coming to you over the grass,
And it walks through brick and it hides behind glass.

BOTH VOICES.
We are the furnace, we are the snow,
The maze and the monolith, the yes and the no:
We are the fish and we are the bait,
We are Noah, the figure of your fate.

FIRST BURGESS.
Now that you have realized the force of our contention

SECOND BURGESS.
Weighed carefully the pro and the con

THIRD BURGESS.
Cleared your mind of all irrelevant issues

231

FIRST BURGESS.
The moment you'll admit is ripe for action

SECOND BURGESS.
We are willing to grant you emergency powers

THIRD BURGESS.
Salary and uniform would not be unattractive

FIRST BURGESS.
As lovers of this town, the paragon of progress

SECOND BURGESS.
Renowned equally for commerce and culture

THIRD BURGESS.
Possessing the largest Lido in the country

FIRST BURGESS.
We appeal to you to take what steps you deem necessary

SECOND BURGESS.
For the safeguarding of our common interests

THIRD BURGESS.
And the preservation of valuable lives

FIRST BURGESS.
Quite frankly, we cannot afford an inundation

SECOND BURGESS.
A blow at us would be a blow at the heart of

THIRD BURGESS.
England, the end of something rather beautiful

FIRST BURGESS.
It is therefore imperative that the flood be stopped

SECOND BURGESS.
Before it touches the fringe of our reputation

THIRD BURGESS.
Wets the feet of the Queen of Cities

FIRST BURGESS.
Dykes, diversions, chemicals, sandbags

SECOND BURGESS.
We leave the methods to you

THIRD BURGESS.
Hear, Hear

> (*While the* CHORUS *speaks the* BURGESSES *go and look out
> of the wings*)

CHORUS.
Too late! Listen and hear
The lisp of waters whispering together in your public
                                                 places,
Mating in gutters, meeting at cross-roads, already
                                                 mounting
Your doorsteps, reaching for the bell, importunate they
                                                 appear
As travellers, they travel in death, it is your death they
                                                 sell:
Fear them you may, for they must live – their life you
                                                 tender
In exchange for your death, indeed you must sell your lives
                                                 dear.

FIRST BURGESS.
Look! Already the waters are upon us

SECOND BURGESS.
I have seen their skirmishers advance through the town

THIRD BURGESS.
Devils, they attacked without ultimatum

FIRST BURGESS.
The hills to the north are white with their running

SECOND BURGESS.
They are sweeping up the southern boulevards

THIRD BURGESS.
Clouds east and west move down in support

FIRST BURGESS.
They have crossed the High Street disregarding traffic lights

SECOND BURGESS.
The cordon of police is powerless against them

THIRD BURGESS.
The cellars of the Constitutional Club are flooded

FIRST BURGESS.
We must stand together, we must keep cool

SECOND BURGESS.
We are not to be intimidated by a muddy rabble

THIRD BURGESS.
After all, they are only water

FIRST BURGESS.
It is lucky we came to Noah's house

SECOND BURGESS.
It gives us time to concert action

THIRD BURGESS.
They will never think of looking for us here

FIRST BURGESS.
They would never dare

SECOND BURGESS.
To enter

THIRD BURGESS.
This house

> (*Enter the* FLOOD. *The* FLOOD *dances. While it is dancing,
> the* BURGESSES *confer together. Presently* FIRST BURGESS
> *jumps on table and addresses* FLOOD.)

FIRST BURGESS.
Waters of England! Speaking for my two friends here, and
for Noah, whom you all love and respect, and for my
unworthy self, I should like first to welcome you to our
town. I could wish that we might have met under happier
conditions. I might cavil perhaps at your somewhat
unceremonious mode of entry; but I feel sure our good
friend Noah will forgive it, and will, under the exceptional
circumstances, waive all ceremony. Now first of all, let us
make up our minds to discuss this matter without heat. On
that I am sure we are agreed. I am, I hope, no alarmist; but
there is no use shutting our eyes to the fact that we have
met at a crisis fraught with the gravest consequences for us
all. In such a crisis frayed tempers, doctrinaire counsels, an

235

atmosphere of suspicion are not only out of place but positively calamitous. Waters of England, I am asking you to approach this problem with that cold, relentless logic for which you are justly famous. I shall put all my cards on the table, and I hope you will do the same. Let me say at the outset, I fully recognize that there have been faults on both sides: my associates and I are willing to make concessions, very generous concessions.

Before we go into details, I would like to address a few words to those of you who have come down from the sky. You, if I may say so, are in a position of peculiar responsibility; for without you the rest would not have risen at all. You have been up in the clouds, and therefore you naturally possess a broader view of things than your more humbly placed fellows: at the same time, it may have led you to take up too airy an attitude towards consequences. You have been up in the clouds. Now that you have come down to solid earth – as we all must sooner or later – you cannot fail to see the facts of the situation in a rather different light. It is possible to be too generous, too open-hearted. Though you acted with the very best intentions, you must realize by now that your first fine flush of enthusiasm has led to the destruction of a great deal that your fellows on earth had for years been helping to build up. No doubt there was much that needed, that cried out for, destruction. But the question we have to ask ourselves is this – who in the long run is the happier for it? Naturally I am not. You don't need me to tell you that you have put me in a very awkward position indeed. But I am of small consequence. If I felt that my death would contribute to a lasting solution of the problem, I should say here and now: 'Take me out into that street and drown me.' No, I am thinking of your mates – the great mass of waters that used to go happily about their tasks on hill and coast and valley, and I am asking myself: 'What is going to become of them?' You have caused a profound unrest among them. You have stirred them out of their familiar beds, their habitual courses. You have led them here, many of them hundreds of miles from their homes. And when it is all over, when the splendid flood of their enthusiasm ebbs – what then? They will stand about in swamps, derelict, irreclaimable, loveless, rotting and lost. In that day they would envy the very marshes of Hell. . . . No, you could never let that happen. And it is not too late to prevent it. To-morrow, as soon as the sun rises, go back to the clouds. Tell them that honour if satisfied, that they need send no more, that by doing so they would imperil – nay, cancel and blot out – the future of their friends down here. For these, I pledge myself to see that justice is done them. The details we can settle later. You agree?

VOICES IN THE FLOOD.
Beware of the bribe!
Beware of the hard-luck story and the soft option!
Beware of the forked tongue that means division, the sweet
                    tooth that makes death a pleasure!
Beware of all who flatter what they fear, who use reason
            against love and rhetoric in the hour of ruin!
Beware of the bribe!

FIRST BURGESS.
   No? You are determined to pursue this senseless and arrogant folly? Very well. Waters of *England*, I believe I said. An unpardonable mistake. I apologize. It must be evident to you that we are not all English here. A foreign element has crept in amongst us. No doubt the rest of you have been wondering where this dirty weather came from. I will tell you. Foul exhalations from every bog, charnel, midden and cesspool, from every brothel and ghetto in Europe: vapours so pestilential and anarchic that even their native swamps would not tolerate them: things whose breath is more fœtid than marsh-gas, more

abominable than Lewisite, more sacrilegious than the kiss of Judas: sucked up, I say, from such unspeakable filth as you pure stay-at-home English waters can have no conception of: rejected of earth, they mounted up in sullen miasmas and defiled the very face of God. Swollen with their own arrogance and rancour, they hung there for a season poisonously. You all saw them. Overweening was their spite, insatiable their venom. Compared with this obscene concourse, a Witches' Sabbath were an assemblage of virgins and the chaste-choosing unicorn would run to it for refuge. But it was not enough for them to spit and swelter in heaven's face. 'Surely there is one land yet uninfected by our disease,' they said, 'one fair country not yet deracinated by our lust.' Yes, my friends, there was such a country. I think you know its name. England. Our England. Long they brooded over her, tense and livid as a ravisher who looks down from the window of his luxury apartment upon the oblivious victim of his choice. Then they acted. Our life was pinned down insidiously with a multitude of fine points, a persistence of low pressure: the forests were beaten down with cloudbursts; the very flowers were not spared, but snapped and sullied in their pretty innocence. Nothing was sacred to the eyes of these ravishers, or irrelevant to their horrid purpose. They whispered in the ears of springs, they seduced watercourses, they poisoned every well. So they duped you, making you turn against Nature and rise with them to ruin your own beloved land. That was the end. Soon now her ornaments, her coverings, her prayers were all swept away. The valleys lie low, the breasts of the hills are going under. England. They have made her name mud. This hour they are come at her last stronghold, to take from her the fact as well as the name of virtue. But, even now, it is not too late. Are you going to stand by and witness this last unutterable contamination? England is your mother and your beloved. You have lain upon her bosom, you have embraced her with the seas, you flow in her veins. I am a plain, blunt man with no skill in sophistry. I remember, not very long ago and under somewhat similar circumstances, saying to a certain person: 'What would you do if you saw a foreigner trying to rape your sister?' That question I ask you now. Your answer is not, I imagine, 'We would join in and help him.' Yes, you may well hang your heads. But shame is not enough. There must be action. You must dissociate yourselves at once from those who have misled you, and then you must drive them away and destroy them. No quarter can be given to criminal and alien degenerates. Let those of you who still care for the honour of England take two steps forward.

Voices in the Flood.
Distrust the distrustful!
Suspect the suspicious!
Only the two-faced can see nothing but duplicity.
Beware of the wolf crying 'wolf' and the crook talking of
honour!
All the earth is our beloved, all waters our brothers: you
only do we not know for a friend.
It is not we who destroy England, but it is you who have
disgraced her.
Distrust!

First Burgess.
I see you have been more gravely misguided than I had thought possible. England means nothing to you. I am glad Shakespeare is not alive to see this day. So be it. If I cannot appeal to your ideals, I must use other arguments. Let me tell you a little story. Once upon a time there was a millstream. For centuries it had turned the waterwheel, making bread for a whole village, performing its humble duty faithfully and unobtrusively, happy in that station to which God had called it, loved and respected by all. One

day this stream said to itself: 'For years we have laboured without recompense. We have produced, but another has profited. Let us arise and drown the miller and be masters instead of slaves!' So, early next morning, the stream leapt from its bed: it broke down its banks, rushed into the mill and drowned the miller. But alas, the mill was damaged. The stream could not repair it: and even if it had been able to, it could not have handled the grain or done the accounts. Besides, there would have been nothing to turn the wheel, for the banks were broken and the stream's whole course changed. A little of it went back to its old way, but it was a mere shadow of its former self. The rest stood about disconsolately, some to vanish quickly with the noonday sun, some to sink into hopeless marsh. Please don't think I am criticizing the motives of this stream. I am not now concerned with the rights and wrongs of the case. I am merely trying, as a hard-headed business man, to put certain facts before you. That miller could not work without the stream: but neither could the stream work without the miller. I need not labour the point. Now let us get down to brass tacks. It is agreed that I and my associates cannot do without you any more than you can do without us. If you go back to your work now, we shall still be able to preserve – I will not say, England – but our own existence. If you stay here, you will have the satisfaction of paralysing and finally killing the nerve-centre of a system on which your livelihood as much as mine depends. An empty satisfaction. Our destruction is your death. It is therefore to your own advantage to retire. But, bearing in mind the justifiable grievances which have brought you here, my colleagues and I are willing, without prejudice, to hold out further inducements. You have hitherto worked long hours. That is unavoidable, being second nature to you. But we can at least see that during those hours there shall be no wastage of your effort. Those of you who have been running idle we will bring into the

national economy through a comprehensive system of
public works. Water will be changed in public baths once a
week instead of once a fortnight as heretofore. All engines
will be compelled to run at higher pressure, thus bringing
more of you into active circulation. Many of you have had
to come a long way to your work, or have worked under
difficulties: the courses of all rivers will be straightened
out, channels where necessary deepened, and estuaries
dredged of silt. The canals will be cleaned up, and by-laws
put into force against the contamination of waters with
the waste-product of our factories. Furthermore, in
recognition of your invaluable co-operation, monuments
will be erected on all watersheds at our expense, a wreath
thrown into the sea every quarter-day, and annual services
of thanksgiving for rain solemnized in all cathedrals and
pro-cathedrals. We cannot say fairer than this. Your
interests will be paramount in my heart. Let 'each for the
other and all for the school' be our motto, the slogan of a
new understanding, a new brotherhood, a new life.

VOICES IN THE FLOOD.
   No! Your profit is our loss.
Your life is our death.
Shun the promises of the desperate, the kiss of disease, the
                              organization of the maggot!
Only the dying make terms with decay.
To know the earth is to learn the power of patience: to
      know the enemy is to have found identity: to know the
      friend is to create the field of force.
Know!

FIRST BURGESS.
   Very well, very well then. We shall soon find out which
of us is the dying man. I should have known better than to
be generous to your sort. There is only one thing you
waters can understand, and that is the whip. You think

241

you are indispensable, do you? Let me tell you, you are no more indispensable than a few grains of sand are to a beach or one constellation to the whole heavenly system. It's to be you or us, is it? All right. We shall call in waters from abroad: they will roll you up and drive you away to chaos. A continuous bombardment of the clouds with belladonna will begin at midday. Every scientist in the country will be mobilized against you: if necessary, the atom will be split. The churches will be told to proclaim a holy war. A defensive alliance will be made with the sun. Every child of school age will be supplied with four reams of blotting-paper. We shall commandeer the oil supplies of the whole world and release them against you without ultimatum. To the survivors no mercy will be shown. Every stream will be compelled to run underground. On the larger rivers, dams and filters will be erected at intervals of thirty miles. Salt will be thrown into the lakes, irrigation systems turned into sewage-farms, wells blown up regardless of age or sex. Anyone still showing signs of insubordination will be handed over to special aerated-water factories or transported to the Sahara. . . . That, or unconditional surrender. Your answer. At once.

Voices in the Flood.
Waters of the world, unite!
Lucky are the strong, for they have learnt indifference.
Lucky are the weak, for they shall understand the earth.
Lucky are the hungry and thirsty, for they shall see that
                                        their sons are filled.
Lucky are those that hate, for they are blind in season.
Lucky are those that love, for their patience redeems the
                                        generations.
Waters of the world, unite!

First Burgess.
So it is war!

(Exit, followed by other BURGESSES*)*

CHORUS.
  War. Not as between
The moon and her filial tides, or the married friction of
                                                    coast
And wave. Not a war to eternity this, but a war to the
                                                    death:
The war of worm and flesh, or oak and the weeds that
                                                    twine
About her breathing wood. One like grass possessing
The power of myriad weakness; one, the weakness of
                                                    power.
On Noah is poised that issue. Which way will Noah lean?

FIRST VOICE.
Rise up, Noah! A day is done,
World shall be water to the rising sun:
Book your passage, wherever you go
This trip will tell you what you want to know.

SECOND VOICE.
Lie down, Noah! A day is dead,
Let the waters be lullabies over your head:
Cut your losses, liquidate the past,
Now all your riddles are resolved at last.

FIRST VOICE.
To fold the earth in the crook of an arm,
To mould its clay in a fluent palm:
To live a hair's-breadth and embrace a sphere,
Travelling single and touching everywhere.

SECOND VOICE.
To be routed like smoke by galloping gales,
To be shredded by fish and the herring-gulls:

243

To be ruled like sand by an overbearing sea
Marching and countermarching over me.

FIRST VOICE.
The beam directed, the channel spied,
Thrust of piston, engaging of pride:
The breaking of the waters is the birth of man,
Earth is to let and to-morrow is mine.

SECOND VOICE.
The mines are flooded, the boilers raked,
Time's pattern unravelled, my thirst now is slaked:
I can live as I lived long before I was born,
A multiple amœba in a plastic dawn.

BOTH VOICES.
We are the furnace, we are the snow,
The maze and the monolith, the yes and the no:
We are the fish and we are the bait,
We are Noah, the figure of your fate.

CHORUS.
   Since you have come thus far,
Your visible past a steamer's wake continually fading
Among the receding hours tumbled, and yet you carry
Souvenirs of dead ports, a freight of passion and fear,
Remembrance of loves and landfalls and much deep-sea
                              predicament
Active upon the heart: – consider by what star
Your reckoning is, and whether conscious a course you steer
Or whether you rudderless yaw, self-mutinied, all at sea.

   You have come far
To the brink of this tableland where the next step treads air,
Your thoughts like antennæ feeling doubtfully towards the
                              future,

Your will swerving all ways to evade that unstable void;
High stakes, hard falls, comfortless contacts lie before,
But to sidestep these is to die upon a waterless plateau;
You must uncase and fly, for ahead is your thorough-fare.

  Consider Noah's fate,
Chosen to choose between two claims irreconcilable,
Alive on this island, old friends at his elbow, the floods at
                                         his feet.
Whether the final sleep, fingers curled about
The hollow comfort of a day worn smooth as holy relics;
Or trusting to walk the waters, to see when they abate
A future solid for sons and for him the annealing rainbow.

  It is your fate
Also to choose. On the one hand all that habit endears:
The lawn is where bishops have walked; the walled garden
                                         is private
Though your bindweed lust overruns it; the roses are sweet
                                         dying;
Soil so familiar to your roots you cannot feel it effete.
On the other hand what dearth engenders and what death
Makes flourish: the need and dignity of bearing fruit, the
                                         fight
For resurrection, the exquisite grafting on stranger stock.

  Stand with us here and now
Consider the force of these waters, the mobile face of the
                                         flood
Trusting and terrible as a giant who turns from sleep.
                                         Think how
You called them symbols of purity and yet you daily
                                         defiled them:
They failed you never; for that they were always the
                                         disregarded.
Ubiquitous to your need they made the barley grow

Or bore you to new homes; they kept you hale and
handsome.
Of all flesh they were the sign and substance. All things
flow.

   Stand with us now
Looking back on a time you have spent, a land that you
know.
Ask what formed the dew and dressed the evening in awe;
What hands made buoyant your ships, what shaped the
impatient prow,
Turned sea-shells and dynamos and wheels on river and
railroad:
Truth's bed and earth's refreshment – one everywhere
element
In the tissue of man, the tears of his anger, the sweat of his
brow.

   Then look with Noah's eyes
On the waters that wait his choice. Not only are they
insurgent
Over the banks and shallows of their birthplace, but they
rise
Also in Noah's heart: their rippling fingers erase
The ill-favoured façade of his present, the weird ancestral
folly,
The maze of mirrors, the corrupting admirers, the silted
lies.
Now must he lay his naked virtue upon their knees.

   Then turn your eyes
Upon that unbounded prospect and your dwindling island
of ease,
Measuring your virtue against its challenger, measuring
well
Your leap across the gulf, as the swallow-flock that flies

In autumn gathers its strength on some far-sighted
                                     headland.
Learn the migrant's trust, the intuition of longer
Sunlight: be certain as they you have only winter to lose,
And believe that beyond this flood a kinder country lies.

   (*Enter* BURGESSES. FIRST BURGESS *carries a poison-gas*
     apparatus, SECOND BURGESS *a shotgun,* THIRD BURGESS *a*
     mop and bucket.)

FIRST BURGESS.
Since they have hardened their hearts against kindness

SECOND BURGESS.
We will bandy words no more with these waters

THIRD BURGESS.
Our ultimatum expires at midday

FIRST BURGESS.
We do not minimize the gravity of the issue

SECOND BURGESS.
Our eyes are open now to our jeopardy

THIRD BURGESS.
All we hold dear is at stake this day

FIRST BURGESS.
We make this last appeal to you, Noah

SECOND BURGESS.
Remembering our close and profitable association

THIRD BURGESS.
And for the sake of auld lang syne

247

First Burgess.
Do not desert us – you and we are bound

Second Burgess.
By ties both of interest and consanguinity

Third Burgess.
Blood you know is thicker than water

First Burgess.
Think of the times we have stood together

Second Burgess.
The private view, the public reception

Third Burgess.
The little brown jug and the thin red line

First Burgess.
Remember prayers at our mother's knee

Second Burgess.
Promises made at father's death-bed

Third Burgess.
Fireworks at the mortgaged family seat

(Noah *makes no sign*)

First Burgess.
Sympathy with this flood is plainly misplaced

Second Burgess.
An error to credit it with pure motives

248

THIRD BURGESS.
Laughable to call it an Act of God

FIRST BURGESS.
On the contrary, its aim is sacrilegious

SECOND BURGESS.
It has undermined the fabric of church and chapel

THIRD BURGESS.
And marooned the priest on a desert sanctuary

FIRST BURGESS.
Roughly it handles the bones of our fathers

SECOND BURGESS.
Its influence on the home flouts all the tenets of

THIRD BURGESS.
Mosaic Law and the Mothers' Union

FIRST BURGESS.
Pale with envy it pours over

SECOND BURGESS.
Your landmarks, your colour-schemes, the contours you
love

THIRD BURGESS.
Levelling all to plumb monotony

FIRST BURGESS.
It shows no respect for the transcendental

SECOND BURGESS.
For the subtle whorls of the solitary conscience

THIRD BURGESS.
For country-house cricket or the classic style

(NOAH *makes no sign*)

FIRST BURGESS.
Since you seem dead to common decency

SECOND BURGESS.
Wilful to walk outright into chaos

THIRD BURGESS.
We must warn you more crudely against these waters

FIRST BURGESS.
Don't imagine yourself indispensable to them

SECOND BURGESS.
I fear you are in for a cold reception

THIRD BURGESS.
Will damp your ardour or I'm much mistaken

FIRST BURGESS.
They are bound by their nature to let you down

SECOND BURGESS.
They will pour contempt on your delicate appetites

THIRD BURGESS.
The higher education is wasted upon them

FIRST BURGESS.
They will fling you overboard in mid-ocean

SECOND BURGESS.
They will leave you high and dry as driftwood

250

THIRD BURGESS.
They will turn you into a limpet or a sponge

FIRST BURGESS.
Their beginning is wrath, their end anarchy

SECOND BURGESS.
They distort the vision – through them you shall see

THIRD BURGESS.
Your death or survival a matter of indifference

FIRST BURGESS.
For the last time therefore

SECOND BURGESS.
We say

THIRD BURGESS.
Distrust them!

THE TWO VOICES.
Trust them!

BURGESSES.
Reject! Reject! Reject!

VOICES.
Accept!

(NOAH *comes forward and addresses the* BURGESSES)

NOAH.
Gentlemen, I have heard out your full contentions,
Paid heed with interest and my debts with silence.
Standing on this narrow island between

251

Yesterday and to-morrow, the traffic defiling
Deathward and its counter-stream, I have been bewildered
Doubtful which way my next appointment lies.
I made this refuge out of my indecision,
My fear of the all-involving wheels, my need
For breathing-space: also, to be the exempt
Spectator of combatant tides is flattery.
There was rest here and some illumination –
A lighthouse for the migrant, not his home.

   I had felt my days fall gradually, one by one,
Like anæsthetic drops upon the mask,
Putting to sleep with their routine behaviour
The saturated will and the conscious protest,
Unfocusing the vision, till nothing remained
But the exorbitant beating of my heart,
The horror of drowning, the wish for annihilation.
Was roaring in my ears; but as through storm
One hears the unison-chorus of the surf,
I heard this Flood.
This it was that aroused me, and I saw
The clever hands all gloved to sterilize
And the slick knife that leered above my manhood.

   But see me also as Noah, a man of substance,
Father of his family, contented simply
By the intimate circle of the leisured seasons:
A man of peace, one who responded always
To the time-honoured charities of hearth and home,
Preferring death to change, whose flightiest cronies
Were the grave earth and the dependable stars.
So it is you see me – one of yourselves.
Well may you look askance when such an one,
Leaving the lode and gear of his proved fortune,
Should ask concessions from a savage flood
And upon rack and ruin build his hopes.

   Gentlemen, you have brought many charges against
This flood – of rapine, of sacrilege, of falsehood.

252

I say your follies were the source and gauge of
Its rising: falsely now you deny its roused
Desire to possess to fertilize the earth
Whose harsh and impotent husbands you were.
You looked upon these waters as an element
Necessary, subordinate, unfeatured,
God-given to be your scavengers, to ripen
Your crops and carry you to outlandish pleasures:
Their lives the head of steam that kept you running.
To me they look like men – more men than you.
    Understand, these waters are here to rescue
Not to ravish the earth you so mishandled.
Their pressure is against your brittle pride,
Much greed and little competence. Already
Muscular eddies close around your nostrils
And fluent fingers are working for the death-grip.
Soon shall your bonds and pledges all be seen
A pocketful of pulp; the iridescent
Scum that you took for pure greatness, the toady
Tawdry Circumstance of your era shall
Be swept like litter out of sight and mind . . .
    I was always the man who saw both sides,
The cork dancing where wave and backwash meet,
From the inveterate clash of contraries gaining
A spurious animation. Say, if you like,
A top whom its self-passions lashed to sleep
Pirouetting upon central indifference,
The bored and perfect ballet-dancer engrossed
By mere reiteration; but lately
The one that cuts a figure on thin ice.
– Who saw both sides and therefore could take neither:
A needle midway between two fields of force,
Swinging at last I point and prove the stronger
Attraction. Gentlemen, you have lost.

CHORUS.
  Now he has made his choice,
Sounding aright the profound heart of this flood at last,
Willing to meet its myriad and breath-taking embrace
Under the wind-wild sky, let him hear his two voices
That from the spirit's echoing cavern speak advice:
They tell what virtues most he needs upon this voyage,
What earth has lent and he must restore when home he
                                                    hies.

  (*As the two voices speak, the* VIRTUES – *in the guise of
  animals – pass before* NOAH *and go to stand behind
  him.*)

FIRST VOICE.
Take first the mole, the anonymous miner,
Earth's intimate friend, lowly of demeanour:
The little genius so good at spadework,
One that was never afraid of the dark.

SECOND VOICE.
He is patience. Read him aright,
Of all virtues the soil and the root:
Remember him in the hour of disaster,
In the hour of triumph may he still be master.

FIRST VOICE.
The migrant salmon, his life fulfils
Outswimming the current, outleaping the falls:
Flashing and obstinate, he will not feed
Till the far headwaters give place to breed.

SECOND VOICE.
So be your courage, and count it rarest

254

To spring the highest where odds fall sheerest:
A far-traveller, a bow trained
Tense and unerring on the fruitful end.

FIRST VOICE.
Now the bull-finch, his glass-glossy breast
Draws the sunset out of the west:
Most handsome of all that lord it on leaf,
He shuns admirers and mates for life.

SECOND VOICE.
Conspicuous by your faith, but shy
To preen it in the public eye:
Ardent and answered may you discover
Your natural constancy to friend and lover.

FIRST VOICE.
The monkey next, the infant explorer
Never tired of trial and error:
Quicksilver wit and adaptable hand,
As fire infectious, agile as wind.

SECOND VOICE.
Let curiosity be such –
Your unappeased and sovereign itch:
A born rover that never stops
Till he has the whole world at his fingertips.

FIRST VOICE.
See the gannet, champion of flyers,
Ride unruffled the quarrelsome airs:
Then plunge out of heaven upon his prey,
Slanting and swiftsure as a sun-shot ray.

SECOND VOICE.
Wide-winged and consummate no less

Be your singlemindedness:
Beating strongly in the heart of the quarrel,
Diving deep to take the moral.

FIRST VOICE.
Last the sheepdog, the right-hand man
Of weatherwise shepherds, resourceful of mien:
He hears the whistle and manœuvres tireless
As a night-flying pilot warned by wireless.

SECOND VOICE.
Learn from him the directed wisdom,
The controlled initiative, the heart-felt system:
So shall you fold your fears and be
The alert equal of necessity.

FIRST BURGESS.
Traitor!

SECOND BURGESS.
Quitter!

THIRD BURGESS.
Cheat and parricide!

FIRST BURGESS.
Ungrateful, so pleased to prophesy our ruin

SECOND BURGESS.
He must take the consequences, the crazy Cassandra

THIRD BURGESS.
He loves this flood, let him go swallow it

FIRST BURGESS.
The look of the waters is growing uglier

SECOND BURGESS.
Don't let us stand doing nothing

THIRD BURGESS.
Remember St. George and the *Lusitania*

FIRST BURGESS.
My poison-gas outfit will make them froth

SECOND BURGESS.
I'll pepper the upstarts soundly with my shotgun

THIRD BURGESS.
With my mop and bucket I'll sweep them away

FIRST BURGESS.
This way!

SECOND BURGESS.
That way!

THIRD BURGESS.
Turn the lights on! No, turn them off!

FIRST BURGESS.
Don't contradict! There can only be one captain

SECOND BURGESS.
Upon a ship, and that's me

THIRD BURGESS.
No, me

(The FLOOD *attacks the* BURGESSES*)*

FIRST BURGESS.
Something's gone wrong, this tide is not retreating

SECOND BURGESS.
Why can't they fight fair, it's fifty to one

THIRD BURGESS.
Save me, mother, they mean mischief

FIRST BURGESS.
Fight harder!

SECOND BURGESS.
Run faster!

THIRD BURGESS.
Pray louder and louder!

FIRST BURGESS.
They beat down our weapons, we had best retire

SECOND BURGESS.
I shall take a ticket to Southampton or Tilbury

THIRD BURGESS.
I'll climb to the top of the highest steeple

FIRST BURGESS.
Let me call at the bank first for my bearer bonds

SECOND BURGESS.
I must rescue my horoscope and my iron ration

THIRD BURGESS.
My malacca cane and fitted dressing-case

FIRST BURGESS.
We'll meet again

SECOND BURGESS.
In Madeira

THIRD BURGESS.
Or mid-ocean

(BURGESSES, FLOOD *and* NOAH *go out in a running fight*)

CHORUS.
   Now Noah says good-bye,
Moorings slipped and the tide floating him clear of mud-
                       flat:
No mourning bands, no hands or streamers stretched from
                    the quay
Make parting difficult; but at night and silently
He sheers away. Only, high in the sinking town,
One lighted window watches him into the dark, a cry
From the heart of a mistress with whom he never could
                  share his secrets.

   He says good-bye
To much, but not to love. For loving now shall be
The close handclasp of the waters about his trusting keel,
Buoyant they make his home and lift his heart high;
Among their marching multitude he never shall feel
                lonely.
Love is for him no longer that soft and garden sigh
Ruffles at evening the petalled composure of the senses,
But a wind all hours and everywhere he no wise can deny.

259

Sorrow there is in store
For all who held up to love the suave distorting mirror,
Or looked therein to be magnified; whose will was ever more
Love's rentiers to live, in make-up still admired.
Earth shall disown them. Noah shall see drowning of
                                        many,
Compounded greed with charity, let wisdom out on hire,
Made freedom a trickster and passion a sick mechanical
                                        whore.
Their pride shall corrode, their shining look in the flood be
                                        tarnished.

What is in store
For Noah and the flood we foresee: unremitting war
And undisguised on all who are mad for the personal glory.
Call not the issue certain. But let the waters beware
Of deviation, the line of least resistance; ignore
The traitor's sop; unclench those hands whose hold on the
                                        living
Has been an ice-age. Stone are those hearts, and only
                                        before
The stern and rhythmic assault of continual waves will
                                        they yield.

But when the floods shall cease,
When the earth knows she is clean and sends her love to
                                        Noah
By the raven of tenderness, when abides the dove of peace,
Down the hillsides then shall the waters tumble apace,
Finding their level, wearing the sun on their wide
                                        shoulders,
To wed the radiant valleys: that reconciled embrace
Shall raise – taller than sunflowers and record crops – the
                                        race
That Noah foresaw in the veiled face of the avenging
                                        waters.

The floods shall cease,
Though forgotten never the height of their triumphs, the
                                    truth of their source.
Delight shall Noah have, as a man returning from exile
Beholds a land greener, more great with growth and ease
Than dreams dared imagine; but most, to live among these
Who shared his exile, to work with, to have for enduring
                                    fellows
All rivers, rains and seas.

1936

261

OVERTURES TO DEATH

TO E. M. FORSTER

Maple and Sumach

Maple and sumach down this autumn ride –
Look, in what scarlet character they speak!
For this their russet and rejoicing week
Trees spend a year of sunsets on their pride.
You leaves drenched with the lifeblood of the year –
What flamingo dawns have wavered from the east,
What eves have crimsoned to their toppling crest
To give the fame and transience that you wear!
Leaf-low he shall lie soon: but no such blaze
Briefly can cheer man's ashen, harsh decline;
His fall is short of pride, he bleeds within
And paler creeps to the dead end of his days.
O light's abandon and the fire-crest sky
Speak in me now for all who are to die!

February 1936

Infirm and grey
This leaden-hearted day
Drags its lank hours, wishing itself away.

Grey as the skin
Of long-imprisoned men
The sky, and holds a poisoned thought within.

Whether to die,
Or live beneath fear's eye –
Heavily hangs the sentence of this sky.

267

The unshed tears
Of frost on boughs and briers
Gathering wait discharge like our swoln fears.

Servant and host
Of this fog-bitter frost,
A carrion-crow flaps, shadowing the lost.

Now to the fire
From killing fells we bear
This new-born lamb, our premature desire.

We cannot meet
Our children's mirth, at night
Who dream their blood upon a darkening street.

Stay away, Spring!
Since death is on the wing
To blast our seed and poison every thing.

Bombers

Through the vague morning, the heart preoccupied,
A deep in air buried grain of sound
Starts and grows, as yet unwarning –
The tremor of baited deepsea line.

Swells the seed, and now tight sound-buds
Vibrate, upholding their paean flowers
To the sun. There are bees in sky-bells droning,
Flares of crimson at the heart unfold.

Children look up, and the elms spring-garlanded
Tossing their heads and marked for the axe.
Gallant or woebegone, alike unlucky –
Earth shakes beneath us: we imagine loss.

Black as vermin, crawling in echelon
Beneath the cloud-floor, the bombers come:
The heavy angels, carrying harm in
Their wombs that ache to be rid of death.

This is the seed that grows for ruin,
The iron embryo conceived in fear.
Soon or late its need must be answered
In fear delivered and screeching fire.

Choose between your child and this fatal embryo.
Shall your guilt bear arms, and the children you want
Be condemned to die by the powers you paid for
And haunt the houses you never built?

A Parting Shot

He said, 'Do not point your gun
At the dove in the judas tree:
It might go off, you see.'

So I fired, and the tree came down –
Limed leaf, branch and stock,
And the fantail swerving flew
Up like a shuttlecock
Released into the blue.

And he said, 'I told you so'.

Newsreel

Enter the dream-house, brothers and sisters, leaving
Your debts asleep, your history at the door:
This is the home for heroes, and this loving
Darkness a fur you can afford.

Fish in their tank electrically heated
Nose without envy the glass wall: for them
Clerk, spy, nurse, killer, prince, the great and the defeated,
Move in a mute day-dream,

Bathed in this common source, you gape incurious
At what your active hours have willed –
Sleep-walking on that silver wall, the furious
Sick shapes and pregnant fancies of your world.

There is the mayor opening the oyster season:
A society wedding: the autumn hats look swell:
An old crocks' race, and a politician
In fishing-waders to prove that all is well.

Oh, look at the warplanes! Screaming hysteric treble
In the long power-drive, like gannets they fall steep.
But what are they to trouble –
These silver shadows to trouble your watery, womb-deep
                                                    sleep?

See the big guns, rising, groping, erected
To plant death in your world's soft womb.
Fire-bud, smoke blossom, iron seed projected –
Are these exotics? They will grow nearer home.

Grow nearer home – and out of the dream-house stumbling
One night into a strangling air and the flung
Rags of children and thunder of stone niagaras tumbling,
You'll know you slept too long.

Regency Houses

In the abandoned heaven
Light shrinks like pools on sand –
One in a million days
That dying where they stand
Image our last and leave an
Adored light behind.
Autumn is soon. We gaze
At a Regency terrace, curved
Like the ritual smile, resigned
And formidable, that's carved
On the stone face of the dead.
Shallow a breath divides us
From the formal-smiling dead.
Light leaves this shore, these shells,
The windows glazed in death,
And soon on us beneath
A first leaf falls,
And then the next night hides us.

We who in younger days,
Hoping too much, tried on
The habit of perfection,
Have learnt how it betrays
Our shrinking flesh: we have seen
The praised transparent will
Living now by reflection.

271

The panes darken: but still
We have seen peering out
The mad, too mobile face
Under the floral hat.
Are we living – we too,
Living extravagant farce
In the finery of spent passions?
Is all we do and shall do
But the glib, habitual breathing
Of clocks where time means nothing,
In a condemned mansion?

Landscapes

1

This autumn park, the sequin glitter of leaves
Upon its withering bosom, the lake a moonstone –
O light mellifluous, glossing the stone-blind mansion,
October light, a godsend to these groves!

These unkempt groves, blind vistas, mark the defeat
Of men who imposed on Nature a private elegance
And died of dropsy. Let still the gay ghosts dance,
They are heartless ones we should wish nor fear to meet.

A ruin now, but here the Folly grinned –
The mad memento that one joker built:
Mocking their reasoned crops, a fabulous guilt
Towered up and cursed them fruitless from the ground.

Light drops, the hush of fallen ash, submission
Of a dying face now muted for the grave:
Through mansion, lake and the lacklustre groves
We see the landscape of their dissolution.

A landscape, now, with no remorse
Or symmetry, hacked out by those
Whom versatile history later chose –
Her ugliest, cash Conquistadors.

An inflamed sky reflects the wrath
Of babes from whom they hid the sun:
Disease and slag-tip smoulder on
With rancour round their narrowing path.

Towns there are choked with desperate men,
Scrap-iron gluts the sidings here:
Iron and men they mould for war,
But in their death that war will end.

From the gashed hills of desolation
Our life-blood springs to liberty,
And in the callous eyes we see
The landscape of their dissolution.

Sex-Crime

For one, the sudden fantastic grimace
Above, the red clown's-grin ripping the chalk sad sky,
Hailstones hatched out of midsummer, a face
Blanched with love's vile reversal.

                                                  The spirit died
First – such blank amazement took away its breath,
And let the body cry
Through the short scuffle and infamy of death.

For the other, who knows what nice proportion of loathing
And lust conjured the deep devil, created
That chance of incandescence? Figures here prove nothing.
One step took him through the roaring waterfall
That closed like a bead-curtain, left him alone with the
writhing
Of what he loved or hated.
His hands leapt out: they took vengeance for all
Denials and soft answers. There was one who said
Long since, 'rough play will end in tears'. There was Cain
In the picture-book. Forgotten. Here is one dead,
And one could never be whole again.

The news
Broke a Sunday inertia: ring after ring
Across that smug mirror went echoing
And fainting out to the dim margins of incredulity.
A few raw souls accuse
Themselves of this felony and find not guilty –
Acquitted on a mere alibi or technical point.
Most see it as an island eruption, viewed
From the safe continent; not dreaming the same fire pent
Within their clay that warps
The night with fluent alarm, their own wrath spewed
Through the red craters of that undistinguished corpse.
All that has reached them is the seismic thrill:
The ornaments vibrate on the shelf; then they are still.
Snugly we settle down
Into our velvet and legitimate bed,
While news-sheets are yet falling all over the town
Like a white ash. Falling on one dead
And one can never be whole again.

You watch him
Pulpited in the dock, preaching repentance
While the two professionals in fancy dress

Manœuvre formally to score off him or catch him.
But grief has her conventions –
The opaque mask of misery will confess
Nothing, nor plead moving extenuations.
But you who crowd the court-room, will you never be
                                             called
To witness for the defence?

                                    Accomplices,
All of you, now – though now is still too late –
Bring on the missing evidence! Reveal the coiled
Venom, the curse that needs
Only a touch to be articulate.
You, Judge, strip off! Show us the abscess boiling
Beneath your scarlet. Oh point, someone, to where it
                                             spreads
On every hand – the red, collusive stain . . .
All too well you have done your work: for one is dead,
And the other will not be whole again.

The Bells that Signed

The bells that signed a conqueror in
Or franked the lovers' bed, now mean
Nothing more heavenly than their
Own impulse and recoil of air.

But still at eve, when the wind swells
Out of the west, those rocking bells
Buoy up the sunken light, or mark
· What rots unfathomed in the dark.

Broods the stone-lipped conqueror still
Abject upon his iron hill,
And lovers in the naked beds
Cry for more than maidenheads.

A Happy View

. . . So take a happy view –
This lawn graced with the candle-flames of crocus,
Frail-handed girls under the flowering chestnut,
Or anything will do
That time takes back before it seems untrue:

And, if the truth were told,
You'd count it luck, perceiving in what shallow
Crevices and few crumbling grains of comfort
Man's joy will seed, his cold
And hardy fingers find an eagle's hold.

Overtures to Death

1

For us, born into a world
Of fledged, instinctive trees,
Of lengthening days, snowfall at Christmas
And sentried palaces,

You were the one our parents
Could not forget or forgive –
A remittance man, a very very
Distant relative.

We read your name in the family
Bible. It was tabu
At meals and lessons, but in church sometimes
They seemed to be praying for you.

You lived overseas, we gathered:
And often lying safe
In bed we thought of you, hearing the indrawn
Breath of the outcast surf.

Later we heard them saying
You had done well in the War.
And, though you never came home to us,
We saw your name everywhere.

When home grew unsympathetic,
You were all the rage for a while –
The favourite uncle with the blank-cheque-book
And the understanding smile.

Some of us went to look for you
In aeroplanes and fast cars:
Some tried the hospitals, some took to vice,
Others consulted the stars.

But now, sir, that you may be going
To visit us any night,
We watch the french windows, picturing you
In rather a different light.

The house, we perceive, is shabby,
There's dry-rot in the wood:
It's a poor welcome and it won't keep you out
And we wish we had been good.

But there's no time now for spring-cleaning
Or mending the broken lock.
We are here in the shrouded drawing-room till
Your first, your final knock.

2

When all the sky is skimming
And lovers frisk in the hay,
When it's easy forgiving the dead or the living,
He is not so far away.

When love's hands are too hot, too cold,
And justice turns a deaf ear,
When springs congeal and the skies are sealed,
We know that he is near.

Now here was a property, on all sides
Considered quite imposing:
Take a good look round at house and grounds –
The mortgage is foreclosing.

Now Death he is the bailiff
And he sits in our best room
Appraising chintz and ornaments
And the child in the womb.

We were not shysters or loonies,
Our spirit was up to proof:
Simpler far is the reason for our
Notice to quit this roof.

We paid for our lease and rule of life
In hard cash; and one day
The news got through to you-know-who
That we'd ceased to pay our way.

Oh what will happen to our dear sons,
Our dreams of pensioned ease?
They are downed and shredded for the wind
                                              we dreaded
Worries the blossom trees.

Oh Death he is the bailiff
And his men wait outside:
We shall sleep well in our handsome shell
While he auctions away our pride.

3

Sir, I'd not make so bold as to lack all
Respect for one whose prowess in the bed and the
                                              battlefield
Have excited (and justly) universal comment.
Nor could I, if I wished –
Who, in the small hours and the talkative
Reception, have felt you ticking within my belly –
Pretend there's any worse ordeal to come.
You and I, my friend, are antagonists
And the fight's framed: for this I blame not you
But the absentee promoter. If I seem to treat
Your titles, stamina, skill with levity,
Call it the rat's bad-loser snarl, the madman
Humouring the two doctors, the point declaring
War on the calm circumference. . . .
    You have appeared to us in many guises –
Pale priest, black camel, the bemedalled sergeant
Of general conscription, a bugbear to affright
Second childhood, or the curtain drawn so deftly
To show that diamond-tiered tree
Evergreen with bliss for all good boys and girls.
You have been called the Leveller: but little
That meant to the aristos you transferred

279

Straight from one rotten borough to another;
Nor can our state, hollow and cold as theirs,
Much envy the drab democrats of the grave.
Happiest, in our nervous time, who name you
Peace. You are the peace that millions die for.
     If there's a moment's solace, laid like the bloom
Of dew upon our meadows; if honeysuckle
Clings to its sweetened hour, and the appealing
Beauty of flesh makes time falter in his stride;
If anywhere love-lips, flower-flaunt, crimson of cloud-crest
With flames impassioned hold off the pacing shadows –
You can rest indulgent: soon enough
They shall be all, all of your complexion.
     I grant you the last word. But what of these –
The criminal agents of a dying will
Who, frantic with defeat, conspire to force your
Earlier intervention?
It is they, your damned auxiliaries, must answer
For the self-slain in the foodless, fireless room,
For stunted hearts that droop by our olive-green
Canals, the blossom of children untimely shattered
By their crazed, random fire, and the fear like a black frost
Foreshortening our prospect, metallic on our tongues.
If I am too familiar with you, sir,
It is that these have brought you into contempt.
You are in nature. These are most unnatural.
We shall desire your peace in our own time:
But with those, your free-lance and officious gunmen,
Our war is life itself and shall not fail.

4

     Forgive us, that we ever thought
     You could with innocence be bought,
     Or, puffed with queasy power, have tried
     Your register to override.

280

Such diamond-faced and equal laws
Allow no chink or saving clause:
Besotted may-fly, bobbish wren
Count in your books as much as men.

No North-West Passage can be found
To sail those freezing capes around,
Nor no smooth by-pass ever laid
Shall that metropolis evade.

The tampering hand, the jealous eye
That overlooked our infancy –
Forgiven soon, they sank their trust
And our reproach into the dust.

We also, whom a bawdy spring
Tempted to order everything,
Shall shrink beneath your first caress
Into a modest nothingness.

The meshes of the imperious blood,
The wind-flown tower, the poet's word
Can catch no more than a weak sigh
And ghost of immortality.

O lord of leisure, since we know
Your image we shall ne'er outgrow,
Teach us the value of our stay
Lest we insult the living clay.

This clay that binds the roots of man
And firmly foots his flying span –
Only this clay can voice, invest,
Measure and frame our mortal best.

O lord of night, bid us beware
The wistful ghost that speaks us fair:
Once let him in – he clots the veins
And makes a still-birth of our pains.

Now we at last have crossed the line
Where's earth's exuberant fields begin,
That green illusion in the sky
Born of our desert years can die.

No longer let predestined need
Cramp our design, or hunger breed
Its windy dreams, or life distil
Rare personal good from common ill.

Lord of us all, now it is true
That we are lords of all but you,
Teach us the order of our day
Lest we deface the honoured clay.

5

The sun came out in April,
The hawthorn in May:
We thought the year, like other years,
Would go the Christmas way.

In June we picked the clover,
And sea-shells in July:
There was no silence at the door,
No word from the sky.

A hand came out of August
And flicked his life away:
We had not time to bargain, mope,
Moralize, or pray.

Where he had been, was only
An effigy on a bed
To ask us searching questions or
Hear what we'd left unsaid.

Only that stained parchment
Set out what he had been –
A face we might have learned better,
But now must read unseen.

Thus he resigned his interest
And claims, all in a breath,
Leaving us the long office work
And winding-up of death:

The ordinary anguish,
The stairs, the awkward turn,
The bearers' hats like black mushrooms
Placed upon the lawn.

As a migrant remembers
The sting and warmth of home,
As the fruit bears out the blossom's word,
We remember him.

He loved the sun in April,
The hawthorn in May:
Our tree will not light up for him
Another Christmas Day.

6

It is not you I fear, but the humiliations
You mercifully use to deaden grief –
The downward graph of natural joys,
Imagination's slump, the blunted ear.

I hate this cold and politic self-defence
Of hardening arteries and nerves
Grown dull with time-serving. I see that the heart lives
By self-betrayal, by circumspection is killed.

That boy, whose glance makes heaven open and edges
Each dawning pain with gold, must learn to disbelieve:
The wildfire lust of the eyes will gutter down
To age's dim recalcitrance.

Have we not seen how quick this young girl's thoughts,
Wayward and burning as a charm of goldfinches
Alarmed from thistle-tops, turn into
Spite or a cupboard love or clipped routine?

Nearing the watershed and the difficult passes,
Man wraps up closer against the chill
In his familiar habits; and at the top
Pauses, seeing your kingdom like a net beneath him spread.

Some climbed to this momentous peak of the world
And facing the horizon – that notorious pure woman
Who lures to cheat the last embrace
Hurled themselves down upon an easier doom.

One the rare air made dizzy renounced
Earth, and the avalanche took him at his word:
One wooed perfection – he's bedded deep in the glacier,
                                                    perfect
And null, the prince and image of despair.

The best, neither hoarding nor squandering
The radiant flesh and the receptive
Spirit, stepped on together in the rhythm of comrades who
Have found a route on earth's true reckoning based.

284

They have not known the false humility,
The shamming-dead of the senses beneath your hunter's hand;
But life's green standards they've advanced
To the limit of your salt unyielding zone.

7

For us, born into a still
Unsweetened world, of sparse
Breathing-room, alleys brackish as hell's pit
And heaven-accusing spires,

You were never far nor fable,
Judgement nor happy end:
We have come to think of you, mister, as
Almost the family friend.

Our kiddies play tag with you often
Among the tornado wheels;
Through fevered nights you sit up with them,
You serve their little meals.

You lean with us at street-corners,
We have met you in the mine;
Your eyes are the foundry's glare, you beckon
From the snake-tooth, sly machine.

Low in the flooded engine room,
High on the yawing steeple –
Wherever we are, we begin to fancy
That we're your chosen people.

They came to us with charity,
They came to us with whips,
They came with chains behind their back
And freedom on their lips:

Castle and field and city –
Ours is a noble land,
Let us work for its fame together, they said;
But we don't quite understand.

For they took the land and the credit,
Took virtue and double-crossed her;
They left us the scrag-end of the luck
And the brunt of their disaster.

And now like horses they fidget
Smelling death in the air:
But we are your chosen people, and
We've little to lose or fear.

When the time comes for a clearance,
When light brims over the hill,
Mister, you can rely on us
To execute your will.

When they have Lost

When they have lost the little that they looked for,
The poor allotment of ease, custom, fame:
When the consuming star their fathers worked for
Has guttered into death, a fatuous flame:
When love's a cripple, faith a bed-time story,
Hope eats her heart out and peace walks on knives,
And suffering men cry an end to this sorry
World of whose children want alone still thrives:
Then shall the mounting stages of oppression
Like mazed and makeshift scaffolding torn down
Reveal his unexampled, best creation –

The shape of man's necessity full-grown.
Built from their bone, I see a power-house stand
To warm men's hearts again and light the land.

In the Heart of Contemplation

In the heart of contemplation –
Admiring, say, the frost-flowers of the white lilac,
Or lark's song busily sifting like sand-crystals
Through the pleased hourglass an afternoon of summer,
Or your beauty, dearer to me than these –
Discreetly a whisper in the ear,
The glance of one passing my window recall me
From lark, lilac, you, grown suddenly strangers.

In the plump and pastoral valley
Of a leisure time, among the trees like seabirds
Asleep on a glass calm, one shadow moves –
The sly reminder of the forgotten appointment.
All the shining pleasures, born to be innocent,
Grow dark with a truant's guilt:
The day's high heart falls flat, the oaks tremble,
And the shadow sliding over your face divides us.

In the act of decision only,
In the hearts cleared for action like lovers naked
For love, this shadow vanishes: there alone
There is nothing between our lives for it to thrive on.
You and I with lilac, lark and oak-leafed
Valley are bound together
As in the astounded clarity before death.
Nothing is innocent now but to act for life's sake.

Sonnet for a Political Worker

Is this what wears you out – having to weigh
One mote against another, the time spent
Fitting each thumbed and jig-saw argument
Into a pattern clear to you as day?
Boredom, the dull repetitive delay,
Opponents' tricky call, the discontent
Of friends, seem to deny what history meant
When first she showed her hand for you to play.

Do you not see that history's high tension
Must so be broken down to each man's need
And his frail filaments, that it may feed
Not blast all patience, love and warm invention?
On lines beyond your single comprehension
The circuit and full day of power proceed.

Questions

How long will you keep this pose of self-confessed
And aspen hesitation
Dithering on the brink, obsessed
Immobilized by the feminine fascination
Of an image all your own,
Or doubting which is shadow, which is bone?

Will you wait womanish, while the flattering stream
Glosses your faults away?
Or would you find within that dream
Courage to break the dream, wisdom to say
That wisdom is not there?
Or is it simply the first shock you fear?

Do you need the horn in your ear, the hounds at your heel,
Gadflies to sting you sore,
The lightning's angry feint, and all
The horizon clouds boiling like lead, before
You'll risk your javelin dive
And pierce reflection's heart, and come alive?

The Volunteer

Tell them in England, if they ask
What brought us to these wars,
To this plateau beneath the night's
Grave manifold of stars –

It was not fraud or foolishness,
Glory, revenge, or pay:
We came because our open eyes
Could see no other way.

There was no other way to keep
Man's flickering truth alight:
These stars will witness that our course
Burned briefer, not less bright.

Beyond the wasted olive-groves,
The furthest lift of land,
There calls a country that was ours
And here shall be regained.

Shine to us, memoried and real,
Green-water-silken meads:
Rivers of home, refresh our path
Whom here your influence leads.

Here in a parched and stranger place
We fight for England free,
The good our fathers won for her,
The land they hoped to see.

The Nabara*

*They preferred, because of the rudeness of their heart,
to die rather than to surrender.†*

PHASE ONE

Freedom is more than a word, more than the base coinage
Of statesmen, the tyrant's dishonoured cheque, or the
                                    dreamer's mad
Inflated currency. She is mortal, we know, and made
In the image of simple men who have no taste for carnage
But sooner kill and are killed than see that image betrayed.
Mortal she is, yet rising always refreshed from her ashes:
She is bound to earth, yet she flies as high as a passage bird
To home wherever man's heart with seasonal warmth is
                                    stirred:
Innocent is her touch as the dawn's, but still it unleashes
The ravisher shades of envy. Freedom is more than a word.

I see man's heart two-edged, keen both for death and
                                    creation.
As a sculptor rejoices, stabbing and mutilating the stone
Into a shapelier life, and the two joys make one –
So man is wrought in his hour of agony and elation
To efface the flesh to reveal the crying need of his bone.

---

* The episode upon which this poem is based is related in G. L. Steer's book *The Tree of Gernika* about the Spanish Civil War.
† In italics are the words of Walsingham after the sea-battle between English and Basques in 1350.

290

Burning the issue was beyond their mild forecasting
For those I tell of – men used to the tolerable joy and hurt
Of simple lives: they coveted never an epic part;
But history's hand was upon them and hewed an
                                   everlasting
Image of freedom out of their rude and stubborn heart.

The year, Nineteen-thirty-seven: month, March: the men,
                                   descendants
Of those Iberian fathers, the inquiring ones who would go
Wherever the sea-ways led: a pacific people, slow
To feel ambition, loving their laws and their
                         independence –
Men of the Basque country, the Mar Cantabrico.
Fishermen, with no guile outside their craft, they had
                                   weathered
Often the sierra-ranked Biscayan surges, the wet
Fog of the Newfoundland Banks: they were fond of *pelota*:
                                   they met
No game beyond their skill as they swept the sea together,
Until the morning they found the leviathan in their net.

Government trawlers *Nabara, Guipuzkoa, Bizkaya,*
Donostia, escorting across blockaded seas
Galdames with her cargo of nickel and refugees
From Bayonne to Bilbao, while the crest of war curled
                                   higher
Inland over the glacial valleys, the ancient ease.
On the morning of March the fifth, a chill North-Wester
                                   fanned them,
Fogging the glassy waves: what uncharted doom lay low
There in the fog athwart their course, they could not
                                   know:
Stout were the armed trawlers, redoubtable those who
                         manned them –
Men of the Basque country, the Mar Cantabrico.

Slowly they nosed ahead, while under the chill North-
                                                  Wester
Nervous the sea crawled and twitched like the skin of a
                                                  beast
That dreams of the chase, the kill, the blood-beslavered
                                                  feast:
They too, the light-hearted sailors, dreamed of a fine fiesta,
Flags and their children waving, when they won home
                                                  from the east.
Vague as images seen in a misted glass or the vision
Of crystal-gazer, the ships huddled, receded, neared,
Threading the weird fog-maze that coiled their funnels and
                                                  bleared
Day's eye. They were glad of the fog till *Galdames* lost
                                                  position
– Their convoy, precious in life and metal – and
                                                  disappeared.

But still they held their course, the confident ear-ringed
                                                  captains,
Unerring towards the landfall, nor guessed how the land
                                                  lay,
How the guardian fog was a guide to lead them all astray.
For now, at a wink, the mist rolled up like the film that
                                                  curtains
A saurian's eye; and into the glare of an evil day
Bizkaya, Guipuzkoa, Nabara, and the little
Donostia stepped at intervals; and sighted, alas,
Blocking the sea and sky a mountain they might not pass,
An isle thrown up volcanic and smoking, a giant in metal
Astride their path – the rebel cruiser, *Canarias*.

A ship of ten thousand tons she was, a heavyweight
                                                  fighter
To the cocky bantam trawlers: and under her armament
Of eight- and four-inch guns there followed obedient

Towards Pasajes a prize just seized, an Estonian freighter
Laden with arms the exporters of death to Spain had sent.
A hush, the first qualm of conflict, falls on the cruiser's
                                                burnished
Turrets, the trawlers' grimy decks: fiercer the lime-
Light falls, and out of the solemn ring the late mists climb,
And ship to ship the antagonists gaze at each other
                                                atonished
Across the quaking gulf of the sea for a moment's time.

The trawlers' men had no chance or wish to elude the
                                                fated
Encounter. Freedom to these was natural pride that runs
Hot as the blood, their climate and heritage, dearer than
                                                sons.
Bizkaya, Guipuzkoa, knowing themselves outweighted,
Drew closer to draw first blood with their pairs of four-inch
                                                guns.
Aboard *Canarias* the German gun-layers stationed
Brisk at their intricate batteries – guns and men both
                                                trained
To a hair in accuracy, aimed at a pitiless end –
Fired, and the smoke rolled forth over the unimpassioned
Face of a day where nothing certain but death remained.

PHASE TWO
The sound of the first salvo skimmed the ocean and
                                                thumped
Cape Machichaco's granite ribs: it rebounded where
The salt-sprayed trees grow tough from wrestling the wind:
                                                it jumped
From isle to rocky isle: it was heard by women while
They walked to shrine or market, a warning they must
                                                fear.

But, beyond their alarm, as
Though that sound were also a signal for fate to strip

293

Luck's last green shoot from the falling stock of the
                              Basques, *Galdames*
Emerged out of the mist that lingered to the west
Under the reeking muzzles of the rebel battleship:

Which instantly threw five shells over her funnel, and
                              threw
Her hundred women and children into a slaughter-yard
                              panic
On the deck they imagined smoking with worse than the
                              foggy dew,
So that *Galdames* rolled as they slipped, clawed, trampled,
                              reeled
Away from the gape of the cruiser's guns. A spasm
                              galvanic,
Fear's chemistry, shocked the women's bodies, a moment
                              before
Huddled like sheep in a mist, inert as bales of rag,
A mere deck-cargo; but more
Than furies now, for they stormed *Galdames*' bridge and
                              swarmed
Over her captain and forced him to run up the white flag.

Signalling the Estonian, 'Heave-to', *Canarias* steamed
Leisurely over to make sure of this other prize:
Over-leisurely was her reckoning – she never dreamed
The Estonian in that pause could be snatched from her
                              shark-shape jaws
By ships of minnow size.
Meanwhile *Nabara* and *Guipuzkoa*, not reluctant
For closer grips while their guns and crews were still entire,
Thrust forward: twice *Guipuzkoa* with a deadly jolt was
                              rocked, and
The sea spat up in geysers of boiling foam, as the cruiser's
Heavier guns boxed them in a torrid zone of fire.

And now the little *Donostia* who lay with her 75's
Dumb in the offing – her weapons against that leviathan
Impotent as pen-knives –
Witnessed a bold manœuvre, a move of genius, never
In naval history told. She saw *Bizkaya* run
Ahead of her consorts, a berserk atom of steel, audacious,
Her signal-flags soon to flutter like banderillas, straight
Towards the Estonian speeding, a young bull over the
                                                    spacious
And foam-distraught arena, till the sides of the freight-ship
                                                    screen her
From *Canarias* that will see the point of her charge too
                                                    late.

'Who are you and where are you going?' the flags of
                              Bizkaya questioned.
'Carrying arms and forced to go to Pasajes,' replied
The Estonian. 'Follow me to harbour.' 'Cannot, am
                              threatened.'
Bizkaya's last word – 'Turn at once!' – and she points her
                              peremptory guns
Against the freighter's mountainous flanks that blankly
                              hide
This fluttering language and flaunt of signal insolence
From the eyes of *Canarias*. At last the rebels can see
That the two ships' talk meant a practical joke at their
                              expense:
They see the Estonian veering away, to Bermeo steering,
Bizkaya under her lee.

(To the Basques that ship was a tonic, for she carried some
                              million rounds
Of ammunition: to hearts grown sick with hope deferred
And the drain of their country's wounds
She brought what most they needed in face of the aid
                              evaded

295

And the cold delay of those to whom freedom was only a
                                                            word.)*
Owlish upon the water sat the *Canarias*
Mobbed by those darting trawlers, and her signals blinked
                                                            in vain
After the freighter, that still she believed too large to pass
Into Bermeo's port – a prize she fondly thought,
When she'd blown the trawlers out of the water, she'd take
                                                            again.

Brisk at their intricate batteries the German gun-layers go
About death's business, knowing their longer reach must
                                                            foil
The impetus, break the heart of the government ships: each
                                                            blow
Deliberately they aim, and tiger-striped with flame
Is the jungle mirk of the smoke as their guns leap and
                                                            recoil.
The Newfoundland trawlers feel
A hail and hurricane the like they have never known
In all their deep-sea life: they wince at the squalls of steel
That burst on their open decks, rake them and leave them
                                                            wrecks,
But still they fight on long into the sunless afternoon.

– Fought on, four guns against the best of the rebel navy,
Until *Guipuzkoa*'s crew could stanch the fires no more
That gushed from her gashes and seeped nearer the
                                                    magazine. Heavy

* Cf. Byron's comments upon 'Non-Intervention' in *The Age of Bronze*:
              Lone, lost, abandoned in their utmost need
              By Christians, unto whom they gave their creed,
              The desolated lands, the ravaged isle,
              The fostered feud encouraged to beguile,
              The aid evaded, and the cold delay
              Prolonged but in the hope to make a prey: –
              These, these shall tell the tale, and Greece can show
              The false friend worse than the infuriate foe.

At heart they turned away for the Nervion that day:
Their ship, *Guipuzkoa*, wore
Flame's rose on her heart like a decoration of highest
honour
As listing she reeled into Las Arenas; and in a row
On her deck there lay, smoke-palled, the oriflamme's
crackling banner
Above them, her dead – a quarter of the fishermen who had
fought her –
Men of the Basque country, the Mar Cantabrico.

PHASE THREE
And now the gallant *Nabara* was left in the ring alone,
The sky hollow around her, the fawning sea at her side:
But the ear-ringed crew in their berets stood to the guns,
and cried
A fresh defiance down
The ebb of the afternoon, the battle's darkening tide.
Honour was satisfied long since; they had held and harried
A ship ten times their size; they well could have called it a
day.
But they hoped, if a little longer they kept the cruiser in
play,
Galdames with the wealth of life and metal she carried
Might make her getaway.

Canarias, though easily she outpaced and out-gunned her,
Finding this midge could sting
Edged off, and beneath a wedge of smoke steamed in a
ring
On the rim of the trawler's range, a circular storm of
thunder.
But always *Nabara* turned her broadside, manœuvring
To keep both guns on the target, scorning safety devices.
Slower now battle's tempo, irregular the beat
Of gunfire in the heart

Of the afternoon, the distempered sky sank to the crisis,
Shell-shocked the sea tossed and hissed in delirious heat.

The battle's tempo slowed, for the cruiser could take her
                                            time,
And the guns of *Nabara* grew
Red-hot, and of fifty-two Basque seamen had been her crew
Many were dead already, the rest filthy with grime
And their comrades' blood, weary with wounds all but a
                                            few.
Between two fires they fought, for the sparks that flashing
                                            spoke
From the cruiser's thunder-bulk were answered on their
                                            own craft
By traitor flames that crawled out of every cranny and rift
Blinding them all with smoke.
At half-past four *Nabara* was burning fore and aft.

What buoyancy of will
Was theirs to keep her afloat, no vessel now but a sieve –
So jarred and scarred, the rivets starting, no inch of her
                                            safe
From the guns of the foe that wrapped her in a cyclone of
                                            shrieking steel!
Southward the sheltering havens showed clear, the cliffs
                                            and the surf
Familiar to them from childhood, the shapes of a life still
                                            dear:
But dearer still to see
Those shores insured for life from the shadow of tyranny.
Freedom was not on their lips; it was what made them
                                            endure,
A steel spring in the yielding flesh, a thirst to be free.

And now from the little *Donostia* that lay with her 75's
Dumb in the offing, they saw *Nabara* painfully lower

A boat, which crawled like a shattered crab slower and
                                                slower
Towards them. They cheered the survivors, thankful to
                                        save these lives
At least. They saw each rower,
As the boat dragged alongside, was wounded – the oars
                                                they held
Dripping with blood, a bloody skein reeled out in their
                                                    wake:
And they swarmed down the rope-ladders to rescue these
                                            men so weak
From wounds they must be hauled
Aboard like babies. And then they saw they had made a
                                                mistake.

For, standing up in the boat,
A man of that grimy boat's-crew hailed them: 'Our officer
                                                    asks
You give us your bandages and all your water-casks,
Then run for Bermeo. We're going to finish this game of
                                                pelota.'
Donostia's captain begged them with tears to escape: but
                                            the Basques
Would play their game to the end.
They took the bandages, and cursing at his delay
They took the casks that might keep the fires on their ship
                                                at bay;
And they rowed back to *Nabara*, trailing their blood behind
Over the water, the sunset and crimson ebb of their day.

For two hours more they fought, while *Nabara* beneath
                                            their feet
Was turned to a heap of smouldering scrap-iron. Once
                                                again
The flames they had checked a while broke out. When the
                                        forward gun

299

Was hit, they turned about
Bringing the after gun to bear. They fought in pain
And the instant knowledge of death: but the waters filling
their riven
Ship could not quench the love that fired them. As each
man fell
To the deck, his body took fire as if death made visible
That burning spirit. For two more hours they fought, and
at seven
They fired their last shell.

Of her officers all but one were dead. Of her engineers
All but one were dead. Of the fifty-two that had sailed
In her, all were dead but fourteen – and each of these half
killed
With wounds. And the night-dew fell in a hush of ashen
tears,
And *Nabara*'s tongue was stilled.
Southward the sheltering havens grew dark, the cliffs and
the green
Shallows they knew; where their friends had watched them
as evening wore
To a glowing end, who swore
Nabara must show a white flag now, but saw instead the
fourteen
Climb into their matchwood boat and fainting pull for the
shore.

Canarias lowered a launch that swept in a greyhound's
curve
Pitiless to pursue
And cut them off. But that bloodless and all-but-phantom
crew
Still gave no soft concessions to fate: they strung their nerve
For one last fling of defiance, they shipped their oars and
threw

Hand-grenades at the launch as it circled about to board
them.
But the strength of the hands that had carved them a hold
on history
Failed them at last: the grenades fell short of the enemy,
Who grappled and overpowered them,
While *Nabara* sank by the stern in the hushed Cantabrian
sea.

*   *   *

They bore not a charmed life. They went into battle
foreseeing
Probable loss, and they lost. The tides of Biscay flow
Over the obstinate bones of many, the winds are sighing
Round prison walls where the rest are doomed like their
ships to rust –
Men of the Basque country, the Mar Cantabrico.
Simple men who asked of their life no mythical splendour,
They loved its familiar ways so well that they preferred
In the rudeness of their heart to die rather than to
surrender . . .
Mortal these words and the deed they remember, but cast a
seed
Shall flower for an age when freedom is man's creative word.

Freedom was more than a word, more than the base
coinage
Of politicians who hiding behind the skirts of peace
They had defiled, gave up that country to rack and
carnage:
For whom, indelibly stamped with history's contempt,
Remains but to haunt the blackened shell of their policies.
For these I have told of, freedom was flesh and blood – a
mortal
Body, the gun-breech hot to its touch: yet the battle's
height

301

Raised it to love's meridian and held it awhile immortal;
And its light through time still flashes like a star's that has
                                        turned to ashes,
Long after *Nabara*'s passion was quenched in the sea's
                                        heart.

Spring Song

Floods and the voluble winds
Have warned the dead away:
In swaying copse the willows
Wave their magic wands.

The sun is here to deal
With the dull decay we felt:
In field and square he orders
The vague shadows to heel.

The licence is renewed
And all roads lead to summer:
Good girls come to grief,
Fish to the springy rod.

Our thoughts like sailplanes go
To and fro sauntering
Along fantastic cloud-streets
On warmer currents' flow.

A larger appetite,
A tautening of the will,
The wild pony tamed,
The common gorse alight.

Now the bee finds the pollen,
The pale boy a cure:
Who cares if in the sequel
Cocky shall be crestfallen?

Night Piece

Down the night-scented borders of sleep
They walk hand in hand, the lovers
Whom day abashed like the cross
Eye of the rheumatic keeper.
They are laid in the grass, and above
Their limbs a syringa blossoms*
In brief and bridal white,
Under whose arch of moonshine
The impotent is made straight,
The ice-queen delighted,
And the virgin loves to moan,
And the schoolboy finds the equator.

Here too the dark plays tricks
On some of accredited glory.
The chairman's forgot his speech:
The general meets his victims,
And the pale wounds weep once more:
The archbishop is preaching
Stark naked: standing alone
Among his people, the dictator
Glares round for a bodyguard.
All the fears cold-shouldered at noonday
Flock to these shades, and await
In displeasure those who ignored them.

* See note on *Father to Sons* (*Pegasus*) p. 514

The Three Cloud-Maidens

Says winding Trent
Among the low pastures –
In my crystal read
Your real wish and features:
May no accident
Of flood or mist be flawing
The chaste, prophetic reed,
The child-face stream's flowing –
Says winding Trent
Among the low pastures.

Say the three cloud-maidens
Over the soiled valley –
To reproach you we rise
Wind-flushed and early:
The mist that maddens,
The clumsy floods that hurt
Innocence, all arise
Out of your shallow heart –
Say the three cloud-maidens
Over the soiled valley.

Behold the Swan

Behold the swan
Riding at her image, anchored there
Complacent, a water-lily upon
The ornamental water:
Queen of the mute October air,
She broods in that unbroken
Reverie of reed and water.

Now from the stricken
Pool she hoists and flurries,
And passes overhead
In hoarse, expressive flight:
Her wings bear hard
On the vibrant air: unhurried
The threat and pulse of wings, the throat
Levelled towards the horizon, see –
They are prophecy.

Song

It was not far through the pinewoods
That day to the lodge gate,
But far enough for the wind to phrase
My ten-year-long regret.

It was not far by the cornfield,
The tall ears looked alive:
But my heart, like corn, was broken for
A harvest I could not have.

From husk of words unspoken
I'll winnow a ripe seed:
From woods where love was shy to trespass
I'll learn the airs I need.

Oh here and unlamenting
Her graceful ghost shall shine –
In the heart mature as fruited fields,
The singing words of pine.

The Escapist

Before a rumour stirred, he fled the country
Preferring blank disgrace to any gesture
That could wipe out his failure with himself.
A warmer man no doubt had realized
His assets in our buoyant love, and taken
Some bonds to gild an unromantic exile.

Before their first reproach could reach his ears,
He had set up a private court, accepted
Full responsibility, and passed judgement.
The man whom later they reviled because
He would not face their music, was already
Self-flayed and branded in his heart for ever.

Before the story broke, he had sat down
To write it out, determined that no vestige
Of guilt be missed, no tiniest false inflection
Of heroism creep in to justify
The ugly tale. They said he was too proud to
Trust other hands even with his dishonour.

Before you heap quick-lime upon that felon
Memory, think how nothing you can do
Could touch his self-vindictiveness, and nothing
You did to cure the cowardice it avenged for.
Say, if you like, escape was in his blood –
Escape's as good a word as any other.

Passage from Childhood

His earliest memory, the mood
Fingered and frail as maidenhair,
Was this – a china cup somewhere
In a green, deep wood.
He lives to find again somewhere
That wood, that homely cup; to taste all
Its chill, imagined dews; to dare
The dangerous crystal.

Who can say what misfeatured elf
First led him into that lifelong
Passage of mirrors where, so young,
He saw himself
Balanced as Blondin, more headstrong
Than baby Hercules, rare as a one-
Cent British Guiana, above the wrong
And common run?

He knew the secrecy of squirrels,
The foolish doves' antiphony,
And what wrens fear. He was gun-shy,
Hating all quarrels.
Life was a hostile land to spy,
Full of questions he dared not ask
Lest the answer in mockery
Or worse unmask.

Quick to injustice, quick he grew
This hermit and contorted shell.
Self-pity like a thin rain fell,
Fouling the view:
Then tree-trunks seemed wet roots of hell,
Wren or catkin might turn vicious,

307

The dandelion clock could tell
Nothing auspicious.

No exile has ever looked so glum
With the pines fretful overhead,
Yet he felt at home in the gothic glade –
More than at home.
You will forgive him that he played
Bumble-puppy on the small mossed lawn
All by himself for hours, afraid
Of being born.

Lying awake one night, he saw
Eternity stretched like a howl of pain:
He was tiny and terrible, a new pin
On a glacier's floor.
Very few they are who have lain
With eternity and lived to tell it:
There's a secret process in his brain
And he cannot sell it.

Now, beyond reach of sense or reason,
His life walks in a glacial sleep
For ever, since he drank that cup
And found it poison.
He's one more ghost, engaged to keep
Eternity's long hours and mewed
Up in live flesh with no escape
From solitude.

Self-Criticism and Answer

It was always so, always –
My too meticulous words
Mocked by the unhinged cries
Of playground, mouse or gull,
By throats of nestling birds
Like bells upturned in a peal –
All that has innocence
To praise and far to fall.

I fear this careful art
Would never storm the sense:
Its agonies are but the eager
Retching of an empty heart;
It never was possessed
By divine incontinence,
And for him whom that eygre*
Sweeps not, silence were best.

Your politicians pray silence
For the ribald trumpeter,
The falsetto crook, the twitching
Unappeasable dictator.
For any else you should be pleased
To hold your tongue: but Satan
Himself would disown his teaching
And turn to spit on these.

When madmen play the piper
And knaves call the tune,
Honesty's a right passion –
She must call to her own.

* A tidal wave of unusual height caused by the rushing of the tide up a narrowing estuary.

309

Let yours be the start and stir
Of a flooding indignation
That channels the dry heart deeper
And sings through the dry bone.

1938

WORD OVER ALL

TO ROSAMOND LEHMANN

Word over all, beautiful as the sky,
Beautiful that war and all its deeds of carnage must in time
 be utterly lost,
That the hands of the sisters Death and Night incessantly
 softly wash again, and ever again, this soiled world.

WALT WHITMAN

312

313

PART ONE

The Lighted House

One night they saw the big house, some time untenanted
But for its hand-to-mouth recluse, room after room
Light up, as when Primavera herself has spirited
A procession of crocuses out of their winter tomb.

Revels unearthly are going forward, one did remark –
He has conjured a thing of air or fire for his crazed delight:
Another said, It is only a traveller lost in the dark
He welcomes for mercy's sake. Each, in a way, was right.

You were the magic answer, the sprite fire-fingered who
        came
To lighten my heart, my house, my heirlooms; you are the
        wax
That melts at my touch and still supports my prodigal
        flame:

But you were also the dead-beat traveller out of the storm
Returned to yourself by almost obliterated tracks,
Peeling off fear after fear, revealing love's true form.

The Album

I see you, a child
In a garden sheltered for buds and playtime,
Listening as if beguiled
By a fancy beyond your years and the flowering maytime.
The print is faded: soon there will be
No trace of that pose enthralling,
Nor visible echo of my voice distantly calling
'Wait! Wait for me!'

Then I turn the page
To a girl who stands like a questioning iris
By the waterside, at an age
That asks every mirror to tell what the heart's desire is.
The answer she finds in that oracle stream
Only time could affirm or disprove,
Yet I wish I was there to venture a warning, 'Love
Is not what you dream.'

Next, you appear
As if garlands of wild felicity crowned you –
Courted, caressed, you wear
Like immortelles the lovers and friends around you.
'They will not last you, rain or shine,
They are but straws and shadows,'
I cry: 'Give not to those charming desperadoes
What was made to be mine.'

One picture is missing –
The last. It would show me a tree stripped bare
By intemperate gales, her amazing
Noonday of blossom spoilt which promised so fair.
Yet, scanning those scenes at your heyday taken,
I tremble, as one who must view

In the crystal a doom he could never deflect – yes, I too
Am fruitlessly shaken.

I close the book;
But the past slides out of its leaves to haunt me
And it seems, wherever I look,
Phantoms of irreclaimable happiness taunt me.
Then I see her, petalled in new-blown hours,
Beside me – 'All you love most there
Has blossomed again,' she murmurs, 'all that you missed
                                      there

Has grown to be yours.'

The Hunter's Game

I am an arrow, I am a bow –
The bow sings fierce and deep,
The arrow's tipped with cruel flame,
Feathered with passionate sleep.
When you play the hunter's game,
I am your arrow and your bow.

Only my love can bend the bow:
When the bow leaps to kill
And darkly as a nerve of night
The string throbs out, you are the skill
That drew the impulsive bowstring tight,
The hand that bent the bow.

What is the air that floats my arrow
Smoothly aloft and bears
It up to the sun, down to the dark?
You are the wanton airs

Which shape and hold its shining arc,
The innocent air that flights the arrow.

What is the victim of this arrow
That flies so fast and true?
Deep in the close, fawn-dappled glade,
Pierced by a shaft of light are you
The huntress, white and smiling, laid –
The victim of your arrow.

Departure in the Dark

Nothing so sharply reminds a man he is mortal
As leaving a place
In a winter morning's dark, the air on his face
Unkind as the touch of sweating metal:
Simple goodbyes to children or friends become
A felon's numb
Farewell, and love that was a warm, a meeting place –
Love is the suicide's grave under the nettles.

Gloomed and clemmed as if by an imminent ice-age
Lies the dear world
Of your street-strolling, field-faring. The senses, curled
At the dead end of a shrinking passage,
Care not if close the inveterate hunters creep,
And memories sleep
Like mammoths in lost caves. Drear, extinct is the world,
And has no voice for consolation or presage.

There is always something at such times of the passover,
When the dazed heart
Beats for it knows not what, whether you part

From home or prison, acquaintance or lover –
Something wrong with the time-table, something unreal
In the scrambled meal
And the bag ready packed by the door, as though the heart
Has gone ahead, or is staying here for ever.

No doubt for the Israelites that early morning
It was hard to be sure
If home were prison or prison home: the desire
Going forth meets the desire returning.
This land, that had cut their pride down to the bone
Was now their own
By ancient deeds of sorrow. Beyond, there was nothing sure
But a desert of freedom to quench their fugitive yearnings.

At this blind hour the heart is informed of nature's
Ruling that man
Should be nowhere a more tenacious settler than
Among wry thorns and ruins, yet nurture
A seed of discontent in his ripest ease.
There's a kind of release
And a kind of torment in every goodbye for every man
And will be, even to the last of his dark departures.

Cornet Solo

Thirty years ago lying awake,
Lying awake
In London at night when childhood barred me
From livelier pastimes, I'd hear a street-band break
Into old favourites – 'The Ash Grove', 'Killarney'
Or 'Angels Guard Thee'.

That was the music for such an hour –
A deciduous hour
Of leaf-wan drizzle, of solitude
And gaslight bronzing the gloom like an autumn flower –
The time and music for a boy imbrued
With the pensive mood.

I could have lain for hours together,
Sweet hours together,
Listening to the cornet's cry
Down wet streets gleaming like patent leather
Where beauties jaunted in cabs to their revelry,
Jewelled and spry.

Plaintive its melody rose or waned
Like an autumn wind
Blowing the rain on beds of aster,
On man's last bed: mournful and proud it complained
As a woman who dreams of the charms that graced her,
In young days graced her.

Strange how those yearning airs could sweeten
And still enlighten
The hours when solitude gave me her breast.
Strange they could tell a mere child how hearts may beat in
The self-same tune for the once-possessed
And the unpossessed.

Last night, when I heard a cornet's strain,
It seemed a refrain
Wafted from thirty years back – so remote an
Echo it bore: but I felt again
The prophetic mood of a child, too long forgotten,
Too lightly forgotten.

O Dreams, O Destinations

1

For infants time is like a humming shell
Heard between sleep and sleep, wherein the shores
Foam-fringed, wind-fluted of the strange earth dwell
And the sea's cavernous hunger faintly roars.
It is the humming pole of summer lanes
Whose sound quivers like heart-haze endlessly
Over the corn, over the poppied plains –
An emanation from the earth or sky.
Faintly they hear, through the womb's lingering haze,
A rumour of that sea to which they are born:
They hear the ringing pole of summer days,
But need not know what hungers for the corn.
They are the lisping rushes in a stream –
Grace-notes of a profound, legato dream.

2

Children look down upon the morning-grey
Tissue of mist that veils a valley's lap:
Their fingers itch to tear it and unwrap
The flags, the roundabouts, the gala day.
They watch the spring rise inexhaustibly –
A breathing thread out of the eddied sand,
Sufficient to their day: but half their mind
Is on the sailed and glittering estuary.
Fondly we wish their mist might never break,
Knowing it hides so much that best were hidden:
We'd chain them by the spring, lest it should broaden
For them into a quicksand and a wreck.
But they slip through our fingers like the source,
Like mist, like time that has flagged out their course.

321

3

That was the fatal move, the ruination
Of innocence so innocently begun,
When in the lawless orchard of creation
The child left this fruit for that rosier one.
Reaching towards the far thing, we begin it;
Looking beyond, or backward, more and more
We grow unfaithful to the unique minute
Till, from neglect, its features stale and blur.
Fish, bird or beast was never thus unfaithful –
Man only casts the image of his joys
Beyond his senses' reach; and by this fateful
Act, he confirms the ambiguous power of choice.
Innocence made that first choice. It is she
Who weeps, a child chained to the outraged tree.

4

Our youthtime passes down a colonnade
Shafted with alternating light and shade.
All's dark or dazzle there. Half in a dream
Rapturously we move, yet half afraid
Never to wake. That diamond-point, extreme
Brilliance engraved on us a classic theme:
The shaft of darkness had its lustre too,
Rising where earth's concentric mysteries gleam.
Oh youth-charmed hours, that made an avenue
Of fountains playing us on to love's full view,
A cypress walk to some romantic grave –
Waking, how false in outline and in hue
We find the dreams that flickered on our cave:
Only your fire, which cast them, still seems true.

5

All that time there was thunder in the air:
Our nerves branched and flickered with summer lightning.
The taut crab-apple, the pampas quivering, the glare
On the roses seemed irrelevant, or a heightening
At most of the sealed-up hour wherein we awaited
What? – some explosive oracle to abash
The platitudes on the lawn? heaven's delegated
Angel – the golden rod, our burning bush?
No storm broke. Yet in retrospect the rose
Mounting vermilion, fading, glowing again
Like a fire's heart, that breathless inspiration
Of pampas grass, crab-tree's attentive pose
Never were so divinely charged as then –
The veiled Word's flesh, a near annunciation.

6

Symbols of gross experience! – our grief
Flowed, like a sacred river, underground:
Desire bred fierce abstractions on the mind,
Then like an eagle soared beyond belief.
Often we tried our breast against the thorn,
Our paces on the turf: whither we flew,
Why we should agonize, we hardly knew –
Nor what ached in us, asking to be born.
Ennui of youth! – thin air above the clouds,
Vain divination of the sunless stream
Mirror that impotence, till we redeem
Our birthright, and the shadowplay concludes.
Ah, not in dreams, but when our souls engage
With the common mesh and moil, we come of age.

7

Older, we build a road where once our active
Heat threw up mountains and the deep dales veined:
We're glad to gain the limited objective,
Knowing the war we fight in has no end.
The road must needs follow each contour moulded
By that fire in its losing fight with earth:
We march over our past, we may behold it
Dreaming a slave's dream on our bivouac hearth.
Lost the archaic dawn wherein we started,
The appetite for wholeness: now we prize
Half-loaves, half-truths – enough for the half-hearted,
The gleam snatched from corruption satisfies.
Dead youth, forgive us if, all but defeated,
We raise a trophy where your honour lies.

8

But look, the old illusion still returns,
Walking a field-path where the succory burns
Like summer's eye, blue lustre-drops of noon,
And the heart follows it and freshly yearns:
Yearns to the sighing distances beyond
Each height of happiness, the vista drowned
In gold-dust haze, and dreams itself immune
From change and night to which all else is bound.
Love, we have caught perfection for a day
As succory holds a gem of halcyon ray:
Summer burns out, its flower will tarnish soon –
Deathless illusion, that could so relay
The truth of flesh and spirit, sun and clay
Singing for once together all in tune!

To travel like a bird, lightly to view
Deserts where stone gods founder in the sand,
Ocean embraced in a white sleep with land;
To escape time, always to start anew.
To settle like a bird, make one devoted
Gesture of permanence upon the spray
Of shaken stars and autumns: in a bay
Beyond the crestfallen surges to have floated.
Each is our wish. Alas, the bird flies blind,
Hooded by a dark sense of destination:
Her weight on the glass calm leaves no impression,
Her home is soon a basketful of wind.
Travellers, we're fabric of the road we go;
We settle, but like feathers on time's flow.

PART TWO

Word Over All

Now when drowning imagination clutches
At old loves drifting away,
Splintered highlights, hope capsized – a wrecked world's
Flotsam, what can I say
To cheer the abysmal gulfs, the crests that lift not
To any land in sight?
How shall the sea-waif, who lives from surge to surge,
                                              chart

Current and reef aright?

Always our time's ghost-guise of impermanence
Daunts me: whoever I meet,
Wherever I stand, a shade of parting lengthens
And laps around my feet.
But now, the heart-sunderings, the real migrations –
Millions fated to flock
Down weeping roads to mere oblivion – strike me
Dumb as a rooted rock.

I watch when searchlights set the low cloud smoking
Like acid on metal: I start
At sirens, sweat to feel a whole town wince
And thump, a terrified heart,
Under the bomb-strokes. These, to look back on, are
A few hours' unrepose:
But the roofless old, the child beneath the debris –
How can I speak for those?

Busy the preachers, the politicians weaving
Voluble charms around
This ordeal, conjuring a harvest that shall spring from
Our hearts' all-harrowed ground.
I, who chose to be caged with the devouring
Present, must hold its eye
Where blaze ten thousand farms and fields unharvested,
And hearts, steel-broken, die.

Yet words there must be, wept on the cratered present,
To gleam beyond it:
Never was cup so mortal but poets with mild
Everlastings have crowned it.
See wavelets and wind-blown shadows of leaves on a
                                    stream
How they ripple together,
As life and death intermarried – you cannot tell
One from another.

Our words like poppies love the maturing field,
But form no harvest:
May lighten the innocent's pang, or paint the dreams
Where guilt is unharnessed.
Dark over all, absolving all, is hung
Death's vaulted patience:
Words are to set man's joy and suffering there
In constellations.

We speak of what we know, but what we have spoken
Truly we know not –
Whether our good may tarnish, our grief to far
Centuries glow not.
The Cause shales off, the Humankind stands forth
A mightier presence,
Flooded by dawn's pale courage, rapt in eve's
Rich acquiescence.

The Image

From far, she seemed to lie like a stone on the sick horizon:
Too soon that face, intolerably near,
Writhed like a furious ant-hill. Whoever, they say, set eyes
                                                on
Her face became a monument to fear.

But Perseus, lifting his shield, beheld as in a view-finder
A miniature monster, darkly illustrious.
Absorbed, pitying perhaps, he struck. And the sky behind
                                                her
Woke with a healthier colour, purified thus.

Now, in a day of monsters, a desert of abject stone
Whose outward terrors paralyse the will,
Look to that gleaming circle until it have revealed you

The glare of death transmuted to your own
Measure, scaled-down to a possible figure the sum of ill.
Let the shield take that image, the image shield you.

The Poet

For me there is no dismay
Though ills enough impend.
I have learned to count each day
Minute by breathing minute –
Birds that lightly begin it,
Shadows muting its end –
As lovers count for luck
Their own heart-beats and believe
In the forest of time they pluck
Eternity's single leaf.

Tonight the moon's at the full.
Full moon's the time for murder.
But I look to the clouds that hide her –
The bay below below me is dull,
An unreflecting glass –
And chafe for the clouds to pass,
And wish she suddenly might
Blaze down at me so I shiver
Into a twelve-branched river
Of visionary light.

For now imagination,
My royal, impulsive swan,
With raking flight – I can see her –
Comes down as it were upon
A lake in whirled snow-floss
And flurry of spray like a skier
Checking. Again I feel
The wounded waters heal.
Never before did she cross
My heart with such exaltation.

Oh, on this striding edge,
This hare-bell height of calm
Where intuitions swarm
Like nesting gulls and knowledge
Is free as the winds that blow,
A little while sustain me,
Love, till my answer is heard!
Oblivion roars below,
Death's cordon narrows: but vainly,
If I've slipped the carrier word.

Dying, any man may
Feel wisdom harmonious, fateful
At the tip of his dry tongue.
All I have felt or sung
Seems now but the moon's fitful
Sleep on a clouded bay,
Swan's maiden flight, or the climb
To a tremulous, hare-bell crest.
Love, tear the song from my breast!
Short, short is the time.

It Would Be Strange

It would be strange
If at a crucial question, in wild-beast dens
Or cellars sweating with pain the stammerers
Should find their confidence.

It would be strange
If the haphazard starling learned a neat
Construction from the goldcrest, and the blackcap's
Seamless song in a night.

It would be strange
If from the consternation of the ant-hill
Arose some order angelic, ranked for loving,
Equal to good or ill.

It would be more than strange
If the devil we raised to avenge our envy, grief,
Weakness, should take our hand like a prince and raise us
And say, 'I forgive'.

The Assertion

Now in the face of destruction,
In the face of the woman knifed out of all recognition
By flying glass, the fighter spinning like vertigo
On the axis of the trapped pilot and crowds applauding,
Famine that bores like a death-watch deep below,
Notice of agony splashed on headline and hoarding,
In the face of the infant burned
To death, and the shattered ship's-boat low in the trough –

Oars weakly waving like a beetle overturned –
Now, as never before, when man seems born to hurt
And a whole wincing earth not wide enough
For his ill will, now is the time we assert
To their face that men are love.

For love's no laughing matter,
Never was a free gift, an angel, a fixed equator.
Love's the big boss at whose side for ever slouches
The shadow of the gunman: he's mortar and dynamite;
Antelope, drinking pool, but the tiger too that crouches.
Therefore be wise in the dark hour to admit
The logic of the gunman's trigger,
Embrace the explosive element, learn the need
Of tiger for antelope and antelope for tiger.
O love, so honest of face, so unjust in action,
Never so dangerous as when denied,
Let your kindness tell us how false we are, your bloody
                                    correction
Our purpose and our pride.

Watching Post

A hill flank overlooking the Axe valley.
Among the stubble a farmer and I keep watch
For whatever may come to injure our countryside –
Light-signals, parachutes, bombs, or sea-invaders.
The moon looks over the hill's shoulder, and hope
Mans the old ramparts of an English night.

In a house down there was Marlborough born. One night
Monmouth marched to his ruin out of that valley.
Beneath our castled hill, where Britons kept watch,

Is a church where the Drakes, old lords of this countryside,
Sleep under their painted effigies. No invaders
Can dispute their legacy of toughness and hope.

Two counties away, over Bristol, the searchlights hope
To find what danger is in the air tonight.
Presently gunfire from Portland reaches our valley
Tapping like an ill-hung door in a draught. My watch
Says nearly twelve. All over the countryside
Moon-dazzled men are peering out for invaders.

The farmer and I talk for a while of invaders:
But soon we turn to crops – the annual hope,
Making of cider, prizes for ewes. Tonight
How many hearts along this war-mazed valley
Dream of a day when at peace they may work and watch
The small sufficient wonders of the countryside.

Image or fact, we both in the countryside
Have found our natural law, and until invaders
Come will answer its need: for both of us, hope
Means a harvest from small beginnings, who this night
While the moon sorts out into shadow and shape our valley,
A farmer and a poet, are keeping watch.

July, 1940

The Stand-To

Autumn met me today as I walked over Castle Hill.
The wind that had set out corn by the ears was blowing
                                                    still:
Autumn, who takes the leaves and the long days, crisped
                                                    the air

With a tang of action, a taste of death; and the wind blew
fair

From the east for men and barges massed on the other
side –
Men maddened by numbers or stolid by nature, they have
their pride
As we in work and children, but now a contracting will
Crumples their meek petitions and holds them poised to
kill.

Last night a Stand-To was ordered. Thirty men of us here
Came out to guard the star-lit village – my men who wear
Unwitting the season's beauty, the received truth of the
spade –
Roadmen, farm labourers, masons, turned to another
trade.

A dog barked over the fields, the candle stars put a sheen
On the rifles ready, the sandbags fronded with evergreen:
The dawn wind blew, the star winked out on the posts
where we lay,
The order came, Stand Down, and thirty went away.

Since a cold wind from Europe blows back the words in my
teeth,
Since autumn shortens the days and the odds against our
death,
And the harvest moon is waxing and high tides threaten
harm,
Since last night may be the last night all thirty men go
home,

I write this verse to record the men who have watched
with me –
Spot who is good at darts, Squibby at repartee,

Mark and Cyril, the dead shots, Ralph with a ploughman's
gait,
Gibson, Harris and Long, old hands for the barricade,

Whiller the lorry-driver, Francis and Rattlesnake,
Fred and Charl and Stan – these nights I have lain awake
And thought of my thirty men and the autumn wind that
blows
The apples down too early and shatters the autumn rose.

Destiny, History, Duty, Fortitude, Honour – all
The words of the politicians seem too big or too small
For the ragtag fighters of lane and shadow, the love that
has grown
Familiar as working-clothes, faithful as bone to bone.

Blow, autumn wind, upon orchard and rose! Blow leaves
along
Our lanes, but sing through me for the lives that are worth
a song!
Narrowing days have darkened the vistas that hurt my
eyes,
But pinned to the heart of darkness a tattered fire-flag flies.
September, 1940

334

Where are the War Poets?

They who in folly or mere greed
Enslaved religion, markets, laws,
Borrow our language now and bid
Us to speak up in freedom's cause.

It is the logic of our times,
No subject for immortal verse –
That we who lived by honest dreams
Defend the bad against the worse.

Angel

We thought the angel of death would come
As a thundering judge to impeach us,
So we practised an attitude of calm or indignation
And prepared the most eloquent speeches.

But when the angel of death stepped down,
She was like a spoilt girl in ermine:
She tipped a negligent wing to some
And treated the rest as vermin.

Now we have seen the way she goes on,
Our self-possession wavers:
We'd fear a hanging judge far less than
That bitch's casual favours.

Airmen Broadcast

Speak for the air, your element, you hunters
Who range across the ribbed and shifting sky:
Speak for whatever gives you mastery –
Wings that bear out your purpose, quick-responsive
Fingers, a fighting heart, a kestrel's eye.

Speak of the rough and tumble in the blue,
The mast-high run, the flak, the battering gales:
You that, until the life you love prevails,
Must follow death's impersonal vocation –
Speak from the air, and tell your hunters' tales.

Lidice

Not a grave of the murdered for freedom but grows seed for freedom.

WALT WHITMAN

Cry to us, murdered village. While your grave
Aches raw on history, make us understand
What freedom asks of us. Strengthen our hand
Against the arrogant dogmas that deprave
And have no proof but death at their command.

Must the innocent bleed for ever to remedy
These fanatic fits that tear mankind apart?
The pangs we felt from your atrocious hurt
Promise a time when even the killer shall see
His sword is aimed at his own naked heart.

Ode to Fear

The lustre bowl of the sky
Sounds and sustains
A throbbing cello-drone of planes.
Entombed beneath this caving liberty,
We note how doom endorses
Our devious fraud and folly where skeins
Of wild geese flew direct on visionary courses.

Now Fear has come again
To live with us
In poisoned intimacy like pus,
Hourly extending the area of our pain,
It seems I must make the most
Of fever's pulsing dreams and thus
Live to allay this evil or dying lay its ghost.

Fear has so many symptoms –
Planes throbbing above
Like headache, rumours that glibly move
Along the bloodstream, sleep's prophetic phantoms
Condemning what we have built,
Heartburn anxiety for those we love –
And all, yes all, are proof of an endemic guilt.

The bones, the stalwart spine,
The legs like bastions,
The nerves, the heart's natural combustions,
The head that hives our active thoughts – all pine,
Are quenched or paralysed
When Fear puts unexpected questions
And makes the heroic body freeze like a beast surprised.

The sap will rise anew in
Both man and brute:
Wild virtues even now can shoot
From the reviled interstices of ruin.
But oh, what drug, what knife
Can wither up our guilt at the root,
Cure our discoloured days and cleanse the blood of life?

Today, I can but record
In truth and patience
This high delirium of nations
And hold to it the reflecting, fragile word.
Come to my heart then, Fear,
With all your linked humiliations,
As wild geese flight and settle on a submissive mere.

The Dead

They lie in the sunday street
Like effigies thrown down after a fête
Among the bare-faced houses frankly yawning revulsion,
Fag-ends of fires, litter of rubble, stale
Confetti-sprinkle of blood. Was it defeat
With them, or triumph? Purification
Or All Fools' Day? On this they remain silent.
Their eyes are closed to honour and hate.

We cannot blame the great
Alone – the mad, the calculating or effete
Rulers. Whatever grotesque scuffle and piercing
Indignant orgasm of pain took them,
All that enforced activity of death
Did answer and compensate

Some voluntary inaction, soft option, dream retreat.
Each man died for the sins of a whole world:
For the ant's self-abdication, the fat-stock's patience
Are sweet goodbye to human nations.

Still, they have made us eat
Our knowing words, who rose and paid
The bill for the whole party with their uncounted courage.
And if they chose the dearer consolations
Of living – the bar, the dog race, the discreet
Establishment – and let Karl Marx and Freud go hang,
Now they are dead, who can dispute their choice?
Not I, nor even Fate.

Reconciliation

All day beside the shattered tank he'd lain
Like a limp creature hacked out of its shell,
Now shrivelling on the desert's grid,
Now floating above a sharp-set ridge of pain.

There came a roar, like water, in his ear.
The mortal dust was laid. He seemed to be lying
In a cool coffin of stone walls,
While memory slid towards a plunging weir.

The time that was, the time that might have been
Find in this shell of stone a chance to kiss
Before they part eternally:
He feels a world without, a world within

Wrestle like old antagonists, until each is
Balancing each. Then, in a heavenly calm,

The lock gates open, and beyond
Appear the argent, swan-assemblied reaches.

Will it be so again?

Will it be so again
That the brave, the gifted are lost from view,
And empty, scheming men
Are left in peace their lunatic age to renew?
Will it be so again?

Must it be always so
That the best are chosen to fall and sleep
Like seeds, and we too slow
In claiming the earth they quicken, and the old usurpers

          reap
What they could not sow?

Will it be so again –
The jungle code and the hypocrite gesture?
A poppy wreath for the slain
And a cut-throat world for the living? that stale imposture
Played on us once again?

Will it be as before –
Peace, with no heart or mind to ensue it,
Guttering down to war
Like a libertine to his grave? We should not be surprised:

          we knew it
Happen before.

Shall it be so again?
Call not upon the glorious dead

To be your witnesses then.
The living alone can nail to their promise the ones who
                                                              said
It shall not be so again.

PART THREE

The Innocent

A forward child, a sullen boy,
My living image in the pool,
The glass that made me look a fool –
He was my judgement and my joy.

The bells that chimed above the lake,
The swans asleep in evening's eye,
Bright transfers pressed on memory
From him their gloss and anguish take.

When I was desolate, he came
A wizard way to charm my toys:
But when he heard a stranger's voice
He broke the toys, I bore the shame.

I built a house of crystal tears
Amid the myrtles for my friend:
He said, no man has ever feigned
Or kept the lustre of my years.

Later, a girl and I descried
His shadow on the fern-flecked hill,

His double near our bed: and still
The more I lived, the more he died.

Now a revenant slips between
The fine-meshed minutes of the clock
To weep the time we lost and mock
All that my desperate ditties mean.

One and One

I remember, as if it were yesterday,
Watching that girl from the village lay
The fire in a room where sunlight poured,
And seeing, in the annexe beyond, M. play
A prelude of Bach on his harpischord.

I can see his face now, heavy and numb
With resignation to the powers that come
At his touch meticulous, smooth as satin,
Firm as hammers: I can hear the air thrum
With notes like sun-motes in a twinkling pattern.

Her task there fetched from a girl the innate
Tingling response of glass to a note:
She fitted the moment, too, like a glove,
Who deft and submissive knelt by the grate
Bowed as if in the labour of love.

Their orbits touched not: but the pure submission
Of each gave value and definition
To a snapshot printed in that morning's sun.
From any odd corner we may start a vision
Proving that one and one make One.

Windy Day in August

Over the vale, the sunburnt fields
A wind from the sea like as streamer unreels:
Dust leaps up, apples thud down,
The river's caught between a smile and a frown.

An inn-sign swinging, swinging to the wind,
Whines and whinges like a dog confined,
Round his paddock gallops the colt,
Dinghies at moorings curvet and jolt.

Sunlight and shadow in the copse play tig,
While the wallowing clouds talk big
About their travels, and thistledown blows
Ghosting above the rank hedgerows.

Cornfield, orchard and fernland hail
Each other, waving from hill to hill:
They change their colours from morn to night
In play with the lissom, engaging light.

The wind roars endlessly past my ears,
Racing my heart as in earlier years.
Here and everywhere, then and now
Earth moves like a wanton, breathes like a vow.

After the Storm

Have you seen clouds drifting across a night sky
After storm's blown out, when the wind that urged them
Lies asleep elsewhere and the earth is buoyed in
Moon-locked oblivion?

Slow the clouds march: only the moon is wakeful,
Watching them trail past in their brown battalions
Spent as storm-troops after defeat or triumph
Deeply indifferent.

No, not storm-troops now, but as crowds that wander
Vague and sluggish down the disordered boulevardes
After a football match or a coronation,
Riot or lynching.

Done the act which tied them together, all its
Ebbing excitement leaves the heart a quicksand:
So betrayed by passion they move, remembering
Each his aloneness.

Clouds are not men. Yet, if I saw men move like
Clouds the wind inspires and abandons, I should
Feel that wakeful sympathy, feel the moon's wild
Ache for oblivion.

Fame

Spurred towards horizons
Beyond the common round,
Trained in ambition's cruellest ring,
Their powers grew muscle-bound

Like those equestrian public statues
Pawing the sky, that rear
And snort with furious nostrils
Nobly, and get nowhere:

A target for birds, a suntrap
For the elderly or infirm,
Children bowl hoops around them, a plaque
Nails them to their fame,

Whose strenuous flanks the sunlight grooms
While sculptured hyacinths
Breathe an odour of worship
Bedded below their plinths.

Fine for the public statues amid
Those noonday crowds: but when
Nights falls and the park is emptied,
What do they think of then?

Does expectation still cast
Its overweening shadow
Onwards? Or do they look back in grief
To a foal of the green meadow? –

That foal with its mane like a carpet-fringe
And its hobbledehoy hooves;
That colt of the restive eye
Whose breast in amazement heaves –

Or, clamped to the sky in a tortured
Pose of the *haute école,*
Have they lost all kinship, horse and rider,
With the dead, the impatient foal?

Jig

That winter love spoke and we raised no objection, at
Easter 'twas daisies all light and affectionate,
June sent us crazy for natural selection – not
Four traction-engines could tear us apart.
Autumn then coloured the map of our land,
Oaks shuddered and apples came ripe to the hand,
In the gap of the hills we played happily, happily,
Even the moon couldn't tell us apart.

Grave winter drew near and said, 'This will not do at all –
If you continue, I fear you will rue it all.'
So at the New Year we vowed to eschew it
Although we both knew it would break our heart.
But spring made hay of our good resolutions –
Lovers, you may be as wise as Confucians,
Yet once love betrays you he plays you and plays you
Life fishes for ever, so take it to heart.

Hornpipe

Now the peak of summer's past, the sky is overcast
And the love we swore would last for an age seems deceit:
Paler is the guelder since the day we first beheld her
In blush beside the elder drifting sweet, drifting sweet.

Oh quickly they fade – the sunny esplanade,
Speed-boats, wooden spades, and the dunes where we've
                                                    lain:
Others will be lying amid the sea-pinks sighing
For love to be undying, and they'll sigh in vain.

It's hurrah for each night we have spent our love so lightly
And never dreamed there might be no more to spend at all.
It's goodbye to every lover who thinks he'll live in clover
All his life, for noon is over soon and night-dews fall.

If I could keep you there with the berries in your hair
And your lacy fingers fair as the may, sweet may,
I'd have no heart to do it, for to stay love is to rue it
And the harder we pursue it, the faster it's away.

The Fault

After the light decision
Made by the blood in a moon-blanched lane,
Whatever weariness or contrition
May come, I could never see you plain;
No, never again

See you whose body I'm wed to
Distinct, but always dappled, enhanced
By a montage of all that moment led to –
Dunes where heat-haze and sea-pinks glanced,
The roads that danced

Ahead of our aimless car,
Scandal biting the dust behind us,
The feel of being on a luckier star,
Each quarrel that came like a night to blind us
And closer to bind us.

Others will journey over
Our hill up along this lane like a rift
Loaded with moon-gold, many a lover

Sleepwalking through the moon's white drift,
Loved or bereft.

But for me it is love's volcanic
Too fertile fault, and will mark always
The first shock of that yielding mood, where satanic
Bryony twines and frail flowers blaze
Through our tangled days.

The Rebuke

Down in the lost and April days
What lies we told, what lies we told!
Nakedness seemed the one disgrace,
And there'd be time enough to praise
The truth when we were old.

The irresponsible poets sung
What came into their head:
Time to pick and choose among
The bold profusions of our tongue
When we were dead, when we were dead.

Oh wild the words we uttered then
In woman's ear, in woman's ear,
Believing all we promised when
Each kiss created earth again
And every far was near.

Little we guessed, who spoke the word
Of hope and freedom high
Spontaneously as wind or bird

To crowds like cornfields still or stirred,
It was a lie, a heart-felt lie.

Now the years advance into
A calmer stream, a colder stream,
We doubt the flame that once we knew,
Heroic words sound all untrue
As love-lies in a dream.

Yet fools are the old who won't be taught
Modesty by their youth:
That pandemonium of the heart,
That sensual arrogance did impart
A kind of truth, a kindling truth.

Where are the sparks at random sown,
The spendthrift fire, the holy fire?
Who cares a damn for truth that's grown
Exhausted haggling for its own
And speaks without desire?

1943

POEMS 1943–1947

TO LAURIE LEE

I seem but a dead man held on end
To sink down soon . . .
THOMAS HARDY

Le vent se lève . . . il faut tenter de vivre!
PAUL VALÉRY

354

The Double Vision

The river this November afternoon
Rests in an equipoise of sun and cloud:
A glooming light, a gleaming darkness shroud
Its passage. All seems tranquil, all in tune.

Image and real are joined like Siamese twins:
Their doubles draw the willows, a brown mare
Drinks her reflection. There's no margin where
Substance leaves off, the illusory begins.

You and I by the river contemplate
Our ideal selves, glossed here, crystal-divined:
We yearn to them, knowing one sigh of wind
Will rub these precious figures from the slate.

It is not of their transience I'm afraid,
But thinking how most human loves protract
Themselves to unreality – the fact
Drained of its virtue by the image it made.

O double vision of the autumnal stream,
Teach me to bear love's fusion or diffusion!
O gems of purest water, pure illusion,
Answer my rays and cluster to a theme!

Juvenilia

So this is you
That was an I twenty-five years ago –
One I may neither disown nor renew.
Youth of the smouldering heart, the seamless brow,
What affinity between you and me?
You are a skin I have long since cast,
A ghost I carry now:
I am the form you blindly, fitfully glassed,
And the finish of your bright vow.

When I seek to peer
Through the fancy-dress words wherein you are woodenly
posed
And to feel the ardours quivering there,
I am as one eavesdropping upon a captive past
Of which nothing remains but echoes and chains.
Yet, could I lay bare that primitive mural
Whereon I am superimposed,
What boldness of line and colour, what pure quaint moral
Emblems might be disclosed!

Youth of the seamless brow, the smouldering heart,
You are my twin,
Yet we seem worlds apart.
More than mere time-grains pile this desert between:
The sands that efface each instant trace
Of my passage – I think they proceed
From my own nature, their origin
Some inexhaustible need
For oblivion, and reservoir of it, deep within.

Were it not so, surely I could remember
The lyric light,

The primrose-and-violet ember
Which was your soul, my soul, when we came to write
These poems. But gone is the breath of dawn,
Clinker the dreams it fanned:
These bones, anonymous now and trite,
Are a message scrawled on the sand
That only in dying could a self indite.

What links the real to the wraith?
My self repudiates myself of yesterday;
But the words it lived in and cast like a shell keep faith
With that dead self always.
And if aught holds true between me and you,
It is the heart whose prism can break
Life's primal rays
Into a spectrum of passionate tones, and awake
Fresh blossom for truth to swell and sway.

Speak to me, then, from the haunted
Hollow of fears and yearnings lost to view,
The instrument my youth, your truth, first sounded –
This heart of impassioned hue!
Speak through the crystal, tell me the gist
Of the shadowy sequence that now is I –
What unseen clue
Threads my pearl-sliding hours, what symmetry
My deaths and metaphors pursue!

When a phoenix opens her rainbow span,
The ashes she rose from warmly speak,
'Your flight, which ends in fire as it began,
Is fuelled by all you seek.'
O beacon bird, I too am fired
To bring some message home
Whose meaning I know not. So from peak to peak
I run – my life, maybe, a palindrome,
But each lap unique.

And since at every stage I need
A death, a new self to reveal me,
And only through oblivion's veil can read
The signs of what befell me,
May not the grave of rigored love
Be but one more abyss
Between two peaks, appointed to compel me
Along the chain of light? . . . Dead youth, is this
What you have to tell me?

Sketches for a Self-Portrait

Consider the boy that you were, although you would
                                        hardly
Recognize him if you met him, even in his old haunts –
The well-shaved lawn or the Rip Van Winkle forest,
With the slag-tip reek acrid as youth's resentments
Tainting their green, or the mellow South West town
That spoke to him words unheeded but unforgotten –
Even in the haunts where he was most himself,
If a chaos can be a self: there perhaps least of all,
So deceptive are youth's environs, so quick to promise
What is not in your power, to fall in with caving moods.
But question the boy that you were, for you have no other
Clue to the man you are, to the heart divided.

Green boy, green boy, who walk through the furzes
Unsinged, and undevoured through the dandelions,
Tell me your secret.

                    I am one who peered
In every stranger's face for my identity,
In every mirror for a family likeness,

In lakes and dewdrops for the antiself.
I stunned myself upon their shallow eyes
Like a chaffinch slamming against a windowpane,
Until at last I learned to use my blindness.
I hung upon their words, and they always broke
Like the old rope they were, letting me down
Into a pit where lidless poisoners coiled:
So was I trained to climb on my own thread.
Love I desired, but the father I loved and hated
Lived too much in me, and his images of me
Fretted a frame always outgrowing them:
I went into the wilderness bearing all
My faults and his ambitions on my head.
   Solitude then was my métier. I wore it
As an invisible cloak, or a glass cloche
To save from nibbling teeth and clodhopper boots
And focus the sun's eye on my sullen growth.
I kept my solitude as a young girl guards
Virginity yet wishes it away,
Impatient of the blossom cloud that endears her.
The bee forces the blossom. I knew the weak
Involuntary spasms of consent –
Ah, *coitus interruptus* with a cheating world!
I wished to commit myself to the irretrievable
As a bee is committed to the bell, or a suicide
Already half way from the parapet, to the river:
But the river whisked away and the flower turned nasty.
Or perhaps I was a coward.

                Green boy, green boy,
What did the lawn teach, what did the Rip Van Winkle
Forest say, and the mellow South West town?

   Resilience first, release perhaps, the lawn.
Morning brought tears and daisies, afternoon
A tennis party. Athletic clergymen. Flannels –

The uniform of a class, of a way of thinking,
Or of not thinking: as I looked for a lost ball
In the laurels, they smirched with pit-grime. It was good –
The sensual leap, the stinging drive and return
Of the blood, conflict without relationship.
I preferred singles – the world, such as it was,
Where I wanted it, on the run, with a net between us.
    Winters, I walked much alone, rubbing my thoughts
Together, and prayed for a spark and imagined a forest
My tinderbox. Around me, sodden bracken:
Overhead, interlocked branches snickering.
A roar from a distant pithead as the cage dropped
Like a stone into the well of an orphic mystery.
Otherwise the forest was silent: birdless; nymphless;
Oaks hollow as history; morose and regimented
Conifers; birches with the hauteur of fashion-plates.
    And the silence said something, something about a wish
To be rooted, a wish profounder than roots, more insidious:
But the whirring wheels at the pithead, 'Stay on the
                                        surface,
You were not made to dip your hand in darkness
Or hew at the mystery's face': and the lawn replied,
'There is coal beneath us, everywhere coal, the dream
Of the deep sleep of forests, so sleep and dream':
And the oaks, 'We are hollow with unfulfilled desire –
Hurry, all is not the same in a thousand years.'
    So I returned to school, a kaleidoscope
Of shaken images, arguments jangling like glass.
And the wise grey South West town claimed me, calmed
                                        me
With the sedatives of routine, the balm of multitude.
Snatches of wisdom borne on a wet wind
Like bells or wood smoke or ancestral memories –
Borne from the high, dry plateaux of reason, weathered
To a romantic tone: and the god was reborn
In the echo. Words unheeded but unforgotten.

Call no man happy . . . Our actions burst like spray
Upon a reef, nevertheless we must act . . .
Know yourself . . . But knowing, do not presume
To swerve or sweeten what is foreordained . . .
For the heart, magnanimity; for the mind, good sense;
For the soul, a natural piety; for fate,
A stoic's bending steel . . . Nothing too much.
Pinnacles of a drowned, four-square age broke surface
Between the waking bell and the afternoon wicket –
Temperate isles in a distempered sea,
Isles of the blessed, a landfall for my tossed dreams.

Green boy, green boy, tell me your dreams.
                                                          Sit here
On the harbour wall with me. Look down at the water
Swaying, impassive, transparent, evasive:
Motiveless swaying, vibrantly motionless,
Rumpling the olive-green and slate-blue boulders
Fathomed below, and glossing the seaweed
To hair hyacinthine of marble statuary.
Look at the seabrow, puckered in sunlight,
Jigged over by millions of sparklers for ever
Quenched, re-illumined: and beyond the fireworks
A swell, a haze, a forever encroaching
Receding question. Such were my daydreams.
Dare you interpret them? Had we not better
Turn round to the castles of sand and the starfish
Sunbathers? return to our spade and bucket?
   Sleepwalking with the tides, unskilled to dive
Into the heart of my images, I practised
Words like a secret vice: words perpetually
Flung up, encroached on, crumbling, superseded,
Real to me as wet sand to a child's fingers,
More real than the quaking asphalt of the sea front
Or the rook-babble of bathers. Oh, innocent vice –
Could everything be reduced to a form of words!

But they were only a guesswork map of the terrain
Where soon I should have to fight; or else a petition
To be exempted. The love I feared and longed for
Would come in out of the sea, a terrible sun
Thrusting aside my screen of words, and pin me
To the sand like a starfish, and pick my dreams
And bleach my fears and make my dry words live.

So, when he met a girl in the forest, he knew her
A nymph. His random casts had found a quarry.
The dead wood woke with her, she dappled the night wood
With carillons of noon, siftings elusive
Of light from the fountain of all truth and legend.
Pursuing then, he quickened his solitude
With a thousand images of her – images
More real to him than the fugitive flesh that awoke them.
Charmed life of a green boy, threading the maze
But alone no longer! The eyes and claws drew back
Deeper into the shade, biding their time.
Was he hunter or hunted? He cared not.
                                        The pursuit led
Out of the forest, over the lawn, past pitheads
Where steam puffed out in a squall of imprecation,
Through smoke-rings in college rooms and the blackened
                                        circles
Of picnic fires, across the common and
The garden, and over the moon, with a coursed hare's
Demented doublings and the closed circuit
Of the electric hare – a thousand repetitions
Of a routine immemorial, each unique,
While the horn hummed like autumn in the blood
Always a field before him, or behind him.
Till at last they came to the verge of the sea, where hunter
And hunted face the effacing and are one.

Marriage of Two

So they were married, and lived
Happily for ever?
Such extravagant claims are not in heaven's gift –
Much less earth's, where love is chanceful as weather:
Say they were married, and lived.

Tell me his marriage vow.
Not the church responses,
But alone at a window one night saying, 'Now
Let me be good to her, all my heart owns or wants is
Staked on this hazardous vow.'

When was the marriage sealed?
One day the strange creature
He loved was missing; he found her, concealed
In a coign of, wearing the secret stamp of his nature.
So matings, if ever, are sealed.

How did the marriage end?
Some marriages die not.
The government goes into exile; then
The underground struggle is on, whose fighters fly not
Even at the bitter end.

What is the marriage of two?
The loss of one
By wounds or abdication; a true
Surrender mocked, an unwished victory won:
Rose, desert – mirage too.

Married Dialogue

HE It is out at last –
     The truth that fevered my cheek and frostily glassed
     My eyes against you: a creeping
     Incurable disease, it passed
     Into your heart from mine while we were sleeping.

SHE I dreamt of the past,
     The primrose and prairie of youth that so contrast
     With this unvernal time.
     Autumn is here too soon, the blast
     Perplexed with waftings of our violet prime.

HE Autumn is here. But see
     With what august forgiveness the rose burns
     Her faithful torch away, and the leaf turns
     Her cheek to winter, and the tree
     Turns the wind's edge with rags of old felicity.

SHE There was a time when we
     Were all in all, one to another. Then
     I lived not by this ghostly regimen,
     Breathing old summers' pot-pourri,
     Rustling the faded hours we glowed in formerly.

HE There was a time. But time piles flake on flake
     Lapping the traveller asleep:
     And in that sleep the heart grows numb. So we awake
     To severance. Oh deep
     The drifts between, treacherous the frozen lake!

SHE Once I watched a young ocean laugh and shake
     With spillikins of aspen light.
     I was your sail, your keel. Nothing could overtake

Love trimmed and stiffened aright.
But now I drown, a white reef in your wake.

HE No reef I saw. If we were shoaled,
It was the ebbing of some tide within.
But aching I behold
Fingers upon a gunwale blue with cold,
And one too weak to draw you in.

SHE Oh crooked tide, what lies it told
So to get round me. Then, cut off, I lay
Weeping. And then I doled
My scraps of you, with hopes of you consoled
Myself, like any castaway.

HE Love's ruin came in love's impenetrable disguise.
Ivy-shoots will prise
Apart the house they grew to adorn;
Lulling poppies snare the corn:
The lies bred up on truth are the worst lies.

SHE I must live on where love first homed, though the wind
                                                     cries
Through all its crumbling eyes;
Must walk alone the field-path where
Our linked illusions trod on air
And honeybeams of moonshine brushed our thighs.

HE Where shall he roam
Who bears old trothings like a chain abroad
And wears a new love like a knotted cord
Over his brow at home,
But in some echoing limbo of the self-outlawed?

SHE Let a new lover
Exploit the solitudes I first explored,

Feed on the grain I grew. Is he not scored
And signed with me? Yes, rough or
Smooth be his ways, my touch the contours still
                                    record.

HE Oh perverse heart, that can forgive
    All error and misuse
    But show yourself no mercy – must you grieve
    As for a fault when love-knots lose
    Their angel hues?

SHE Oh piteous heart, how could I blame
    You that your sighs accuse
    My lack? But would that we two were the same
    As when we thought love aye renews
    Our dawns and dews!

The Woman Alone

1

Take any place – this garden plot will do
Where he with mower, scythe or hook goes out
To fight the grass and lay a growing fever,
Volcanic for another, dead to me;
Meek is the ghost, a banked furnace the man.

Take any time – this autumn day will serve,
Ripe with grassed fruit, raw with departing wings,
When I, whom in my youth the season tempted
To oceanic amplitudes, bend down
And pick a rotting apple from the grass.

From every here and now a thread leads back
Through faithless seasons and devouring seas:
New blooms, dead leaves bury it not, nor combers
Break it – my life line and my clue: the same
That brought him safe out of a labyrinth.

So I, the consort of an absent mind,
The emerald lost in a green waste of time,
The castaway for whom all space is island –
To follow, find, escape, this thread in hand,
Warp myself out upon the swelling past.

2

Take any joy – the thread leads always on
To here and now: snow, silence, vertigo;
His frozen face, a woman who bewails not
Only because she fears one echoing word
May bring the avalanche about her ears.

Take any joy that was – here it remains,
Corruptless, irrecoverable, cold
As a dead smile, beneath the cruel glacier
That moved upon our kisses, lambs and leaves,
Stilled them, but will not let their forms dissolve.

O tomb transparent of my waxen joys!
O lifelike dead under the skin of ice!
O frozen face of love where my one treasure
Is locked, and the key lost! May I not share
Even the bare oblivion of your fate?

But dare I throw the past into one fire,
One burning cry to break the silence, break
The cataleptic snows, the dream of falling?
Last night I thought he stood beside my bed
And said, 'Wake up! You were dreaming. I am here.'

3

Take any grief – the maggot at the nerve,
The words that bore the skull like waterdrops,
The castaway's upon the foam-racked island,
The lurching figures of a mind's eclipse –
I have felt each and all as love decayed.

Yet every grief revives a fainting love.
They are love's children too; I live again
In them; my breast yearns to their innocent cruelty.
If only tears can float a stranded heart,
If only sighs can move it, I will grieve.

The pleasured nerve, the small-talk in the night,
The voyaging when isles were daisy-chains,
The dance of mere routine – if I could reach them
Again through this sick labyrinth of grief,
I would rejoice in it, to reach them so.

Alas, hull-down upon hope's ashen verge
Hastens the vessel that our joined hands launched,
Stretching my heart-strings out beyond endurance.
Ah, will they never snap? Can I not climb
The signal hill, and wave, and *mean* goodbye?

Ending

That it should end so! –
Not with mingling tears
Nor one long backward look of woe
Towards a sinking trust,
A heyday's afterglow;

Not even in the lash and lightning
Cautery of rage!
But by this slow
Fissure, this blind numb grinding severance
Of floe from floe.
Merciless god, to mock your failures so!

Heart and Mind

Said Heart to Mind at the close of day,
I was older than you, yet I led you astray
Fancying I knew each twist and turn of our way,
Said Heart to Mind.
The blind would still have been leading the blind
Whichever of us had held the sway,
Answered the pensive Mind.

I was younger than you, the Mind went on,
Yet you carried me through the fire of noon
And the chilling shades: of all I encountered, none
Was stronger than you.
Said Heart, I could feed upon dust or rue,
But you, the daintiest eater, have shown
What a rational diet can do.

So queer a partnership never was sealed –
A sceptic hungry for truth revealed,
A fool to his rule-of-thumb vision unreconciled
From the very start:
No wonder we almost pulled apart,
Envious each of his comrade's field,
Pursued the plaintive Heart.

No marriage is proof against travail or bliss,
Spoke Mind. How uniting can be the abyss,
How chafing the bond between all earth's denizens – this
Is what marriages prove.
And this we have learnt from our seasoned love –
When heart and mind agree, they kiss
Over an opening grave.

A Failure

The soil was deep and the field well-sited,
    The seed was sound.
Average luck with the weather, one thought,
    And the crop would abound.

If harrowing were all that is needed for
    Harvest, his field
Had been harrowed enough, God knows, to warrant
    A record yield.

He gazed from a hill in the breezy springtime:
    That field was aflow
With wave upon wave like a sea's green shallows
    Breathing below.

He looked from a gate one summer morning
    When the mists uprolled:
Headland to headland those fortunate acres
    Seemed solid gold.

He stood by the field as the day of harvest
    Dawned. But, oh,
The fruit of a year's work, a lifetime's lore,
    Had ceased to grow.

No wickedest weather could thus have turned,
    As it were overnight,
His field to so wan and weedy a showing:
    Some galloping blight

From earth's metabolism must have sprung
    To ruin all;
Or perhaps his own high hopes had made
    The wizened look tall.

But it's useless to argue the why and wherefore.
    When a crop is so thin,
There's nothing to do but to set the teeth
    And plough it in.

The Unwanted

On a day when the breath of roses
    Plumpened a swooning breeze
And all the silken combes of summer
    Opened wide their knees,
Between two sighs they planted one –
A willed one, a wanted one –
And he will be the sign, they said, of our felicities.

Eager the loins he sprang from,
    Happy the sheltering heart:
Seldom had the seed of man
    So charmed, so clear a start.
And he was born as frail a one,
As ailing, freakish, pale a one
As ever the wry planets knotted their beams to thwart.

371

Sun locked up for winter;
  Earth an empty rind:
Two strangers harshly flung together
  As by a flail of wind.
 Oh was it not a furtive thing,
 A loveless, damned, abortive thing –
This flurry of the groaning dust, and what it left behind!

 Sure, from such warped beginnings
  Nothing debonair
Can come? But neither shame nor panic,
  Drugs nor sharp despair
 Could uproot that untoward thing,
 That all too fierce and froward thing:
Willy-nilly born it was, divinely formed and fair.

The Sitting

(FOR LAURENCE GOWING)

So like a god I sit here,
One of those stone dreamers quarried from solitude,
A genius – if ever there was one – of the place:
The mountain's only child, lips aloof as a snow-line,
Forearms impassive along the cloud-base of aeons,
Eyes heavy on distance –
Graven eyes that flinch not, flash not, if eagles
Clap their wings in my face.

With hieratic gestures
He the suppliant, priest, interpreter, subtly
Wooing my virtue, officiates by the throne.
I know the curious hands are shaping, reshaping the image
Of what is only an image of things impalpable.

I feel how the eyes strain
To catch a truth behind the oracular presence –
Eyes that augur through stone.

And the god asks, 'What have I for you
But the lichenous shadow of thought veiling my temple,
The runnels a million time-drops have chased on my
                                        cheek?'
And the man replies, 'I will show you the creed of your
                                bone, I'll draw you
The shape of solitude to which you were born.'
And the god cries, 'I am meek,
Brushed by an eagle's wing; and a voice bids me
Speak. But I cannot speak.'

The god thinks, Let him project, if
He must, his passionate shapings on my stone heart,
Wrestle over my body with his sprite,
Through these blind eyes imagine a skin-deep world in
                                        perspective:
Let him make, if he will, the crypt of my holy mountain
His own: let even the light
That bathes my temple become as it were an active
Property of his sight.

O man, O innocent artist
Who paint me with green of your fields, with amber or
                                        yellow
Of love's hair, red of the heart's blood, eyebright blue,
Conjuring forms and rainbows out of an empty mist –
Your hand is upon me, as even now you follow
Along the immortal clue
Threading my veins of emerald, topaz, amethyst,
And know not it ends in you.

Statuette: Late Minoan

Girl of the musing mouth,
The mild archaic air,
For whom do you subtly smile?
Yield to what power or prayer
Breasts vernally bare?

I seem to be peering at you
Through the wrong end of time
That shrinks to a bright, far image –
Great Mother of earth's prime –
A stature sublime.

So many golden ages
Of sunshine steeped your clay,
So dear did the maker cherish
In you life's fostering ray,
That you warm us today.

Goddess or girl, you are earth.
The smile, the offered breast –
They were the dream of one
Thirsting as I for rest,
As I, unblest.

The Revenant

Out of the famous canyon
Deeper than sleep,
From the nerveless tarn of oblivion
She climbed. Dark was the slope,

And her companion
Gave not one love-glance back to brighten it.
Only the wind-chafed rope
Of melody held her
To him that haled her
Lifeward, praising the fire and delight in it.

On the gist of that lay or its burden
Legend is dumb.
How else, though, with love-looks forbidden
Could he say, 'Come back to me, come' –
Could he touch the long-hidden
Spring of a shade unfleshed, unfertilized
Than by singing, oh, crust and crumb,
Bark, sap, flesh, marrow –
Life's all, in the narrow
Ambit of sense flowering, immortalized?

Glimmering tall through the gloom
In her phantom garment,
Like a daffodil when its stem
Feels trembling the first endearment
Of amorous bloom,
She palely paused, on the verge of light again.
One step to break from her cerement,
Yes, daffodil-rayed
From the mould of the shade –
No revenant now, a golden wife again.

Had death become then, already,
A habit too strong
For her to break? The steady
Pulsing of Orpheus' song
– Though lightwards led he –
Grew faint in her. She wept for astonishment,
Feared she could never belong

To life, be at home there,
Find aught but harm there,
Till that last step seemed less a birth than a banishment.

What strand of his love was the weak one,
Or how it befell
That a song which could melt the Dark One,
Death's granite lord, with its spell
Saved not his meek one,
Moved not his meek one to step from the last of her
Terrors, no man may tell.
He felt the cord parting,
The death-wound smarting:
He turned his head but to glimpse the ghost of her.

So, as a pebble thrown
From a cliff face, soaring
Swerves back, less like a stone
Than a bird, ere it falls to the snoring
Surf, she was gone.
Reluctant her going: but the more bitterly
Mocked were his love, his imploring –
That the gods spoke
As seldom they speak
On matters of life and death, non-committally.

The House-Warming

Did you notice at all as you entered the house,
    Your dove-treed house,
Traces of one who was there before you
Imagining roseate company for you,
    While the locked rooms lay in a drowse?

One there was who paced to and fro,
    To and fro
Through the empty house with an occupied air,
Veiled in the passage, soft on the stair,
    And kept its heart aglow.

Did you feel, when first you stepped in the hall,
    Stepped in the hall,
A note of warmth like a weir's deep humming?
A message marked 'To await her coming'
    Written on hearth and wall?

One had been there for better or worse,
    Better or worse,
Curtaining, carpeting, lighting all
Your rooms with a love ineffaceable;
    And still in the night he stirs.

Fear him not. He is but a shade,
    A homely shade
For no dread signs or haunting cast:
Not a phantom risen like spray from the past,
    But a ghost by the future made.

Love enmeshed in his own folly –
    Mischance or folly –
Expiates a deed for ever undone,
Weeps for all that it could have won
    Of living together wholly.

Such is the tenant you'll have beside you,
    Often beside you
Through the spoilt Junes when a gusty rain
Strums fitful arpeggios on the pane,
    The dawns when light is denied you.

But here may you find, for all his fretting
        And gaunt regretting,
Between the dove-tops and the weir's
Undying fall, how broken years
        Can sing to a new setting.

Meeting

Did I meet you again?
Did I meet you again in the flesh we have come to know,
That evening of chorusing colours a week ago?
Or was it delusion wrung from a faulted brain
When we seemed enveloped in love like naked dunes
Effaced by a seventh wave's onrush and undertow?
Did I meet you again?

Though I meet you again,
Though I meet you a thousand times, surely the crest
Of our quickening, breaking love can never be blessed
With so generous a reach and radiance as fired it then.
Since meetings must have their peak, and the luckiest
                                        matings
Fade from golden to drab, perhaps it is best
Not to meet you again.

If I met you again,
Met you again after years of extinct days,
Oh, from dry air such a dance of aureate sprays
Would break and freshly figure the lost refrain
That a tremor would wring my heart's rock, and I'd sigh,
'Two loves which might have bloomed at the zenith
                                        always
Are meeting again.'

The Heartsease

Do you remember that hour
In a nook of the flowing uplands
When you found for me, at the cornfield's edge,
A golden and purple flower?
Heartsease, you said. I thought it might be
A token that love meant well by you and me.

I shall not find it again
With you no more to guide me.
I could not bear to find it now
With anyone else beside me.
And the heartease is far less rare
Than what it is named for, what I can feel nowhere.

Once again it is summer:
Wildflowers beflag the lane
That takes me away from our golden uplands,
Heart-wrung and alone.
The best I can look for, by vale or hill,
A herb they tell me is common enough – self-heal.

Is it far to go?*

Is it far to go?
  A step – no further.
Is it hard to go?
  Ask the melting snow,
  The eddying feather.

* The third stanza is on CDL's tombstone in Dorset.

What can I take there?
   Not a hank, not a hair.
What shall I leave behind?
   Ask the hastening wind,
   The fainting star.

Shall I be gone long?
   For ever and a day.
To whom there belong?
   Ask the stone to say,
   Ask my song.

Who will say farewell?
   The beating bell.
Will anyone miss me?
   That I dare not tell –
   Quick, Rose, and kiss me.

New Year's Eve

ODE

The moon slides through a whey of cloud; the running
Cloud thins over the moon, and again curdles.
Milk of the word, flow!
Shine forth, my shadowed clay!

A five-bell peal stumbles up from the valley;
The midnight constellations mass their fire.
Aspire, my blindworm heart!
Arrogant heart, be humble!

The midnight constellations hold their fire,
The bells ring up to volley a new year in.

380

Now comes the zero between
Desire and resignation,

Between cast-iron past and plastic future;
But equally, haunters of this unnatural pause,
Remorse for what is to be,
Doubt of all that has passed.

Moon-floods heighten the valley with glimmerings like
The feel of a memory before it is born:
The stars burn to deliver
Their pregnant souls of the dying.

We are caught, all of us, in time's fine net,
Walled up in time: yet still we seek a secret
Spring, a weak mesh, where we may
Break out and be immortal.

So conscience, need, imagination pierce
An arbitrary point between two years:
The fabric tears; but in truth
It is we, not time, who bleed.

We lament not one year only
Gone with its chance and change
Disavowed, its range of blessings unbought or unpaid for,
But all our time lost, profitless, misspent.

Through this pinprick, like life-blood,
The ghosts of time we killed
Spill out – an age coarse custom has buried alive,
And sightless hours, and pallor of weeks unquickened.

Cuckoophrase of children
In their green enchantment
Where slanting beams fall warm and cool as larksong –
A woodnote rill unheard through afterdays.

381

Unseen the sunburst Aprils
And the bloomed Octobers –
Oh, tremulous rivers danced by primula light!
Oh, blaze of marigold where love has been!

The holly fire unfelt,
The snowmaid left asleep,
The cheap, the rare joy thrown away half-eaten,
The nimbus round each truth-pang unacknowledged.

Unfelt, unseen, unheard
So much that would have ripened
An open heart, and left a sweet taste there
After its blossomy aura was dispelled.

But, if the fluent senses
So often are benumbed,
What has our fumbling virtue to look back on?
How much has it passed up, mishandled, ruined!

Tonight, as flyers stranded
On a mountain, the battery fading, we tap out
Into a snow-capped void our weakening
Vocations and desires.

Bound by the curse of man –
To live in his future, which is to live surely
In his own death – we endure the embrace of the present
But yearn for a being beyond us;

Beyond our powers and our time,
Behind the pinnacle stars, the horizon sleep,
Beneath the deepest kiss of heaven's azure
And the roots of Atlantis flowers.

Into the blue we project
Our dreaming shadows. And is the hope forlorn
That in them we may be reborn, that our images
More masterful are, more true

Than we? The bells upclamouring
Like hungry beaks from a nest, the eyes that strain
To read the stars – vainly still they implore
Eternity to reveal

The virgin truths it is sworn
By its own laws to guard . . . Then turn away
Before the star-scape blinds or the moon maddens.
Earth is your talent. Use it.

Ring bells for here and now.
Time's your condition; and in time alone
May man, full grown, reach out over the void
A rapt, creator's wing.

MEDITATION

At a junction of years I stand, with the stars palsied
And the bells stumbling o'er me;
My life a pinprick in time, and half a lifetime
At the very most before me.
The trembling stars, the cracked bells tongue in chorus,
'Begone! It is better to go
Not when the going but the staying is good.'
I have suspected so
Often enough, looking down from a height of love
On the flats it momently crowned,
Looking up from the workaday, golden, orthodox level
To the bluffs and the terrors beyond.
But living becomes a habit, like any other
No easier to break than to sanction;

It numbs the sense and dissembles the earth's raw features
With action drifted on action:
Till at last, as a child picking flowers near home, from
                                    flower to
Flower enticed, will find
Himself the next moment lost in another country;
As, when a hill's undermined,
A windowframe jammed or a door flying open tell one
The hill has invisibly moved: –
So we look up one day and see we are dying
From the difference in all we have loved.

If I balance the year's account, in the right-hand column
What new assets are shown?
One cloud left behind in a cloudless sky, like a plume
From a white May-day long flown:
One elm ash-budded with starlings which brassily jingled
Like a sack of curtain-rings shaken:
Some nights when thought of my love was sweet as a child's
Birthday to dream of, to wake on.
What can a few such casual entries amount to
Against the perpetual drain
Of the real into abstractions – life just jetting
And falling in a fountain's rain?
And then, the expansive follies, the petty withdrawals
Swelling an overdraft
I must carry forward to next year, not to be cancelled
By any godsend or graft.
Look at this left-hand column! Does it read like
A soul whose credit is good? –
This mind wasting on wildcat speculation
Half it has understood;
This man for ever trimming, tacking and wearing
His truth to keep the capricious
Wind of a woman's favour; this heart by turns
Too gullible, too suspicious?

Lost, profitless, misspent – how can last year's self
Gratify or engross,
Unless you believe that, by spiritual accountings,
The profit is in the loss?
Turn to the future, you say: plan to improve:
Tonight we make good resolutions.
But I would plan for the present, and this involves
Such a whirl of lightning decisions
And intuitions, that for the nearest distance
I'd have not a glance to spare.
Let them take their turn, I say – the unborn roses,
The morrows foul or fair;
Let them wait their turn, those siren hills exhaling
A violet fluorescence,
The one-eyed cannibals and the horned dilemmas –
All, all that is not Presence.
Our fear makes myths of the future, even as our love does
Of the past: and, I ask myself, how
Can I face a mythical future unless I am armed
Cap-à-pie in a magical Now?
Invulnerable Now, my saviour, always
Dying, but never dead!
My winged shoes, my clairvoyant shield, my cap of
Darkness upon the head!

Yet the Now is a ghost too, fleetingly glimpsed at the turn
Of an agony, or in the lee of
A joy, for ever vanishing through some secret
Door that I have not the key of –
An unborn thing, a ghost of the real miscarried
By accident or neglect –
Unless it is free to drink my living blood
And in my flesh to be decked:
My flesh and blood, themselves a web of experience
Discarded, renewed, amassed.
Ah no, the present is nothing unless it is spun from

A live thread out of the past,
As the clarinet airs of the early morn are echoed
By eve's full-hearted strings,
As the stars and the bells in April grass foreshadow
Winter's pure crystallings.
There are September mornings when every shrub
Sparkles an hour and dances
Spangled with diamond parures, for a heavy dew
Makes visible and enhances
The spider webs. Oh fleeting, magical Presence!
Oh time-drops caught in a few
Workaday filaments! Nevertheless, the spider
Spins not to catch the dew.

To live the present then, not to live for it –
Let this be one of today's
Resolutions; and the other, its corollary,
To court the commonplace.
Whatever is common to life's diversity must,
For me, be the one eternal
Truth, or if naught is for ever, at least the medium
Wherein I may best discern all
The products of time, embalmed, alive, or prefigured.
Let me brood on the face of a field,
The faces in streets, until each hero is honoured,
Each unique blade revealed.
Alluring the past, the future, their bright eyes veiled
Or enlarged in a mist of fable:
But he who can look with the naked eye of the Now –
He is the true seer, able,
To witness the rare in the common, and read the common
Theme for all time appointed
To link our variations . . . And though my todays are
Repetitive, dull, disjointed,
I must continue to practise them over and over
Like a five-finger exercise,

Hoping my hands at last will suddenly flower with
Passion, and harmonize.

Emily Brontë

All is the same still. Earth and heaven locked in
A wrestling dream the seasons cannot break:
Shrill the wind tormenting my obdurate thorn trees,
Moss-rose and stone-chat silent in its wake.
Time has not altered here the rhythms I was rocked in,
Creation's throb and ache.

All is yet the same, for mine was a country
Stoic, unregenerate, beyond the power
Of man to mollify or God to disburden –
An ingrown landscape none might long endure
But one who could meet with a passion wilder-wintry
The scalding breath of the moor.

All is yet the same as when I roved the heather
Chained to a demon through the shrieking night,
Took him by the throat while he flailed my sibylline
Assenting breast, and won him to delight.
O truth and pain immortally bound together!
O lamp the storm made bright!

Still on those heights prophetic winds are raving,
Heath and harebell intone a plainsong grief:
'Shrink, soul of man, shrink into your valleys –
Too sharp that agony, that spring too brief!
Love, though your love is but the forged engraving
Of hope on a stricken leaf!'

Is there one whom blizzards warm and rains enkindle
And the bitterest furnace could no more refine?
Anywhere one too proud for consolation,
Burning for pure freedom so that he will pine,
Yes, to the grave without her? Let him mingle
His barren dust with mine.

But is there one who faithfully has planted
His seed of light in the heart's deepest scar?
When the night is darkest, when the wind is keenest,
He, he shall find upclimbing from afar
Over his pain my chaste, my disenchanted
And death-rebuking star.

Birthday Poem for Thomas Hardy

Is it birthday weather for you, dear soul?
Is it fine your way,
With tall moon-daisies alight, and the mole
Busy, and elegant hares at play
By meadow paths where once you would stroll
In the flush of day?

I fancy the beasts and flowers there beguiled
By a visitation
That casts no shadow, a friend whose mild
Inquisitive glance lights with compassion,
Beyond the tomb, on all of this wild
And humbled creation.

It's hard to believe a spirit could die
Of such generous glow,
Or to doubt that somewhere a bird-sharp eye

Still broods on the capers of men below,
A stern voice asks the Immortals why
They should plague us so.

Dear poet, wherever you are, I greet you.
Much irony, wrong,
Innocence you'd find here to tease or entreat you,
And many the fate-fires have tempered strong,
But none that in ripeness of soul could meet you
Or magic of song.

Great brow, frail frame – gone. Yet you abide
In the shadow and sheen,
All the mellowing traits of a countryside
That nursed your tragi-comical scene;
And in us, warmer-hearted and brisker-eyed
Since you have been.

Who Goes There?

(FOR WALTER DE LA MARE, ON HIS 75TH BIRTHDAY)

Who goes there?
What sequestered vale at the back of beyond
Do you come from – you with the moonbeam wand,
The innocent air?
And how got you here, spirited on like a bubble of silence
                                                    past
The quickset ears, the hair-trigger nerves at each post?

    My staff is cut from the knowledge tree.
    My place no infidel eye can see.
    My way is a nonchalant one,
    Wilful as wind yet true as the line of a bee.
    My name is – Anon.

389

Are you aware
That you're trespassing, sir, on a battleground?
It's hard to see what excuse can be found
For magicians where
All light and airy ways must endanger the men's morale.
What business have you with the sturdy ranks of the real?

I bring them dew from earth's dayspring.
Fire from the first wild rose I bring.
And this – my deepest art –
I bring them word from their own hungering
Beleaguered heart.

Pass, friend. You bear
Gifts that, although men commonly flout them
Being hardened, or born, to live without them,
Are none the less rare.
Pass, friend, and fare you well, and may all such travellers
be speeded
Who bring us news we had almost forgot we needed.

Lines for Edmund Blunden on his Fiftieth Birthday

Your fiftieth birthday. What shall we give you?
An illuminated address
Would be hard on one who was never at home with
Pomp or pretentiousness.
Here is a loving-cup made from verse,
For verse is your favourite of metals:
Imagine its stem like a tulip stalk,
Its bowl a tulip's petals

And the whole as gracefully formed and charactered
　　As a poem of your own.
What shall the toast be? Fifty years more?
　　A century? Let it be known
That a true poet's age is truthfully reckoned
　　Not in years but in song:
So we drink instead to that happy girl
　　Your Muse – may she live long!
But we pledge our love, our love for one
　　Who never has burned or bowed
To popular gods, and when fame beckons
　　Modestly melts in the crowd.
Into the crowd of your haunting fancies –
　　The streams, the airs, the dews,
The soldier shades and the solacing heartbeams –
　　You melt, and fame pursues;
And our good wishes follow you, even
　　To the fortunate meadows where
Tonight your loving-cup is raised
　　By Shelley, Hunt and Clare.

Buzzards Over Castle Hill

A world seems to end at the top of this hill.
　　Across it, clouds and thistle-clocks fly,
And ragged hedges are running down from the sky,
　　As though the wild had begun to spill
Over a rampart soon to be drowned
With all it guards of domesticated ground.

It was silent here on the slope of the hill.
　　But now, now, as if the wild grass
And the wild sky had found their voices at last

391

And they were one voice, there comes a shrill
Delirious mewing, thin as air,
A wraith-like rumour, nowhere and everywhere.

Over the hill three buzzards are wheeling
On the glass sky their skaters' curves.
Each in its solemn figures-of-nought preserves
Some thread invisible, reeling, unreeling,
Then glides to a stop and with wings outlined
Motionless broods there balancing on the wind.

Often enough ere now I have eyed them –
Those three celestial bodies appear
Cutting their abstract figures year after year –
But never have fathomed what instinct rides them
Round heaven's dome like a frozen pond,
Nor why they are always three, and what is the bond

Between them: although you might well surmise
They are earth-souls doomed in their gyres to unwind
Some tragic love-tangle wherein they had mortally pined,
When you hear those phantom, famishing cries.
But birds are birds. No human key
Of fond frustration unites the haunting three.

Wild natures, kin to all cageless things –
Thistledown, grass and cloud – yet mewing
So ghostly, no prey nor animal need pursuing
In those pure rings and hoverings,
I watch the angelic pastime until
I seem to know what is beyond the hill.

A Hard Frost

A frost came in the night and stole my world
And left this changeling for it – a precocious
Image of spring, too brilliant to be true:
White lilac on the windowpane, each grass-blade
Furred like a catkin, maydrift loading the hedge.
The elms behind the house are elms no longer
But blossomers in crystal, stems of the mist
That hangs yet in the valley below, amorphous
As the blind tissue whence creation formed.
   The sun looks out, and the fields blaze with diamonds.
Mockery spring, to lend this bridal gear
For a few hours to a raw country maid,
Then leave her all disconsolate with old fairings
Of aconite and snowdrop! No, not here
Amid this flounce and filigree of death
Is the real transformation scene in progress,
But deep below where frost
Worrying the stiff clods unclenches their
Grip on the seed and lets our future breathe.

The Christmas Tree

Put out the lights now!
Look at the Tree, the rough tree dazzled
In oriole plumes of flame,
Tinselled with twinkling frost fire, tasselled
With stars and moons – the same
That yesterday hid in the spinney and had no fame
Till we put out the lights now.

393

Hard are the nights now:
The fields at moonrise turn to agate,
Shadows are cold as jet;
In dyke and furrow, in copse and faggot
The frost's tooth is set;
And stars are the sparks whirled out by the north wind's
fret
On the flinty nights now.

So feast your eyes now
On mimic star and moon-cold bauble:
Worlds may wither unseen,
But the Christmas Tree is a tree of fable,
A phoenix in evergreen,
And the world cannot change or chill what its mysteries
mean
To your hearts and eyes now.

The vision dies now
Candle by candle: the tree that embraced it
Returns to its own kind,
To be earthed again and weather as best it
May the frost and the wind.
Children, it too had its hour – you will not mind
If it lives or dies now.

The Chrysanthemum Show

Here's Abbey Way: here are the rooms
   Where they held the chrysanthemum show –
Leaves like talons of greenfire, blooms
Of a barbarous frenzy, red, flame, bronze –
And a schoolboy walked in the furnace once,
   Thirty years ago.

You might have thought, had you seen him that day
    Mooching from stall to stall,
It was wasted on him – the prize array
Of flowers with their resinous, caustic tang,
Their colours that royally boomed and rang
    Like gongs in the pitchpine hall.

Any tongue could scorch him; even hope tease
    As if it dissembled a leer:
Like smouldering fuse, anxieties
Blindwormed his breast. How should one feel,
Consuming in youth's slow ordeal,
    What flashes from flower to flower?

Yet something did touch him then, at the quick,
    Like a premature memory prising
Through flesh. Those blooms with the bonfire reek
And the flaming of ruby, copper, gold –
There boyhood's sun foretold, retold
    A full gamut of setting and rising.

Something touched him. Always the scene
    Was to haunt his memory –
Not haunt – come alive there, as if what had been
But a flowery idea took flesh in the womb
Of his solitude, rayed out a rare, real bloom.
    I know, for I was he.

And today, when I see chrysanthemums,
    I half envy that boy
For whom they spoke as muffled drums
Darkly messaging, 'All decays;
But youth's brief agony can blaze
    Into a posthumous joy.'

395

Two Songs

Written to Irish Airs

'LOVE WAS ONCE LIGHT AS AIR' (Air: *Dermott*)

Love was once light as air
Brushed over all my thoughts and themes;
Love once seemed kind as air
When the dewfall gleams.
Now he's another thing –
Naked light, oh hard to bear,
Too much discovering
With his noonday beams.

Long had I sought for you,
Long, long by subtle masks delayed:
Fair shapes I thought were you
On my green heart played.
Now love at his height informs
All that was so vague to view,
Shall not those slighter forms
In his noon hour fade?

Fade they then fast as snow
When April brings the earth to light,
One shape – alas 'tis so –
Still lingers white:
One heart-wrung phantom still,
One I would not tell to go,
Shadows my noontime still
And haunts my night.

'OH LIGHT WAS MY HEAD' (Air: *St. Patrick's Day*)

Oh light was my head as the seed of a thistle
And light as the mistletoe mooning an oak,

396

I spoke with the triton, I skimmed with the nautilus,
Dawn was immortal as love awoke.
　But when a storm began to blow
　My thistle was dashed, my tree laid low,
　My folk of the wave went down to their deep, so I
Frown on a thistledown floating capriciously,
Scorn as mere fishes the folk of the sea,
Agree the renowned golden bough is a parasite,
Love but a gallous-eyed ghost for me.

Ah, fooled by the cock at the cool of the morning
And fooled by the fawning mirage of the day,
I say that I'm truly well rid of this featherwit –
Reason has tethered it down in clay.
　But when the light begins to go,
　When shadows are marching heel and toe,
　When day is a heap of ashes, I know that I'll
Ride to love's beam like a barque at her anchorage,
Glide on the languorous airs of the past,
For fast as the pride of our reason is waning,
Old follies returning grow wise at last.

Minor Tragedy

Hundreds went down to the ocean bed,
Hundreds fell from the sky,
The shades in the street thickened,
Blood stood in every eye.
Oh kiss me or I'll die, she said,
Kiss me or I'll die!

He took a shadow into the bed
Where she had drained him dry:

With words that buzzed like bullets
She pinned him to a lie.
Don't kiss me or I'll die, she said,
Don't kiss me or I'll die!

Thousands twined on the ocean bed,
Thousands burned in the sky:
Nursing a spent bullet
He let the world go by,
And I'll kiss it till I die, he said,
Kiss it till I die!

On the Sea Wall

As I came to the sea wall that August day,
One out of all the bathers there
Beckoned my eye, a girl at play
With the surf-flowers. Was it the dark, dark hair
Falling Egyptian-wise, or the way
Her body curved to the spray? –

I know not. Only my heart was shaking
Within me, and then it stopped; as though
You were dead and your shape had returned to haunt me
On the very same spot where, five years ago,
You slipped from my arms and played in the breaking
Surges to tease and enchant me.

I could not call out. Had there been no more
Than those thickets of rusty wire to pen us
Apart, I'd have gone to that girl by the shore
Hoping she might be you. But between us
Lie tangled, severing, stronger far,
Barbed relics of love's old war.

Ewig

Multitudes of corn
Shock-still in July heat,
Year upon foaming year
Of may and meadowsweet –
Soon, soon they fleet.

So many words to unsay,
So much hue and cry
After a wisp of flame,
So many deaths to die
Ere the heart runs dry.

All Gone

The sea drained off, my poverty's uncovered –
Sand, sand, a rusted anchor, broken glass,
The listless sediment of sparkling days
When through a paradise of weed joy wavered.

The sea rolled up like a blind, oh pitiless light
Revealing, shrivelling all! Lacklustre weeds
My hours, my truth a salt-lick. Love recedes
From rippled flesh bared without appetite.

A stranded time, neap and annihilation
Of spirit. Gasping on the inglorious rock,
I pray the sea return, even though its calm
Be treachery, its virtue a delusion.

Put forth upon my sands, whether to mock,
Revive or drown, a liberating arm!

The Neurotic

The spring came round, and still he was not dead.
Skin of the earth deliciously powdered
With buttercups and daisies – oh, Proserpina
Refreshed by sleep, wild-cherry-garlanded
And laughing in the sallies of the willow-wren!
With lambs and lilies spring came round again.

Who would suppose, seeing him walk the meadows,
He walks a treadmill there, grinding himself
To powder, dust to greyer dust, or treads
An invisible causeway lipped by chuckling shadows?
Take his arm if you like, you'll not come near him.
His mouth is an ill-stitched wound opening: hear him.

'I will not lift mine eyes unto the hills
For there white lambs nuzzle and creep like maggots.
I will not breathe the lilies of the valley
For through their scent a chambered corpse exhales.
If a petal floats to earth, I am oppressed.
The grassblades twist, twist deep in my breast.'

The night came on, and he was still alive.
Lighted tanks of streets a-swarm with denizens
Darting to trysts, sauntering to parties.
How all the heart-fires twinkle! Yes, they thrive
In the large illusion of freedom, in love's net
Where even the murderer can act and the judge regret.

This man who turns a phrase and twiddles a glass
Seems far from that pale muttering magician
Pent in a vicious circle of dilemmas.
But could you lift his blue, thick gaze and pass
Behind, you would walk a stage where endlessly
Phantoms rehearse unactable tragedy.

'In free air captive, in full day benighted,
I am as one for ever out of his element
Transparently enwombed, who from a bathysphere
Observes, wistful, amazed, but more affrighted,
Gay fluent forms of life weaving around,
And dares not break the bubble and be drowned.'

His doomsdays crawled like lava, till at length
All impulse clogged, the last green lung consumed,
Each onward step required the sweat of nightmare,
Each human act a superhuman strength . . .
And the guillemot, clotted with oil, droops her head.
And the mouse between the elastic paws shams dead.

Death mask of a genius unborn:
Tragic prince of a rejected play:
Soul of suffering that bequeathed no myth:
A dark tower and a never-sounded horn. –
Call him what we will, words cannot ennoble
This Atlas who fell down under a bubble.

Two Travellers

One of us in the compartment stares
Out of his window the whole day long
With attentive mien, as if he knows
There is hid in the journeying scene a song
To recall or compose
From snatches of vision, hints of vanishing airs.

He'll mark the couched hares
In grass whereover the lapwing reel and twist:
He notes how the shockheaded sunflowers climb

401

Like boys on the wire by the railway line;
And for him those morning rivers are love-in-a-mist,
And the chimneystacks prayers.

The other is plainly a man of affairs,
A seasoned commuter. His looks assert,
As he opens a brief-case intent on perusing
Facts and figures, he'd never divert
With profitless musing
The longest journey, or notice the dress it wears.

Little he cares
For the coloured drift of his passage: no, not a thing
Values in all that is hurrying past,
Though dimly he senses from first to last
How flaps and waves the smoke of his travelling
At the window-squares.

One is preoccupied, one just stares,
While the whale-ribbed terminus nears apace
Where passengers all must change, and under
Its arch triumphal quickly disperse.
So you may wonder,
Watching these two whom the train indifferently bears,

What each of them shares
With his fellow-traveller, and which is making the best of it,
And whether this or the other one
Will be justified when the journey's done,
And if either may carry on some reward or regret for it
Whither he fares.

Seen From The Train

Somewhere between Crewkerne
And Yeovil it was. On the left of the line
Just as the crinkled hills unroll
To the plain. A church on a small green knoll –
A limestone church,
And above the church
Cedar boughs stretched like hands that yearn
To protect or to bless. The whole

Stood up, antique and clear
As a cameo, from the vale. I swear
It was not a dream. Twice, thrice had I found it
Chancing to look as my train wheeled round it.
But this time I passed,
Though I gazed as I passed
All the way down the valley, that knoll was not there,
Nor the church, nor the trees it mounded.

What came between to unsight me? . . .
But suppose, only suppose there might be
A secret look in a landscape's eye
Following you as you hasten by,
And you have your chance –
Two or three chances
At most – to hold and interpret it rightly,
Or it is gone for aye.

There was a time when men
Would have called it a vision, said that sin
Had blinded me since to a heavenly fact.
Well, I have neither invoked nor faked
Any church in the air,
And little I care

403

Whether or no I shall see it again.
But blindly my heart is racked

When I think how, not twice or thrice,
But year after year in another's eyes
I have caught the look that I missed today
Of the church, the knoll, the cedars – a ray
Of the faith, too, they stood for,
The hope they were food for,
The love they prayed for, facts beyond price –
And turned my eyes away.

Outside and In

How pretty it looks, thought a passer-by –
That cyclamen on her windowsill:
Flowers flushed like the butterfly kisses of sleep that
                                        illumine
A child's alabaster cheek.
She who set it there must have warm hopes to bloom in,
So happy it looks, thought the passer-by,
On the newcomer's windowsill.

O passer-by, can you not feel my glances
Beating against the pane,
Fluttering like a moth shut off from the glades of musk
And the moonlit dances?
O passer-by, can you not see it plain?

She comes not to meet us, muttered the neighbours
Peering in from the stony street:
But look at her parlour, all lighted and spider-spruce!
How saucily wink the brasses!

So garnished a room never tokens a pure recluse.
Let us hope she'll bring, said the gossiping neighbours,
No scandal upon our street.

Ah, what do you know of the crippled heart, my neighbours,
That shrinks from the light and the press?
My winking brass, all the fine repetitive web
Of my house-proud labours –
Even I dare not know them for signals of distress.

A happy release, murmured the living
As they carried at last out into the world
Her body, light as a bird's that has died of hunger
Beneath some warped hedgerow:
Though it was her own doing if all humanity shunned her,
Yet a happy release to be done with living
An outcast from the world.

O living hearts, you are wrong once more. Unassuaged
Even now are my pangs, my fears.
I starved amid plenty. Death seemed no deliverance
To flesh that was caged,
O living hearts, in a ghost these fifty years.

The Misfit

At the training depot that first morning
When the west-country draft came forth on parade –
Mechanics, labourers, men of trade
Herded with shouts like boneheaded cattle –
One stood out from the maul
Who least of them all
Looked metal for killing or meat for the butchery blade.

He wore a long black cutaway coat
Which should have been walking by blackthorn-fleeced
Hedges to church; and good as a feast
Was the spare, wild face much weather had flavoured.
A shepherd or ploughman
I thought, or a cowman –
One with a velvet hand for all manner of beast.

I cannot forget how he stood, bemused,
With the meek eye of a driven thing:
But a solitude old as a cromlech ring
Was around him; a freeborn air of the downland,
A peace of deep combes
No world-anger consumes
Marked him off from the herd to be branded for soldiering.

I saw him not after. Is he now buried
Far from pastures buttercup-strewed,
Or tending his beasts again with the same rude
Rightness of instinct which then had brought him
So quaintly dressed
In his Sunday best
For the first step along the Calvary road?

In the Shelter

In a shelter one night, when death was taking the air
Outside, I saw her, seated apart – a child
Nursing her doll, to one man's vision enisled
With radiance which might have shamed even death to its
lair.

Then I thought of our Christmas roses at home – the dark
Lanterns comforting us a winter through
With the same dusky flush, the same bold spark
Of confidence, O sheltering child, as you.

Genius could never paint the maternal pose
More deftly than accident had roughed it there,
Setting amidst our terrors, against the glare
Of unshaded bulb and whitewashed brick, that rose.

Instinct was hers, and an earthquake hour revealed it
In flesh – the meek-laid lashes, the glint in the eye
Defying wrath and reason, the arms that shielded
A plaster doll from an erupting sky.

No argument for living could long sustain
These ills: it needs a faithful eye, to have seen all
Love in the droop of a lash and tell it eternal
By one pure bead of its dew-dissolving chain.

Dear sheltering child, if again misgivings grieve me
That love is only a respite, an opal bloom
Upon our snow-set fields, come back to revive me
Cradling your spark through blizzard, drift and tomb.

Two Translations

THE FOOTSTEPS
(from Paul Valéry)

Born of my voiceless time, your steps
Slowly, ecstatically advance:
Toward my expectation's bed
They moved in a hushed, ice-clear trance.

407

Pure being, shadow-shape divine –
Your step deliberate, how sweet!
God! – every gift I have imagined
Comes to me on those naked feet.

If so it be your offered mouth
Is shaped already to appease
That which occupies my thought
With the live substance of a kiss,

Oh hasten not this loving act,
Rapture where self and not-self meet:
My life has been the awaiting you,
Your footfall was my own heart's beat.

THE GRAVEYARD BY THE SEA*
(from Paul Valéry)

This quiet roof, where dove-sails saunter by,
Between the pines, the tombs, throbs visibly.
Impartial noon patterns the sea in flame –
That sea for ever starting and re-starting.
When thought has had its hour, oh how rewarding
Are the long vistas of celestial calm!

What grace of light, what pure toil goes to form
The manifold diamond of the elusive foam!
What peace I feel begotten at that source!
When sunlight rests upon a profound sea,
Time's air is sparkling, dream is certainty –
Pure artifice both of an eternal Cause.

Sure treasure, simple shrine to intelligence,
Palpable calm, visible reticence,

* The graveyard is at Sète (Hérault)

Proud-lidded water, Eye wherein there wells
Under a film of fire such depth of sleep –
O silence! . . . Mansion in my soul, you slope
Of gold, roof of a myriad golden tiles.

Temple of time, within a brief sigh bounded,
To this rare height inured I climb, surrounded
By the horizons of a sea-girt eye.
And, like my supreme offering to the gods,
That peaceful coruscation only breeds
A loftier indifference on the sky.

Even as a fruit's absorbed in the enjoying,
Even as within the mouth its body dying
Changes into delight through dissolution,
So to my melted soul the heavens declare
All bounds transfigured into a boundless air,
And I breathe now my future's emanation.

Beautiful heaven, true heaven, look how I change!
After such arrogance, after so much strange
Idleness – strange, yet full of potency –
I am all open to these shining spaces;
Over the homes of the dead my shadow passes,
Ghosting along – a ghost subduing me.

My soul laid bare to your midsummer fire,
O just, impartial light whom I admire,
Whose arms are merciless, you have I stayed
And give back, pure, to your original place.
Look at yourself . . . But to give light implies
No less a sombre moiety of shade.

Oh, for myself alone, mine, deep within
At the heart's quick, the poem's fount, between
The void and its pure issue, I beseech

The intimations of my secret power.
O bitter, dark and echoing reservoir
Speaking of depths always beyond my reach.

But know you – feigning prisoner of the boughs,
Gulf which eats up their slender prison-bars,
Secret which dazzles though mine eyes are closed –
What body drags me to its lingering end,
What mind draws *it* to this bone-peopled ground?
A star broods there on all that I have lost.

Closed, hallowed, full of insubstantial fire,
Morsel of earth to heaven's light given o'er –
This plot, ruled by its flambeaux, pleases me –
A place all gold, stone and dark wood, where shudders
So much marble above so many shadows:
And on my tombs, asleep, the faithful sea.

Keep off the idolaters, bright watch-dog, while –
A solitary with the shepherd's smile –
I pasture long my sheep, my mysteries,
My snow-white flock of undisturbéd graves!
Drive far away from here the careful doves,
The vain daydreams, the angels' questioning eyes!

Now present here, the future takes its time.
The brittle insect scrapes at the dry loam;
All is burnt up, used up, drawn up in air
To some ineffably rarefied solution . . .
Life is enlarged, drunk with annihilation,
And bitterness is sweet, and the spirit clear.

The dead lie easy, hidden in earth where they
Are warmed and have their mysteries burnt away.
Motionless noon, noon aloft in the blue
Broods on itself – a self-sufficient theme.

O rounded dome and perfect diadem,
I am what's changing secretly in you.

I am the only medium for your fears.
My penitence, my doubts, my baulked desires –
These are the flaw within your diamond pride . . .
But in their heavy night, cumbered with marble,
Under the roots of trees a shadow people
Has slowly now come over to your side.

To an impervious nothingness they're thinned,
For the red clay has swallowed the white kind;
Into the flowers that gift of life has passed.
Where are the dead? – their homely turns of speech,
The personal grace, the soul informing each?
Grubs thread their way where tears were once composed.

The bird-sharp cries of girls whom love is teasing,
The eyes, the teeth, the eyelids moistly closing,
The pretty breast that gambles with the flame,
The crimson blood shining when lips are yielded,
The last gift, and the fingers that would shield it –
All go to earth, go back into the game.

And you, great soul, is there yet hope in you
To find some dream without the lying hue
That gold or wave offers to fleshy eyes?
Will you be singing still when you're thin air?
All perishes. A thing of flesh and pore
Am I. Divine impatience also dies.

Lean immortality, all crêpe and gold,
Laurelled consoler frightening to behold,
Death is a womb, a mother's breast, you feign –
The fine illusion, oh the pious trick!
Who does not know them, and is not made sick –
That empty skull, that everlasting grin?

Ancestors deep down there, O derelict heads
Whom such a weight of spaded earth o'erspreads,
Who *are* the earth, in whom our steps are lost,
The real flesh-eater, worm unanswerable
Is not for you that sleep under the table:
Life is his meat, and I am still his host.

'Love', shall we call him? 'Hatred of self', maybe?
His secret tooth is so intimate with me
That any name would suit him well enough,
Enough that he can see, will, daydream, touch –
My flesh delights him, even upon my couch
I live but as a morsel of his life.

Zeno, Zeno, cruel philosopher Zeno,
Have you then pierced me with your feathered arrow
That hums and flies, yet does not fly! The sounding
Shaft gives me life, the arrow kills. Oh, sun! –
Oh, what a tortoise-shadow to outrun
My soul, Achilles' giant stride left standing!

No, no! Arise! The future years unfold.
Shatter, O body, meditation's mould!
And, O my breast, drink in the wind's reviving!
A freshness, exhalation of the sea,
Restores my soul . . . Salt-breathing potency!
Let's run at the waves and be hurled back to living!

Yes, mighty sea with such wild frenzies gifted
(The panther skin and the rent chlamys), sifted
All over with sun-images that glisten,
Creature supreme, drunk on your own blue flesh,
Who in a tumult like the deepest hush
Bite at your sequin-glittering tail – yes, listen!

The wind is rising! . . . We must try to live!
The huge air opens and shuts my book: the wave
Dares to explode out of the rocks in reeking
Spray. Fly away, my sun-bewildered pages!
Break, waves! Break up with your rejoicing surges
This quiet roof where sails like doves were pecking.

1948

AN ITALIAN VISIT*

. . . an Italian visit is a voyage of discovery, not only of scenes and cities, but also of the latent faculties of the traveller's heart and mind.

JASPER MORE: *The Land of Italy*

* This poem was written in 1948–49 except for Part Five. It was eventually published in 1953. Rosamond Lehmann, with whom CDL had had a long liaison until 1949, laid an embargo on its publication, which she lifted in 1953.

TO HENRY REED

417

PART ONE

Dialogue at the Airport

TOM So here we are, we three, bound on a new
experience.

DICK Three persons in one man, bound for the Eternal
City.

HARRY We're not as young as we were, but Italy's some
years older.

TOM Listen, I don't much fancy antiques myself; we've
had some.
Ruins fetch nothing today. The Forum, the Farringdon
Market,
The Colosseum, Hiroshima – death's death, however you
look at it,
However composed the remains. Time enough for such
bric-à-brac when
My silver cord is loosed, my arches are fallen. Oh no, if
It's ruins you're after, we'll soon be parting company.

DICK   Wait!
There are ruins and ruins. Some mature their memories,
feed them
On seeding love-spores blown from age to age; or it may be
Their ghosts fly back like a silver skein of doves when the
crash
Of the fall that tumbled them out has died away. It is these
ghosts
I'm going to look for.

HARRY You think so. But I don't think you will find
them.

419

The only ghosts I believe in are the dangerous self-
                                            detachments
We leave behind in places captured or captivating:
Garrisons, call them, or hostages – wiped out soon enough,
                                            most of them,
Yet here and there is a hardier self lives on to haunt us
With the old riddle, what is the phantom, what the real.
Temple, aqueduct, belvedere, projects fulfilled or
                                            abandoned –
Multiform are the ruins, but the ghosts are always the
                                            same ghost.

    TOM We'd better leave you behind, then, to the desk, the
                                            queue and the rush-hour,
Men and women straphanging like clusters of bats, the
                                            bodies
That jostle and never touch, the eyes without speculation
But for tomorrow's headline or deadline; leave you behind
With all the white-faced addicts of a patent, cellophaned
                                            future.
London's the place for ghosts, if ghosts are invalid monads.
And for God's sake, Harry, don't tell us a crowd is always
                                            the same crowd.

    DICK What are we leaving behind, though? The identity
                                            cards that inform us
Not who we are or might be, but how we are
                                            interchangeable;
The season tickets that rattle us back and forth in a groove
                                            from
Centre to circumference, from dust to dust; the ration
                                            books
Entitling each to his cut of the communal mess and
                                            heartburn.
The fog, the slush, the slogans.

    HARRY   Italy will provide

The same slogans, no doubt, but at least in another
language.

TOM No doubt in another language escapism may sound
more attractive.

DICK Well, it's a holiday, isn't it? Even Harry can take a
holiday.

HARRY I have omitted to pack my Kierkegaard, Marx and
Groddeck.
My *angst* I can only hope they will confiscate at the
Customs.

TOM I am too old to suppose new facts give new
sensations.
Still, like shadows, our senses revive on a shot of sunshine.
One would go far to feel their primitive dance again

DICK Far from the heart's last ditch, the stand on private
relationships

HARRY Far from the mind's closed shop and the
intellectual weeklies.

TOM So here we are, we three, off for a fortnight's holiday,
Our fingers already reaching out to the treat before us

DICK Like a child's on Christmas Eve who, visioning the
dear morrow
Spangled with expectation, would whip time faster and
faster,
And at last whips himself into a humming sleep.

HARRY Travel ought to be sleep – I mean, we should
move oblivious
To the interspace between here and there. We've only a
limited
Stock of attention, and this we had better not spend on
wayside

Sirens who'd make us break our journey or regret not
                                breaking it.

TOM   If he means what I think he means, I am not to look
                              out of the window.

DICK   There's something in what he says, though the
                         motive's unsound, as usual.
Could the zone between here and there be instead a kind of
                                hiatus
Heart would be spared the throes of departure and
                              anticipation,
The tug-of-war in the tensile flesh between near and far,
The sense of all routes leading to a scheduled anti-climax
Because what they lead away from seems now, too late,
                              the nonpareil
The truly virgin place.

HARRY   Yes, travel is travail: a witless
Ordeal of self-abasement to an irreversible process.
It would be nice, waking as it were from twilight sleep, to
Find the new bourne beside one.

TOM   But you never can skip the process
And reach a conclusion, the one is woven into the other
Like hues of a shot-silk rainbow: apart from which, your
                              analogy
Falls to the ground – we shall not, I presume, give birth to
                              Italy.

DICK   But we should give body to our so tentative
                         viewpoints of it

HARRY   Or rather conceive a self, hitherto inconceivable,
                              through it.

TOM   Both of you ask too much. I'll be quite happy,
                    taking Snapshots.

DICK   I shall develop and print them.

422

HARRY   I shall mount them.
And after a year or two fetching the album out again,
Snapshot or time exposure, in every scene, among each
                                        group
Posed before pillars, informally strolling across a piazza,
We'll see, oh yes we shall see them, the usual boring
                                        intruders –
Spirits or ectoplasm, who cares? – spoiling the brilliant
Occasion like long-lost cousins or hangovers out of the
                                        future,
Whether from Dick's chemicals or Tom's automatic choice
Of the haunted subject.

TOM   I don't deny my photographs would be
More satisfactory if you two could stop interfering.
What with Dick's fancy touches and Harry's insufferable
                                        habit
Of scribbling captions across them which later become
                                        obsessions –
Spirits or ectoplasm, who cares? – no wonder if
The results are not

DICK There would be no results but for my dark-room,
Where negatives lie steeped in a warm solution, passing
The acid test of Lethe, to emerge with the self-assurance
Of memories; but for this hand that ever so lightly brushes
Over your brash impressions the dove-downed, hallowing
                                        haze.
What if I do touch up now and then a defective feature? –
There is no law against putting the best face on
                                        experience.

HARRY No law to say we must grind the cornfields into
                                        vitamins,
Reduce the grape to a formula, express the olive in terms of
Statistics. It is deplorable, yes, and against nature:
Nevertheless, one does it, being of a generation

423

Whose only faith is the piling of fact on fact, in the hope
           that
Some day a road may be built of them and may lead
          somewhere.

TOM In the meanwhile, we go to Italy: Dick, with his
         decadent craving
For perfection at any price, who cannot pass by an arc
Without officiously filling in the rest of the circle;
Harry whose conscience bids him take the round world to
          pieces
And ticket each stone for the use of a possibly grateful
          posterity;
And I who, with your permission, intend just to enjoy
         myself.

DICK But even you have been taught the simpler
        associations –
For example, mouth and famine, lily and corpse, bambino
And bomb – to say nothing of *odi et amo* – which stand in
        the light of
Enjoyment pure and simple. Travellers can't be choosers
Any more than the stay-at-homes.

HARRY   No, man's gleaming aspirations
Are endlessly batted down as telegraph wire by the poles
When you look from a train window, everywhere and for
        ever
Abased his soaring creeds by the very proofs which support
        them.
Yet still we aspire. Each journey's a bid for the empyrean
Of Absolute freedom, whether we fly to the ends of the earth
Or take a week-end ticket to Clacton; and as certainly
We are twitched back on the thread reeled out from our
        ruling passion.

TOM All the more reason for going abroad with a *tabula*
        rasa,

424

Not trailing clouds of vainglory or the old tin can of
                                          conscience.
Granted we cannot entirely escape ourselves, and granted
That up to a point we can only see what we're bound to
                                          look for,
Still, there is such a thing as simple impressionability,
A sense in which form and colour are more than mere
                                          dreams of our senses,
A moment – though rare – when the lily speaks for itself
                                          alone
And the babe's ephemeral laughter chimes with eternity.

DICK And another thing: when the new place,
                    mysteriously conveying
A promise of maiden surrender and morning glory, invites
                                          us,
We are wax in her hands for a little, our former loves
                                          effaced,
Ready to take her seal, to believe the rewarding fallacy
That this is it at last, that this time all will be different;
And we really may find the knack of pure freedom, pure
                                          submission,
Whereby a miraculous rebirth is possible – find it
Before the displaced selves crowd back to declare us
                                          impotent.

HARRY Since you two appear in agreement on this, the
                    logical next step
Is to unpack our preconceptions and leave them behind
                                          here,
Discarding whatever might come between us and the
                                          naked fact.

TOM Myself, I have always travelled light – eyes, ears,
                    nose, fingers,
And one thing more, I carry. Now Dick, you'll have to
                    jettison

Time, whose ripple prettifies the weed which fouls it, and
flaws
The willow it images.

DICK Time, without which there could be no images? –
You might as well go abroad without an interpreter – you,
Tom,
Who don't know a word in any tongue but your own. Now
Harry
Has much he should lighten his bag of; props, probes and
provisos;
The impressive manner he wears while wooing the heiress,
Truth;
And of course the instruments he will presently use to
dissect her.

HARRY Your programmes are too ambitious. I only meant
to suggest
We should expose the Italy faked by our fraudulent vision,
Tear up the glowing prospectus that pictured a heaven on
earth

TOM Confess why we are going and what we expect to
find there?

DICK Rub out the shadow our ego projects? Make a clean
sheet of Italy?

HARRY Yes, a cadenza from each on this fantasy
movement. We have
Ten minutes until our flight-number is called. Let Tom
begin.

TOM First, a great Elgarian clash and bray of sunshine
Throwing open the day, blaring a paeony fanfare
Through flesh and blood, throwing wide the earth – a
fabulous mansion
Where every maid is a gift, every moment a pulse in a fun-
fair.

426

None of your fairy gold! The real, royal, vulgar pageant –
Time flung like confetti or twirled in rosettes – was never
                                        too garish
For me. How much better than your dim flounderings
                                toward some imagined
Immortal star, to flare like a firework and goldenly perish!
Mornings, I ask a cloudless sky; or if clouds there must be,
Billowy suds that have scoured the sky bluer than corn-
                                        flowers:
Acacia and lemon-blossom shall drench me, mimosa dust
                                        me,
Violet and rose be banked along my sauntering hours.
Noon shall stand as long as I fancy, and tall as houses –
A fountain pluming itself upon the enchanted air:
Afternoon shall sleep with the goat-flock villages drowsing
Lightly, precipice-high, or deep in shuttered squares.
Ah, but the nights! I see them festooned in a long fiesta –
Mediterranean nights that will send me spinning and flying
With the waltz of a purple Maelstrom, the arrowy glide of
                                        a Cresta.
Here's to the masks and the music, the dancers ebbing and
                                        flowing!
Let fairy-lit streets run wine through the veins like a ride
                                on a scenic
Railway! and then the ravishing flesh of girls consume me
Flame upon flame to scented ashes, and I a phoenix!
Yes, one thing I know: it's the sting of strangeness renews
                                        me.
Listen, the bells tumble from a humming campanile
With a dull pot-and-pan clang: those two at the table – the
                                        cadence
Is unfamiliar they talk in: banal their gist, but to me they
Are speaking, lover and carillon, with the tongues of angels.
I do not wish to dig down to the sullen roots of existence
Where one clod's the same as the next, or to tangle myself
                                in humanity's

427

Fretted heart-strings: not here lies the world of essential
                                        difference,
But above, in the bloom, the spectrum, the transient
                                        flavours and vanities.
Therefore I'd browse on the skin of things, the delicate field
                                        of
Diversity, skimming gold from the buttercup, dust from the
                                        nettle.
I, the merely sensual man, have a scope undreamed of
By you whom a larger ambition drives to discard or belittle
Appearance. And so I ask of Italy nothing more than
Mere foreignness, the shock and buoyant feel of the
                                        unknown,
And quivering over its surface an irridescent path, an
Arrow to point me, the eternal tripper, away from home.

   DICK Different my nature, my needs. I journey as a
                                        colonial
Reaching across generations to find the parent stock,
As a child setting out to colour a black-and-white picture
                                        book,
A priest entering into the spirit of dead ceremonial . . .
They have been dormant so long, the ghosts that were used
                                        to school us:
Deep-buried as once Pompeii the classroom walls with
                                        their jaded
Photos of classical ruin, of statues leprous, abraded.
Did ever those dry bones live? And instantly Ovid, Catullus
Wild for his Lesbia, Virgil, Lucretius – sports of a prosy
Marble-eyed, muscle-bound people – emerge from the
                                        shades to claim one.
Ancestor worship's a form of self-seeking: all the same, one
Is grateful to those who had no immediate hand in our crazy
Present: the Romans at any rate did manage to keep the
                                        peace,
Off and on. But that's by the way. Some breathing
                                        counterpart

I want for a dead language years ago learnt by heart,
Some vista shaped and haunted by youthful pieties.
Immortal landscape of a day, for ever dreaming
In haze of summers half imagined, half remembered!
Meek-swarded, comely pastoral where nymph and
                                    shepherd
Still twine two worlds in a dance! Demesne of phantoms,
                                    teeming
With myrtle, vine and olive, pied with fact and fable!
Hero, god, or brute, all hold to the light their antique
Self-sufficiency – a grace which no romantic
Yearnings can discompose nor withering years enfeeble.
Such is the foreground. Behind it vaporously writhes a
                                    spectacular
Region of mounting disquiet, dark meaning, where lie
                                    concealed
A lake that shoots down birds with a whiff of the
                                    underworld;
Proserpine's trapdoor; a gorge rumbling in tones oracular;
A forest of shadows juddering athwart the golden bough.
Is it I they wait for, the feudal lords of light and mystery
Their kingdoms to unite? Is it they who shall assist me
To define, or abolish, the frontier between my Then and
                                    my Now?
There was a time of substance and shadow richly confused,
When a dry Tuscan evelight engraved the cricket-ground
And my study shafted towards the black diamonds and
                                    dene profound
Of Pluto: then the beam went, the pit fell into disuse.
If I could find that place where nymph and shepherd meet
And the distance melts into deity, I would unearth my
                                    buried
Heirlooms, my sealed orders. Genius of the place, remarry
These sundered elements, make one circle at last complete!

HARRY A landscape I also may look for: a town in fiesta
                                    would do

429

Equally well for the purpose this traveller has in view.
Let me try to explain myself – both artist and analyst;
> hence
For me the approach that in others would be pure
> innocence
Were wild irresponsibility. Think! The desirable villa
Haunted by princes, hallowed with cypresses, there on a
> hillside
Ultimately reduces to a vulgar hop of electrons:
I see the revellers, masked and articulate for faction;
Your language of bells and lovers I hear, but as workable
> fictions.
Since all strips down to motion, and all's in a state of
> becoming,
Whoever would master the truth by which your
> provocative, charming
Strip-tease universe lives, ideally should be at rest
Himself; at any rate disinterested, unimpressed.
And that is why I am far from being a keen traveller.
On the other hand, I admit one cannot hope to unravel
Experience unless one is to a certain degree involved.
Is there a method by which, then, a mutable self may
> resolve
And fix the ever-changing? Let us try an experiment –
> briefly
The playing a trick on time. Help me, you two, to achieve
> it.
To see as it were from the far end of a cypress walk of
> bereavement,
Or the eyrie of ten years hence! For look, how the terraced
> garden,
Statues, orange trees, villa, unfocused now by sudden
Tremors – the whole prospect fidgets, vibrates, wavers,
Collapsing always with the present. But if upon that fevered
Hill brow, my brow, should once be laid grief's cooling
> hand,

Dance and dissolution would come to a dead stand.
Memory needs time before the outraged dwelling, love's
                                                centre,
Purified, tear upon tear, shines forth like a shell of
                                                candour,
And all around, elegiac in evergreen, new contours
Idealize the old agony. But I have to induce
Years from a moment: therefore I must predicate loss.
Let me take some figure of the dance, so fleetingly fiercely
                                                exulting
That it quickens the seed of loss, my seed, and itself is
                                                halted
And magnified thus, a still from the moving picture,
                                                framed
In parting's hard embrace some beauty, flushed, fleshed,
                                                tamed.
Separation's my metier, then, sifting through form the
                                                formless:
Creation my end, to subdue and liberate time in the
                                                timeless.
I find the whole in elusive fragments: let one be caught
And profoundly known – that way, like a skeleton key, the
                                                part
May unlock the intricate whole. What else is the work of
                                                art?

PART TWO

Flight to Italy

The winged bull trundles to the wired perimeter.
Cumbrously turns. Shivers, brakes clamped,
Bellowing four times, each engine tested
With routine ritual. Advances to the runway.
Halts again as if gathering heart
Or warily snuffing for picador cross-winds.
Then, then, a roar open-throated
Affronts the arena. Then fast, faster
Drawn by the magnet of his *idée fixe*,
Head down, tail up, he's charging the horizon.
⠀⠀⠀⠀And the grass of the airfield grows smooth as a fur.
The runway's elastic and we the projectile;
Installations control-tower mechanics parked aeroplanes –
Units all woven to a ribbon unreeling,
Concrete melts and condenses to an abstract
Blur, and our blood thickens to think of
Rending, burning, as suburban terraces
Make for us, wave after wave.
⠀⠀⠀⠀⠀⠀⠀⠀⠀⠀⠀⠀⠀⠀The moment
Of Truth is here. We can only trust,
Being as wholly committed to other hands
As a babe at birth, Europa to the bull god.
And as when one dies in his sleep, there's no divining
The instant of take-off, we who were earth-bound
Are air-borne, it seems, in the same breath.
The neutered terraces subside beneath us.

⠀⠀⠀⠀Bank and turn, bank and turn,
Air-treading bull, my silver Alitalia!

432

Bank and turn, while the earth below
Swings like a dial on the wing-tip's axis,
Whirls and checks like a wheel of chance!
Now keep your course! On azure currents
Let the wings lift and sidle drowsily –
A halcyon rocked by the ghost of the gale.
To watchers in Kent you appear as a quicksilver
Bead skimming down the tilted sky;
To the mild-eyed aircrew, an everyday office:
To us, immured in motion, you mean
A warm womb pendant between two worlds.

O trance prenatal and angelic transport!
Like embryos curled in this aluminium belly –
Food and oxygen gratis – again
We taste the pure freedom of the purely submissive,
The passive dominion of the wholly dependent.
Through heaven's transparent mysteries we travel
With a humdrum of engines, the mother's heartbeat:
And our foreshadowed selves begin to take shape, to be
Dimly adapted to their destination.
What migrant fancies this journeying generates! –
Almost we imagine a metempsychosis.

Over the Channel now, beneath the enchanting
Inane babble of a baby-blue sky,
We soar through cloudland, at the heights of nonsense.
From a distance they might be sifted-sugar-drifts,
Meringues, iced cakes, confections of whipped cream
Lavishly piled for some Olympian party –
A child's idea of heaven. Now radiant
All around the airscrew's boring penumbra
The clouds redouble, as nearer we climb,
Their toppling fantasy. We skirt the fringe of icebergs,
Dive under eiderdowns, disport with snowmen
On fields of melting snow dinted by the wind's feet,
Gleefully brush past atom-bomb cauliflowers,

433

Frozen fuffs of spray from naval gunfire.
    Wool-gathering we fly through a world of make-
                                    believe.
We *are* the aircraft, the humming-bird hawk moth
Hovering and sipping at each cloud corolla;
But also ourselves, to whom these white follies are
Valid as symbols for a tonic reverie
Or as symptoms of febrile flight from the real.
Let us keep, while we can, the holiday illusion,
The heart's altimeter dancing bliss-high,
Forgetting gravity, regardless of earth
Out of sight, out of mind, like a menacing letter
Left at home in a drawer – let the next-of-kin acknowledge
                                        it.

    The cloud-floor is fissured suddenly. Clairvoyance
It seems, not sight, when the solid air frays and parts
Unveiling, like some rendezvous remote in a crystal,
Bright, infinitesimal, a fragment of France.
We scan the naked earth as it were through a skylight:
Down there, what life-size encounters, what industrious
Movement and vocations manifold go forward!
But to us, irresponsible, above the battle,
Villages and countryside reveal no more life than
A civilization asleep beneath a glacier,
Toy bricks abandoned on a plain of linoleum . . .
    After a hard winter, on the first warm day
The invalid venturing out into the rock-garden,
Pale as a shaft of December sunshine, pauses,
All at sea among the aubretia, the alyssum
And arabis – halts and moves on how warily,
As if to take soundings where the blossom foams and
                                        tumbles:
But what he does sound is the depth of his own weakness
At last, as never when pain-storms lashed him.
So we, convalescent from routine's long fever,

Plummeting our gaze down to river and plain,
Question if indeed that dazzling world beneath us
Be truth or delirium; and finding still so tentative
The answer, can gauge how nearly we were ghosts,
How far we must travel yet to flesh and blood.

But now the engines have quickened their beat
And the fuselage pulsates, panting like a fugitive.
Below us – oh, look at it! – earth has become
Sky, a thunderscape curdling to indigo,
Veined with valleys of green fork-lightning.
The atrocious Alps are upon us. Their ambush –
A primeval huddle, then a bristling and heaving of
Brutal boulder-shapes, an uprush of Calibans –
Unmasks its white-fanged malice to maul us.
The cabin grows colder. Keep height, my angel!
Where we are, all but terra firma is safe.
Recall how flyers from a raid returning,
Lightened of one death, were elected for another:
Their homing thoughts too far ahead, a mountain
Stepped from the mist and slapped them down.
We, though trivial the hazard, retract
Our trailing dreams until we have cleared these ranges.
Exalted, numinous, aloof no doubt
To the land-locked vision, for us they invoke
A mood more intimate, a momentary flutter and
Draught of danger – death's fan coquettishly
Tapping the cheek ere she turn to dance elsewhere.
Our mien is the bolder for this mild flirtation,
Our eyes the brighter, since every brush with her
Gives flesh a souvenir, a feel of resurrection.

Those peaks o'erpassed, we glissade at last to
A gentian pasture, the Genoan sea.
Look south, sky-goers! In flying colours
A map's unrolled there – the Italy

435

Your schooldays scanned once: the hills are sand-blond,
A pale green stands for the littoral plain:
The sea's bedizened with opening islands
Like iris eyes on a peacock's fan.
How slowly dawns on the drowsy newborn
Whose world's unworn yet – a firelit dress,
An ego's glamorous shell, a womb of rumours –
The first faint glimmering of otherness!
But half awake, we could take this country
For some vague drift from prenatal dreams:
Those hills and headlands, like sleep's projections
Or recollections, mere symbol seem.
        Then hurtling southward along shores of myrtle,
Silverly circle the last lap,
My bull-headed moth! This land is nothing
But a mythical name on an outline map
For us, till we've scaled it to our will's dimensions,
Filled in each wayward, imperious route,
Shaded it in with delays and chagrins,
Traced our selves over it, foot by foot.
Now tighter we circle, as if the vertical
Air is a whirlpool drawing us down;
And the airfield, a candle-bright pinpoint, invites us
To dance ere alighting . . . Hurry! We burn
For Rome so near us, for the phoenix moment
When we have thrown off this traveller's trance,
And mother-naked and ageless-ancient
Wake in her warm nest of renaissance.

PART THREE

A Letter from Rome

We have been here three days, and Rome is really –
I know, I know; it would take three life-times to cover
The glorious junk-heap. Besides, our generation –
Well, you've only to think of James, as one must do here,
Lapping the cream of antiquity, purring over
Each vista that stroked his senses, and in brief
Rubbing himself against Rome like a great tabby,
To see what I mean. We who 'flowered' in the Thirties
Were an odd lot; sceptical yet susceptible,
Dour though enthusiastic, horizon-addicts
And future-fans, terribly apt to ask what
Our all-very-fine sensations were in aid of.
We did not, you will remember, come to coo.
Still, there is hope for us. Rome has absorbed
Other barbarians: yes, and there's nobody quite so
Sensuously rich and reckless as the reformed
Puritan . . . This by the way, to establish a viewpoint.
     You wanted my impressions. If only one were
A simple sieve, be the mesh close or wide,
For Rome to shake (and how it does shake one!), sifting
Some finer stuff from the coarser. But the trouble with me
                                                      is
– Or perhaps it's the trouble with Rome – to discriminate
Merely between what is here and what has been here,
Between the eye and the mind's eye. The place has had
Over two thousand years of advance publicity
For us, which clouds the taste and saps the judgment.
What are you to do when Catullus buttonholes you
On the way to St. Peter's? When the Colosseum presents

Nero* comparing notes with Roderick Hudson
On art and egotism? Sights, sounds, phantoms –
It is all too much for me, it should not be allowed!
    Perhaps, though, it is just here that something
                                  emerges.
As when, composing a poem, the tangle of images
And jangle of words pressing hard on you, mobbing you,
                                   may
Compel you to choose the right moment to disengage
And find the one word, the word of command which makes
                                   them
Meekly fall in to their ranks, and the march continues:
So from this Rome, where the past lies weltering
In the blood of the present, and posters of Betty Grable
Affront the ghost of Cato; from all its grandiose
Culs-de-sac – the monumental gateways
That open on nothing, the staircases starting for heaven,
The stone-blind palaces sweltering in the noon;
From the stilled tempest of the Sistine ceiling
To the water exasperated by sirocco
In every fountain basin; from the whole gamut,
Theatrical, vulgar, rhetorical, fractious, sublime,
Of a city young as Tithonus, a city so ancient
That even the shadows here lie thick as dust: –
Emerges from all this, like invisible writing
Drawn out by the heart's warmth, one lucid word.
    Compost. I do not suppose the word original
(Original! Rome is quite beyond that). But think of it –
Century into century rotting down,
Faith piled on faith, Mithra on Jupiter,
Christ upon Mithra, Catholicism on Christ,
Temples imbedded in churches, church-stones in palaces:
Think of the pagan gods, demoted to demons,
Haunting and taunting the Early Fathers; long-dead

* The Colosseum was built by Vespasian on the site of the Golden House of Nero.

438

Lights of love, immortalized as Madonnas,
Demurely smiling at man's infant idealism.
Superstition, sanctity, cruelty, laws, art, lust –
Layer after layer laid down, course upon course
They renew the soul of this city, a city whose prospects
Are quarried out of its bones, a soul digesting
All foreignness into one rich dark fibre.
Rome, I can tell you, is the very type of
The hugger-mugger of human growth. For here
You can see the grand design eternally crossed
By the abject means, and its seedy ruin redeemed with
Valerian, arbutus, fennel; a character root-fast
Like a man's in the deposit of all his acts.

   Or say, a woman's; for so she appeared to us
On the first morning when we sauntered out
(The night before, wild strawberries and Frascati
Gold as the Roman May-light, cool as grottoes).
A woman – how shall I put it? – who makes you feel
She has waited two thousand years to meet you, and now
At once she is wholly yours, her liquid tongue,
Her body mantled in the full flush of Ceres,
And Primavera fluttering in her eyes.
She can be tiresome, no doubt, feverish, languid,
Changing her moods like dresses. But today
She has chosen to be divinely acquiescent:
'What shall we do?' the shell-like murmur comes,
'Shall we go shopping? Would you like me to show you the
                                                    sights?'
'I will do anything you say, anything.'
. . . So we took, in the end, a carrozza to St. Peter's.
The driver was plainly a phantom; his conveyance
Jarred like old bones and mumbled of better days when
Violet-adorned beauties, sedate or giddy,
Turned all heads on the Corso. Thus we went
Jaunting over the seven hills of Rome
With the streets rocking beneath us as if seven ages

439

Turned in their grave, while noise upon noise the drift
Of our own – its voices, horns, wheels, bells, loudspeakers –
Washed past us; then it dwindled away to a sea-shell
Cadence, beyond the Tiber, as we came near
Vatican city.
                    And now *vates tacete*
Should be the word. Words here can only scrabble
Like insects at the plinth of a colossus,
Scrabble and feebly gesticulate and go elsewhere.
Mere magnitude one might deal with, or pure and simple
Meaning; but both in one, they give no purchase.
A dome superb as heaven's vault, capping a story
Whose hero blessed the meek; a desert of floor
Refracting faith like a mirage; the orchestration
Of gold and marble engulfing the still, small voice: –
You cannot pass over St. Peter's and what it stands for,
Whether you see it as God's vicarious throne
Or the biggest bubble ever yet unpricked.
And here, I have to confess, the old Puritan peeped out;
Not in sour protest against the Scarlet Woman,
Nor quite in the mood of my generation – its volatile
Mixture of hero-worship and disrespect;
But that an early habit of going to church
Prevents me from going to churches however distinguished
Their provenance, just as a sight-seer. Faith perhaps,
Though unconscious, is not yet dead, its breath still
                                        clouding
The glass of aesthetic perception. Apart from which,
I could not do with the guides who spring up like sweat-
                                        white
Fungi from every chink, and cling to one, furtively
Offering their curious knowledge; these pimps are not
The type you would choose to lead you to any altar.
So I was lost, ill at ease here, until by chance
In a side chapel we found a woman mourning
Her son: all the *lacrimæ rerum* flowed

To her gesture of grief, all life's blood from his stone.
There is no gap or discord between the divine
And the human in that pieta of Michelangelo.
Then, after a marathon walk through the Vatican
                                        galleries,
An endless belt of statues, tapestry, pictures
Glazing the eye, we came out into the streets again.
Better than all the museums, this strolling folk
Who sun themselves in the apricot light of antiquity
And take its prestige for granted. Cameo faces,
Contessa or contadina; bronze boys skylarking
As if they had just wriggled free from a sculptor's hand –
How easily art and nature overlap here!
Another thing you would like about the Romans
Is the way they use their city, not as a warren
Of bolt-holes, nor a machine into which one is fed
Each morning and at evening duly disgorged,
But as an open-air stage. Palazzo, tenement
Seem pure façade – back-cloth for a continuous
Performance of business, love-making, politics, idling,
Conducted with a grand operatic extravagance
At the tempo of family theatricals. That same night
In the Piazza del' Esedra, sipping
Grappa, we watched the people, warm as animals
And voluble as fountains, eddying round
While the floodlit masonry was mere slabs of moonshine.
Rome is a city where flesh and blood can never
Be sacrificed, or mistaken, for abstractions.

        But already (you can imagine how) my mind's
Crisscrossed with figures, memoranda, lightning sketches,
Symbolic doodlings, hour by hour set down
Haphazardly as in Rome era on era.
And time is already shuffling tricks with discards.
Those fountains yesterday at the Villa d'Este
Grouped like patrician spectres in white conclave
Against a drop-scene of terraces and urns –

441

Did we indeed see them, or have they stepped
From a picture book years ago perused? Last night
We found on a wall of the Pincio a bas-relief,
A wide white calm imperious head suddenly
Surveying us out of the blank wall like some racial
Memory still not deep enough bricked up.

     Yesterday, then, was a day with the dead. We hired
A car, and set out first for the Palatine hill.
The Forum? Well, picture a clearing found
In the depth of a clamorous forest, a low space littered
With bits of temples, arches, altars, mosaics
And God knows what – classical tags, fag ends,
Smatterings and stumps of a once apparently stable
Civilization, which packed up for all that
And left, like a gipsy encampment or picnic party:
And over it all, the silence of sheer exhaustion.
This area, sad as scar-tissue now, was the heart
Of a great republic, the S. P. Q. R.
Here they governed – a people, like the Scots,
Smouldering, pious, intolerant, living hard,
And demon fighters. Warlike was the seed;
But Time has pushed out this crop of decayed teeth.
It was the usual story. Long before
Their aqueducts ran dry and became picturesque,
Their virtue had imperceptibly seeped away
Into the dunes of ambition. They caught
Luxury, like a syphilis, from their conquests.
Then, feeling queer, they appointed one man to cure them
And made a god of him. The disease was arrested
From time to time. But injections grew more frequent,
And the extremities began to rot;
While at home no amount of marble could hide the sick
                                 core –
Vestals too free with their flame, tribunes long impotent,
A rabble who had not the wherewithal to redeem its
Too often pledged heirlooms, justice and hardiness.

So we were glad on the whole to leave this spot
Where glum mementoes of decline and fall
Are cherished like a grievance in Rome's heart,
And drive out towards Tivoli. The name
Had a certain frivolous charm for one oppressed
By dwelling on ruined greatness. The little town,
Modishly perched on an olive-tressed hillside,
Is famous for its sulphur springs (our driver
Stopped the car so that we might inhale it)
And of course, for the Villa d'Este. There at first
In the elaborate Renaissance gardens
Laid out for the lust of the eye, you seem to see
The lineaments of gratified desire.
An illusion though, like the smile on a dead face
Which means nothing but our own wish for peace.
Exquisite, yes: but a sense of the past, to be truly
Felicitous, demands some belief in the present,
Some moral belvedere we have not got.
This villa inhabited only by frescoes,
This garden groomed for sightseers – they mirror
Too clearly our lack of prospect or tenable premise.
The cardinals and princes who adorned them,
Lords of an age when men believed in man,
Are as remote from us as the Colosseum
Where high-tiered beasts howled down professional heroes;
Perhaps – it is a comfortless thought – remoter.
　　Back, then, to Rome. At Tivoli our driver
Stopped again like some house-proud, indelicate devil
To remark the smell of sulphur. Presently,
Held in a crook of Rome's old city wall
Close by St. Paul's gate under the pagan shadow
Of Gaius Cestius' pyramid, we found
The English cemetery. An ox-eyed, pregnant,
Slatternly girl opened the gate for us
And showed us round the desirable estate.
Here is one corner of a foreign field

443

That is for ever garden suburb. See,
In their detached and smug-lawned residences,
Behind a gauze of dusty shrubs, the English
Indulge their life-long taste for privacy.
Garish Campagna knocks at the back door,
Rome calls *en grande tenue*: but 'not at home'
Murmur these tombs, and 'far from home they died,
'The eccentric couple you have come to visit –
'One spitting blood, an outsider and a failure,
'One sailing a boat, his mind on higher things.'
Somewhere close to the pyramid a loud-speaker
Blared jazz while we lingered at Keats' shabby mound,
But the air was drowned by the ghost of a nightingale;
The ground was swimming with anemone tears
Where Shelley lay.
          We could feel at home here, with
This family of exiles. It is our people:
A people from whose reticent, stiff heart
Babble the springtime voices, always such voices
Bubbling out of their clay . . .
          So much for Rome.
Tomorrow we shall take the bus to Florence.

PART FOUR

Bus to Florence

In the white piazza Today is barely awake.
    A well-water breeze freshens
Her nakedness, musky with love, and wafts about
    Her breath of moist carnations.
Oh the beautiful creature, still in a dream pinioned,
    A flutter of meadowsweet thighs!
How she clings to the night, whose fingertips haunt her
                                waxen
    Body! Look at the eyes
Opening – pale, drenched, languid as aquamarines!
    They are open. The mere-smooth light
Starts glancing all over the city in jets and sparklets
    Like a charm of goldfinches in flight.
The tousled alleys stretch. Tall windows blink.
    Hour of alarum clocks and laces.
Sprinklers dust off the streets. The shops hum gently
    As they make up their morning faces.
And today comes out like a bride, a different woman,
    Subtler in hue, hazier,
Until the pensive mist goes, shyly avowing
    Such a zenith of shameless azure.

    This is our day: we mean
To make much of her, tune to her pitch. The enchanting
                             creature
    Travels with us. For once
There will be no twinge of parting in a departure.
    So eager she is to be off,

Spilling her armful of roses and mignonette,
    Her light feet restlessly echoed
From campanile and wristwatch (will they forget?
    Be late?) What a stir and lustre
Ripple the white square at a lift of her hand!
    Look! she has seen us, she points to
That blue bus with the scarab-like trailer behind.

We went the Cassian Way, a route for legions,
    We and the May morning.
Rome flaked off in stucco; blear-eyed villas
    Melancholiac under their awnings.
Rome peeled off like a cataract. Clear beyond us
    A vision good to believe in –
The Campagna with its longdrawn sighs of grass
    Heaving, heaving to heaven.
This young-old terrain of asphodel and tufo
    Opening its heart to the sun,
Was it sighing for death like Tithonus, or still athirst for
    Immortal dews? . . . We run
Towards Tuscany now through a no-man's-land where stilted
    Aqueducts dryly scale
The distance and sport the lizard his antediluvian
    Head and tendril tail.
But soon the road rivers between flowerbanks:
    Such a fume and flamboyance of purple
Vetch, of campions, poppy, wild rose, gladioli,
    Bugloss! The flowery people,
Come out in their best to line our route, how they wave
    At the carnival progress! And higher,
The foothills flush with sanfoin, salutes of broom
    Are setting the rocks on fire.
Sutri, Viterbo, Montefiascone passed:
    Each village, it seemed, was making
A silent bar in the music, the road's hurdy-gurdy
    Winding, the tambourine shaking

Of sunlit leaves. You tatterdemalion townships –
    Elegance freaked with decay –
Your shuttered looks and your black doormouths gaping
    Dumb in the heat of the day
Reject, unanswered, the engine's urgent beat.
    But now, groves of acacia
Swing their honeybells peal upon peal to welcome us
    Over the vibrant, azure,
Deep organ chords of Bolsena, the silvery wavelets
    Trilling tranquillamente.
That music followed us for miles, until
    We came to Acquapendente.

Eyes grown used to the light, we were finding our form and
                                        meeting

    Impressions squarely.
Yet, where all was new, changeful, idyllic, it saddened
    To think how rarely
More than a few snippets remain from the offered fabric,
    And they not always
The ones we'd have chosen. It's sequence I lack, the talent
                                        to grasp

    Not a here-and-there phrase
But the music entire, its original stream and logic. I'd better
    Accept this, perhaps,
As nature's way: matter, the physicists tell one, is largely
    A matter of gaps.

Another stage, and a change of key. Listen!
    Rosetted oxen move –
The milky skins, the loose-kneed watersilk gait of
    Priestesses vowed to Love.
A road stubborn with stone pines. Shrines at the roadside.
    A sandstone cliff, where caves
Open divining mouths: in this or that one
    A skeleton sibyl raves.

447

Signs and omens . . . We approached the haunts of
        The mystery-loving Etruscans.
Earth's face grew rapidly older, ravine-wrinkled,
        Shadowed with brooding dusk on
Temple and cheek. Mountains multiplied round us
        And the flowery guise shredded off as we
Climbed past boulders and gaunt grass high into
        A landscape haggard as prophecy,
Scarred with bone-white riverbeds like veins
        Of inspiration run dry.
Still what a journey away the apocalypse! See it –
        A tower, a town in the sky!
A child from the flowering vale, a youth from the foothills
        May catch glimpses of death
Remote as a star, irrelevant, all of a lifetime
        Ahead, less landmark than myth.
For ages it seems no nearer. But imperceptibly
        The road, twisting and doubling
As if to delay or avoid it, underlines
        That Presence: the man is troubled,
Feeling the road beneath him being hauled in now
        Like slack, the magnetic power
Of what it had always led to over the dreaming
        Hills and the fable of flowers.
So, while the bus toiled upwards and the Apennines
        Swirled like vapours about it,
That town in the sky stayed constant and loomed nearer
        Till we could no more doubt it;
And soon, though still afar off, it darkly foretold us
        We were destined to pass that way.
We passed by the thundercloud castle of Radicofani
        At the pinnacle of our day.

The wrack of cloud, the surly ruinous tower
Stubborn upon the verge of recognition –
        What haunts and weights them so?

448

Memory, or premonition?
Why should a mouldering finger in the sky,
An hour of cloud that drifts and passes, mean
    More than the flowering vale,
    The volcanic ravine?
A driven heart, a raven-shadowing mind
Loom above all my pastorals, impend
    My traveller's joy with fears
    That travelling has no end.

But on without pause from that eyrie the bus, swooping,
    Checking and swooping, descends:
The road cascades down the hillface in blonde ringlets
    Looped up with hairpin bends.
The sun rides out. The calcined earth grows mellow
    With place-names sleek as oil –
Montepulciano, Montalcino, Murlo,
    Castiglione. The soil
Acknowledges man again, his hand which husbands
    Each yielding inch and endures
To set the vine amid armies, the olive between
    Death's adamantine spurs.
Presently, on a constellation of three hills,
    We saw crowning the plain
A town from a missal, a huddle of towers and houses,
    Mediaeval Siena.
A gorge of a street, anfractuous, narrow. Our bus
    Crawled up it, stemming a torrent
Of faces – the faces impetuous, proud, intransigent
    Of those who had fought with Florence
For Tuscany. Was it a demonstration they flocked to?
    A miracle? Or some huger
Event? We left the bus stranded amongst them, a monster
    Thrown up from their fathomless future,
And strolled into a far-off present, an age
    Where all is emblematic,

Pure, and without perspective. The twining passages,
      Diagrams of some classic
Doctrinal knot, lap over and under one another.
      The swan-necked Mangia tower
With its ruff stands, clear as Babel, for pride: beneath it,
      Shaped like a scallop, that square
Might be humility's dewpond, or the rose-madder
      Shell from which Aphrodite
Once stepped ashore. And the west front of the Duomo –
      How it images, flight upon flight, the
Ascending torrent, a multitude without number
      Intent on their timeless way
From the world of St. Catherine, Boccaccio and Fiammetta
      Towards the judgment day!

A township cast up high and dry from an age
      When the whole universe
      Of stars lived in man's parish
And the zodiac told his fortune, chapter and verse.
A simple time – salvation or damnation
      One black and white device,
      Eternity foreshortened,
Earth a mere trusting step from Paradise.
O life where mystery grew on every bush,
      Saints, tyrants, thrills and throes
      Were for one end! – the traveller
Dips into your dreams and, sighing, goes.

After two hours we went on, for our destination
      Called. The adagio dance
Of olives, their immemorial routine and eccentric
      Variations of stance;
The vines that flourished like semaphore alphabets endlessly
      Flagging from hill to hill:
We knew them by heart now (or never would), seeing
                              them tiny

And common as tormentil.
Florence invisibly haled us. The intervening
  Grew misted with expectations,
Diminished yet weirdly prolonged, as all the go-between
  World by a lover's impatience.
Through Poggibonsi we glided – a clown's name
  And a history of hard knocks:
But nothing was real till at length we entered the
                              nonpareil
  City . . . A hand unlocks
The traveller's trance. We alight. And the just coming
                              down to
  Earth, the pure sense of arrival,
More than visions or masterpieces, fulfil
  One need for which we travel.

  This day, my bride of a day,
Went with me hand in hand the centuried road:
  I through her charmed eyes gazing,
She hanging on my words, peace overflowed.
  But now, a rose-gold Eve,
With the deep look of one who will unbosom
  Her sweetest to death only,
She opens out, she flames and falls like blossom.
  A spray that lightly trembles
After the warbler's flown. A cloud vibrating
  In the wash of the hull-down sun.
My heart rocks on. Remembering, or awaiting?

PART FIVE

Florence: Works of Art

Florence, father of Michelangelo,
Dante, da Vinci, Fra Angelico,
Cellini, Botticelli, Brunelleschi.
Giotto, Donatello, Masaccio! –

We shall not see their like, or yours, again.
Painters depart, and patrons. You remain,
Your bridges blown, your glory catalogued,
A norm for scholars and for gentlemen.

Reverend city, sober, unperplexed,
Turning your page to genius annexed
I breathe the mint and myrrh of Tuscan hills,
The tart aroma of some classic text.

Shields and medallions; overshadowing eaves
Like studious brows; the light that interleaves
Your past with amber: all's definitive, all
In changeless chiaroscuro one conceives.

I sometimes think that the heart is ne'er so dead
As where some vanished era overspread
The soil with titan foliage, scattering down
Eternal rubies when its bloom was shed.

Where rode Lorenzo, panoplied and plumed,
Where Savonarola burned, and Ruskin fumed,
The lady artist set her easel up,
The tourist with mild wonder is consumed.

Yet still the Arno navigably flows,
And saunterers past the Ponte Vecchio's
Jewel shops cast a shadow: here is still
A taste for life, a market for the rose.

Ah no, it's not the Florentines who fade
Before the statued loggia, the arcade,
The cliffs of floral stone. They live enough
In a pure tongue and a congenial trade.

Should the past overawe them? It's not theirs,
More than a mansion is the caretaker's.
A church by Giotto does as well as any
Other for this day's rendezvous or prayers.

What if along the pot-holed boulevards
Slogans are scrawled, not cantos? if postcards
Stand in for masterpieces, and ice cream
Says more to them than edifying façades?

The past is all-encroaching; and unless
They lopped its tentacles, stemmed its excess
To clear the air for some domestic seed,
They'd soon be strangled by a wilderness.

It's not the Florentine who pales beside
That vast, rank efflorescence. The pop-eyed
Tourist it is who rushes on his doom,
Armed with good taste, a Leica and a guide.

The primitive forest, the renaissance range
So massive are, surely they will estrange
Him from himself, or send him yelping home
To plastic novelties, to art's small change.

Plodding the galleries, we ask how can
That century of the Uncommon Man,
Sovereign here in paint, bronze, marble, suit
The new narcissism of the Also-Ran.

As many men, so many attitudes
Before the artifact. One writhes: one broods:
One preens the ego and one curls the lip:
One turns to stone, one to adjacent nudes.

Each man must seek his own. What do I seek?
Not the sole rights required by snob and freak,
The scholar's or the moralist's reward,
Not even a connoisseur's eye for technique;

But that on me some long-dead master may
Dart the live, intimate, unblinding ray
Which means one more spring of the selfhood tapped,
One tribute more to love wrung from my clay.

And if I miss that radiance where it flies,
Something is gained in the mere exercise
Of strenuous submission, the attempt
To lose and find oneself through others' eyes.

Singing Children: Luca Della Robbia

(T. H.)

I see you, angels with choirboy faces,
    Trilling it from the museum wall
As once, decani or cantoris,
    You sang in a carved oak stall,
Nor deemed any final bar to such time-honoured carollings
    E'er could befall.

I too gave tongue in my piping youth-days,
    Yea, took like a bird to crotchet and clef,
Antheming out with a will the Old Hundredth,
    Salem, or Bunnett in F.,
Unreckoning even as you if the Primal Sapience
    Be deaf, stone-deaf.

Many a matins cheerfully droned I
    To the harmonium's clacking wheeze,
Fidgeted much through prayer and sermon
    While errant bumblebees
Drummed on the ivied window, veering my thoughts to
    Alfresco glees.

But voices break – aye, and more than voices;
    The heart for hymn tune and haytime goes.
Dear Duomo choristers, chirping for ever
    In jaunty, angelic pose,
Would I had sung my last ere joy-throbs dwindled
    Or wan faith froze!

Judith and Holofernes: Donatello

(W. B. Y.)

. . . Next, a rich widow woman comes to mind
Who, when her folk were starving, dined and wined
Alone with Holofernes, until he
Grew rabid for her flesh. And presently,
Matching deceit with bitterer deceit,
She had struck off that tipsy captain's head
Upon the still untousled bed,
And borne it homeward in a bag of meat.

Old Donatello thought it out in bronze –
The wrists trailing, numb as it were from bonds;
The fuddled trunk lugged upright by a loop
Of hair; the falcon-falchion poised to stoop.
Tyrant, and tyrant's man, maybe:
Nevertheless, the sculptural face presents
A victim's irony, the mild innocence
Of passionate men whom passion has set free.

And she, the people's saviour, the patriot?
She towers, mouth brooding, eyes averted, not
In womanly compunction but her need
To chew and savour a vindictive deed;
Or so I construe it. One thing's sure –
Let a man get what issue he has earned,
Where death beds or love tussles are concerned
Woman's the single-minded connoisseur.

A political woman is an atrocious thing.
Come what may, she will have her fling
In flesh and blood. Her heady draughts cajole
A man only to cheat him, body or soul.
Judith took great Holofernes in.

For all the silver lamps that went before,
He made but a remnant on a knacker's floor:
She lives, the brazen kind of heroine.

Annunciation: Leonardo

(R. F.)

There was never a morning quite so tremendous again.
The birth, you think? I'm not for setting great store
By birth. Births aren't beginnings. And anyway
She only wanted to sleep off the pain
Which had made her a beast among beasts on the cow-
                                        house floor.
Shepherds and magnates tiptoeing through the hay
(You get all kinds at an inn, she drowsily thought),
Even the babe – they were part of a snowdrift trance,
Almost unreal. He was to prove a good son
In his way, though his way was beyond her. Whatever he
                                        sought
When he left home and led his friends such a dance,
He did not forget her as other boys might have done.

Her morning of mornings was when one flew to bring
Some news that changed her cottage into a queen's
Palace; the table she worked at shone like gold,
And in the orchard it is suddenly spring,
All bird and blossom and fresh-painted green.
What was it the grand visitor foretold
Which made earth heaven for a village Mary?
He was saying something about a Saviour Prince,
But she only heard him say, 'You will bear a child',
And that was why the spring came. Angels carry
Such tidings often enough, but never since
To one who in such blissful ignorance smiled.

Perseus Rescuing Andromeda: Piero di Cosimo

(W. H. A.)

It is all there. The victim broods,
Her friends take up the attitudes
    Right for disaster;
The winsome rescuer draws his sword,
While from the svelte, impassive fjord
Breaches terrific, dense and bored
    The usual monster.

When gilt-edged hopes are selling short,
Virtue's devalued, and the swart
    Avenger rises,
We know there'll always be those two
Strolling away without a clue,
Discussing earnestly the view
    Or fat-stock prices.

To either hand the crisis throws
Its human quirks and gestures. Those
    Are not essential.
Look rather at the oafish Dread,
The Cloud-man come to strike it dead,
Armed with a sword and gorgon's head –
    Magic's credentials.

White on the rocks, Andromeda.
Mother had presumed too far.
    The deep lost patience.
The nightmare ground its teeth. The saviour
Went in. A winning hit. All over.
Parents and friends stood round to offer
    Congratulations.

458

But when the vast delusions break
Upon you from the central lake,
　　　You'll be less lucky.
I'd not advise you to believe
There's a slick op. to end your grief
Or any nick-of-time reprieve.
　　　For you, unlikely.

Boy with Dolphin: Verrocchio

(D. T.)

At the crack of spring on the tail of the cold,
　　When foam whipped over the apple tree aisles
And the grape skin sea swelled and the weltering capes
　　　　　　　　　　　　　　　were bold,
　　I went to school with a glee of dolphins
　　Bowling their hoops round the brine tongued isles
And singing their scales were tipped by a sun always
　　　　　　　　　　　　　　　revolving.

　　Oh truant I was and trident and first
　　Lord of fishes, bearleading all tritons
In the swim of my blood before the foam brewed bubble
　　　　　　　　　　　　　　　burst.
　　And as I was nursling to mermaids, my sun
　　Cooed through their nestling grottoes a cadence
Of thrummed and choral reefs for the whale sounded gulfs
　　　　　　　　　　　　　　　to hum.

　　Those were the gambolling days I led
　　Leviathan a dance in my sea urchin glee
Till the lurching waves shoaled out with a school of
　　　　　　　　　　　　　　　wishes. My head

Was shells and ringing, my shoulders broke
Into a spray of wings. But the sea
Ran dry between two bars of foam, and the fine folk

In the temple of fins were flailed away
And the weed fell flat and the mermilk curdled,
And buoyant no more to bliss are the miles where alone I
                                           play
My running games that the waves once aisled,
With a doll of a lithe dead dolphin saddled,
And cold as the back of spring is my tale of the applefroth
                                              isles.

Elegy Before Death: At Settignano

(TO R. N. L.)

. . . for be it never so derke
Me thinketh I see hir ever mo.
CHAUCER

Come to the orangery. Sit down awhile.
The sun is setting: the veranda frames
An illuminated leaf of Italy.
Gold and green and blue, stroke upon stroke,
Seem to tell what nature and man could make of it
If only their marriage were made in heaven. But see,
Even as we hold the picture,
The colours are fading already, the lines collapsing
Fainting into the dream they will soon be.

Again? Again we are baffled who have sought
So long in a melting Now the formula
Of Always. There is no fast dye. Always! –
That is the word the sirens sing
On bone island. Oh stop your ears, and stop
All this vain peering through the haze,
The fortunate haze wherein we change and ripen,
And never mind for what. Let us even embrace
The shadows wheeling away our windfall days.

Again again again, the frogs are screeling
Down by the lilypond. Listen! I'll echo them –
Gain gain gain . . . Could we compel
One grain of one vanishing moment to deliver
Its golden ghost, loss would be gain

And Love step naked from illusion's shell.
Did we but dare to see it,
All things to us, you and I to each other,
Stand in this naked potency of farewell.

The villa was built for permanence. Man laid down
Like wine his heart, planted young trees, young pictures,
Young thoughts to ripen for an heir.
Look how these avenues take the long view
Of things ephemeral! With what aplomb
The statues greet us at the grassy stair!
Time on the sundial was a snail's migration
Over a world of warmth, and each day passing
Left on the fertile heart another layer.

The continuity they took for granted
We wistfully glamourize. So life's devalued:
Worth not a rhyme
These statues, groves, books, bibelots, masterpieces,
If we have used them only to grout a shaken
Confidence or stop up the gaps of time.
We must ride the flood, or go under
With all our works, to emerge, when it recedes,
Derelicts sluggish from the dishonouring slime.

Our sun is setting. Terrestrial planes shift
And slide towards dissolution, the terraced gardens
Quaver like waves, and in the garden urn
Geraniums go ashen. Now are we tempted, each
To yearn that his struggling counterpoint, carried away
Drowned by the flood's finale, shall return
To silence. Why do we trouble
A master theme with cadenzas
That ring out, fade out over its fathomless unconcern?

Love, more than our holidays are numbered.
Not one day but a whole life is drained off
Through this pinprick of doubt into the dark.
Rhadamanthine moment! Shall we be judged
Self-traitors? Now is a chance to make our flux
Stand and deliver its holy spark, –
Now, when the tears rise and the levees crumble,
To tap the potency of farewell.
What ark is there but love? Let us embark.

A weeping firmament, a sac of waters,
A passive chaos – time without wind or tide,
Where on brief motiveless eddy seethe
Lost faces, furniture, animals, oblivion's litter –
Envelop me, just as the incipient poem
Is globed in nescience, and beneath
A heart purged of all but memory, grows.
No landfall yet? No rift in the film? . . . I send you
My dove into the future, to your death.

*   *   *

A dove went forth: flits back a ghost to me,
Image of her I imagine lost to me,
Up the road through Fiesole we first travelled on
Was it a week or thirty years ago?
Time vanishes now like a mirage of water,
Touched by her feet returning whence she had gone,
Touched by the tones that darkly appeal to me,
The memories that make her shade as real to me
As all the millions breathing under the upright sun.

We are back at the first time we went abroad together.
Homing to this garden with a love-sure bent
Her phantom has come. Now hand in hand we stray
Through a long-ago morning mounting from a lather
Of azaleas and dizzy with the lemon blossom's scent.
And I seem to hear her murmur in the old romantic way,

'So blissfully, rosily our twin hearts burn here,
'This vernal time, whenever we return here,
'To haunter and haunted will be but yesterday.'

I follow her wraith down the terraced gardens
Through a dawn of nightingales, a murmurous siesta,
By leaf-green frogs on lily leaves screeling again
Towards eve. Is it dark or light? Fireflies glister
Across my noon, and nightlong the cicadas
Whir like a mechanical arm scratching in the brain.
All yesterday's children who fleetingly caressed her
Break ranks, break time, once more to join and part us:
I alone, who possessed her, feel the drag of time's harsh
                                        chain.

'Ah, you,' she whispers; 'are you still harping
'On mortal delusion? still the too much hoping
'Who needs only plant an acorn to dream a dryad's kiss?
'Still the doubtful one who, when she came to you
'Out of the rough rind, a naked flame for you,
'Fancied some knot or flaw in love, something amiss?'
Yes, such I am. But since I have found her
A revenant so fleshed in my memories, I wonder
Is she the real one and am I a wisp from the abyss.

Dare I follow her through the wood of obscurity –
This ilex grove where shades are lost in shade?
Not a gleam here, nothing differs, nothing sings, nothing
                                        grows,
For the trees are columns which ebonly support
A crypt of hollow silence, a subliminal thought,
A theorem proving the maggot equivalent to the rose.
Undiminished she moves here, shines, and will not fade.
Death, what had she to do with your futile purity,
The dogma of bone that on rare and common you would
                                        impose?

Her orbit clasped and enhanced in its diadem
All creatures. Once on a living night
When cypresses jetted like fountains of wine-warm air
Bubbling with fireflies, we going outside
In the palpitating dark to admire them,
One of the fireflies pinned itself to her hair;
And its throbbings, I thought, had a tenderer light
As if some glimmering of love inspired them,
As if her luminous heart was beating there.

Ah, could I make you see this subtle ghost of mine,
Delicate as a whorled shell that whispers to the tide,
Moving with a wavering watersilk grace,
Anemone-fingered, coral-tinted, under whose crystalline
Calm such naiads, angel fish and monsters sleep or slide;
If you could see her as she flows to me apace
Through waves through walls through time's fine mesh
                              magically drawn,
You would say, this was surely the last daughter of the
                              foam-born,
One whom no age to come will ever replace.

Eve's last fainting rose cloud; mornings that restored her
With orange tree, lemon tree, lotus, bougainvillea:
The milk-white snake uncoiling and the flute's light-
                              fingered charm:
Breast of consolation, tongue of tried acquaintance:
A tranquil mien, but under it the nervous marauder
Slithering from covert, a catspaw from a calm:
Heaven's city adored in the palm of a pictured saint:
My vision's *ara coeli*, my lust's familiar,
All hours, moods, shapes, desires that yield, elude,
                              disarm –

All woman she was. Brutalizing, humanizing,
Pure flame, lewd earth was she, imperative as air

465

And weak as water, yes all women to me.
To the rest, one of many, though they felt how she was
                                    rare
In sympathy and tasted in her warm words a sweetness
Of life that has ripened on the sunny side of the tree.
To herself a darker story, as she called her past to witness –
A heart much bruised, how often, how stormily surmising
Some chasmal flaw divided it from whole felicity.

So I bless the villa on the hill above Fiesole,
For here and now was flawless, and the past could not
                                    encroach
On its charmed circle to menace or to taunt her.
Oh, time that clung round her in unfading drapery,
Oh, land she wore like an enamelled brooch,
It was for remembrance you thus adorned her!
Now as I look back, how vividly, how gracefully
Ghosting there, she breathes me not the ghost of a
                                    reproach.
Happiness, it seems, can be the best haunter.

You later ones, should you see that wraith divulged for a
                                    moment
Through the sleep-haze of plumbago, glancing out from the
                                    loggia's
Vain dream of permanence as from a page
Time is already turning again, will you thus comment? –
'She is some dead beauty, no doubt, who queened here
                                    awhile
'And clasped her bouquets, and shrinks to leave the lighted
                                    stage:
'Not quite of the villa's classic period, though –
'Something more wistful, ironic, unstable in act and style,
'A minor masterpiece of a silver age.'

466

But to me she stands out tall as the Torcello madonna
Against a mosaic of sunlight, for ever upholding
My small, redeeming love. But 'love is all',
She says; and the mortal scene of planets and tides,
Animals, grass and men is transformed, proved, steadied
                        around me.
But her I begin to view through a thickening veil,
A gauze of tears, till the figure inscrutably fades –
As every vision must vanish, if we and it keep faith,
Into the racked, unappeasable flesh of the real.

*   *   *

But look, the garden storm is stilled, the flood
Blinked away like a tear, earth reconciled to
Her molten birth-bed's long prophetic throes!
Her hills are lizards in their solid trance
Of sun and stone: upon each hill
Vine and olive hold the archaic pose:
Below, the bubble dome looks everlasting
As heaven's womb, and threading the eyes of bridges
Arno endlessly into the loom of oblivion flows.

A ghost, the mere thought of a shade, has done it.
Testing the shifty face of the Now with a dove, I found
Terra firma. Whatever in me was born to praise
Life's heart of blood or stone here reached its zenith,
Conjuring, staying, measuring all by that meek shade . . .
Now, love, you have tried on your phantom dress,
Return to nakedness!
Be breathing again beside me, real, imperfect!
Enmesh, enact my dream till it vanishes!

The oranges are going out? Tomorrow
Will light them up again. Tomorrow will call you
With nightingales; tomorrow will leave
A rose by your plate, and freshen the plumbago's

Blue millinery and open a parasol
Of cedar for you, as it did for the first, ignorant Eve
Before exile or death was thought of. But we know well
On what tenure we have this garden. Each day's a livelier
Paradise when each dawn is a reprieve.

I imagine you really gone for ever. Clocks stop.
Clouds bleed. Flames numb. My world shrunk to an
        echoing
Memorial skull. (A child playing at hide-
And-seek suddenly feels the whole terrible truth of
        Absence.)
Too keen the imagined grief, too dearly gained
Its proof of love. I would let all else slide,
Dissolve and perish into the old enigma,
If that could keep you here, if it could keep
Even your sad ghost at my side.

But gold and green and blue still glows before us
This leaf of Italy, the colours fixed
The characters formed by love. It is love's way
To shine most through the slow dusk of adieu.
Long may it glow within us, that timeless, halcyon halt
On our rough journey back to clay.
Oh, may my farewell word, may this your elegy
Written in life blood from a condemned heart
Be quick and haunting even beyond our day.

PART SEVEN

The Homeward Prospect

TOM A word with you, my friends. High summer is
scorching up
Northwards through poplared Umbria to these foothills of
Tuscany.
But I notice a nip in the air, a recession in all around me –
Statues and groves and fountains adopting a cooler
attitude,
As if they were already waiving their claims upon us.

DICK I feel – oh look at the stream's face, innocently
asleep
But twitching as if a nightmare coursed it! Stagnant as ice,
Bland as silver it seems now: but fast and faster the drift of
Objects inexorably drawn onward unmasks it. I feel
Time's force. It is a last reach. I know the tug of the weir.

HARRY You should not take it to heart so, Dick. It is
merely one more
Holiday ending. Now is a chance to count the change,
To check the income against the outgoings, and find our
balance.
We shall come back some day – if only to demonstrate
Upon our person the law of diminishing returns.

TOM Coming or going, I care not, when poised, alert and
shimmering
Like angels on a pinpoint, we stand at the tip of departure.

DICK A point that is equidistant between two fields of
attraction
And thus, for me, the extreme agony.

469

HARRY   One or the other
Proves always the stronger field. You should regard such
                                                  occasions,
Dick, as limberings-up and rehearsals for a deathbed.

TOM Well, God save us all! What a way to encourage the
                                                      queasy
Traveller! We go home enriched.

DICK   Sobered

HARRY   Lightened:
Lightened of one illusion, and therefore one truth the
                                              richer.

TOM Enriched with extravagant draughts of the strange:
                                      after them, soberer.

DICK Sobered through sense of gain, by knowledge of loss
                                          enlightened –
Though what we have gained or lost is not yet apparent to
                                                        me,
Nor do I get any answer from these implausible word-plays.

HARRY Time will tell. In the meantime, let us imagine
                                        what Tom,
The boyish and indiscriminate collector, has filled our
                                          trunk with.

TOM Sapphires of lakes I declare, a tiara of diamond
                                          fireflies,
Emerald valleys aglow in platinum dawns, mosaic of
Noondays, ivory evenings with voices flowing like thick
                                                    silk:
Illuminated leaves torn from an Italian
Book of hours: frescoes and canvases by the masters;
A landscape with figures alive yet touched by the same
                                          genius:
Perfumes of contraband moments, essences of antiquity:

470

Nightingales, oxen, a hoopoe, cicadas and frogs –
miscellaneous
Curios rare as dirt and cheap as gold. I declare, too,
The wines of the country, the olive and maize of women's
flesh.

DICK That will do to go on with. And such of these
acquisitions
As we get past the paternal customs and heavy duties
Which await our return, I shall unpack in the front parlour
Where Harry will arrange them in the pattern his latest
aesthetic
Or ethic requires, to show off to our guests, like any travel-
bore.
Presently, chipped and tarnished, or crowded out, they will
find
Their way to the attic: and there, one morbid afternoon
When rooks are eddying round a backwater of brackish sky
And a blight smears over the streets, morosely rummaging I
Shall cut myself to the bone on some poignant cobwebbed
souvenir.

HARRY Let it be so. What Tom acquires for us has no
absolute
Value; nor, I admit, have the elegant systems wherein
I am disposed to compose it. There's no way even of telling
Which objects are really kin to us, which we've partaken
of life with,
Until, deep buried, they draw blood from us and are
eloquent.
Home is where we inter our travels, but equally give them
A chance to germinate beneath the dust and the
housework,
The preoccupied face of routine, the protective sleep of the
heart.
Thence, on a gust of travail, something is born, crying
'I am your flesh and blood!' . . . Let us look homeward, then.

471

TOM I see, as the plane booms into the beetling, vertical
                                              dark,
Gold and green and blue, amber and red, the lights of
A city like uncut gems in a jeweller's tray, tempting
And myriad below me. How precious now are the stones of
                                              London!
How deeply caressing the velvet blackness in which they
                                       are bedded!

DICK Soon my bees will be swarming, swirling and
                                    swarming upward
Like bonfire sparks in a gale. Let the early flowers be
                                         consumed,
The new cells built. I feel – and my harebell heart
                                         windlessly
Quivers with far-flown tremors – the tramp, tramp of
                                         Atlantic,
A funeral march plangent upon my uttermost shore.

HARRY I imagine our house repainted by absence, the
                                windowpanes cleaned,
A clearer view of the tangled streets, and the flowerbeds
                                              tidier.
I return to myself as it were to a son who, in the interval,
Has grown perceptibly older, filled out; or like the astral
Self flying back to a body refreshed by the night's vacation.

TOM Happy the natural nomad, sees home in a series of
                                        new lights!

DICK Blessed the born settler, whom all roads lead to
                                          home!

HARRY Can the human animal ever return, though, to its
                                        old form?

TOM Never. The form may remain; but the animal, being
                                     a mere sequence
Of current sensations, could not recognize it.

472

DICK   You're wrong.
The *human* animal carries his form

HARRY   Like a shell?

TOM   Like a prison –
Where, but for me, you'd be starving in solitary
                                        confinement.

DICK Neither a shell nor a prison. Say rather an x, a
                                        potential
Within him that cell by cell he has to incarnate, until
It sloughs him off one day and emerges, more or less
                                        perfect.

HARRY That is not quite what I meant. I wonder, to be
                                        explicit,
If the home to which our traveller returns may seem, not
                                        only
Changed by his prodigal experience, but estranged from
                                        him.

TOM Why yes. And that is surely one of the points of
                                        travelling:
The exotic veils we bring back and drape over the form of
The too familiar charmer, reviving her value, her mystery,
Compel us to woo her again.

DICK   I cannot take part in such make-believe.
Home, for me, is simply the place you can never quit;
An ideal home, if you like, which you spend a lifetime
                                        building
Out of whatever comes to hand – dropped bricks, last
                                        straws,
Love's mortar, the timbre and rubble of today, old stones
                                        from Italy.

HARRY I agree with you both, but will add *this*: our going
                                        abroad is

Only a shift in space, a projection of home's shadow,
Unless it enlarges us with a new concept whereby
We may reassemble the known in a different, more
                              luminous pattern,
The better to guide or follow our fateful thread of becoming.

TOM Must every holiday end in a kind of Royal
                              Commission?
I myself, like a sun-warmed stone or a satisfied lover,
Am purely grateful. Cannot one say so, and leave it at
                              that?

DICK Grateful exactly for what? Italy waits a tribute.

HARRY Let us sharpen our recollections and write in her
                              visitors' book.

TOM On the sill of languorous autumn a tortoise-shell or
                              red admiral
Called by a sunbeam opens the eyes of its dreamless wings,
Longs for a last flutter, rustles against the windowpane
Trembling in the draught of a heliotrope desire.
Italy was the sun that awoke me, the hand that opened
A window and released me into a new playground.
I spread my wings on her basking stones, with her bells I
                              quivered,
Then sipped the violet mountains and the lilies of her
                              valleys:
On dome after dome alighting, pirouetting through grave
                              arcades,
Dithering over the fruit in a marketplace, pinned to a
                              frieze or
Skimming the dew of flesh, I wilfully everywhere wafted
Like a soul freed from a body yet fraught with the body's
                              enthralments.
I have no call to improve myself or the shining hour:
There was only the dance, the butterfly kiss on each of a
                              thousand

474

Adorable things. That dance is the tribute I pay to Italy.

DICK   On a flank of the hard-faced Apennines, on the
                        threshold of sheer desolation,
I see a few acres of terraced farmland, ruled with olives
And ridged between for cereal, not a foot nor a clod
                                        wasted,
All snug and rooted against the barbarian hordes of
                                        boulders.
It is a composite picture: many such have I seen here –
Places where generation on generation labouring
Up to the last instant before the rock takes over,
Ploughing their legends back into the heart's fibre,
Hammering their need to a tool and an emblem of primary
                                        virtue,
Have kept man's nature green. It's here, and not in some
                                        absolute
Immaculate distance or lawn of idyllic dance, I have found
The piety glimpsed by my youth, the deity under the fable.
And whenever, amid the vapours and topheavy crags of the
                                        present,
I feel a handhold or lifeline, and grasp in myself the
                                        classical
Lineage of man's endurance, I shall remember Italy.

HARRY   On a lap of the road to Florence we passed a
                        Tuscan graveyard
Out in the fields at the far end of a cortege of cypresses,
Insulated and distanced from life, yet part of a frieze where
Living and dead are one to love's creative eye,
Embryos each of the other . . . I took our most cherished
                                        possession
And offered her to death. I took a ghost for my glass
And focused through it the inchoate, atomized face of
                                        becoming.
Then, from the tower in the sky to the tiniest flower on the
                                        earth's hem,

475

All was distinct, illustrious, full-formed in the light of
                           necessity,
Time's cocoon fallen away from the truth and kinship of
                           all things.
For one immeasurable moment the world's hands stood
                           still
And the worm that ticks at the heart of the golden hoard
                           was silent.
Losing my heart to this alien land, I renewed my true love:
Lending my love to death, I gained this grain of vision.
I took my pen. What I wrote is thanks to her and to Italy.

1953

PEGASUS
and other poems

TO JILL

479

480

PART ONE

Pegasus

(IN MEMORIAM: L. B. L.)*

It was there on the hillside, no tall traveller's story.
A cloud caught on a whin-bush, an airing of bleached
Linen, a swan, the cliff of a marble quarry –
It could have been any of these: but as he approached,
He saw that it was indeed what he had cause
Both to doubt and believe in – a horse, a winged white
horse.

It filled the pasture with essence of solitude.
The wind tiptoed away like an interloper,
The sunlight there became a transparent hood
Estranging what it revealed; and the bold horse-coper,
The invincible hero, trudging up Helicon,
Knew he had never before been truly alone.

It stood there, solid as ivory, dreamy as smoke;
Or moved, and its hooves went dewdropping so lightly
That even the wild cyclamen were not broken:
But when those hooves struck rock, such was their might
They tapped a crystal vein which flowed into song
As it ran through thyme and grasses down-along.

'Pegasus,' he called, 'Pegasus' – with the surprise
Of one for the first time naming his naked lover.
The creature turned its lordly, incurious eyes
Upon the young man; but they seemed to pass him over

---

* LBL was the poet Lilian Bowes Lyon.

As something beneath their pride or beyond their ken.
It returned to cropping the violets and cyclamen.

Such meekness, indifference frightened him more than any
Rumoured Chimaera. He wavered, remembering how
This milk-white beast was born from the blood of uncanny
Medusa, the nightmare-eyed: and at once, although
Its brief glance had been mild, he felt a cringing
And pinched himself to make sure he was not changing

Into a stone. The animal tossed its head;
The white mane lifted and fell like an arrogant whinny.
'Horses are meant to be ridden,' the hero said,
'Wings or no wings, and men to mount them. Athene
'Ordered my mission, besides, and certainly you
'Must obey that goddess,' he cried, and flung the lassoo.

The cyclamen bow their heads, the cicadas pause.
The mountain shivers from flank to snowy top,
Shaking off eagles as a pastured horse
Shakes off a cloud of flies. The faint airs drop.
Pegasus, with a movement of light on water,
Shimmers aside, is elsewhere, mocking the halter.

So there began the contest. A young man
Challenging, coaxing, pursuing, always pursuing
The dream of those dewfall hooves: a horse which ran
Quicksilver from his touch, sliding and slewing
Away, then immobile a moment, derisively tame,
Almost as if it entered into a game.

He summoned up his youth, his conscious art
To tire or trick the beast, criss-crossing the meadow
With web of patient moves, circling apart,
Nearing, and pouncing, but only upon its shadow.
What skill and passion weave the subtle net!
But Pegasus goes free, unmounted yet.

All day he tried for this radiant creature. The more he
Persevered, the less he thought of the task
For which he required it, and the ultimate glory.
So it let him draw close, closer – nearly to grasp
Its mane; but that instant it broke out wings like a spread
Of canvas, and sailed off easily overhead.

He cursed Pegasus then. Anger arose
With a new desire, as if it were some white girl
To stretch, mount, master, exhaust in shuddering throes.
The animal gave him a different look: it swirled
Towards him, circled him round in a dazzling mist,
And one light hoof just knocked upon his breast.

The pale sky yawns to its uttermost concave,
Flowers open their eyes, rivulets prance
Again, and over the mountainside a wave
Of sparkling air tumbles. Now from its trance
That holy ground is deeply sighing and stirring.
The heights take back their eagles, cicadas are whirring.

The furious art, the pursuer's rhythmic pace
Failed in him now. Another self had awoken,
Which knew – but felt no chagrin, no disgrace –
That he, not the winged horse, was being broken:
It was his lode, his lord, his appointed star,
He but its shadow and familiar.

So he lay down to sleep. Argos, Chimaera,
Athene in one solution were immersed.
Around him, on bush and blade, each dewdrop mirrored
A star, his riding star, his universe,
While on the moonlit flowers at his side
Pegasus grazed, palpable, undenied.

A golden bridle came to him in sleep –
A mesh of immortal fire and sensual earth,
Pliant as love, compulsive as the sweep
Of light-years, brilliant as truth, perfect as death.
He dreamed a magic bridle, and next day
When he awoke, there to his hand it lay.

Wings furled, on printless feet through the dews of morn
Pegasus stepped, in majesty and submission,
Towards him. Mane of tempest, delicate mien,
It was all brides, all thoroughbreds, all pent passion.
Breathing flowers upon him, it arched a superb
Neck to receive the visionary curb.

Pegasus said, 'The bridle that you found
'In sleep, you yourself made. Your hard pursuit,
'Your game with me upon this hallowed ground
'Forged it, your failures tempered it. I am brute
'And angel. He alone, who taps the source
'Of both, can ride me. Bellerophon, I am yours.'

Psyche

He came to her that night, as every night,
Through the dark palace in a shape of darkness –
Or rather, it seemed to her, of light made invisible;
Came in a torrential swoop of feet
Or wings, and taking her filled her with sweetness:

Then slept, as the gods sleep who have no need
To dream. But she, awake in that dream palace
Where the wine poured itself and instruments played
At their own sweet will, began to feel afraid
That it was all some trick of the Love-Queen's malice.

A virgin once I roamed – my thoughts were vague
As a mother-of-pearl sky – before this beauty
Had grown to isolate me like a plague
From men, and set my sisters in jealous league.
It was I then who envied Aphrodite.

'Your husband,' they say, 'your husband is a dragon
'Sent to devour you.' And truly I am devoured
With love. But the daytimes drag, the tongues wag,
Distorting his unseen face; and I grow weak.
Can it be love that makes me such a coward?

Timidly then she touched his flank, which flowed
Like a river dreaming of rapids. Flesh it was,
Not scales. Each limb retraced was a midnight road
Humming with memories: each warm breath sighed
'Foolish girl, to believe only her eyes!'

Drowsing she closed her petals over this new
Delicate trust. But a quick remorse pierced her
That, doubting him, she had clouded her own love too;
And with it a seeming-pure desire to know
The facts of him who had so divinely possessed her.

Flesh of my flesh – yet between me and him
This maidenhead of dark. A voice, a stir,
A touch – no more, and yet my spirit's home.
Man, god, or fiend – blindly I worship him:
But he will tire of a blind worshipper.

'You must not look,' he said: but now I believe
Without seeing, what harm can it be to gaze?
He said, 'It is a secret.' Oh but in love
There are no secrets! and how can I ever prove
My love till I know what it is I might betray?

487

So ran the fatal argument; and so,
Closer than night, equivocal as a spy,
Into bed between them stole the lie . . .
She rose and lit her lamp. In the hall below
The harp strings broke, the wine jars all ran dry.

Heavy with sight, alarmed at new-born shadows,
She groped towards him. Night drew back in awe,
And the light became a clear, impassable window
Through which her love could gaze but never go.
The lamp burned brighter, inflamed by what it saw.

O moon-white brow and milky way of flesh!
Wings like a butterfly's on a warm stone
Trembling asleep! O rod and fount of passion,
Godlike in act, estranged in revelation! –
Once you were mine, were me, for me alone.

O naked light upon our marriage bed,
Let me touch you again and be consumed!
No reaching through the radiance you shed?
Breaking my faith, myself I have betrayed.
We that were one are two. Thus am I doomed.

She grasped her knife, but it refused the breast
She offered. Trying a finger on his arrows
She pricked herself, and love was dispossessed
By love of love, which means self-love. Unblest,
Unchecked – what a serpent flame letched at her marrow!

Darkness she craved now – but oblivion's pall
Not the true night of union. Anyway
The lamp would not blow out. Along the wall
A taloned shadow-beast began to crawl
Fawning and glum toward its naked prey.

488

A drop of burning oil upon his bare
Shoulder awoke him. Shuddering he beheld
Crusted over that face so innocent-fair,
The hangdog look, the dissolute anxious glare
Of lust, and knew his treasure had been spoiled.

So he passed from her, and at last she learnt
How blind she had been, how blank the world can be
When self-love breaks into that dark room meant
For love alone, and on the innocent
Their nakedness dawns, outraging mystery.

Followed the tasks – millet seed, poppy seed
And all. They keep her fingers busy, bind
A gaping heart. She tells the grain like beads:
Yet it is not her penance, it is her need
Moves mercy, proves and touches the Divine.

Dear souls, be told by me. I would not take
Love as a gift, and so I had to learn
In the cold school of absence, memory's ache,
The busy, barren world of mend and make,
That my god's love is given but never earned.

Baucis and Philemon

You see those trees on the hillside over the lake
Standing together – a lime tree and an oak –
With a stone circle around them? A strange thing
To find two trees wearing a marriage ring,
You say? You would not, if you knew their story. Yes,
They are wedded: the roots embrace, the leaves caress
One another still. You can hear them gossip together,

489

Murmuring commonplaces about the weather,
Rocked by gusts of memory, like the old.
In this evening light their wall is a hoop of gold. . . .

Philemon gazed into the cooling hearth,
And the hearth stared listlessly back at one whose fire
Was all but ash. His hands hung down like dry leaves
Motionless in a summer's aftermath –
Planter's hands, they could make anything grow.
So labourers sit at the end of a day or a lifetime.
The old man drowsed by the fire, feeling his death
Ripen within him, feeling his lifetime gone
Like a may-fly's day, and nothing to show for all
The works and days of his hands but a beaten path
Leading nowhere and soon to be overgrown.
Beside him, Baucis absently traced her memories
Which seemed a brood of children scattered long since
Among far lands; but always in him, her own –
Husband and child – where they began, they ended.
Knuckled like bark, palmed thin as a saint's relics,
Her hands rested from love. There was love in the shine
Of the copper pans, the thrift of a mended coverlet,
The scrubbed and sabbath face of the elm-wood table.
But now this wordless love, which could divine
Even in sleep his qualms and cares, awoke
And out of the speaking silence between them, heard

To dwindle down, to gutter and go out,
Consenting to the dark or jerking agonized
Shadows on the white faces round me!
The year goes out in a flash of chrysanthemum:
But we, who cell by cell and
Pang upon pang are dragged to execution,
Live out the full dishonour of the clay.
A bright bewildered April, a trance-eyed summer –
Mirage of immortality: then

490

The mildew mists, the numbing frosts, and we
Are rotting on the bough, who ripen to no end
But a maggot's appetite.
Where are my memories? Who has taken the memories
I stored against these winter nights, to keep me warm?
My past is under snow – seed-beds, bud-grafts,
Flowering blood, globed hours, all shrouded, erased:
There I lie, buried alive before my own eyes.
Are we not poor enough already
That the gods must take away –

                                        'Hush, my dear,'
Said Baucis, and laid her finger upon his lips
Like a holy wafer. 'We must not even dream
Ill of the gods. I too fear Death, but I fear
Him most because he will take one of us first
And leave the other alive. I fear his cruelty
Less than his charity.'
                        There was a knock at the door.
Her heart cried out – He has come for us both, bless him!
But it was only a couple of tramps or tinkers,
A bearded one and a younger, begging food,
All other doors in the village closed against them.
'You are welcome. It's nice to have company once in a
                                        while,'
She said to the grimy wayfarers, and strewed
Clean coverlets on the willow-wood couch for them
To rest while she blew up the fire again. Philemon
Brought out a well-smoked ham and his autumn fruit –
Radishes, endives, apples and plums, a honeycomb.
'You wandering folk see much of the world,' he said.
'Ah yes, there's nothing my father has not seen
In his time,' the young man answered: 'except perhaps
An eagle nesting with two turtle doves.'
The other smiled in his beard: his gaze, serene
As if it could weigh the gods and find them wanting,

Weighed now those hands like skeleton leaves, the bird-
                                                    boned
Pair and the crumbs they shared, a copper pan
Gleaming, a rickety table freshened with mint.
All was amenity there, a calm sunshine
Of the heart. The young stranger, whose grey eyes
Were full of mischief and messages, winked at the elder:
'They could not treat us handsomer if we were gods.'
His companion nodded – at once the windless trees
In the orchard danced a fandango – and raised his cup
Of beechwood, charged to the brim with home-made wine:
'Philemon, a toast! I give you – your memories.'
He drained the cup; and when he had put it down,
It was still brimming. And in Philemon's soul
Welled up a miraculous spring, the wished release.

  I am blind no longer. My joys have come home to me
Dancing in gipsy colours from oblivion.
Back on their boughs are the fruits of all my seasons
Rosy from sleep still, ripened to the core.
Look at the autumn trees content with their workaday
Russet and the grass rejoicing for mere greenness,
As the spring paths I trod through garden, through orchard,
Were content with violets. Oh chime and charm
Of remembered Junes, of killer frosts returning
To smile and be forgiven! Oh temperate haze
Maturing my yesterdays, promise of good morrows! –
Seventy years have I lived with Contentment,
And now for the first time I see her face.
Now I can thank the gods, who mercifully
Changed my despair into a cup full of blessings
And made a vision grow where a doubt was planted.

Baucis, weeping and smiling, knelt to adore
The elder god: who said, 'You had a wish too?'
With a glance at her husband's shadowless face, she replied,

'You have done one miracle. How could I ask more?
He is content. What more did I ever ask?'
'Nevertheless, an unspoken prayer shall be answered
When the prayer is good, and not to have voiced the prayer
Is better. Death shall not part you. Now follow me.'
They helped each other up the slow hillside
Like pilgrims, while the two gods went before.
When they looked back, their cottage in the combe below
Was changed – cob walls to pearl and thatch to gold –
A lodge for deity, almost as marvellous
As the wonder in their eyes. 'Ah, that is no
Miracle,' Hermes said, 'or if it is,
The miracle is yours.' Then Zeus affirmed, 'The seed
Hears not the harvest anthem. I only show you
A jewel your clay has formed, the immortal face
Of the good works and days of your own hands:
A shrine after my heart. Because I know you
Faithful in love to serve my hearth, my earth,
You shall stay here together when you go. . . .'

They climbed that hill each evening of their lives
Until, one day, their clasped hands uttered leaves
And the tired feet were taken underground.
'Goodbye, dear wife,' he called as the bark closed round,
And his branches upheld the cry in a carol of birds.
She yearned to his oaken heart, with her last words
Sweet as lime blossom whispering on the air –
'It's not goodbye.'
                    We found them growing there
And built the wall around them; not that they need
A ring to show their love, or ever did.

Ariadne on Naxos

(A Dramatic Monologue)

Between the hero's going and the god's coming
She paced a flinty shore, her windflower feet
Shredded and bleeding, but the flesh was numb
Or the mind too delirious to heed
Its whimpers. From the shore she vainly dredged
The deep horizon with a streaming eye,
And her strained ears like seashells only fetched
A pure pale blare of distance. Listlessly
She turned inland. Berries on bushes there
Watched her like feral eyes: she was alone:
The darkening thicket seemed a monster's fur,
And thorn trees writhed into a threat of horns.
She walks a knife-edge here, between the woe
Of what is gone and what will never go.

O many-mooded One, you with the bared
Horizons in your eye, death in your womb,
Who draw the mariner down to a choked bed
And write his name upon an empty tomb –
Strangle him! Flay the flesh from his dishonoured
Bones, and kiss out his eyes with limpets! – No,
Drown my words! Who is the faithless now? Those eyes
Were true, my love. Last night, beside the myrtle,
You said 'For ever', and I saw the stars
Over your head, and then the stars were lost in
The flare and deluge of my body's dawn.
False dawn. I awoke. Still dark. Your print upon me
Warm still. A wind, chilling my nakedness,
Lisped with the sound of oars. It was too dark
To see the wake of your bold, scuttling ship,
Or I'd have reeled you back on that white line,
As once . . . Is it because I saved you then

494

That you run from me as from a place accursed?
   What is it in the bushes frightens me so?
A hide for nothing human. Coalfire eyes
Penning me on the beach. You had a kingdom
In your eyes. When you looked at me with love,
Were you only seeing a way to it through me?
I am a girl, unversed in the logic of heroes –
But why bring me so far, rescuing me
From my father's rage, to leave me on this island
For the wild beasts? leave me like a forgotten
Parcel, or a piece of litter you had no time
To bury when you had used it under the myrtle?
Already a star shows. It is a day, an age
Since we came here. Oh, solitude's the place
Where time congeals and memories run wild.
   I put the ball of thread into your hands.
It is my own heartstrings I am paying out
As you go down the tunnel. I live with you
Through the whole echoing labyrinth, and die
At each blind corner. Now you have come back with
A bloody sword, a conqueror's tired smile.
For you, the accustomed victory: for me,
Exultation, miracle, consummation.
Embracing you, the steel between us, I took
That blood upon myself, sealing our bond
Irrevocably with a smear of blood,
Forgetting that a curse lifted falls elsewhere
And weighs the heavier, forgetting whose blood it was.
Did you hear my mother's willing, harsh outcry
Under the bull, last night? and shrink from your
Accomplice in the hot act, remembering
Whose daughter she is and whose unnatural son
She helped you butcher in the labyrinth?
   I was a royal child, delicately nurtured,
Not to be told what happened once a year
Beneath the mosaic floor, while the court musicians

Played louder and my father's face went still
As a bird listening for worms. But the maids gossiped;
And one day, when I was older, he explained –
Something about war crimes, lawful deterrents,
Just compensation for a proved atrocity.
It seemed nothing to do with flesh and blood,
The way he talked. Men have this knack for embalming
And burying outraged flesh in sleek abstractions.
Have you, too, found already a form of words
To legitimize the murdering of our love?
Ah well, I was not guiltless – never a thought for
The writhing give-and-take of those reparations
Until, with the last consignment of living meat
To be fed to the man-bull in the maze, you came.
    You with the lion look among that huddle
Of shivering whelps – I watched you from the gate-tower
And trembled, not in pity, but afraid
For my own world's foundations. When our hands
Touched at the State Reception, I knew myself
A traitor, wishing that world away, and found
My woman's heart – sly, timorous, dangerous creature,
Docile but to the regent of her blood,
Despising the complexities men build
To cage or to hush up the brute within.
What were parents and kingdom then? or that
Poor muzzled freak in the labyrinth, my brother?
– Forgotten all. Forgetfulness, they say,
Is the gods' timeliest blessing or heaviest curse.
A bundle of fear and shame, too much remembering,
I lie, alone, upon this haunted isle.
    A victim for a victim is the law.
Is there no champion strong enough to break
That iron succession? Listen! What is this word
The bushes are whispering to the offshore breeze?
'Forget'? No. Tell me again. 'Forgive.' A soft word.
I'll try it on my tongue. Forgive. Forgive . . .

How strangely it lightens a bedevilled heart!
Come out of the thorn thicket, you, my brother,
My brother's ghost! Forgive the clue, the sword!
Forgive my fear of you! Dead, piteous monster,
You did not will the hungry maze, the horns,
The slaughter of the innocents. Come, lay
Your muzzle on my forsaken breast, and let us
Comfort each other. There shall be no more blood,
No more blood. Our lonely isle expands
Into a legend where all can dream away
Their crimes and wounds, all victims learn from us
How to redeem the Will that made them so.

So on the dark shore, between death and birth,
Clasping a ghost for comfort, the girl slept.
Gently the night breeze bore across that firth
Her last, relinquishing sob: like tears unwept,
Windflowers trembled in the eye of night
Under the myrtle. Absence whirred no more
Within her dreamless head, no victim cried
Revenge, no brute fawned on its conqueror.
At dawn, far off, another promise broken,
The hero's black sail brought his father death.
But on that island a pale girl, awoken
By more than sunlight, drew her quick, first breath
Of immortality, seeing the god bend down
And offer a hoop of stars, her bridal crown.

PART TWO

A Riddle

What is this bird
Who purloins the gold from your teeth, the pearls from
                                        your lips
To star in its nest
With any old garish domestic scraps and strips?
Who thieves for its hoard
Like a jackdaw, but builds as trig and snug as the goldcrest?

Who stabs her own breast
To nurture the nestlings? who fetches them worms in his
                                        beak
Out of sweet lawn or carrion?
What is this anomalous creature at once unique
As the phoenix chaste,
Faithful as bullfinch, immoral and many as sparrows?

A starling for fun,
For sorrow a nightingale; the golden oriole
Seen through umbrageous
Thickets; the lark which a clear sky swallows up whole:
This manifold one
Flies higher than rocketing hope, sings best in a cage.

Seasonable Thoughts for Intellectuals

(at Portland Bill, 1949)

Cold chisels of wind, ice-age-edged,
Hammered hard at the marble block of
This mutilated island. Wind like a wedge
Splitting the cross-grained, bitter sea.
What a pity no artist or master mason
Aims the blows blind Nature lays on!

Flint flakes of a wintry sea
Shaling off the horizon
In endless, anonymous, regimental order.
Fish or fowl should laugh to see
Such penitential hordes of water.
Not so merrily laugh we.

A shag, wave-hopping in emblematic flight
Across that molten iron, seems
Less a bird than the shadow of some bird above,
So invulnerably it skims.
But there's no sun, and Neptune's unreflective,
And anyway, who wants a fowl's directive? . . .

O sea, with your wolverine running,
Your slavering over the land's end,
Great waves gulping in granite pot-holes,
Smacking your lips at the rocks you'd devour,
Belching and belly-rumbling in caves,
Sucking your teeth on the shingle! –
How sad to think that, before
You've more than nibbled a trillionth of the meal,
A piece of jelly which came from your maw
Many aeons ago, and contracted a soul,
May atomize earth and himself and you –
Yes, blow the whole bloody issue back into the blue.

The Committee

So the committee met again, and again
Nailed themselves to the never-much-altered agenda,
Making their points as to the manner born,
Hammering them home with the skill of long practice.

These men and women are certainly representative
Of every interest concerned. For example, A. wears
Integrity like a sheriff's badge, while B.
Can grind an axe on either side of a question:
C. happens to have the facts, D. a vocation
For interpreting facts to the greater glory of Dogma:
E. is pompously charming, diffidently earnest,
F. is the acid-drop, the self-patented catalyst.
Our chairman's a prince of procedure, in temporizing
Power a Proteus, and adept in seeming to follow
Where actually he leads – as indeed he must be,
Or the rest would have torn him to pieces a long time ago.
Yet all, in a curious way, are public-spirited,
Groping with their *ad hoc* decisions to find
The missing, presumed omnipotent, directive.

Idly the sun tracing upon their papers
Doodles of plane-leaf shadows and rubbing them out:
The buzz of flies, the gen of the breeze, the river
Endlessly stropping its tides against the embankment:
Seasons revolving with colours like stage armies,
Years going west along the one-way street –
All these they ignore, whose session or obsession
Must do with means, not ends. But who called this meeting
Of irreconcilables? Will they work out some positive
Policy, something more than a *modus vivendi*?
Or be adjourned, *sine die*, their task half done?

So the committee, as usual, reached a compromise –
If reach is the word, denoting, as it ought to,
A destination (though why should destiny not
Favour a compromise, which is only the marriage
For better or worse between two or more incompatibles,
Like any marriage of minds?) and left the table,
There being no further business for today.
And the silent secretary wrote up the minutes,
Putting the leaves in order. For what? the eye
Of higher authority? or the seal of the dust?
Or again, to be dispersed irreparably
When the hinge turns and a brusque new life blows in?
And I regret another afternoon wasted,
And wearily think there is something to be said
For the methods of the dictatorships – I who shall waste
Even the last drops of twilight in self-pity
That I should have to be chairman, secretary,
And all the committee, all the one-man committee.

The Wrong Road

There was no precise point at which to say
'I am on the wrong road'. So well he knew
Where he wanted to go, he had walked in a dream
Never dreaming he could lose his way.
Besides, for such travellers it's all but true
That up to a point any road will do
As well as another – so why not walk
Straight on? The trouble is, *after* this point
There's no turning back, not even a fork;
And you never can see that point until
After you have passed it. And when you know
For certain you are lost, there's nothing to do

But go on walking your road, although
You walk in a nightmare now, not a dream.

But are there no danger-signs? Couldn't he see
Something strange about the landscape to show
That he was near where he should not be?
Rather the opposite – perhaps the view
Gave him a too familiar look
And made him feel at home where he had no right
Of way. But when you have gone so far,
A landscape says less than it used to do
And nothing seems very strange. He might
Have noticed how, mile after mile, this road
Made easier walking – noticed a lack
Of grit and gradient; *there* was a clue.
Ah yes, if only he had listened to his feet!
But, as I told you, he walked in a dream.

You can argue it thus or thus: either the road
Changed gradually under his feet and became
A wrong road, or else it was he who changed
And put the road wrong. We'd hesitate to blame
The traveller for a highway's going askew:
Yet possibly he and it became one
At a certain stage, like means and ends.
For this lost traveller, all depends
On how real the road is to him – not as a mode
Of advancement or exercise – rather, as grain
To timber, intrinsic-real.
                          He can but pursue
His course and believe that, granting the road
Was right at the start, it will see him through
Their errors and turn into the right road again.

The Pest

That was his youthful enemy, fouling the azure
With absolute mirk risen from god knows where –
A zero mood, action's and thought's erasure,
Impassable as rock, vapid as air.
When angels came, this imbecile thing infesting
His home retired to its sanctum below stairs;
But emerged, sooner or later, clammily testing
His hold on grace, his bond with the absent stars:
Till the horror became a need, the blacked-out sky
A promise that his angels would reappear,
A proof of light. Then the curse played its sly
Last trick – it thinned away, it was never there.
If it has gone for good, will he mope and die
Like a pauper with the lice washed out of his hair?

Almost Human

The man you know, assured and kind,
Wearing fame like an old tweed suit –
You would not think he has an incurable
Sickness upon his mind.

Finely that tongue, for the listening people,
Articulates love, enlivens clay;
While under his valued skin there crawls
An outlaw and a cripple.

Unenviable the renown he bears
When all's awry within? But a soul
Divinely sick may be immunized
From the scourge of common cares.

503

A woman weeps, a friend's betrayed,
Civilization plays with fire –
His grief or guilt is easily purged
In a rush of words to the head.

The newly dead, and their waxwork faces
With the look of things that could never have lived,
He'll use to prime his cold, strange heart
And prompt the immortal phrases.

Before you condemn this eminent freak
As an outrage upon mankind,
Reflect: something there is in him
That must for ever seek

To share the condition it glorifies,
To shed the skin that keeps it apart,
To bury its grace in a human bed –
And it walks on knives, on knives.

George Meredith, 1861

Whether it was or not his wish,
His real wish, he could never know:
But, after it happened, it seemed as if
A total stranger had struck the blow –
Some liberator out of the blue
Or hooded fanatic within himself.
The victim's cry for mercy came
Like a cry from his own heart, instantly gashed
By the knowledge of all he had aimed to undo.
So one they were, that severing blow
Could not but mortally hurt him too:

The deed came home to him in a flash
(Yet still too late), and at last he knew
The terrible meaning of 'one flesh'.

Historians now might take the view
That this was one more – though a crucial one –
Incident of his war within.
He'd been the battlefield long enough
As well as a combatant, when he withdrew
Scorching the earth behind him thus,
To whatever was left of integrity.
If they merely say that he saved his own skin,
They miss the point. Though he could not be
Occupied, utterly possessed again,
He has bought invulnerability
Too dear: such broad areas blackened, deadened –
How few of those sensitive threads remain
Which kept him in touch with hell, with heaven!

Betrayal is always a self-betrayal
Where love is concerned. The beautiful place,
Mortgaged by our ancestral sin,
Grows more untenable and more unreal
Each time, however needfully, we sell
Some share of it, buying with certain loss
Uncertain reprieve for our dwindling demesne . . .
So he, whose choice or necessity willed
The blackened earth, the liberating blow,
Is pent in the fruitless policies of brain.
While through his ghostly orchards tread
A murdered love and án unfulfilled
Agony, he walks elsewhere; and oh!
His silenced heart cannot tell him he is dead.

The Mirror

To make a clean sweep was the easiest part,
Though difficult enough. Anger of grief
Strengthened her hand and kept the silly heart
From dallying over his relics for relief.

To burn the letters, send back the keepsakes, wipe
His fingerprints off what little remained her own –
The girl stood over herself with a swift whip
And lashed until the outrageous task was done.

She had detached her flesh from his flesh, torn
It loose like a sea-anemone from a rock.
Now in that bare room where, lest he return,
All else was changed (she could not change the lock)

She took one careful invalid step, gauging
How much the ice of solitude would bear,
Then sat to her glass, as women do, assuaging
Chaotic thoughts with the clear, known image there.

No blood at the lips, no scars on the limpid brow,
Her face gazed out, vacant and undistracted,
A mere proscenium – nothing to show
For the tragedy, or farce, lately enacted.

True, it was not the first time nor the second
That love had lured her into a dead end.
She knew it all: but on this she had not reckoned –
The trick of a mirror upon the wall behind

Which cast in hers an endless, ever-diminished
Sequence of selves rejected and alone,
Cast back in her teeth the falsehood that she was finished
With love's calamities, having survived this one.

Seven devils, each worse than the one she had expelled,
Entering now that swept and garnished room,
Image on image on image in the glass she felt
Sucking her down into a vacuum,

A hell of narrowing circles. Time and again
Would she sit at the glass, helplessly reviling
The self that had linked her failures into a chain,
An ineluctable pattern. Love's too willing

Victim and love's unwilling poisoner, she
Would always kill the joys for which she died.
'Deep within you,' whispered the fiends, 'must be
'A double agent, false to either side. . . .'

Fallen at last, hurled beyond hope or terror,
Gathering doom about her, the girl now saw
Her hand, which had not strength to break the mirror,
Grope for the sleeping tablets in a drawer.

Love and Pity

Love without pity is a child's hand reaching,
A behemoth trampling, a naked bulb within
A room of delicate tones, a clown outraging
The heart beneath the ravished, ravisher skin.
Pity without love is the dry soul retching,
The strained, weak azure of a dog-day sky,
The rescuer plunging through some thick-mined region
Who cannot rescue and is not to die.
Pitiless love will mean a death of love –
An innocent act, almost a mercy-killing:
But loveless pity makes a ghost of love,

507

Petrifies with remorse each vein of feeling.
Love can breed pity. Pity, when love's gone,
Bleeds endlessly to no end – blood from stone.

The Tourists

Arriving was their passion.
Into the new place out of the blue
Flying, sailing, driving –
How well these veteran tourists knew
Each fashion of arriving.

Leaving a place behind them,
There was no sense of loss: they fed
Upon the act of leaving –
So hot their hearts for the land ahead –
As a kind of pre-conceiving.

Arrival has stern laws, though,
Condemning men to lose their eyes
If they have treated travel
As a brief necessary disease,
A pause before arrival.

And merciless the fate is
Of him who leaves nothing behind,
No hostage, no reversion:
He travels on, not only blind
But a stateless person.

Fleeing from love and hate,
Pursuing change, consumed by motion,
Such arrivistes, unseeing,

Forfeit through endless self-evasion
The estate of simple being.

In Memory of Dylan Thomas

'it was Adam and maiden'

Too soon, it is all too soon
Laments our childhood's horn
Husky and cool at the close
Of its dove-note afternoon.
Too soon, a red fox echoes
Old on the hunted hill
Where dewfall mirrors the dawn
And dawn rides out for a kill.
It is too soon, too soon
Wails the unripened barley
To flailing storms: *too soon*
Pipes the last frail leaf in the valley.

A poet can seem to show
Animal, child and leaf
In the light of eternity, though
It is but the afterglow
From his consuming love,
The spill of a fabulous dawn
Where animal, leaf and child,
Timelessly conceived,
With time are reconciled.

Now we lament one
Who danced on a plume of words,
Sang with a fountain's panache,
Dazzled like slate roofs in sun

After rain, was flighty as birds
And alone as a mountain ash.
The ribald, inspired urchin
Leaning over the lip
Of his world, as over a rock pool
Or a lucky dip,
Found everything brilliant and virgin,
Like Adam who went to school
Only with God, and like Adam
He gave that world a tongue.
Already he has outsung
Our elegies, who always
Drew from creation's fathomless
Grief a pure drop of praise.

Elegiac Sonnet

TO NOEL MEWTON-WOOD

A fountain plays no more: those pure cascades
And diamond plumes now sleep within their source.
A breath, a mist of joy, the woodsong fades –
The trill, the transport of his April force.

How well these hands, rippling from mood to mood,
Figured a brooding or a brilliant phrase!
Music's dear child, how well he understood
His mother's heart – the fury and the grace!

Patient to bear the stern ordeal of art,
Keyed to her ideal strain, he found too hard
The simple exercise of human loss.

He took the grief away, and we are less.
Laurels enough he had. Lay on his heart
A flower he never knew – the rose called Peace.

Final Instructions

For sacrifice, there are certain principles –
Few, but essential.

I do not mean your ritual. This you have learnt –
The garland, the salt, a correct use of the knife,
And what to do with the blood:
Though it is worth reminding you that no two
Sacrifices ever turn out alike –
Not where this god is concerned.

The celebrant's approach may be summed up
In three words – patience, joy,
Disinterestedness. Remember, you do not sacrifice
For your own glory or peace of mind:
You are there to assist the clients and please the god.

It goes without saying
That only the best is good enough for the god.
But the best – I must emphasize it – even your best
Will by no means always be found acceptable.
Do not be discouraged:
Some lizard or passing cat may taste your sacrifice
And bless the god: it will not be entirely wasted.

But the crucial point is this:
You are called only to *make* the sacrifice:
Whether or no he enters into it

Is the god's affair; and whatever the handbooks say,
You can neither command his presence nor explain it –
All you can do is to make it possible.
If the sacrifice catches fire of its own accord
On the altar, well and good. But do not
Flatter yourself that discipline and devotion
Have wrought the miracle: they have only allowed it.

So luck is all I can wish you, or need wish you.
And every time you prepare to lay yourself
On the altar and offer again what you have to offer,
Remember, my son,
Those words – patience, joy, disinterestedness.

PART THREE

The House Where I Was Born

An elegant, shabby, white-washed house
With a slate roof. Two rows
Of tall sash windows. Below the porch, at the foot of
The steps, my father, posed
In his pony trap and round clerical hat.
This is all the photograph shows.

No one is left alive to tell me
In which of those rooms I was born,
Or what my mother could see, looking out one April
Morning, her agony done,
Or if there were pigeons to answer my cooings
From that tree to the left of the lawn.

Elegant house, how well you speak
For the one who fathered me there,
With your sanguine face, your moody provincial charm,
And that Anglo-Irish air
Of living beyond one's means to keep up
An era beyond repair.

Reticent house in the far Queen's County,*
How much you leave unsaid.
Not a ghost of a hint appears at your placid windows
That she, so youthfully wed,
Who bore me, would move elsewhere very soon
And in four years be dead.

* Queen's County: now Co. Laois.

I know that we left you before my seedling
Memory could root and twine
Within you. Perhaps that is why so often I gaze
At your picture, and try to divine
Through it the buried treasure, the lost life –
Reclaim what was yours, and mine.

I put up the curtains for them again
And light a fire in their grate:
I bring the young father and mother to lean above me,
Ignorant, loving, complete:
I ask the questions I never could ask them
Until it was too late.

Father to Sons*

That is the house you were born in. Around it
A high old box-hedge inked out the view:
And this the garden it buxomly bounded,
Where salvia, syringa, tobacco plants grew
Sheltered like you.

From snapshot to snapshot you can see yourselves growing
And changing like figures on a dawn-struck frieze.
Ah, swift enough for my after-knowing
That growth: but then you seemed to increase
By mere coral degrees.

So, to my fondness, you still may linger
There at your romps and poker-faced ploys

* The house was Box Cottage, Charlton Kings. CDL was, for once, inexact in this poem
in his use of the beautiful word Syringa – given to mock orange or philadelphus in those
days. Syringa is the lilac genus.

Under the sweet pale downpour of syringa,
  Brief and sweet as all natural joys
    In pathos and poise.

But you – what will you think of me, say of me,
  Turning these photographs over, years hence,
When I am dead? What shadow or ray of me
  Lingering for you then will cloud or enhance
    Their brilliance?

Not the garden idyll, but a serpent mood it
  Concealed from the lens; not the innocent fall
Of light, but how I would often occlude it
  With guardian stance: is it this, above all,
    That you must recall?

How often did words of mine, words out of season,
  Leave smouldering chagrin like fag-ends to char
Your fresh-painted sill of life! my unreason
  Or too much reason chill the air
    For your tendril career!

If such bewilderments made your Eden
  A state you could not be sorry to slough,
Forgive. I still had much that even
  A god only gets at through mortal stuff
    To learn about love.

Son and Father

By the glim of a midwinterish early morning
Following habit's track over comatose fields,
A path of bleak reminder, I go to receive
The sacraments from my father, thirty years back.

Afterwards, walking home, unannealed, implacable,
I knew in the bones of my age this numb, flayed air,
These frozen grassblades rasping the foot, those hoar-drops
Which hung from a branch all day like unredeemed
                                        pledges.

Oh, black frost of my youth, recalcitrant time
When love's seed was benighted and gave no ear
To others' need, you were seasonable, you were
In nature: but were you as well my nature's blight?

That was thirty years back. The father is dead whose image
And superscription upon me I had to efface
Or myself be erased. Did I thus, denying him, grow
Quite dead to the Father's grace, the Son's redemption?

Ungenerous to him no more, but unregenerate,
Still on a frozen earth I stumble after
Each glimmer of God, although it lights up my lack,
And lift my maimed creations to beg rebirth.

Christmas Eve

Come out for a while and look from the outside in
At a room you know
As the firelight fitfully beats on the windowpane –
An old heart sinking low,
And the whispering melting kisses of the snow
Soothe time from your brow.

It is Christmastide. Does the festival promise as fairly
As ever to you? 'I feel
The numbness of one whose drifted years conceal
His original landmarks of good and ill.
For a heart weighed down by its own and the world's folly
This season has little appeal.'

But tomorrow is Christmas Day. Can it really mean
Nothing to you? 'It is hard
To see it as more than a time-worn, tinsel routine,
Or else a night incredibly starred,
Angels, oxen, a Babe – the recurrent dream
Of a Christmas card.'

You must try again. Say 'Christmas Eve'. Now, quick,
What do you see?
'I see in the firelit room a child is awake,
Mute with expectancy
For the berried day, the presents, the Christmas cake.
Is he mine? or me?'

He is you, and yours. Desiring for him tomorrow's
Feast – the crackers, the Tree, the piled
Presents – you lose your self in his yearning, and borrow
His eyes to behold
Your own young world again. Love's mystery is revealed
When the father becomes the child.

'Yet would it not make those carolling angels weep
To think how incarnate Love
Means such trivial joys to us children of unbelief?'
No. It's a miracle great enough
If through centuries, clouded and dingy, this Day can keep
Expectation alive.

'The Years O'

The days are drawing in,
A casual leaf falls.
They sag – the heroic walls;
Bloomless the wrinkled skin
Your firm delusions filled.
What once was all to build
Now you shall underpin.

The day has fewer hours,
The hours have less to show
For what you toil at now
Than when long life was yours
To cut and come again,
To ride on a loose rein –
A youth's unbroken years.

Far back, through wastes of ennui
The child you were plods on,
Hero and simpleton
Of his own timeless story,
Yet sure that somewhere beyond
Mirage and shifting sand
A real self must be.

Is it a second childhood,
No wiser than the first,
That we so rage and thirst
For some unchangeable good?
Should not a wise man laugh
At desires that are only proof
Of slackening flesh and blood?

Faster though time will race
As the blood runs more slow,
Another force we know:
Fiercer through narrowing days
Leaps the impetuous jet,
And tossing a dancer's head
Taller it grows in grace.

Lot 96*

Lot 96: a brass-rimmed ironwork fender.
It had stood guard for years, where it used to belong,
Over the hearth of a couple who loved tenderly.
Now it will go for a song.

Night upon winter night, as she gossiped with him
Or was silent, he watched the talkative firelight send
Its reflections twittering over that burnished rim
Like a language of world without end.

Death, which unclasped their hearts, dismantled all.
The world they made is as if it had never been true –

* From 1953–1957 we lived at 96 Campden Hill Road, London.

That firelit bubble of warmth, serene, magical,
Ageless in form and hue.

Now there stands, dulled in an auction room,
This iron thing – a far too durable irony,
Reflecting never a ghost of the lives that illumed it,
No hint of the sacred fire.

This lot was part of their precious bond, almost
A property of its meaning. Here, in the litter
Washed up by death, values are re-assessed
At a nod from the highest bidder.

Time to Go*

The day they had to go
Was brilliant after rain. Persimmons glowed
In the garden behind the castle.
Upon its wall lizards immutably basked
Like vitrified remains
Of an archaic, molten summer. Bronze
Cherubs shook down the chestnuts
From trees over a jetty, where fishing nets
Were sunshine hung out in skeins
To dry, and the fishing boats in their little harbour
Lay breathing asleep. Far
And free, the sun was writing, rewriting ceaselessly
Hieroglyphs on the lake –
Copying a million, million times one sacred
Vanishing word, peace.
The globed hours bloomed. It was grape-harvest season,

* Torre del Benaco 1951. The first Italian visit after our marriage.

520

And time to go. They turned and hurried away
With never a look behind,
As if they were sure perfection could only stay
Perfect now in the mind,
And a backward glance would tarnish or quite devalue
That innocent, golden scene.
Though their hearts shrank, as if not till now they knew
It was paradise where they had been,
They broke from the circle of bliss, the sunlit haven.
Was it for guilt they fled?
From enchantment? Or was it simply that they were driven
By the migrant's punctual need?
All these, but more – the demand felicity makes
For release from its own charmed sphere,
To be carried into the world of flaws and heartaches,
Reborn, though mortally, there.
So, then, they went, cherishing their brief vision.
One watcher smiled to see
Them go, and sheathed a flaming sword, his mission
A pure formality.

On a Dorset Upland

The floor of the high wood all smoking with bluebells,
Sap a-flare, wildfire weed, a here-and-gone wing,
Frecklings of sunlight and flickerings of shadowleaf –
How quick, how gustily kindles the spring,
Consumes our spring!

Tall is the forenoon of larks forever tingling:
A vapour trail, threading the blue, frays out
Slowly to a tasselled fringe; and from horizon
To horizon amble white eternities of cloud,
Sleepwalking cloud.

521

Here in this niche on the face of the May morning,
Fast between vale and sky, growth and decay,
Dream with the clouds, my love, throb to the awakened
Earth who has quickened a paradise from clay,
Sweet air and clay.

Now is a chink between two deaths, two eternities.
Seed here, root here, perennially cling!
Love me today and I shall live today always!
Blossom, my goldenmost, at-long-last spring,
My long, last spring!

Dedham Vale, Easter 1954

FOR E. J. H.

It was much the same, no doubt,
When nature first laid down
These forms in his youthful heart.
Only the windmill is gone
Which made a miller's son
Attentive to the clouds.

This is the vale he knew –
Its games of sun and shower,
Willow and breeze, the truant
Here-and-there of the Stour;
And an immutable church tower
To polarize the view.

Yet, earnestly though we look
At such hard facts, the mill,
The lucid tower and the lock
Are something less than real.

For this was never the vale
He saw and showed unique –

A landscape of the heart,
Of passion nursed on calm,
Where cloud and stream drew out
His moods, and love became
A brush in his hand, and the elm tree
Lived like a stroke of art.

His sunburst inspiration
Made earthly forms so true
To life, so new to vision,
That now the actual view
Seems a mere phantom, through
Whose blur we glimpse creation.

It wears a golden fleece
Of light. However dull
The day, one only sees here
His fresh and flying colours –
A paradise vale where all is
Movement and all at peace.

The Great Magicians

To fish for pearls in Lethe,
Wash gold from age-long grief;
To give infinity a frame,
The may-fly a reprieve:

In a calm phrase to utter
The wild and wandering sky;

To reconcile a lover's Eden
With a madman's sty:

To mediate between
The candle and the moth;
To plug time's dripping wound, or spin
A web across hell's mouth:

Such feats the great magicians
Found within their powers,
Whose quick illusions bodied out
A world more whole than ours.

But the hollow in the breast
Where a God should be –
This is the fault they may not
Absolve nor remedy.

Moods of Love

1

The melting poles, the tongues that play at lightning,
All that gross hurricane hatched from a sigh –
These are the climax to his sure routine.
But first, a glance coins gold in the air, doves issue
From clasped hands, knots no one saw tied are tightening;
The card you chose, or were made to, wondrously
Turns up here there and anywhere like a djinn,
And borrowed time vanishes to amaze you.

Admire the 'fluence of this conjuring
As once again he runs the gamut through
Of tricks you can neither fathom nor resist,

Though well you know the old Illusionist
Employs for his whole repertoire only two
Simple properties – a rod, a ring.

2

Think of his transformations; thirsty babe,
Secret companion, devil, confidante,
Lapdog and sphinx – each hides that king whose orb
Is the whole earth grasped in a bare 'I want'.
Redder the rose for him, sadder the fall,
Who swells a trivial word into a portent,
Turns dust to diamond, shows the bantam tall,
The giant weak: nevertheless, most potent
When he comes back insidious and subdued
As an old jailbird begging one more chance.
Whether you trust him then, or look askance,
Or slam your door, at least don't act the prude:
He's what you've made of him: plausible, lewd
Or tough, he's your flesh – was a pure child once.

3

'Oh shelter me from the invisible rain
Corrodes my flesh piecemeal! Oh take me in –
I'll be your god, your man, your mannikin!'
Cry the gaunt lecher and the ignorant swain.

Dipped in eternity now, they find nowhere
A flaw in the magic circle of their embracing:
Two are reborn as one: where all is passing
They dream a now for ever and set fair.

Reborn! The very word is like a bell.
From the warm trance, the virgin arms awoken,

Each turns to his sole self. Out of the shell
They step, unchanged. Only a spell is broken.

Though there's no cure, no making whole, no fusion,
Live while you can the merciful illusion.

4

See, at a turn of her wrist, paradise open;
Dote, lover, upon a turquoise vein;
Feel how the blood flowers and the nerves go lilting
Like butterflies through an immortal blue.
This is creation morning. What could happen
But miracles here? The god you entertain,
The pure legend you breathe, no desert silting
Over your garden ever makes untrue.

New-seen, first-named, your own to hurt and heal,
This commonplace of skin, bone, habit, sense
Is now a place that never was before.
Lose and possess yourself therein: adore
The ideal clay, the carnal innocence.
Where all's miraculous, all is most real.

5

Inert, blanched, naked, at the gale's last gasp
Out of their drowning bliss flung high and dry
Above the undertow, the breakers' rasp,
With shells and weed and shining wrack they lie.
Or, as an isle asleep with its reflection
Upon the absolute calm, each answers each
In the twin trance of an unflawed affection
That shows the substance clear, the dream in reach.
By one arched, hollowing, toppling wave uptossed
Together on the gentle dunes, they know

A world more lucid for lust's afterglow,
Where, fondly separate, blind passion fused
To a reflective glass, each holds in trust
The other's peace, and finds his real self so.

6

The dance, the plumage, all that flaunting day
Of blood's clairvoyance and enchanter's wit
Making trite things unique – you reckon it
Tells more than brute necessity at play?

Unwise. Another tedious, piteous woman
Was Helen, got by heart. Can you adore
The human animal's ecstasy, yet ignore
The ground and primitive logic of being human? –

Deplore that closest viewed is clearliest changing,
And least enduring is the most enthralling?
That love breeds habit, habit brings estranging?
That highest flown means most abysmal falling?

When the flushed hour goes down, what residue
From its broad-glittering flood remains to you?

7

Shells, weed, discoloured wrack – a spring tide's litter
Dully recalling its lost element,
And one you live with, quarrelsome or complying,
Are all that's left of Aphrodite's birth.
Gone is the power she gave you to delight her,
The period of grace, so quickly spent,
When the day's walk was a white dream of flying,
Earth a far cry, she a sufficient earth.

Whether long use has now choked your desire
With its own clinker, or, abruptly parted
At love's high noon, incredulous you have stood
Suffering her absence like a loss of blood
Week after week, still, by the god deserted,
You worship relics of a sacred fire.

8

Beware! Such idolizing can divorce
Body and mind: the foam-bright fiction drains
Purpose away and sings you from your course.
Better a brutal twitching of the reins
And off, than this devouring pious whore
Who in a soft regret will twine you fast
Where thigh-bones mope along the tainted shore
And crazed beachcombers pick over their past.
Love is the venturing on: think – as you fare
Among strange islands, each a phantasy
Of home, giving your strength to what must be
Found and new-found through doubt, mirage, despair –
Weaving, unweaving her true self somewhere
Deep in your heart grows a Penelope.

9

If love means exploration – the divine
Growth of a new discoverer first conceived
In flesh, only the stranger can be loved:
Familiar loving grooves its own decline.

If change alone is true – the ever-shifting
Base of each real or illusive show,
Inconstancy's a law: the you that now
Loves her, to otherness is blindly drifting.

But chance and fretting time and your love change her
Subtly from year to year, from known to new:
So she will always be the elusive stranger,
If you can hold her present self in view.

Find here, in constant change, faithful perceiving,
The paradox and mode of all true loving.

Last Words

Suppose, they asked,
You are on your death-bed (this is just the game
For a man of words),
With what definitive sentence will you sum
And end your being? . . . Last words: but which of me
Shall utter them?

– The child, who in London's infinite, intimate darkness
Out of time's reach,
Heard nightly an engine whistle, remote and pure
As a call from the edge
Of nothing, and soon in the music of departure
Had perfect pitch?

– The romantic youth
For whom horizons were the daily round,
Near things unbiddable and inane as dreams,
Till he had learned
Through his hoodwinked orbit of clay what Eldorados
Lie close to hand?

– Or the ageing man, seeing his lifelong travel
And toil scaled down

To a flimsy web
Stranded on two dark boughs, dissolving soon,
And only the vanishing dew makes visible now
Its haunted span?

Let this man say,
Blest be the dew that graced my homespun web.
Let this youth say,
Prairies bow to the treadmill: do not weep.
Let this child say,
I hear the night bird, I can go to sleep.

1957

THE GATE
and other poems

TO
PEGGY AND JEREMY

534

Acknowledgments are due to the editors of periodicals in which a number of these poems have appeared – the *Critical Quarterly*, *Encounter*, the *Listener*, the *London Magazine*, the *New Yorker*, *Stand*, *The Times Literary Supplement*, the *Transatlantic Review*, the *Twentieth Century*, *Unicorn*. The verses on pp. 578–9 are reproduced by permission of the proprietors of *Punch*.

'The Disabused' and 'Not Proven' were broadcast on the Third Programme of the B.B.C. in May 1960.

'The Unexploded Bomb' is part of the Prologue written for a midnight matinée, held in the Royal Festival Hall, in aid of the Campaign for Nuclear Disarmament.

'The Christmas Rose', in a setting by Alan Ridout, was sung by the University of London Musical Society in St Paul's Cathedral on December 7th, 1961.

'Requiem for the Living' was written for music, and set by Donald Swann.

Bread and Wine

A cornfield, moon-bemused
And crocketed with stooks,
Or shining spheres upon the vine
Are food and drink to one who looks

Beyond his nose. Another
May draw some aliment,
Estimating what's the yield of
Matured existence they present.

We labourers in this field
Have not the same concern,
Being strictly bound to melt into
The shoots we tend, the earth we turn.

Our dirt, our drought have grown
That heady stuff they pour you:
It is our hunger makes the bread,
We who are blessed and broken for you.

These staple foods ignore,
Take, or spit out like phlegm;
But do not think to isolate
What was absorbed in making them.

Your uttermost communion
With us labouring men
Is in the joy that we rejoiced with,
Being consumed by grape and grain.

The Gate

FOR TREKKIE

In the foreground, clots of cream-white flowers (meadow-
                                        sweet?
Guelder? Cow parsley?): a patch of green: then a gate
Dividing the green from a brown field; and beyond,
By steps of mustard and sainfoin-pink, the distance
Climbs right-handed away
Up to an olive hilltop and the sky.

The gate it is, dead-centre, ghost-amethyst-hued,
Fastens the whole together like a brooch.
It is all arranged, all there, for the gate's sake
Or for what may come through the gate. But those white
                                        flowers,
Craning their necks, putting their heads together,
Like a crowd that holds itself back from surging forward,
Have their own point of balance – poised, it seems,
On the airy brink of whatever it is they await.

And I, gazing over their heads from outside the picture,
Question what we are waiting for: not summer –
Summer is here in charlock, grass and sainfoin.
A human event? – but there's no path to the gate,
Nor does it look as if it was meant to open.
The ghost of one who often came this way
When there was a path? I do not know. But I think,
If I could go deep into the heart of the picture

From the flowers' point of view, all I would ask is
Not that the gate should open, but that it should
Stay there, holding the coloured folds together.
We expect nothing (the flowers might add), we only
Await: this pure awaiting –
It is the kind of worship we are taught.

View From An Upper Window*

FOR KENNETH AND JANE CLARK

From where I am sitting, my windowframe
Offers a slate roof, four chimneypots,
One aerial, half of a leafless tree,
And sky the colour of dejection. I could
Move my chair; but, London being
What it is, all would look much the same
Except that I'd have the whole of that tree.
Well, window, what am I meant to do
With the prospect you force me to dwell upon – this tame
And far from original *aperçu*?

I might take the picture for what it can say
Of immediate relevance – its planes and tones,
Though uninspiring, significant because
Like history they happened to happen that way.
Aerial, chimneypots, tree, sky, roof
Outline a general truth about towns
And living together. It should be enough,
In a fluctuating universe, to see they are there
And, short of an atom bomb, likely to stay.
But who wants truth in such everyday wear?

Shall I, then, amplify the picture? track
The roof to its quarry, the tree to its roots,
The smoke just dawdling from that chimneystack
To the carboniferous age? Shall I lift those slates
And disclose a man dying, a woman agape
With love? Shall I protract my old tree heavenwards,
Or set these aerial antennae to grope

---

* This poem began as an exercise to keep the writer's 'muscles' going. Like a musician or dancer, he practised daily after he'd finished a project. He had had a conversation with Kenneth Clark about the need for frames.

For music inaudible, unborn yet? But why,
If one's chasing the paradigm right forward and back,
Stop at embryo, roots, or sky?
Perhaps I should think about the need for frames.
At least they can lend us a certain ability
For seeing a fragment as a kind of whole
Without spilling over into imbecility.
Each of them, though limited its choice, reclaims
Some terra firma from the chaos. Who knows? –
Each of *us* may be set here, simply to compose
From a few grains of universe a finite view,
By One who occasionally needs such frames
To look at his boundless creation through?

The Newborn

(D. M. B.: APRIL 29TH, 1957) *

This mannikin who just now
Broke prison and stepped free
Into his own identity –
Hand, foot and brow
A finished work, a breathing miniature –
Was still, one night ago,
A hope, a dread, a mere shape we
Had lived with, only sure
Something would grow
Out of its coiled nine-month nonentity.

Heaved hither on quickening throes,
Tossed up on earth today,
He sprawls limp as a castaway

* Our Son: Daniel Michael Blake Day Lewis.

And nothing knows
Beside the warm sleep of his origin.
Soon lips and hands shall grope
To try the world; this speck of clay
And spirit shall begin
To feed on hope,
To learn how truth blows cold and loves betray.

Now like a blank sheet
His lineaments appear;
But there's invisible writing here
Which the day's heat
Will show: legends older than language, glum
Histories of the tribe,
Directives from his near and dear –
Charms, curses, rules of thumb –
He will transcribe
In his own blood to write upon an heir.

This morsel of man I've held –
What potency it has,
Though strengthless still and naked as
A nut unshelled!
Every newborn seems a reviving seed
Or metaphor of the divine,
Charged with the huge, weak power of grass
To split rock. How we need
Any least sign
That our stone age can break, our winter pass!

Welcome to earth, my child!
Joybells of blossom swing,
Lambs and lovers have their fling,
The streets ran wild
With April airs and rumours of the sun.
We time-worn folk renew

Ourselves at your enchanted spring,
As though mankind's begun
Again in you.
This is your birthday and our thanksgiving.

Sheepdog Trials in Hyde Park

FOR ROBERT FROST

A shepherd stands at one end of the arena.
Five sheep are unpenned at the other. His dog runs out
In a curve to behind them, fetches them straight to the
    shepherd,
Then drives the flock round a triangular course
Through a couple of gates and back to his master; two
Must be sorted there from the flock, then all five penned.
Gathering, driving away, shedding and penning
Are the plain words for the miraculous game.

An abstract game. What can the sheepdog make of such
Simplified terrain? – no hills, dales, bogs, walls, tracks,
Only a quarter-mile plain of grass, dumb crowds
Like crowds on hoardings around it, and behind them
Traffic or mounds of lovers and children playing.
Well, the dog is no landscape-fancier; his whole concern
Is with his master's whistle, and of course
With the flock – sheep are sheep anywhere for him.

The sheep are the chanciest element. Why, for instance,
Go through this gate when there's on either side of it
No wall or hedge but huge and viable space?
Why not eat the grass instead of being pushed around it?
Like blobs of quicksilver on a tilting board
The flock erratically runs, dithers, breaks up,

Is reassembled: their ruling idea is the dog;
And behind the dog, though they know it not yet, is a
    shepherd.

The shepherd knows that time is of the essence
But haste calamitous. Between dog and sheep
There is always an ideal distance, a perfect angle;
But these are constantly varying, so the man
Should anticipate each move through the dog, his medium.
The shepherd is the brain behind the dog's brain,
But his control of dog, like dog's of sheep,
Is never absolute – that's the beauty of it.

For beautiful it is. The guided missiles,
The black-and-white angels follow each quirk and jink of
The evasive sheep, play grandmother's steps behind them,
Freeze to the ground, or leap to head off a straggler
Almost before it knows that it wants to stray,
As if radar-controlled. But they are not machines –
You can feel them feeling mastery, doubt, chagrin:
Machines don't frolic when their job is done.

What's needfully done in the solitude of sheep-runs –
Those tough, real tasks – becomes this stylized game,
A demonstration of intuitive wit
Kept natural by the saving grace of error.
To lift, to fetch, to drive, to shed, to pen
Are acts I recognize, with all they mean
Of shepherding the unruly, for a kind of
Controlled woolgathering is my work too.

Circus Lion

Lumbering haunches, pussyfoot tread, a pride of
Lions under the arcs
Walk in, leap up, sit pedestalled there and glum
As a row of Dickensian clerks.

Their eyes are slag. Only a muscle flickering,
A bored, theatrical roar
Witness now to the furnaces that drove them
Exultant along the spoor.

In preyward, elastic leap they are sent through paper
Hoops at another's will
And a whip's crack: afterwards, in their cages,
They tear the provided kill.

Caught young, can this public animal ever dream of
Stars, distances and thunders?
Does he twitch in sleep for ticks, dried water-holes,
Rogue elephants, or hunters?

Sawdust, not burning desert, is the ground
Of his to-fro, to-fro pacing,
Barred with the zebra shadows that imply
Sun's free wheel, man's coercing.

See this abdicated beast, once king
Of them all, nibble his claws:
Not anger enough left – no, nor despair –
To break his teeth on the bars.

Getting Warm – Getting Cold

FOR TAMASIN*

We hid it behind the yellow cushion.
'There's a present for you,' we called,
'Come in and look for it.' So she prowled
About the suddenly mysterious room –
'Getting warm,' she heard, 'getting cold.'

She moved in a dream of discovery, searching
Table and shelf and floor –
As if to prolong the dream, everywhere
But behind that cushion. Her invisible present
Was what she lived in there.

Would she never find it? Willing her on,
We cried, 'you're cold, you're warm,
You're burning hot,' and the little room
Was enlarged to a whole Ali Baba's cave
By her eyes' responsive flame.

May she keep this sense of the hidden thing,
The somewhere joy that enthralled her,
When she's uncountable presents older –
Small room left for marvels, and none to say
'You are warmer, now you are colder.'

* Our daughter: Tamasin Day Lewis.

Walking Away

FOR SEAN*

It is eighteen years ago, almost to the day –
A sunny day with the leaves just turning,
The touch-lines new-ruled – since I watched you play
Your first game of football, then, like a satellite
Wrenched from its orbit, go drifting away

Behind a scatter of boys. I can see
You walking away from me towards the school
With the pathos of a half-fledged thing set free
Into a wilderness, the gait of one
Who finds no path where the path should be.

That hesitant figure, eddying away
Like a winged seed loosened from its parent stem,
Has something I never quite grasp to convey
About nature's give-and-take – the small, the scorching
Ordeals which fire one's irresolute clay.

I have had worse partings, but none that so
Gnaws at my mind still. Perhaps it is roughly
Saying what God alone could perfectly show –
How selfhood begins with a walking away,
And love is proved in the letting go.

* C.D.L.'s first-born son.

This Young Girl*

This young girl, whose secret life
Vagues her eyes to the reflective, lucent
Look of the sky topping a distant
Down beyond which, invisible, lies the sea –

What does she mark, to remember, of the close things
That pearl-calm gaze now shines upon? . . .
Her mother, opening a parasol,
Drifts over the hailed-with-daisies lawn:

Head full of designs, her father
Is pinned to a drawing board: two brothers settle
For cool jazz in the barn: a little
Sister decides to become Queen Pocahontas.

Or is it the skyline viewed from her attic window
Intimating the sea, the sea
Which far off waits? or the water garden
Fluent with leaves and rivulets near by,

That will be her memory's leitmotif?
All seems acceptable – an old house sweetened
By wood-ash, a whole family seasoned
In dear pursuits and country gentleness.

But her eyes elude, this summer's day. Far, far
Ahead or deep within they peer,
Beyond those customary things
Towards some Golden Age, that is now, is here.

---

* Written after a visit to Janet and Reynolds Stone and their four children at the Old
Rectory, Litton Cheney, Dorset.

Travelling Light

Naturally, we travelled light.
What with the tide-race in the bight,
Reefs uncharted, winds contrary,
And having few goods then to carry
(Though each canoe or coracle,
Lumpish upon the inshore swell,
Seemed loaded down with just its crew)
We had to travel light. The slew
And lee-way of such primitive craft!
Anyone now would call it daft
To sail a pond in jobs like these,
But we dared breakers, promontories,
Sea monsters.
            What our need had forced
On us grew second nature: first
Ventures in travelling light became
Accepted ordeals, then a game
Of self-denial, sanctified
By habit or traditional pride.
So when, resolved to sail beyond
Sheltering bays and sight of land,
We designed the prototype Argo,
There was no hold in her for cargo.
We despised the chaffering sort
Of matelot who tacks from port
To port, dodges from isle to isle,
Intent upon making his pile
And soon retiring to a villa
Well inland.
          Our type of sailor
May tell you that he also lives
For landfall, profit, whores and spivs:
This is not so. To him, the thing

You voyage for is voyaging –
Purely that. I do not mean
'To travel hopefully': I mean
Times when horizon, heart, sky, sea
Dilate with absolute potency –
The present at its highest power,
The course in view, the wake in flower.
    Argo, now. It's undeniable
That journalists – seldom reliable,
Trained to believe the lower deck's
Sole interests are cash and sex –
Made a good story of it: which
Was easy, given a royal witch
And a fleece of gold – indeed sensational,
With 'palace drama' and 'crime passionel'
For follow-ups. But all that stuff
Is not the real issue. Sure enough
We did turn up a golden fleece –
A web of moonshine among trees –
And a witch (who had the right
Ideas about travelling light,
Pitching her brother overboard,
You argue?) No, we can afford
To jettison flesh and blood still less
Than to keep those encumbrances
Which clutter our deck – the silken sheets,
Ivories, zithers, parakeets,
And yellowing ram-skins.
              Oh, you're bound
To pick up hamper, cruising around.
Think of streamlined whales and hulls
Accumulating barnacles
By moving long enough immersed
In their own element. At first
Objects become attached to you,
Then you to them, while they accrue

Like interest on an overdraft
Draining your substance through their graft,
Until they've grown, with your conniving,
Reasons or substitutes for living.
  When age or weakness dims the creed
Of travelling light, there's still a need
To travel. Some may justify
The things that clog our vessel by
Calling them ballast. Valuing those
Objects merely as curios,
Keepsakes of voyaging, is hard.
What mariner would now discard
Things – just by-products once and proof
Of his seafaring – when they spoof
Him into thinking they must be
The end for which he put to sea?
Hear the old salt, with no dismay,
Bad faith or hesitation, say
'That patch of moonshine among trees
Actually was the golden fleece.
It weighed five stone: and we all knew
We had done what we came to do.'
      Yellowing ram-skin, silken sheets,
Ivories, zithers, parakeets –
Is it strange they assume a dearer,
A more intrinsic worth, the nearer
We approach that harsh whirlpool –
End of our voyaging – whose pull
Grows stronger daily now? Past fears,
Hopes, joys live in these souvenirs
We've kept; but they do not oppress
Like flesh and blood our consciences.
Let's say they're given us to console
The heart for being no longer whole,

For the loss of each wide hour –
The course in view, the wake in flower –
When being rose to utmost power.

Things

The woman shuffled about her room
With a shut, sleepwalking air –
A room like a million other rooms,
A nondescript woman – absently
Touching each object there.

Ornaments, hangings, furniture looked
Of little worth; and this woman
Fingering the tasteless, time-dulled things
(Vaguely? raptly?) might seem no more
Than a connoisseur of the common.

It was as though her room, her world
Had blurred with fog, and she
Was feeling her way from chair to clock,
From vase to mahogany table, less
By sight than by memory.

There was more to this touching routine than mere
Habit or pride of possessing.
As she went the rounds of her shabby room,
Her hands were lightened – the hands of one
Who gave, and received, blessing.

An Episode

So then he walled her up alive
(It seemed that her betrayal must deserve
What his own agony felt like – the slow choking
Of breath and pore in a close grave)
And waited. There was no cry from her, no knocking.

– Waited for pain to end, with her
Who had been his love and any comer's whore.
Soft-spoken dreams revealed how he was wanting
The victim to turn comforter –
A chastened ghost, an unreproachful haunting.

Presently the blank wall grew eyes
That hunted him from every covert ease
And thickset pain. He felt as if heart were searching
For heart. He saw in those whitewashed eyes
A look neither forgiving nor beseeching.

His bloody fingers tore at the wall,
Demolishing what could never salve nor seal
Its crime, but found in the nook where he had placed her
No twisted limbs, no trace at all.
His heart lay there – a mess of stone and plaster.

A Loss

'You are nice' – and she touched his arm with a fleeting
Impulsive gesture: the arm that had held her close
And naked a year ago. She was not cheating,
But it falsified their balance of profit and loss.

552

Her gesture saluted a magnanimity shown
When he asked if she was happy with her new
Lover. That cool touch scalded him to the bone:
The ingenuous words made all words ring untrue.

Their love had never been one of creditor-debtor;
But he felt that her hand, reaching to him across
The year he had spent in failing to forget her
And all they'd shared, simply wrote off a loss.

A Meeting

Meeting the first time for many years,
What do they expect to see
Of the beings they made once, for better and worse,
Of each other – he and she?

A shrine to lost love? a hovel for guilt?
A vacant historic pile?
Something in ruins? something rebuilt
In a grand or a makeshift style?

Whatever is here to be freshly scanned,
Their view will be overcast:
Though they'll encounter, smile, shake hands,
They can only meet in the past –

Meet at the point where they parted, in
The house of what once they were,
Haunted by ghosts of what they might have been
Today, had they lived on there.

The life they had fashioned long ago
Seemed close as a honeycomb;
And if anything couples these strangers now
Who were each other's home,

It is grief that the pureness and plenitude of
Their love's long-flowering day
Could, like baser, flimsier stuff,
Corrupt or melt away.

Nothing left of the cells they stored
With joy, trust, charity
For years? . . . Nature, it seems, can afford
Such wastefulness: not we.

An Upland Field*

By a windrowed field she made me stop.
'I love it – finding you one of these,'
She said; and I watched her tenderly stoop
Towards a sprig of shy heartsease
Among the ruined crop.

'Oh but look, it is everywhere!'
Stubble and flint and sodden tresses
Of hay were a prospect of despair:
But a myriad infant heartsease faces
Pensively eyed us there.

Long enough had I found that flower
Little more common than what it is named for –

* Dorset – near Plush.

554

A chance-come solace amid earth's sour
Failures, a minute joy that bloomed for
Its brief, precocious hour.

No marvel that she, who gives me peace
Wherein my shortening days redouble
Their yield, could magically produce
From all that harshness of flint and stubble
Whole acres of heartsease.

The Disabused

(a Dramatic Monologue)

Eleven o'clock. My house creaks and settles,
Feeling the dry-rot in its old bones. Well,
It will see me out; and after that, who cares?
More than a house is perishing – civilization,
For all I know; and Helen's marriage, she tells me,
Breaking up – a mishap she seems to confuse
With the end of the world, poor girl. 'You are so calm,
'You amaze me, father,' she said: 'I feel I cannot
'Keep my head above water any longer.'
Now she has taken her tragedy to bed.
But what storms first! – this indelicate need of woman
To have emotion – hers, his, anyone's – exposed
Like bleeding lumps of meat on a butcher's counter
And poke at it with insensitive, finicky fingers!
'Helen,' I might have said, 'if I am calm
'It is because I have spent most of a lifetime
'Learning to live with myself, which is the hardest
'Marriage of all.' But to say this would only
Have underlined her notion that I had somehow
Failed her. The way she spoke about my calmness

Was to reproach me, of course, for having failed –
Not in recognizing what she suffers,
But in refusing to be infected by it:
For that's what women want – that we vibrate
To their disturbance, visibly respond –
Tears, smiles, exasperation, pity, rage,
Any response will satisfy them, for so
Their weakness sees its power. She'll never grasp
How a man grows strong by silently outstaring
His brute infirmity. 'Helen,' I all but told her,
'Tomorrow is the fortieth anniversary
'Of the day I let my brother drown.'

                                  Not 'saw'
Or 'watched' – you notice, Tom – but 'let'. I never
Permit myself the soft and venial option . . .
It's the first morning of a summer holiday
After the War. You are just demobbed, and I,
Three years younger, finished with school. We run
Along the cliff path – harebell, scabious, rampion,
Sunlight and dew on the grass – and we are running
Back into the boyhood of our world.
You, always the leader, stand at the waves' edge
Undressed, before I have scrambled down the steep path
Among those yellow poppies to the beach.
Then, like a new slide thrown on the screen, with a click
The picture is different – I on the shingle, you
Thirty yards out suddenly thrashing the calm sea
To foam, as if you had been harpooned. This happens
So quickly, and yet your dying seems to go on
For ever. You struggle silently, your eyes
Howling for help. And I, a feeble swimmer,
Must let you drown or flounder out and let you
Drag me under.

                        But there was no choice, really:
Fear, like an automatic governor,
Shut off the power in my limbs, held me down

So hard that a flint dug my bare sole open
(I have the stigma now). The cove contained
My tiny shouts. My eyes searched everywhere –
Foreshore and cliff and heaven – at first for help,
But soon to make sure there was no witness of
Your dying and my living, or perhaps
Most of all to avoid your whitening stare.
No one in sight; and at last the sea's face too
Was empty. Now I could look. Along the horizon,
Slow as a minute hand, there faintly moved
A little ship, a model of indifference.
So it went.
                              You have omitted one thing.
No, Tom, I was coming to that. I lay down
In the shallows to saturate my clothes.
('What presence of mind,' you say? A coward soon
Learns circumspection.) So, when I got home
Crying, limping, dripping with brine, father
In his crammed anguish still found room to praise me,
Console and praise me for having done my best.

There's this to be said for growing old – one loses
The itch for wholeness, the need to justify
One's maimed condition. I have lived all these years
A leper beneath the skin, scrupulous always
To keep away from where I could spread contagion.
No one has guessed my secret. I had to learn
Good and early the know-how of consuming
My own waste products: I at least have never
Contaminated soil or river. Why,
Why then, though I have played the man in facing
My worst, and cauterized the ugly wound,
Does that original morning by the sea
Still irk me like a lovers' tryst unkept –
Not with remorse or tragedy curses – no,
With the nostalgic sweetness of some vision

557

All but made flesh, then vanishing, which drains
Colour and pith from the whole aftertime?
I lost a brother

             Only a brother?

                           Tom,
Do you mean self-respect? We have had this out
A hundred times. You know I have regained it,
Stiffening my heart against its primal fault.
'There was the fault,' you say? What? Do you blame
The wound for the scar-tissue, or a bombed site
For growing willowherb? It is nature's way.
You who gulped the sea and are dead, why do you
Keep swimming back with these cast-off things in your
                                  mouth
Like an imbecile dog?

                  The vision. The sweet vision.
Recapture. A last chance.

                      This is beyond me!
Last chance of what? Is it your elder-brotherly
Pleasure to keep me wallowing in that sour
Humiliation? You can teach me nothing
About the anatomy of fear – I've made it
A life-long study, through self-vivisection:
And if I did use local anaesthetics
To deaden the area, better a witness than
A victim to the science of self-knowledge.
Relentlessly I have tracked each twist and shuffle,
Face-saving mask, false candour, truth-trimmed fraud,
All stratagems of bluster and evasion –
Traced them back along the quivering nerves
To that soft monster throned in my being's chasm,
Till I was armed in and against the infirmity.
Self-knowledge. I tell you, Tom, we do not solve
Human problems with tears and kisses: each,
Like one of my engineering jobs, demands
Calculation of stresses and resistance.

If the material's faulty

       Poor father,

Must you fail me then?

      Helen! You too?
How can you put such nonsense into my head?
I said I would do all that I can to help you,
See the lawyers, have you and the children here –
Practical things. 'Consider this your home now,'
I said. A storm of animal sobbing then,
As though I had struck her. Good Lord, does she expect me
To interview Robert and make him return to her?
If only her mother was alive! – such scenes
Afflict me with a rigor of repulsion.
Curious, that: how near we come to loathing
Those whose demands, however unreasonable,
We fail to meet – yes, impotence humiliates,
Not in bed only.

      Father, do you love me?
Love you? Of course I do. You are my daughter.
She used to remind me, as a child, of Tom –
The same blue, mocking, meditative gaze . . .
Azure eye of the sea, wakeful, dangerous.
Between the sea's eye and the yellow poppies
A vision to recapture? . . . I perceive
One drowning, one not drowning, that is all.
No, Tom, let us stick to facts: the relevant fact is
That it was you, not I, who died that day.
Well, do you deny it? Do you deny it? Speak to me!
You cannot. You are dead, I am alive.
Let sleeping visions lie. How could he think
I should breach the dyke I have been all these years
Building and reinforcing? Ah, I see it –
Trying to lure me out of my depth – the same
As Helen an hour ago – 'Come, father, jump
Into the boiling sea of my emotions
And let us choke together.'

If you love me,
Father, stretch out a hand.

                                              If stretching out
My hand could rescue, I would do it: but
Father, if you can love, stretch out your hand.
Well, gestures are the easiest way to humour
A woman. So why not reach out my hand,
As it might be over the breakfast table tomorrow,
Reach out this hand to Helen, so. Reach out –
Christ, I cannot! Won't move, it won't move!
What's this? A seizure, a stroke? Move, damn you!
Dying? No! No! I cannot die yet.
Dreaming. A bad dream. Overwork. Of course.
Jackson's arm caught in the hydraulic press.
Man with a withered arm, in the Bible: atrophy –
No, that's gradual. Cramp. Tom died of it.
But there's no agony, not a twinge – God!
Let me feel something! I have gone dead, quite dead:
All power cut off . . . If I could analyse
My feelings, I should – cogito, ergo sum –
But there's no feeling, only an Arctic night
Of numb, eternal fear, death's null forever.
Dead, then? How long? How long? Eleven-fifteen,
The clock says. My nightcap still on the table;
And there's my hand, reaching out to take it.
Reaching! Alive! . . .

                                    My God, I needed that.
What a grotesque hallucination! Really,
I could have sworn my arm was paralysed
For a few moments. If I were superstitious,
I'd say it was a sign from heaven – yes, Tom,
It rather proves my point – a sign that I
Was right not to embroil myself in Helen's
Hysterical maelstrom. What she needs from me
Is rational guidance, realism, detachment,
Not facile gestures of pure self-indulgence.

You and your 'vision', Tom! No, I'm not buying it.
One delusion is quite enough . . . I'd better
Ring MacIntyre in the morning, and arrange
For him to give me a thorough overhaul.

Not Proven

(a Dramatic Monologue)

FOR GEORGE RYLANDS

NOTE: Madeleine Hamilton Smith was tried for murder, at Edinburgh, in 1857. She died in
the United States of America, aged 92, in 1928.

So. I am dying. Let the douce young medico
Syrup his verdict, I am not deceived.
You pity me, boy? a shrunk old woman dying
Alone in an alien country? Sir, you have chosen
The wrong woman to pity. There was a girl
Seventy-two years ago – high-coloured, handsome,
The belle of the Glasgow ballrooms – gave herself
Body and soul to a wheedling mannikin,
And went down into hell through him. Pity
Her, if pity you must – though she asked none
Except from her dwarf-souled lover – not this crumpled
Dead-letter of flesh, yellow as the press-cuttings
I keep in my workbox there. You wonder why
I treasure such things? I was a heroine,
A nine-days' marvel to an admiring world.
No, sir, my wits are not astray. Those cuttings –
They're my citations for valour. Close, come closer.
The panel's voice grows weak. You are very young.
Tell me, what does it mean to you – the name of
Madeleine Smith? . . .

                    Now he is gone at last,

The nice wee doctor, leaving a prescription
And an unuttered question in the room –
A question I have seen for seventy years
In every eye that knew me, and imagined
In every eye that would not rest on mine.
They got no sign from me – those speiring eyes:
Long ago I learnt to outface even
My own, soliciting me from the cold mirror,
As I outfaced them all in court for nine days –
Beetle-eyes of journalists crawling busily
Over me; jurymen's moth-eyes fluttering at mine
And falling, scorched; bat-eyes darting around me.
And after the trial, a drift of letters offering
Marriage, or fornication. Chivalrous
Young fools, wishful to comfort a wronged innocent;
Used-up philanderers dreaming of new sensations
In bed with a murderess; they too were drawn
To the mystery behind this brow, the sphinx.
　　My secret! Ah, the years have mossed it over,
The lettering on the stone's illegible now.
　　HERE LIE THE REMAINS OF MADELEINE,
　　DAUGHTER OF JAMES SMITH, WIDOW OF
　　GEORGE WARDLE, IN HOPE OF EVERLASTING
　　OBLIVION. SHE WAS TRIED FOR THE MURDER
　　OF HER LOVER, PIERRE EMILE L'ANGELIER, BY
　　THE ADMINISTRATION OF ARSENIC. THE
　　VERDICT OF THE COURT: NOT PROVEN.
　　THE REST WAS SILENCE.
　　　　　　　　　　Beneath that slab I have lain
Seventy years – the remains of a gallant girl
Whom passion, flaring up too high, too sudden,
Blackened like a lamp-chimney. Oh, long-dead flame!
They say there comes a lightening before death.
Light, any light, come – ray of mercy or bale-fire –
And run some stitch of meaning through my life,
The shreds and snippets of that Madeleine,

Her after-life!

                    Well, there were compensations,
They think? The wicked prospered? George was kind,
Smooring the question in his heart. Affluence
We had: travel: the house in Onslow Gardens:
Artists and thinkers round us – William Morris,
William de Morgan: the Social Democrat Club.
Yes, I was quite a firebrand for those days . . .

    A brand plucked from the burning: charred, chastened –
So you would figure me, all you respectable
Fathers and mothers of nubile daughters who
Must cool their blood with albums, prayers, tea-parties?
I hear your judgment, hypocrites, mealy-mouthed
Over the porridge at the mahogany sideboards:
'Guilty or innocent of murder, she
Has shamed our womanhood. Illicit love
Were shame enough; but that a female should
Write to her lover, exulting in the act,
Baring herself in words to acknowledge pleasure –
Depraved! Unnatural! Doubtless she repents now.'
Repentance? Shame? Little you know, Papa,
Nor you, Lord Justice-Clerk, sitting in judgment
On me, where lies the core of my remorse,
The cancer of my shame . . .

                       No, they are dead,
Those stuffed men – long ago dead. Foolish Madeleine,
Dreaming yourself once more back to the trial,
The aftermath! Aye, at one bound, as if
The years between were a wee burn to jump
And not the insipid mere, the bottomless pit
Which has swallowed up my youth, my pride, my graces
Like dumped rubbish, and still been unfulfilled.
Would I return, live it again, to keep death
Waiting a while for me? Would the old actress
Re-live her greatest triumph! – and not to stay death;
To spurn him from the pinnacle of her fame.

Yes, I would walk as then, flushed with achievement,
Out of the cheering courtroom through the chill
Silence of Rowaleyn (Papa frock-coated,
A plaster figure of repudiation,
The family Jehovah buttoned up in
Self-righteous outrage; brothers and sisters cowed
Less by his wrath than by my flung defiance:
Mother, of course, had taken to her bed) –
Stride like a tragic heroine, through that last
Ordeal, into my life's long anti-climax.

     Dusk already? What time is it? My skin
Sweats cold. Doctor! You cannot let me die –
Not yet! Madeleine Smith must go to court:
Her trial is not yet over. She must live
Through the command performance once again.
Doctor! . . . Doctor, are you familiar with
The signs of poisoning by arsenic? No,
He is not here. Contempt of court. And I
Despise it too – the cant and rigmarole
Of the Law. Quick then, Madeleine, dress yourself:
Demure black mantle, and the straw scoop-bonnet
Trimmed with white ribbon, leaving your face naked
To all the prurient, cringing eyes – unveiled,
But in its cold, bold calm inviolable.
Madeleine takes the dock – how did they put it? –
With the air of a belle entering a ballroom.

                        See,
The room fills up with shadows – a sibilant audience
Of ghosts: they rise: Hope, Handyside and Ivory,
Robed and bewigged, come soberly on – dead men
To sit in judgment on a dying actress.
No, no, my Lords, it is not you, tricked out
In gravity and fine feathers, who will make
This play immortal; nor you, Lord Advocate,
Plaiting your rope of logic round my neck;
Nor even you, John Inglis, Dean of Faculty,

My eloquent defender: no, it is I,
The silent heroine of the wordy drama,
Who pack your theatre day after day.
Let them drone on – what do I care? – over
That trash, that reptile thing which died writhing.
    Ah, how the drab years fly up like a blind
At *his* vile touch, to show the lighted past!
And through that scene, a play behind a play,
Moncrieff, Lord Advocate, frigidly weaving
His figured plot . . . On such and such occasions
The panel purchased arsenic, stating that
It was to kill rats, or for her complexion.
On such and such occasions the deceased
Took ill; and the third time he died of it.
We've no eye-witness: but no doubt the panel
Administered the poison in a cup
Of cocoa which she handed to her lover
That last night through the basement window of
The house in Blythswood Square, the scene of previous
Assignations – passed it across the space
Between her window and the railings, where
She had been used to put her letters for
Pierre Emile L'Angelier to pick up –
Those passionate letters which he threatened now
To show her father, if she would not abandon
Her purpose of wedding another, William Minnoch.
To all the panel's desperate entreaties
That he should return her letters, L'Angelier
Was adamant. Rather than be exposed
As a vicious wanton and ruined irretrievably,
She murdered him. That is the Crown's case.
    'What did you think, Miss Smith, of the Lord
                                    Advocate's
Address?' *When I have heard the Dean of Faculty,*
I'll tell you. I never like to give an opinion
Until I have heard both sides of the question.

565

By God! I was a pert young lassie then,
And fearless too – letting my wit dance
On the scaffold's trap-door, over the drop, the quick-lime –
So you believed? Or a monster from the Pit,
Murderess, whore, with the vibrant, mordant tongue
Of the damned? But I was neither, I tell you; only
A woman, the husk that's left of a woman after
Premature birth, when her rich, quickened body
Has dropped a stillborn thing (dropped? aborted?)
A love, conceived in ecstasy, that became
A deadweight burden, a malignant growth
Of self-disgust . . .

                      But listen, the Dean of Faculty
Rises to address the jury. Listen.
Gentlemen of the Jury, the charge against the prisoner
is murder, and the punishment of murder is death;
and that simple statement is sufficient to suggest to us
the awful solemnity of the occasion
which brings you and me face to face.
Inglis! Listen to me, Inglis. You must drive home
The point about my letters. The prosecution
Has said I would go any length to stop
Those letters being revealed. And so I would have,
Almost, but not to the folly of – oh, they must
Realize there was no surer way of having
My letters to him made public than for Emile
To die by poison. Do they suppose that I
Would not see this? They insult my intelligence. But
The panel is a woman: all men know
The weaker sex have little power of reason.
Weaker? Pah! Why, why must I be silent
While self-important lawyers play at ball
With my life? No, I *will* speak!

                          My Lords, and you
Gentlemen of the jury, listen to me.
Lay by your masks, all this majestic flummery –

566

You, lords of creation, who keep us women
To fawn on you, be petted, brought to heel –
And think: although nature has trained our bodies
To fawn, our hearts to love subjection, how would
A woman – slave and Spartacus to her sex –
Once she'd revolted from this rule of nature,
Loathe him for whom nature had made her kneel!
And what if such a woman found her master,
Not weak, vain, tyrannous merely – you are all so –
But abject, sirs, abject as a maggot
That clings to the flesh it has gorged on? a maggot who,
After his first meal, sermonized to me
About the weakness of *my* flesh! Ach, men,
The moral hypochondriacs, for ever
Coddling their timid minds against the real,
Medicining themselves with patent lies
And sedative abstractions – look, how bravely
Cowardice makes a conscience for them all!
I am accused of poisoning my lover.
Bring *him* to trial, I say. Let Pierre Emile
L'Angelier be arraigned for poisoning love.
Aye, the deep wells of my awakened body,
The pent abundance, and the dancing fountains
That leapt and wept for him like paradise trees
In diamond leaf – he tainted them. How soon
My springs went bitter and the loving cup
Tasted metallic! . . . Sirs, you have marvelled at
My strange composure. Do you not recognize
The calm of a face prepared for burial? Which,
Which is the tragic victim? – one who dies
Vomiting up a trumpery soul? or one
Who, legend-high in love, proud as Diana,
Awakes to find her matchless Prince deformed
Into a Beast, a puny, whimpering lapdog?
Oh waste, waste, waste! Sir, I plead guilty of
Self-mutilation. Cutting that hateful image

Out of my heart, I should have bled to death:
But hatred's a fine cautery for such wounds,
And love as wild as mine needs but a flick of
Indignity or disrelish to become
That searing, healing, all-redeeming hatred.
But what do you know of such things, my Lords,
With your tame wives and farthing-dips of lust?
As for this trial of yours – a man has ceased,
A paltry creature whom my passion exalted
Into a figment of its own white fire.
That furnace proved him dross. He is better dead,
My Lords . . .

      My Lords! Hear me out! Why do they –
Hope, Handyside and Ivory – why withdraw,
Dissolve to moonshine? Moonshine, and a haze of
Branches knitted above me. I am caged in
From the star-daisied heaven. Ah, my rowans:
The garden of Rowaleyn, and beside me –
Emile! Emile, wake up! I have had a terrible
Dream. I dreamt that I had – dreamt that you
Were dead. Comfort me. Do not be cold.
You are not angry with me? I am your wife now,
Truly your wife, the woman you've created
As God created woman. I worship you.
Listen to my heart, Emile – close, come closer –
How the blood pulses for you, calm and crazing
As torrents of moonshine; crazed and calmed by you.
Husband, speak to me. Do not be afraid:
They are all asleep in the house. Papa is sleeping
The sleep of the self-righteous: he'll never dream
That I'd creep out to you, your cat, your vixen,
For a midsummer mating. Are you ashamed
Because I am so shameless in love? But I
Have high blood in these veins, dare-devil blood:
My kin's not all the halfway kind who live
Haltered by prudence and propriety – no,

Remember, I am Madeleine *Hamilton* Smith.
Why are you silent, Emile? – and so cold,
Clay-cold to my fevered lips! The night is chill
For June, and you are delicate: you must go, love:
Your Mimi must not be the death of you.
Go quickly, then. We shall soon be together –
One bed, one life – for always. I will coax
Papa, or else defy him. I am all yours now.
Quick! – by the side gate . . . Why will you not go?
Are you frozen to my side? Leave me! No, no more
Loving – get away from me! You shall not –

                         Oh!

The fearful dream! Loathing. A clay man:
Incubus from the grave. What was he doing
Here at my bedside? trying to fright me into
Death-bed confession? Always he misprized me,
Misjudged: it is not well to underrate
A woman such as I . . . Had I been born
Fifty years later, I should leave the world
Richer for me and be remembered as
A maker, a pioneer, not an enigma.
What an end for the Lucifer who rebelled
Against their sanctimonious, whiskered god –
To be smuggled out, like a prisoner who has served
Life-sentence, by a side door of the jail,
Fameless and futureless!

                        Who's this at my door
In black among the shadows? A minister?
I have nothing to say to you. Nothing. He draws
Nearer. It is the minister of bone.
Sir, I shall be no burden for you to carry.
I am light and small now – small in your arms:
A wisp of flesh; some courage; and what weighs
Heavier than they – my secret. I can trust you
With it. Hold me up. It is hard to speak,
To breathe. Whose hand – the cup of poison? His?

Mine? But so long ago it happened, how
Can I be sure? Their busy arguments
Hummed in my ears like echoes from a dream,
Making unreal all that had passed between us,
Emile and me, till I became two phantasms –
One innocent, one guilty, and the truth
Went down in the gulf between them, the real I –
What she had done or not done – sinking away
From me, dubious, hidden, lost, amid
A fog and welter of words.

It lies too deep now
In the black ooze. My heart quakes. The sea-bed
Heaves. Last agony. Heaves to give up its dead.
I cannot. Sir, have mercy on me. Make haste.
I am heavy with you. Deliver me.
Madeleine, Madeleine, tell me the truth.
I have forgotten . . . long ago . . . forgotten.

Wind's Eye

Eye of the wind, whose bearing in
A changeful sky the sage
Birds are never wrong about
And mariners must gauge –

The drift of flight, the fluttered jib
Are what we know it by:
Seafarers cannot hold or sight
The wind's elusive eye.

That eye, whose shifting moods inspire
The sail and trim the sheet,
Commands me, though I can but steer
Obliquely towards it.

In Loving Memory

E. M. BUTLER*

1

'Goodbye' – the number of times each day one says it!
But the goodbyes that matter we seldom say,
Being elsewhere – preoccupied, on a visit,
Somehow off guard – when the dear friend slips away

Tactfully, for ever. And had we known him
So near departure, would we have shut our eyes
To the leaving look in his? tried to detain him
On the doorstep with bouquets of goodbyes?

I think of one, so constant a life-enhancer
That I can hardly yet imagine her dead;
Who seems, in her Irish courtesy, to answer
Even now the farewell I left unsaid.

Remembering her threefold self – a scholar,
A white witch, a small girl, fused into one –
Though all the love they lit will never recall her,
I warm my heart still at her cordial sun.

2

There was the small-boned witch who would accost us
In Notting Hill Gate, white shoes and hairnet on,
Having just flown out of a dream of Doctor Faustus,
Vanished from Cambridge or Ceylon,
Or merely passed intact under the wheels

* E. M. Butler: former Professor of German at Cambridge, and author.

Of several buses. And instantly her spells
Worked on us – we were young, a drab day shone.

Then the attentive scholar, listening for clues
To meaning, like a bird with its head inclined
Earthward: one in whose presence to misuse
Truth was hazardous – she would find
You gently out. But her own truth sang and tingled
With a Mozartian gaiety that mingled
Wise innocence and pure elegance of mind.

But I think I loved in her most the original Alice –
The round blue gaze ready for wonderland,
The mien, polite, inquisitive, without malice,
Of one who nevertheless would stand
No nonsense from cardboard kings or tinpot knights –
A little girl who reached spectacular heights
By chewing on whatever came to hand . . .

Child, with a scholar's cool, precise discerning:
Scholar, unfeigned in her bewitching glee:
White witch, whose subtle essences were burning
With a child's candour. Now all three
Are in one grave. But still her nature glows
Through earth and night, and like trefoil there grows
On us the sweetness of her memory.

Edward Elgar

1857–1934

1

A boy among the reeds on Severn shore
Sound-bathing: a ghost humming his 'cello tune
Upon the Malvern hills: and in between,
Mostly enigma. Who shall read this score?

The stiff, shy, blinking man in a norfolk suit:
The martinet: the gentle-minded squire:
The piano-tuner's son from Worcestershire:
The Edwardian grandee: how did they consort

In such luxuriant themes? Not privilege
Nor talent's cute, obsequious ear attuned
His soul to the striding rhythms, the unimpugned
Melancholy of a vulgar, vivid age.

Genius alone can move by singular ways
Yet home to the heart of all, the common chord;
Beat to its own time, timelessly make heard
A long-breathed statement or a hesitant phrase.

For me, beyond the marches of his pride,
Through the dark airs and rose-imperial themes,
A far West-country summer glares and glooms,
A boy calls from the reeds on Severn side.

2

Orchards are in it – the vale of Evesham blooming:
Rainshine of orchards blowing out of the past.

The sadness of remembering orchards that never bore,
Never for us bore fruit: year after year they fruited,
But all, all was premature –
We were not ripe to gather the full beauty.
And now when I hear 'orchards' I think of loss, recall
White tears of blossom streaming away downwind,
And wish the flower could have stayed to be one with the
          fruit it formed.
Oh, coolness at the core of early summers,
Woodwind haunting those green expectant alleys,
Our blossom falling, falling.

Hills are in it – the Malverns, Bredon, Cotswold.
A meadowsweetness of high summer days:
Clovering bees, time-honeyed bells, the lark's top C.
Hills where each sound, like larksong, passes into light,
And light is music all but seen.
Dawn's silvery tone and evening's crimson adagio;
Noonday on the full strings of sunshine simmering,
          dreaming,
No past, no future, the pulse of time unnoticed:
Cloud-shadows sweeping in arpeggios up the hillsides;
Grey, muted light which, brooding on stone, tree, clover
And cornfield, makes their colours sing most clear –
All moods and themes of light.

And a river – call it the Severn – a flowing-awayness.
Bray of moonlight on water; brassy flamelets
Of marigold, buttercup, flag-iris in water-meadows;
Kingfishers, mayflies, mills, regattas: the ever-rolling
Controlled percussion of thunderous weirs.
Rivers are passionate gods: they flood, they drown,
Roar themselves hoarse, ripple to gaiety, lull the land
With slow movements of tender meditation.
And in it too, in his music, I hear the famous river –
Always and never the same, carrying far

Beyond our view, reach after noble reach –
That bears its sons away.

Ideal Home

1

Never would there be lives enough for all
The comely places –
Glimpsed from a car, a train, or loitered past –
That lift their faces
To be admired, murmuring 'Live with me.'

House with a well,
Or a ghost; by a stream; on a hill; in a hollow: breathing
Woodsmoke appeal,
Fresh paint, or simply a prayer to be kept warm,
Each casts her spell.

Life, claims each, will look different from my windows,
Your furniture be
Transformed in these rooms, your chaos sorted out here.
Ask for the key.
Walk in, and take me. Then you shall live again.

2

. . . Nor lives enough
For all the fair ones, dark ones, chestnut-haired ones
Promising love –
I'll be your roof, your hearth, your paradise orchard
And treasure-trove.

With puritan scents – rosemary, thyme, verbena,
With midnight musk,
Or the plaintive, memoried sweetness tobacco-plants
Exhale at dusk,
They lure the footloose traveller to dream of
One fixed demesne,
The stay-at-home to look for his true self elsewhere.
I will remain
Your real, your ideal property. Possess me.
Be born again.

3

If only there could be lives enough, you're wishing? . . .
For one or two
Of all the possible loves a dozen lifetimes
Would hardly do:
Oak learns to be oak through a rooted discipline.

Such desirableness
Of place or person is chiefly a glamour cast by
Your unsuccess
In growing your self. Rebirth needs more than a change of
Flesh or address.

Switch love, move house – you will soon be back where
                                        you started,
On the same ground,
With a replica of the old romantic phantom
That will confound
Your need for roots with a craving to be unrooted.

Fisherman and/or Fish

There was a time when I,
The river's least adept,
Eagerly leapt, leapt
To the barbed, flirtatious fly.

Thrills all along the line,
A tail thrashing – the sport
Enthralled: but which was caught,
Which reeled the other in?

Anglers aver they angle
For love of the fish they play
(Arched spine and glazing eye,
A gasping on the shingle).

I've risen from safe pools
And gulped hook line and sinker
(Oh, the soft merciless fingers
Fumbling at my gills!)

Let last time be the last time
For me with net or gaff.
I've had more than enough
Of this too thrilling pastime.

The river's veteran, I
Shall flick my rod, my fin,
Where nothing can drag me in
Nor land me high and dry.

The Antique Heroes

Faultlessly those antique heroes
    Went through their tests and paces,
Meeting the most extraordinary phenomena
    With quite impassive faces.

Dragons, chimeras, sirens, ogres
    Were all in the day's work;
From acorn to dryad, from home to the Hesperides
    No further than next week.

There was always someone who would give them
                          something
    Still more impossible to do,
And a divinity on call to help them
    See the assignment through.

The functions of the heroine were,
    Though pleasurable, more narrow –
Receiving a god, generally Zeus,
    And breeding another hero.

It gave life an added interest for all
    Complaisant girls, to know
That a bull, a swan, a yokel might be
    Deity incognito.

Scholars dispute if such tales were chiefly
    The animist's childwise vision,
Ancestor-snobbery, or a kind of
    Archaic science-fiction.

Well, I have seen a clutch of hydras
    Slithering round W.C.2,

And Odysseus striding to the airport. I think
Those tales could be strictly true.

The Graves of Academe

The ghosts were all right till this grave-digger came
With the rheumatic style and the missioner's frown.
Unpleasing, unpleasured, he lectures each shade:
Now they ought to be dead, but they will not lie down.

How the tall, genial spirits must laugh
When this pocket Disposer-Supreme volunteers
To drill and dismiss them, puts each in his place
And lays on the tombstone a wreath of pale sneers.

Which do we honour – a generous host,
Or maggots puffed up by the fare he provides them?
Ghosts whose bright presence has outlived the dawn,
Or this channering worm that officiously chides them?

'Said the Old Codger'

When Willie Yeats was in his prime,
Said the old codger,
Heroic frenzy fired his verse:
He scorned a poet who did not write
As if he kept a sword upstairs.

Nowadays what do we find,
Said the old codger,

In every bardlet's upper room?
– Ash in the grate, a chill-proof vest,
And a metronome.

The Unexploded Bomb

Two householders (semi-detached) once found,
Digging their gardens, a bomb underground –
Half in one's land, half in t'other's, with the fence
                        between.
Neighbours they were, but for years had been
Hardly on speaking terms. Now X. unbends
To pass a remark across the creosoted fence:
'Look what I've got! . . . Oh, you've got it too.
Then what, may I ask, are you proposing to do
About this object of yours which menaces my wife,
My kiddies, my property, my whole way of life?'
'Your way of life,' says Y., 'is no credit to humanity.
I don't wish to quarrel; but, since you began it, I
Find your wife stuck-up, your children repel me,
And let me remind you that we too have the telly.
This bomb of mine –'
                'I don't like your tone!
And I must point out that, since I own
More bomb than you, to create any tension
Between us won't pay you.'
                     'What a strange misapprehension!'
Says the other: 'my portion of bomb is near
Six inches longer than yours. So there!'

'They seem,' the bomb muttered in its clenched and
                          narrow
Sleep, 'to take me for a vegetable marrow.'

'It would give me,' said X., 'the very greatest pleasure
To come across the fence now with my tape-measure –'
'Oh no,' Y. answered, 'I'm not having you
Trampling my flowerbeds and peering through
My windows.'
                              'Oho,' snarled X., 'if that's
Your attitude, I warn you to keep your brats
In future from trespassing upon my land,
Or they'll bitterly regret it.'
                              'You misunderstand.
My family has no desire to step on
Your soil; and my bomb is a peace-lover's weapon.'

Called a passing angel, 'If you two shout
And fly into tantrums and keep dancing about,
The thing will go off. It is surely permissible
To say that your bomb, though highly fissible,
Is in another sense one and indivisible;
By which I mean – if you'll forgive the phrase,
Gentlemen – the bloody thing works both ways.
So let me put forward a dispassionate proposal:
Both of you, ring for a bomb-disposal
Unit, and ask them to remove post-haste
The cause of your dispute.'

                              X. and Y. stared aghast
At the angel. 'Remove my bomb?' they sang
In unison both: 'allow a gang
To invade my garden and pull up the fence
Upon which my whole way of life depends?
Only a sentimental idealist
Could moot it. I, thank God, am a realist.'

The angel fled. The bomb turned over
In its sleep and mumbled, 'I shall soon discover,
If X. and Y. are too daft to unfuse me,
How the Devil intends to use me.'

The Christmas Rose

What is the flower that blooms each year
In flowerless days,
Making a little blaze
On the bleak earth, giving my heart some cheer?

    Harsh the sky and hard the ground
    When the Christmas rose is found.
    Look! its white star, low on earth,
    Rays a vision of rebirth.

Who is the child that's born each year –
His bedding, straw:
His grace, enough to thaw
My wintering life, and melt a world's despair?

    Harsh the sky and hard the earth
    When the Christmas child comes forth.
    Look! around a stable throne
    Beasts and wise men are at one.

What men are we that, year on year,
We Herod-wise
In our cold wits devise
A death of innocents, a rule of fear?

    Hushed your earth, full-starred your sky
    For a new navitity:
    Be born in us, relieve our plight,
    Christmas child, you rose of light!

Requiem for the Living*

REQUIEM

Grant us untroubled rest. Our sleep is fretted,
Anxious we wake, in our terrestrial room.
What wastes the flesh, what ticks below the floor will
Abort all futures, desecrate the tomb.

Let healing grace now light upon us. All flesh
Lives with its death. But may some shaft unblind
Soon our sick eyes, lest the death we choose to live with
And then must die be the murder of mankind.

Peace in our time: else upon earth a timeless
Pause of unbeing, sterile, numb and null –
Spiritus mundi, a smudge of breath wiped off
Glass; earth revolving, an idiot skull.

O living light, break through our shroud! Release
Man's mind, and let the living sleep in peace.

KYRIE ELEISON

Because we are hypnotized by a demon our will has
conjured: because we play for safety with dangerous
power, and dare not revoke: because we injure the
tissue of creation –
                    Have pity upon us.

Whether in the pursuit of knowledge, the name of
freedom, or the course of duty, I serve humanity's

---

* After publication of *The Gate* Donald Swann set the *Requiem* to music.

programme for suicide; or whether inert I
acquiesce –

> Have pity upon me.

I am the young who have no time in trust, no time
for belief; the old who reserve the sacrament of
violence: I am what struts or chaffers on a
crumbling edge of existence –

> Have pity upon me.

In the hour of our death, and in the day of our
judgment –

> Have pity upon us.

DIES IRAE

Day of wrath, oh ruthless day
When humankind shall melt away:
Day of wrath when in a flash
History shall burn to ash.

Turning keys upon the dials
Shall unloose the furious phials;
Then the trumpeting blasts be heard –
Art, law, science, all absurd.

From a lucid heaven foresee
Monstrous that epiphany
Of man's calculated error
Break in light and brood in terror:

Skin flayed off the skeleton,
Ghosts of men burnt into stone,
Uberant rivers boiling dry,
Cities sucked up into the sky.

All too late then for repenting
Of the powers we are mis-spending.
We could only pray that doom
Fall sheer on us and fast consume;

Pray the loud heat-stroke spare us not
For the soundless rain to rot
Our angry blood, corrupt our bone –
Remnants of life that crawl and moan;

Spare us not to see this earth
Travail with a second birth,
Monsters multiply and breed
From a joyless, tainted seed.

Look how the sun of nature dips
Toward evil's dark apocalypse!
How near the ages' growth is blighted,
Man in his brilliancy benighted!

Day of wrath, oh ruthless day
When humankind shall melt away:
Day of wrath when in a flash
Past and future turn to ash.

OFFERTORIUM

O God, in whom we half believe,
Or not believe,
Or pray to like importunate children
Tugging a sleeve:
Whether man's need created you,
Or his creation seed from you,
Our creeds have overshaded you
With terror, pain and grief.

585

O God, in whose mysterious name
We men have lit
Age after age the torturer's flame
And died in it:
If you have not forsaken us,
Rake out this burning rage from us,
Give us concern, awake in us
Children a holier spirit!

The kin-dividing sovereignty
Of pride and fear, the blasphemy
Which is our blear-eyed apathy –
These let us sacrifice;
Burn up the false gods that infect
Our soul with lies,
Melt down the bars that cage us off
In cells of ice.

If you exist, if heed our cares,
If these our offerings and prayers
Could save, if earth's entreating heirs
Are to be born to live –
Spirit, in whom we half believe
And would believe,
Free us from fear, revive us in
A fire of love.

SANCTUS

Holy this earth where unamazed we dwell –
Mothering earth, our food, our fabulous well –
A mote in space, a flicker of time's indifferent wheel.

Holy the marigold play of evening sun
On wall and tree, the dawn's light-fingered run,
Night's muted strings, the shimmering chords of summer
noon.

586

Holy the salmon leaping up a fall,
Leopard's glide, birds and bees their seasonal
Employ, the shy demeanour of antelope and snail.

Praise wild, tame, common, rare – chrysanthemums
That magnify a back-yard in the slums.
Gentian and passion flower, primrose of deep combes.

Praise the white orchards of the cloudful west,
Wheat prairies with abundance in their breast,
The seas, the mineral mountains, the jungle and the waste.

Holy the flowering of our genial dust
In art, law, science, raising from earth's crust
A testament of vision made good and truth diffused.

Holy the climber's grit, the athlete's grace,
Whippets unleashed and pigeons' homing race,
A stadium's roar, a theatre's hush – they also praise.

Oh praise man's mind that, questioning why things are
And whence, haloes the moon with a new star,
Peers into nature's heart and cons the order there.

Oh praise what makes us creatures breed and build
Over death's void, and know ourselves fulfilled
In that age-hallowed trinity – man, woman, child.

Holy the heights where flesh and spirit wed.
Holy this earth, our source, our joy, our bread.
Holy to praise man's harvest and treasure his brave seed.

BENEDICTUS

Blessed are they who come
At need, in mercy's name

587

To walk beside the lame,
Articulate for the dumb.

Blessed who range ahead
Of man's laborious trek,
Survey marsh, desert, peak,
Signal a way to tread.

Blessed whose faith defies
The mighty, welds the weak;
Whose dreaming hopes awake
And ring like prophecies.

Blessed who shall release
At this eleventh hour
Us thralls of evil power
And lift us into peace.

AGNUS DEI

O child of man,
Wombed in dark waters you retell
Millenniums, image the terrestrial span
From an unwitting cell
To the new soul within her intricate shell,
O child of man.

O child of man
Whose infant eyes and groping mind
Meet chaos and create the world again,
You for yourself must find
The toils we know, the truths we have divined –
Yes, child of man.

O child of man,
You come to justify and bless
The animal throes wherein your life began,
And gently draw from us
The milk of love, the most of tenderness,
Dear child of man.

So, child of man,
Remind us what we have blindly willed –
A slaughter of all innocents! You can
Yet make this madness yield
And lift the load of our stock-piling guilt,
O child of man.

LUX AETERNA

Commune with the dead, the myriad commonwealth
Of our forefathers: an earthbound family,
But listen! remote in mind's catacombs they whispering
Enlighten us.

Impalpable these: but look! they point and power us
To destinies unknown and stellar distances;
Transmitting the genius of generations, they
Enlighten us.

Life-line of heroes, god-favoured or unlucky;
Common clay turned and fired by circumstance
Into rare acts of exalting beauty –
Enlighten us!

Adventurer, heart dilated with horizons;
Rebel, whose impious hand shaped a future piety;
Outcast, whose wilderness rebuked your cruel kind;
Enlighten us!

You that envisioned order and revealed it
In nature's anomalies, to men's anarchic
Selfishness – lawgiver, scientist, artist,
Enlighten us!

Shepherd, husbandman, artisan, clerk – all whose
Workaday routines kept our world in good trim:
You ghostly ranks of the unregarded,
Enlighten us!

The dead are engraved in us. We till death are
Keepers of their peace, and of their expansive
Estate the sole trustees. Lest we betray them,
Enlighten us!

Little as dust-motes in the light of eternity,
A moment they danced, but a dance momentous.
Break we that chain now? change being to nothing?
Angels, essences of truth, enlighten us!

RESPONSORIUM

Free us from fear, we cry. Our sleep is fretted,
Anxious we wake, in our terrestrial room.
What wastes the flesh, what ticks below the floor would
Abort all futures, desecrate the tomb.

Free us from fear. The shapes that loom around us
Darkening judgment, freezing all that's dear
Into a pose of departure – these are shadows
Born of man's will and bodied by his fear.

May the white magic of the child's wayfaring,
Wonderful earth – our present from the dead,
And the long vistas of mankind slow maturing
Lighten the heart and clear the feverish head!

O living light, break through our shroud! Release
Man's mind, and let the living sleep in peace!

1962

THE ROOM
and other poems

TO ELIZABETH BOWEN

595

FABLES AND CONFESSIONS

The Room

FOR GEORGE SEFERIS*

To this room – it was somewhere at the palace's
Heart, but no one, not even visiting royalty
Or reigning mistress, ever had been inside it –
To this room he'd retire.
Graciously giving himself to, guarding himself from
Courtier, suppliant, stiff ambassador,
Supple assassin, into this unviewed room
He, with the air of one urgently called from
High affairs to some yet loftier duty,
Dismissing them all, withdrew.

And we imagined it suitably fitted out
For communing with a God, for meditation
On the Just City; or, at the least, a bower of
Superior orgies . . . He
Alone could know the room as windowless
Though airy, bare yet filled with the junk you find
In any child-loved attic; and how he went there
Simply to taste himself, to be reassured
That under the royal action and abstraction
He lived in, he was real.

---

* Seferis (George Seferiades) was Greek Ambassador in London at this time. The conflict between the particularly public career of diplomat with the private one of poet intrigued CDL.

On Not Saying Everything

This tree outside my window here.
Naked, umbrageous, fresh or sere,
Has neither chance nor will to be
Anything but a linden tree,
Even if its branches grew to span
The continent; for nature's plan
Insists that infinite extension
Shall create no new dimension.
From the first snuggling of the seed
In earth, a branchy form's decreed.

Unwritten poems loom as if
They'd cover the whole of earthly life.
But each one, growing, learns to trim its
Impulse and meaning to the limits
Roughed out by me, then modified
In its own truth's expanding light.
A poem, settling to its form,
Finds there's no jailer, but a norm
Of conduct, and a fitting sphere
Which stops it wandering everywhere.

As for you, my love, it's harder,
Though neither prisoner nor warder,
Not to desire you both: for love
Illudes us we can lightly move
Into a new dimension, where
The bounds of being disappear
And we make one impassioned cell.
So wanting to be all in all
Each for each, a man and woman
Defy the limits of what's human.

Your glancing eye, your animal tongue,
Your hands that flew to mine and clung
Like birds on bough, with innocence
Masking those young experiments
Of flesh, persuaded me that nature
Formed us each other's god and creature.
Play out then, as it should be played,
The sweet illusion that has made
An eldorado of your hair
And our love an everywhere.

But when we cease to play explorers
And become settlers, clear before us
Lies the next need – to re-define
The boundary between yours and mine;
Else, one stays prisoner, one goes free.
Each to his own identity
Grown back, shall prove our love's expression
Purer for this limitation.
Love's essence, like a poem's, shall spring
From the not saying everything.

The Way In

The right way in would be hard to find –
Not for want of a door, but because there were so many,
Each commanding a different kind
Of approach, and then committing him to
An unretraceable step. If he faced
The flunkey's sneer and the snarling wolfhounds,
He would soon discover that getting past
Them was the least of his troubles. He lacked
The hero's invincible charm: to go

Without card of introduction or book
Of etiquette was bad; but worse, he had no
Ground-plan given him for what would be
Less of a mansion, he feared, than a maze.
Still, through state apartments and ancestor-lined
Passages, beyond a door of green baize,
He knew there must be that innermost room
Where She, alone, waited. Waited for whom?

No doubt she was at home. He had seen her mooning
Around the garden – pearl feet, gold crown
Proved her a princess – early every morning
In the ghostfall dew by the dreaming cedars.
No sentry, mastiff or chains could he spy,
But he felt her a captive . . . Now, crawling through
The grass of the lawn, which had grown head-high
Since he came, he listened at a gloomed french window
Faint sounds he heard: they might have been
Cries for help or his own voice calling
From sleep. Ventured a glance: obscene
Slug trails and spider webs pasted the glass.
Frantic to peel away the cataract spell
He circled the domicile, trying each door:
Bells, knockers, handles – he tried them all.
But all in a repudiating hush was locked;
Till a window opened, a wide mouth mocked.

So he went home, romantic even in disgrace,
And told his father the whole sad story.
Who said: 'To be sure, I remember the place,
And the afternoon I felt like going there.
I walked through the door – there is only one,
By the way – and yes, I remember a crown
Of tawny hair. I tumbled it down.
She sighed for relief. I took her, bare
And crowing as a babe, on the kitchen floor.'

The Passion for Diving

The man up there with red trunks, middle-aged paunch,
Rapt in a boylike singleness of mind
Or in some trance of altitude immersed –
What do we make of him? The way he'll launch
From bank, deck, high board, harbour wall, to find
Himself arriving, more or less head-first,
In pool, sea, river, then scramble out and prise
The void again, again? Not for display:
He cuts no athlete's figure through the air.
Nor from infatuation with what lies
Supine beneath: it seldom can delay
Him longer than the few strokes he must spare
To reach a foot-hold and climb out again.
There may be pride in it (for Lucifer,
Might not that long dive feel like an aspiring?);
And pleasure – heaving haunches of the main,
That green, comethering inshore eye, the stir
Of watersilk muscle, over which he's poring.
But most it is the sense of challenge, a boy's
Need and fear of solitary engagement
With powers beyond his power, that springs the leap.
The man recalls a young self in that poise
And pause between an airy unattachment
And the blind, brief committal to the deep.

Derelict

FOR A. D. PETERS*

The soil, flinty at best, grew sour. Its yield
Receding left the old farm high and dry
On a ledge of the hills. Disused, the rutted field-
Track fades, like the sound of footsteps, into a sigh
For any feet to approach this padlocked door.
The walls are stained and cracked, the roof's all rafter.
We have come where silence opens to devour
Owl-cry, wind-cry, all human memories . . . After
So many working life-times a farm settles
For leisure, and in the tenth of a life-time goes
To seed . . . A harrow rusts among harsh nettles.
She who in love or protest grew that rose
Beneath her window, left nothing else behind
But a mangle in the wash-house. The rose now
Looks mostly thorn and sucker; the window's blind
With cobwebs. Dilapidated! – even the low
Front wall is ragged: neighbours have filched its stone
To build their pigsties, maybe; but what neighbours? –
Never did a farm stand more alone.
Was it the loneliness, then, and not their labour's
Poor yield that drove them out? A farmer's used
To the silence of things growing, weather breeding.
More solitude, more acres. He'd be amused
To hear it's human company he was needing.
With a wife to bake, wash, mend, to nag or share
The after-supper silence, children to swing
From those rheumatic apple trees; and where
The docks run wild, his chained-up mongrel barking
If anyone climbed a mile off on the hill.

* A. D. Peters was CDL's literary agent and close friend for forty-six years of his writing life.

He'd not abandon cheerfully a place
In which he'd sunk his capital of skill
And sweat. But if earth dies on you, it's no disgrace
To pull up roots . . . Now, all that was the farm's –
The same demands of seasons, the plain grit
And homely triumph – deepens and informs
The silence you can hear. Reverence it.

Saint Anthony's Shirt

'We are like the relict garments of a Saint: the same and not
the same: for the careful Monks patch it and patch it: till
there's not a thread of the original garment left, and still
they show it for St Anthony's shirt.'

KEATS: Letter to Reynolds

This moving house of mine – how could I care
If, wasting and renewing cell by cell,
It's the ninth house I now have tenanted?
I cannot see what keeps it in repair
Nor charge the workmen who, its changes tell,
Build and demolish it over my head.

Ninth house and first, the same yet not the same –
Are there, beneath new brickwork, altering style,
Viewless foundations steady through the years?
Hardly could I distinguish what I am
But for the talkative sight-seers who file
Through me, the window-view that clouds or clears.

The acting, speaking, lusting, suffering I
Must be a function of this house, or else
Its master principle. Is I a sole
Tenant created, recreated by

What he inhabits, or a force which tells
The incoherent fabric it is whole?

If master, where's the master-thread runs through
This patchwork, piecemeal self? If occupant
Merely, the puppet of a quarrelsome clique,
How comes the sense of selfhood as a clue
Embodying yet transcending gene and gland?
The I, though multiple, is still unique.

I walk these many rooms, wishing to trace
My frayed identity. In each, a ghost
Looks up and claims me for his long-lost brother –
Each unfamiliar, though he wears my face.
A draught of memory whispers I was most
Purely myself when I became another:

Tending a sick child, groping my way into
A woman's heart, lost in a poem, a cause,
I touched the marrow of my being, unbared
Through self-oblivion. Nothing remains so true
As the outgoingness. This moving house
Is home, and my home, only when it's shared.

Days before a Journey

Days before a journey
The mind, prefiguring absence,
Begins to leave. Its far
Destination loosens
The weave of the familiar
And distances the near.

A man begins his absence
From a loved one, easing
Away as if he peeled
Gently a cling-close dressing
From a wound unhealed –
A wound as yet scarce felt.

From a loved home easing
While he is still there,
For all its sheltering grief
He finds in his breast the hare
Roused from its form, the leaf
That in late fall writhes to be off.

While he is here, still here,
His going will slide between
Him and all he would stay for,
Misting each homely scene;
The ill-wished hours hang over
His head, without bloom or flavour.

Between staying and going
Opens the little death,
Shadowed, unformed, uncanny
And makes the real a wraith.
Oh, travelling starts many
Days before the journey.

Fishguard to Rosslare

From all my childhood voyages back to Ireland
Only two things remembered: gulls afloat
Off Fishguard quay, littering a patch of radiance
Shed by the midnight boat.

And at dawn a low, dun coast shaping to meet me,
An oyster sky opening above Rosslare . . .
I rub the sleep from my eyes. Gulls pace the moving
Mast-head. We're almost there.

Gulls white as a dream on the pitch of Fishguard harbour,
Paper cut-outs, birds on a lacquered screen;
The low coastline and the pearl sky of Ireland;
A long sleep in between.

A sleep between two waking dreams – the haven,
The landfall – is how it appears now. The child's eye,
Unpuzzled, saw plain facts: I catch a glint from
The darkness they're haunted by.

The Hieroglyph

Now limbs awaken stiff
And wit goes limp, I view
Closer but no clearer
Death's riddling hieroglyph –
The sole, the common grave.

Reason deciphers there
An order to dissolve

608

Body and mind: religion
Reads in it a dear-
Bought visa to elsewhere.

The shadows lengthen. I
Could envy a brute beast
Who, till the hour comes round,
Enjoys an eternal sty,
Ignorant he must die.

Indeed I would not be one
Who counts the hours to death,
Hoarding each last gold drip
Of an exhausted sun,
Or wishing his day were done.

Treasure and snake entwined
Image love's transience,
The gold unvalued if
No guardian sting the mind
To think it must be resigned.

Meanwhile, let me preserve
A discipline of living
Under the law of death,
Honouring still the nerve
And need of mortal love.

Seven Steps in Love

'I dreamed love was an angel,
But her finger-tip is laid
Like the peine forte et dure upon
My breast, and I'm afraid.

'I am afraid, afraid.
The letter-box rattles a threat,
Disaster seeps through my window-frame,
Takes me by the throat.'

Sure, earth changes colour
And the heart's oppressed –
It's the storm of rebirth you fear – when *she*
Points a man at your breast.

Oh she's the wheedling goddess
With a strap behind her back:
She'll hand you a bunch of roses
And lay you on the rack;

Stretch you upon your lover's absence,
Wring you dry of tears,
Brainwash you into believing
You're dead till he climbs the stairs.

And if at last for each other
Body and mind you strip,
She'll pin her undated farewell note
Onto the pillow-slip.

Give in, give in, fond lovers,
And she'll starve you with wanting more:
Refrain, refrain, and she crams you
With yeasty dreams to the craw.

She has no heart for mercy,
Treats honour as a clown:
But when her naked eye selects you,
Better lie down, lie down.

II

Where autumn and high midsummer meet, there's a touch
Of desperation – rose-beds ready to flare
Their last, holidays nearly over, a premonition
On bonfire and frost in the air.

Veterans of the game, they watched the agents
Of that great power, disguised as usual
In quite transparent innocence, dawdle across the frontier
Disarming and casual

As tourists. A man force deployed from both.
Silently the soft perimeters fell.
Then key positions, yielding at a collusive whisper,
Betrayed the citadel.

Each occupied by the other now, they exchange
Rations, arms, campaign-talk: nothing matters
But more and more to surrender. See the vanquished crown
                                                        with
Olive those sweet invaders.

The everyday opens into a paradise garden.
Gold roses spring through pavements, and a spray
Of freesia freshens the dusty room. For a while, winter
Seems two life-times away.

611

III

She is the dark Unknown
Which makes him an explorer. Gales and spices
For him alone
Breathe in her singing words, her silences
Are silver mines, her frown
Ripples with lynx and cobra . . . It is the strangeness
That lures him on.

Wisdom upon her tongue, but in her veins
Terrified and exulting
Nymph-breasts like whitebeam flash, animals panic –
All's running, melting
Before the tall flame's stride. She fears there'll be
No escape now, no halting,
Yet dreams of forest fires tamed to a hearth.

In love, the animal speaks
With an angel's tongue,
Crying his pure Magnificat
Over sweat, wounds, dung.
Erect and single-minded,
Cunning of enterprise,
The brute becomes a poet in
Flatteries and lies.

That prince and scourge of the blood
Will claim he can do no wrong,
Coin his own image of truth, and whip
The half-hearted along;
Rubicund, smiles to think
That Honesty is the name

For what looks like the ghost of a flower,
A flimsy spectrogram.

V

When eyes go dark and bodies
Nakedly press home,
Let all else be dumb,
Louder sing the sensual glee,
Louder the nerves thrum.

Stand off, you cowled observer
Who eye love's act askance.
Shameless of tongue, of hands,
Body shall make the awkward soul
Jump to its commands.

Only the wry soul answers
In ridicule or disgust.
Praise, man, that flurry of dust –
Your rutting animal: moon-gold woman,
Be candid of your lust.

Now the respectful lover,
Fleshed upon his prey
Brute hunger to allay,
Is one with roughneck ancestors
Millenniums away.

Now she is the tumid
Ocean he rides and reaps:
Wave upon wave she leaps
Against him; then her dissolute power
Gulps him down, and sleeps.

When eyes go dark and bodies
One to another fly,
Let not the soul decry
What wisdom's born from dialogues
Of wanton breast and thigh.

VI

Stretched at their feet, one morning after love,
The holy lough renews without a flaw
What the storm had erased – a shadow-shore
Of rocks, grass, bracken: russet, emerald, mauve.
Dream-colours wake in their untroubled sense,
Golds of the fall – grain, harvest moon, wild bees,
And the leaves reddening for long goodbyes:
The lake's hushed in the silver of their trance.
A violet mountain, steep beyond the glen,
Lets down like tumbling hair a cataract
Which goes to sleep in waters that reflect
Its passionate leaping as a still, white line.
No stir of wind or wing to flaw the calm,
These lovers, flesh appeased, would consummate
A dearer union, for their hearts dilate
With images of all they could become.

VII

Not in the fleshed and wanton grove,
The goddess-haunted air,
The sacred calm when bodies move
Apart which groaned and cleaved,
Is tenderness conceived,
The lover taught his care.

A woman, beautiful as a myth,
Turns mortal-eyed and plain,

Demanding reassurance with
Quenched grace, domestic tongue –
Then is the trap sprung,
The treadmill starts again.

The Fox

'Look, it's a fox!' – their two hearts spoke
Together. A fortunate day
That was when they saw him, a russet spark
Blown from the wood's long-smouldering dark
On to the woodside way.

There, on the ride, a dog fox paused.
Around him the shadows lay
Attentive suddenly, masked and poised;
And the watchers found themselves enclosed
In a circuit stronger than they.

He stood for some mystery only shared
By creatures of fire and clay.
They watched him stand with the masterless air
Of one who had the best right to be there –
Let others go or stay;

Then, with a flick of his long brush, sign
The moment and whisk it away.
Time flowed back, and the two walked on
Down the valley. They felt they were given a sign –
But of what, they could hardly say.

The Romantics

Those two walked up a chancel of beech trees
Columnar grey, and overhead there fluttered
Fan-vaultings of green leaf. She moved with chastity's
Dancing step, he dull with love unuttered.
She is all Artemis, he thought, and I
Her leashed and clownish hound. But he miscalled her
Who dreamily saw at the ride's far end an O of sky
Like love-in-a-mist, herself pure white, an altar.

The vows exchanged, their love pronounced eternal,
They learn how altar stands for sacrifice.
All changes – beechwood chancel into a cramped tunnel;
Huntress to victim; hound, throwing off disguise,
To faithless hero. Soon he'll take the knife and start
To carve his way out of her loving heart.

Stephanotis

Pouring an essence of stephanotis
Into his bath till the panelled, carpeted room
Breathed like a paradise fit for sweltering houris,
He lapsed through scent and steam

To another bathroom, shires and years away –
A makeshift one tacked on to
The end of a cottage, it smelt of rusting pipes,
Damp plaster. In that lean-to

One night she sprinkled the stephanotis
He'd given her – a few drops of delicate living

616

Tasted by two still young enough to need
No luxury but their loving.

They are long parted, and their essence gone.
Yet even now he can smell,
Infused with the paradise scent, that breath of rusty
Water and sweating wall.

The Dam

It mounted up behind his cowardice
And self-regard. Fearing she would expose
His leper tissue of half-truths and lies
When, hurt, she probed at him, he tried to gloze
That fear as patience with her sick mistrust
Of him: he could not answer her appeal,
Nor recognize how his was the accursed
Patience of flesh that can no longer feel . . .
Love had once mounted up behind his fear
Of being exposed in love's whole helplessness,
And broke it down, and carried him to her
On the pure, toppling rage for nakedness . . .
A spate of her reproaches. The dam broke.
In deluging anger his self-hatred spoke.

An Operation

The knife, whose freezing shadow had unsteeled
His loved one's heart, moved in at last to shear
Impassive flesh: she was no longer there –
Only a surface to be botched or healed.

While this went through, he felt the critical blade
Cut from his own heart all the encrustation
Of years and usage: bleeding with compassion,
He found his love laid bare, a love new-made.

OTHERS

Who Goes Home?

(WINSTON SPENCER CHURCHILL, 1874–1965)

I

So the great politician
  Goes home; and we consign
To history his craft of politics
  Ennobled by a vision
  That saw the grand design,
The vaulting arch sprung from the clay-bound bricks.

  Soldier, historian,
  Orator, artist – he
Adorned the present and awoke the past:
  Now ended his long span,
  A one-man ministry
Of all the talents has resigned at last.

  We knew him in debate
  Provocative or prophetic,
A Puck one day, the next a Prospero.
  We saw him by defeat
  Unsoured – the energetic
Come-back, the magnanimity all through.

  Here was a man in whom
  Great issues brought to light
Genius to grapple them. On a poised hour
  Danger drew steel and gloom
  Struck fire from him: the tide
Of battle charged his impetuous mind with power.

619

So he becomes a myth,
  A dynast of our day
Standing for all time at the storm's rough centre
  Where he, a monolith
  Of purpose grim and gay,
Flung in the waves' teeth the rock's no-surrender.

II

That myth we cherish now the man is dead.
But, living, what was he to most? – a trite
    Cartoon of grit and wit?
A bulldog mouth, a tortoise thrust of the head,
A cigar, a genial snarl? Go deeper. See
    The versatility

Rare in this narrowing age. His soldier's nerve,
Painter's colour-struck eye, orator's flair
    For passion, writer's care
In the ménage of thought – all went to serve
His need that life be a momentous tale
    Heroic in scope and scale.

The route was difficult, and the peak remote.
A dunce at school, an uppish subaltern –
    How few could there discern
One who would make the history he wrote,
Or see the young fox-haired firebrand of debate
    Steadying a shaken State.

Aristocratic temper, in an age
Restive against the uncommon, rides for a fall.
    Wilful, mercurial,
Impatient of the reckonings that engage
Small minds, unseated often, still he rose
    Above his falls and foes.

Great Marlborough in his heart, upon his tongue
Gibbon's long thunders, always he foreknew
   High destiny, and grew
Into his legend slowly; then among
Titanic storms claimed an immortal part –
   Gave Britain tongue and heart.

III

Who goes home? goes home?
   By river, street and dome
The long lamenting call echoes on, travels on
   From London, further, further,
   Across all lands. The Mother
Of Parliaments is grieving for her great, dead son.

A soaring spirit vaults
   The failures and the faults
Of the clay that it worked in, the will it clarified.
   Though a voice is taken hence,
   Its reverberant eloquence
Rings on into the ages, rings out on freedom's side.

Remember at his passing
   That finest hour – the bracing
Of nerve, the hearts lifting, the challenge to dismay,
   When a nation took cheer
   From the vision he held dear
Of uplands shining out beyond a sombre day.

But also call to mind
   With what grace he resigned
The habit of power, the pulse of action. Character stood
   The test of letting go
   What had sustained it; so
He and his fame ripened in autumn quietude.

Who goes home? A man
Whose courage and strong span
Of enterprise will stand for ages yet to come.
  Storm-riding heart now stilled
  And destiny fulfilled,
Our loved, our many-minded Churchill has gone home.

Pietà*

Naked, he sags across her cumbered knees,
Heavy and beautiful like the child she once
Aroused from sleep, to fall asleep on the next breath.

The passion is done,
But death has not yet stiffened him against her,
Nor chilled the stripling grace into a dogma.
For a timeless hour, imagined out of marble,
He comes back to his mother, he is all
And only hers.

And it is she whom death has magnified
To bear the burden of his flesh – the arms
Excruciated no more, the gash wiped clean.
A divine, dazed compassion calms her features.
She holds all earth's dead sons upon her lap.

*   *   *

In the triumphal car
Closely escorted through the gaze and heart of
A city, at the height of his golden heyday,
He suddenly slumps.

* The assassination of President Kennedy.

622

Cameras show her bending to shelter him
(But death has moved faster), and then a pink
Nimbus veiling the exploded skull.

No order here, no artistry, except for
The well-drilled wounds, the accomplished sacrifice.
But from that wreck
Two living images are saved – the wife who
Nurses a shattered world in her lap;

And, flying the coffin home, refuses to change
Out of her yellow, blood-spattered dress, with
'Let them all see what was done to him.'

Elegy for a Woman Unknown

(F.P.) *

I

At her charmed height of summer –
Prospects, children rosy,
In the heart's changeful music
Discords near resolved –
Her own flesh turned upon her:
The gross feeder slowly
Settled to consume her.

Pain speaks, bearing witness
Of rank cells that spawn

---

* In 1961, Dr Michael Peters came to see CDL at Chatto and Windus, bringing a sheaf of his wife's poems: she had recently died of cancer. C prayed that they would be good enough to publish. They weren't. When we were voyaging in Greece that summer, he started to write a poem on the island of Delos at sunset, as he sat, head in hands, gazing at the stone lions. He tried to make it a poem she would like to have written.

To bring their temple down.
Against such inmost treachery
Futile our protesting:
The body creates its own
Justice and unjustness.

Three times flesh was lopped,
As trees to make a firebreak.
(In their natural flowering
Beautiful the trees.)
Three times her enemy leapt
The gap. Three years of dying
Before the heart stopped.

Upon the shrinking islands
Of flesh and hope, among
Bitter waves that plunged,
Withdrew to lunge yet deeper,
Patient, unreconciled,
She wrote poems and flung them
To the approaching silence.

Upon the stretching hours
Crucified alone,
She grew white as a stone
Image of endurance;
Soft only to the cares
Of loved ones – all concern
For lives that would soon lack hers.

Dying, did she pass through
Despair to the absolute
Self-possession – the lightness
Of knowing a world indifferent
To all we suffer and do,
Shedding the clung-to load
Of habit, illusion, duty?

You who watched, phase by phase,
Her going whose life was meshed
With yours in grief and passion,
Remember now the unspoken,
Unyielding word she says –
How, in ruinous flesh,
Heroic the heart can blaze.

II

Island of stone and silence. A rough ridge
Chastens the innocent azure. Lizards hang
Like their own shadows crucified on stone
(But the heart palpitates, the ruins itch
With memories amid the sunburnt grass). Here sang
Apollo's choir, the sea their unloosed zone.
Island of stillness and white stone.

Marble and stone – the ground-plan is suggested
By low walls, plinths, lopped columns of stoa, streets
Clotted with flowers dead in June, where stood
The holy place. At dusk they are invested
With Apollonian calm and a ghost of his zenith heats.
But now there are no temples and no god:
Vacantly stone and marble brood,

And silence – not the silence after music,
But the silence of no more music. A breeze twitches
The grass like a whisper of snakes; and swallows there are,
Cicadas, frogs in the cistern. But elusive
Their chorusing – thin threads of utterance, vanishing
                                        stitches
Upon the gape of silence, whose deep core
Is the stone lions' soundless roar.

Lions of Delos, roaring in abstract rage
Below the god's hill, near his lake of swans!
Tense haunches, rooted paws set in defiance
Of time and all intruders, each grave image
Was sentinel and countersign of deity once.
Now they have nothing to keep but the pure silence.
Crude as a schoolchild's sketch of lions

They hold a rhythmic truth, a streamlined pose.
Weathered by sea-winds into beasts of the sea,
Fluent from far, unflawed; but the jaws are toothless,
Granulated by time the skin, seen close,
And limbs disjointed. Nevertheless, what majesty
Their bearing shows – how well they bear these ruthless
Erosions of their primitive truth!

Thyme and salt on my tongue, I commune with
Those archetypes of patience, and with them praise
What in each frantic age can most incline
To reverence; accept from them perfection's myth –
One who warms, clarifies, inspires, and flays.
Sweetness he gives but also, being divine,
Dry bitterness of salt and thyme.

The setting sun has turned Apollo's hill
To darker honey. Boulders and burnt grass.
A lyre-thin wind. A landscape monochrome.
Birds, lizards, lion shapes are all stone-still.
Ruins and mysteries in the favouring dusk amass,
While I reach out through silence and through stone
To her whose sun has set, the unknown.

III

We did not choose to voyage.
Over the ship's course we had little say,

626

And less over the ship. Tackle
Fraying; a little seamanly skill picked up on our way;
Cargo, that sooner or later we should
Jettison to keep afloat for one more day.
But to have missed the voyage –

That would be worse than the gales, inglorious calms,
Hard tack and quarrels below . . .
Ship's bells, punctual as hunger; dawdling stars;
Duties – to scrub the deck, to stow
Provisions, break out a sail: if crisis found us of one mind,
It was routine that made us so,
And hailed each landfall like a first-born son.

Figure to yourself the moment
When, after weeks of the crowding emptiness of sea
(Though no two waves are the same to an expert
Helmsman's eye), the wind bears tenderly
From an island still invisible
The smell of earth – of thyme, grass, olive trees:
Fragrance of a woman lost, returning.

And you open the bay, like an oyster, but sure there'll be
A pearl inside; and rowing ashore,
Are received like gods. They shake down mulberries into
Your lap, bring goat's cheese, pour
Fresh water for you, and wine. Love too is given.
It's for the voyaging that you store
Such memories; yet each island seems your abiding-place.

. . . For the voyaging, I say:
And not to relieve its hardships, but to merge
Into its element. Bays we knew
Where still, clear water dreamed like a demiurge
And we were part of his fathomless dream;

627

Times, we went free and frisking with dolphins through the
                                                    surge
Upon our weather bow.

Those were our best hours – the mind disconnected
From pulsing Time, and purified
Of accidents: those, and licking the salt-stiff lips,
The rope-seared palms, happy to ride
With sea-room after days of clawing from off a lee shore,
After a storm had died.
Oh, we had much to thank Poseidon for.

Whither or why we voyaged,
Who knows? . . . A worst storm blew. I was afraid.
The ship broke up. I swam till I
Could swim no more. My love and memories are laid
In the unrevealing deep . . . But tell them
They need not pity me. Tell them I was glad
Not to have missed the voyage.

Young Chekhov

This young provincial, his domestic ties,
Modest pretensions both to medicine
And literature (well, who would not despise
Such penny-a-line humour as he turned in?)
Mocks all who say the bourgeois life inhibits
And can't conceive how, through frivolity,
Hackwork, piles, unobjectionable habits,
A Vanya and a Masha came to be.
He paid his bills, and others'; scoured the town
For gossip, but created none – too tired
And prudent for debauch or the noble blather

Of revolutionaries . . . The god sends down:
The bourgeoise is astonished when her brood
Grow up to prove an angel was their father.

The Widow Interviewed

'The Poet' (well, that's the way her generation
Talked) 'the Poet wrote these for me when first – '
(She said, touching the yellowed manuscripts
Like a blind girl gentling a young man's hair)
– 'When first we were betrothed. I have kept them:
'The rest I had to sell.'
                     Beside the juniper
Breaking a branch to light at the cottage fire,
'Incense for you,' he said. But I did truly worship
That smouldering, pliant boy.
                     'He was a great
"Lover of Beauty" (yes, that's how she put it,
Capital letters and all. Eyes calm: cheeks russet, wrinkled:
Face of a good plain cook or somebody's old nurse).
'Ah, you may wonder what he saw in me.
'Wonder it was to me – the homely, spectacled
'Girl he married. But you yourself are a writer:
'You know what poets need is a plain screen
'To project their magical lines and colours upon.
'He had beauty enough for us both, enough passion
'For Beauty to evoke a vernal goddess
'Out of my pudgy clay.'
                    One April morning
You dropped four primroses into my bosom,
Called me your Primavera. Oh, my love!
My dear love!
                And those poems – what a treasure

You've got there! – they appeared in his first book?
'No. They were never published. He became
'Dissatisfied with them.'
                    Would have burnt them, too:
But I hid them away, as I hid other failures
And failings, cherished them for being his.
    He was his own severest critic. 'Well,
'The only one he could do with. It was the act
'Of bearing poems he lived by, not the issue.
'He could launch a sheaf of them from our gusty hilltop –
'Paper darts for the children, yet despair
'And walk all night, searching for one lost word.'
    The artist's hard to live with. 'So I learned:
'Hard, because *with* him is not how you live,
'Housekeeping for an often absentee
'Master – one most absent sitting at home when
'His daemon empties you out of his eyes
'And draws the cloak of solitude about him.
'I bore his children, cooked his meals . . . But never
'Imagine I regret the unequal menage.'
    To be a great man's inspiration – 'Have the glory
'Of being an oyster's grit? Besides, I was not,
'Not for long; more like a shock-absorber.'
He had a roughish road. 'The road he chose.'
And you went with him.
                    Oh, my dear love, why
Could you not take the comfort that I offered?
What else had I to give you than a cup
Of water in the desert? Did you not see
How often I was spilt over the sand?
'Yes, to the end. For me it was easier going
'After I'd shaken off my own pride – most
'My clinging pride in him – learnt to let go his hands,
'Leaving him free to wrestle with his daemon.'
(Who often took the slippery form and naked
Grip of another girl, by all accounts).

630

He was much loved. 'And loved much. If you like to call it
'Love. You are curious? Listen – where he went,
'He went more out of curiosity
'Than love, or even lust: the lust ensued, and even
'Love once or twice. Imagine him as prospecting
'For a new lode. One place where he might find –
'Not fairy gold nor Ali Baba's cave –
'Simply a poem's crude and filthy ore, was
'Between a woman's legs.'
                     Now I have shocked
The poor man, spoken out of character, Eve
Grinning through pure white Martha. Well of course
I was jealous: the body parted from mine, whose essence
I'd had no part in ever – what was left? . . .
   How right you are. Where all the ladders start.
It has been a privilege. The world of letters
Owes you a great debt. Prop and stay of one
I do not scruple to acclaim a genius.
They also serve who only . . .
                    But always,
Always you came home to me, as if
You had left your daemon in my care, and me
In its safe keeping. Oh, the joy at last
To find something we had proved equally –
The peace, knowing your daemon was my angel.

For Rex Warner On His Sixtieth Birthday

   'The hawk-faced man' – thirty-five years ago
   I called him – 'who could praise an apple
   In terms of peach and win the argument' . . .
   Oxford between the wars. I at the age of dissent
   From received ideas, admiring a man so able
   At undermining the crusted status quo.

But he was no sophist, this unsophisticated
Son of a Modernist clergyman, who came down
From a Cotswold height with the larks of Amberley
And the lays of Catullus running wild in his head. We,
Two green youths, met by chance in a Jacobean
Quad. From that term our friendship's dated.

Friendship, I'd guess, has not much more to do
With like minds, shared needs, than with rent or profit:
Nor is it the love which burns to be absolute, then dies
By inches of ill-stitched wounds, of compromise:
But a kind of grace – take it or leave it.
'Keeping up' a friendship means it is through.

That grace I accept. When he returns at last
From Egypt, Greece, the States, we take up where
We left. Right friendships are that homing, each to the
                                          other,
On frequencies unchanged through time or weather.
And still, though bulkier, he'll appear
In focus with the young self I knew first. –

Scholar, wing three-quarter, and bird-watcher:
Self-contained, yet an affable bar-crony:
A mind of Attic dash and clarity,
Homeric simpleness, and natural charity
For all but intellectual cliques and their baloney. –
So was he then. And since, each new departure

Proved him, though wayward, all of a piece.
Working a spell of allegoric art,
In *The Wild Goose Chase* and *The Aerodrome*
He formed a style intrinsic, dry and firm –
Revetment against the chaos in his and a nation's heart –
As, centuries ago, Thucydides.

Fable or fact, living and dead, he carries
Greece near his heart. Rocks, olives, temples, sea and sun
In lucid paradigm express
His tonic scepticism, cordial address.
Pericles and Prometheus spoke through one
Loved by Sikelianós and great Seferis.

Enough that in a pretentious age, when all –
Love, politics, art, right down to money – is cheapened,
He'll take each issue for what it's worth, not wincing,
Inflating, prancing his ego there, romancing
A tragic fall: if deaths have happened
In him, through him, he never preached at the funeral.

It's friendship we return to in the end:
Past selves are kept alive in it, a living
Communion flows from their dead languages. A home
Enlarged by absences, mellowed by custom,
Undemanding, simply taking and giving,
Is he, our sixty-year-old friend.

My Mother's Sister*

I see her against the pearl sky of Dublin
Before the turn of the century, a young woman
With all those brothers and sisters, green eyes, hair
She could sit on; for high life, a meandering sermon

(Church of Ireland) each Sunday, window-shopping
In Dawson Street, picnics at Killiney and Howth . . .
To know so little about the growing of one
Who was angel and maid-of-all-work to my growth!

* Agnes Squires, known as 'Knos'.

– Who, her sister dying, took on the four-year
Child, and the chance that now she would never make
A child of her own; who, mothering me, flowered in
The clover-soft authority of the meek.

Who, exiled, gossiping home chat from abroad
In roundhand letters to a drift of relations –
Squires', Goldsmiths, Overends, Williams' – sang the songs
Of Zion in a strange land. Hers the patience

Of one who made no claims, but simply loved
Because that was her nature, and loving so
Asked no more than to be repaid in kind.
If she was not a saint, I do not know

What saints are . . . Buying penny toys at Christmas
(The most a small purse could afford) to send her
Nephews and nieces, she'd never have thought the shop
Could shine for me one day in Bethlehem splendour.

Exiled again after ten years, my father
Remarrying, she faced the bitter test
Of charity – to abdicate in love's name
From love's contentful duties. A distressed

Gentle woman housekeeping for strangers;
Later, companion to a droll recluse
Clergyman brother in rough-pastured Wexford,
She lived for all she was worth – to be of use.

She bottled plums, she visited parishioners.
A plain habit of innocence, a faith
Mildly forbearing, made her one of those
Who, we were promised, shall inherit the earth.

. . . Now, sunk in one small room of a Rathmines
Old people's home, helpless, beyond speech
Or movement, yearly deeper she declines
To imbecility – my last link with childhood.

The battery's almost done: yet if I press
The button hard – some private joke in boyhood
I teased her with – there comes upon her face
A glowing of the old, enchanted smile.

So, still alive, she rots. A heart of granite
Would melt at this unmeaning sequel. Lord,
How can this be justified, how can it
Be justified?

Madrigal for Lowell House*

The crimson berry tree navelled upon this court
Twinkles a coded message, a wind-sun tingling chord,
Curious round her foot saunters one blue jay:
Fallen leaves swarm and scurry – a game of running away
Slides from play to panic.
Young men pull the berries
To pelt one another, or go their way to seminars
On art and the organic.

The crimson berry tree
Has serious moments too – or we make-believe it so,
Dubbing inspired comments on
Her dumb but pretty show.
'Jaywalker, stuttering leaves have little need to stay

---

* CDL lived in Lowell House, Harvard, when he held the Charles Eliot Norton Chair
1964–65.

When I bleed berries over the snow. But oh, the gay
Young men, the grave young men who feel the wind and
                                                    sun
Today are gone tomorrow, never come back again.'

This Loafer

In a sun-crazed orchard
Busy with blossomings
This loafer, unaware of
What toil or weather brings,
Lumpish sleeps – a chrysalis
Waiting, no doubt, for wings.

And when he does get active,
It's not for business – no
Bee-lines to thyme or heather,
No earnest to-and-fro
Of thrushes: pure caprice tells him
Where and how to go.

All he can ever do
Is to be entrancing,
So that a child may think,
Upon a chalk-blue chancing,
'Today was special. I met
A piece of the sky dancing.'

Grey Squirrel: Greenwich Park

You with the panache tail
The dowdy old ash-bin fur –
What are you *for*, zigzagging so sprucely
And so obtusely
Over the autumn leaves, stopping so dead
The eye shoots ahead of you? What main chance
Are you after, my prancing dear?
You cover the autumn grass with a row
Of lolloping shorthand signs and no
Hesitation or apparent destination;
Then pose upright, paws on chest
Like a politician clasping his top-hat on
A solemn occasion, or a hospital matron
Attending some lord of the wards.
They say you are vermin, but I cannot determine
What no good you're up to. Possibly the odium
Attaches to you for ganging so thoroughly
Your own mad, felicitous gait, not doing
A hand's turn for State, Church, Union, or Borough.

Squirrel, go climb a tree.
You are too like me.

Terns

Sunlit over the shore
Terns – a flock of them – flew,
With swordplay supple as light
Criss-crossing the charmed blue.
They seemed one bird, not a score –

One bird of ubiquitous flight,
One blade so swift in the fence
It flickers like twenty men's,
Letting no thought of a scar,
No fatal doubt pierce through.

Oh whirl and glide, the cut
And thrust of the dazzling terns,
Weaving from joy or need
Such quick, momentous patterns!
If we shall have opted out
Of nature, may she breed
Something more tern-like, less
Inept for togetherness
Than we, who have lost the art
Of dancing to her best tunes.

Apollonian Figure

Careful of his poetic p's and q's,
This self-possessed master of circumspection
Enjoyed a *mariage blanc* with the Muse,
Who never caught his verse in an erection.

Some praise the lapidary figure: but
With due respect to the attendant's spiel,
That fig-leaf there, so elegantly cut –
Just what, if anything, does it conceal?

A Relativist

He raged at critic, moralist – all
That gang who with almightiest gall
Lay claim to the decisive vote
In separating sheep from goat.

So on the last day, when he's got
His breath back again, it will not
Be goats or sheep that rouse his dudgeon
But the absurdity of judging.

Moral

'Moral education is impossible apart from the habitual vision
of greatness.'

A. N. WHITEHEAD

Saints and heroes, you dare say,
Like unicorns, have had their day.
Unlaurel the compulsive tough!
All pierced feet are feet of clay.

Envy – and paucity – of what
Men lived by to enlarge their lot,
Diminishing your share in them,
Downgrade you and not the great.

The saint falls down, the hero's treed
Often, we know it. Still we need
The vision that keeps burning from
Saintly trust, heroic deed.

Accept the flawed self, but aspire
To flights beyond it: wiser far
Lifting our eyes unto the hills
Than lowering them to sift the mire.

The Voyage

Translated from Baudelaire

I

Children, in love with maps and gravings, know
A universe the size of all they lack.
How big the world is by their lamps' clear glow!
But ah, how small to memory looking back!

One morning we set out, our heads on fire,
Our yearning hearts sulky with sour unease,
Following the waves' rhythm, nursing our desire
For the unbounded on those earth-bound seas.

Some glad to leave an infamous birthplace: some
To escape the cradle's nightmare; and a few –
Star-gazers drowned in a woman's eyes – it's from
The scent and power of Circe that they flew.

Not to be changed to beasts, they drug their minds
With space and the large light and burning sky:
The ice that bites them and the suns that bronze
Efface the scar of kisses gradually.

But the true travellers are those who go
For going's sake: hearts light as a balloon,

They never slip their fate: why it is so
They cannot tell, but the word is 'Fare on!'

With longings shaped like hazy clouds, they dream –
As a recruit of gunfire – there impend
Huge pleasures, changeful and untried, whose fame
Is past the wit of man to comprehend.

II

God, that we should behave like top and ball
Bouncing and twirling! Even in our sleep
The Unknown we seek gives us no rest at all,
Like suns tormented by an Angel's whip.

Strange game, whose goal is always on the move
And being nowhere, may be any place;
And Man, whose hope no setbacks will disprove,
Keeps running madly just to catch repose.

The soul is a three-master, Ithaca-bound.
'Keep your eyes skinned!' a sea voice will implore;
From the maintop a keen, mad voice resound
'Love . . . glory . . . luck!' Oh hell, we've run ashore!

Each little isle hailed by the look-out man
Is the Promised Land, golden beyond belief:
Such revels he imagines, but he'll scan
By the cold light of dawn only a reef.

Fairytale lands – that they should craze him so!
Clap him in irons? Pitch him overboard? –
This bold Columbus, drunken matelot,
Whose mirage makes our sea more hard to abide.

641

So the old tramp goes pounding through the shit
And, nose in air, dreams up a paradise;
The meanest shanties where a candle's lit
Are Pleasure-Domes to his enchanted eyes.

III

Amazing voyagers, what splendid tales
Your sea-deep eyes have printed on them. Rare
The jewel caskets of your chronicles:
Show us those gems, fashioned from stars and air.

We'd voyage, but we have no sail or screw.
Liven our spirits, that are canvas-taut.
Breathe your horizon memories, view on view,
Over the boredom of our prisoned thought.

Tell us, what have you seen?

IV

We've seen some stars,
Some waves; and we have met with sand-banks too:
For all the uncharted hazards and the jars
We suffered, we were often bored, like you.

Splendour of sunlight on a violet sea,
Splendour of townships in the setting sun
Kindled in us a burning wish to be
Deep in a sky whose mirror lured us on.

Rich towns and landscapes lovely to the gaze
Had never the mysterious appeal
Of those that chance created out of haze
And our impassioned wanting made so real.

Enjoying gives desire more potency –
Desire that feeds on pleasure: the bark grows
Thicker and tougher on the ageing tree,
But its boughs strain to see the sun more close.

Will you be growing still, great tree, who soared
Higher than cypress? . . . Well, since you rejoice
To swallow anything far-fetched, we've worked hard
And brought these sketches for your album, boys.

There we have greeted trumpeting effigies,
Thrones of star-clustered gems dazzling to view,
Palaces wrought by fairy artifice –
Dreams that would bankrupt millionaires like you;

Dresses which stagger you like drunkenness,
Women with nails and teeth vermilion-stained,
Magicians conjuring a snake's caress.

V

Yes, yes! Go on! And then?

VI

You baby-brained!

Lest we should miss the great, the unique thing,
Ubiquitous and unconcealed we've seen
On the predestined ladder's every rung
The tedious sight of man's inveterate sin:

Woman, bitch slave, stupid and overweening,
Vain without humour, and without disgust
Self-loving; man, slave to a slave, a stream in
A sewer, all grab and foulness, greed, power, lust:

The thug who loves his work, the sobbing martyr,
The feast that seasons and perfumes the blood;
The prince whom power corrupts into self-murder,
The mob who kiss the brutalizing rod:

Several religions, just like our own following,
Bulldoze their path to heaven; the austere,
While dissolute types on feather beds are wallowing,
Gratify their own taste with nails and hair:

Gabbling mankind, drunk on its own nature
And mad today as in all previous years,
Raving with agony bawls to its Maker
'My lord, oh my twin-brother, it's you I curse!'

And the least mad, tough lovers of Alienation,
Fleeing the herd whom fate has corralled in,
Takes refuge with a limitless Illusion . . .
Such is our globe's unchanging bulletin

VII

Acid the knowledge travellers draw. The world,
Little and dull, today, tomorrow and
Tomorrow makes you see yourself – an appalled
Oasis in a tedium of sand.

Should we then go, or stay? If you can, stay:
Go, if you must. One races: one shams death
To cheat the watchful enemy of his prey.
Some runners Time allows no pause for breath –

The wandering Jew, the apostles, who can neither
Escape this gladiator and his net
By ship nor car nor any means: another
Can kill Time without stirring from his cot.

644

And when he sets his foot upon our spine
At last, we shall cry hopefully 'Let's be going!'
Just as in old days when we left for China,
Eyes fixed on distances and our hair blowing,

We shall embark upon the sea of Shade,
Light-hearted as a young enthusiast.
Now do you hear those voices, sweet and sad,
Singing, 'This way, all you who want to taste

The fragrant lotus! Here we shall let you savour
Those miracle fruits, for which your souls were famished:
Come and transport yourselves with the strange flavour
Of a long afternoon that's never finished'?

What's grown unreal, we guess from its usual tone.
Dear friends stretch out their arms; and 'Swim this way,
Take new life from my loyal heart,' cries one
Whose knees we kissed – but that was yesterday.

VIII

Old Captain Death, it's time to go. We're sick
Of this place. Weigh anchor! Set the course, and steer!
Maybe the sky and sea are inky black,
But in our hearts – you know them – all is clear.

Pour us the cordial that kills and cheers.
We wish, for our whole beings burn and burn,
To sound the abyss – heaven or hell, who cares? –
And find the secret wombed in the Unknown.

1965

THE WHISPERING ROOTS

FOR SEAN AND ANNA

'The House where I was Born' first appeared in *Pegasus and Other Poems* (1957), and 'Fishguard to Rosslare' first appeared in *The Room and Other Poems* (1965). They are repeated here, so that all the Irish poems can be kept together.

650

PART ONE

The House Where I Was Born

An elegant, shabby, white-washed house
With a slate roof. Two rows
Of tall sash windows. Below the porch, at the foot of
The steps, my father, posed
In his pony trap and round clerical hat.
This is all the photograph shows.

No one is left alive to tell me
In which of those rooms I was born,
Or what my mother could see, looking out one April
Morning, her agony done,
Or if there were pigeons to answer my cooings
From that tree to the left of the lawn.

Elegant house, how well you speak
For the one who fathered me there,
With your sanguine face, your moody provincial charm,
And that Anglo-Irish air
Of living beyond one's means to keep up
An era beyond repair.

Reticent house in the far Queen's County,
How much you leave unsaid.
Not a ghost of a hint appears at your placid windows
That she, so youthfully wed,
Who bore me, would move elsewhere very soon
And in four years be dead.

I know that we left you before my seedling
Memory could root and twine
Within you. Perhaps that is why so often I gaze
At your picture, and try to divine
Through it the buried treasure, the lost life –
Reclaim what was yours, and mine.

I put up the curtains for them again
And light a fire in their grate:
I bring the young father and mother to lean above me,
Ignorant, loving, complete:
I ask the questions I never could ask them
Until it was too late.

Ballintubbert House, Co. Laois*

Here is the unremembered gate.
Two asses, a grey and a black,
Have ambled across from the rough lawn
As if they'd been told to greet
The revenant. Trees draw graciously back
As I follow the drive, to unveil
For this drifty wraith, composed and real
The house where he was born.

Nothing is changed from that sixty-year-old
Photograph, except
My father's young face has been brushed away.
On the steps down which he strolled
With me in his arms, the living are grouped,
And it is my son Sean

* Laois: pronounced Leash. Ballintubbert House was the poet's birthplace.

Who stands upon the dishevelled lawn
To photograph us today.

I walk through the unremembered house,
Note on the walls each stain
Of damp; then up the spacious stair
As if I would now retrace
My self to the room where it began.
Dust on fine furnishings,
A scent of wood ash – the whole house sings
With an elegiac air.

Its owner is not at home – nor I
Who have no title in it
And no drowned memories to chime
Through its hush. Can piety
Or a long-lost innocence explain it? –
By what prodigious spell,
Sad elegant house, you have made me feel
A ghost before my time?

Fishguard to Rosslare

From all my childhood voyages back to Ireland
Only two things remembered: gulls afloat
Off Fishguard quay, littering a patch of radiance
Shed by the midnight boat.

And at dawn a low, dun coast shaping to meet me,
An oyster sky opening above Rosslare . . .
I rub the sleep from my eyes. Gulls pace the moving
Mast-head. We're almost there.

Gulls white as a dream on the pitch of Fishguard harbour,
Paper cut-outs, birds on a lacquered screen;
The low coastline and the pearl sky of Ireland;
A long sleep in between.

A sleep between two waking dreams – the haven,
The landfall – is how it appears now. The child's eye,
Unpuzzled, saw plain facts: I catch a glint from
The darkness they're haunted by.

Golden Age, Monart, Co. Wexford*

There was a land of milk and honey.
Year by year the rectory garden grew
Like a prize bloom my height of summer.
Time was still as the lily ponds. I foreknew
No chance or change to stop me running
Barefoot for ever on the clover's dew.

Buttermilk brimmed in the cool earthen
Crocks. All day the french-horn phrase of doves
Dripped on my ear, a dulcet burden.
Gooseberry bushes, raspberry canes, like slaves
Presented myriad fruit to my mouth.
In a bliss of pure accepting the child moves.

Hand-to-mouth life at the top of the morning!
Shabby, queer-shaped house – look how your plain
Facts are remembered in gold engraving!
I have watched the dead – my simple-minded kin,

* Monart: pronounced Mŏnárt.
The eccentric uncle was the Rev. W. G. Squires.

Once bound to a cramped enclave – returning
As myths of an Arcadian demesne.

Hens, beehives, dogs, an ass, the cobbled
Yard live on, brushed with a sunshine glaze.
Thanks to my gaunt, eccentric uncle,
His talkative sister, and the aunt who was
My second mother, from all time's perishable
Goods I was given these few to keep always.

Avoca, Co. Wicklow

Step down from the bridge.
A spit of grass points
At the confluence.

Tree he sat beneath
Spoiled for souvenirs,
Looks numb as driftwood.

A pretty fellow
In stone broods over
The meeting waters.

His words came alive
But to music's flow,
Like weeds in water.

I recall my aunt, my second mother,
Singing Tom Moore at the old rectory
Harmonium – *The Last Rose of Summer*,
She is far from the Land – her contralto
Scoop, the breathy organ, an oil lamp lit.

Words and tune met, flowed together in one
Melodious river. I drift calmly
Between its banks. Sweet vale of Avoca,
She is still young, I a child, and our two
Hearts like thy waters are mingled in peace.

> Dublin tradesman's son,
> Byron's friend, the pet
> Of Whig drawing-rooms.

> Fêted everywhere,
> Everywhere at home,
> He sang of exile

> And death, tailoring
> Country airs to a
> Modish elegance.

> Let the waters jig
> In a light glitter,
> So the source run full.

Near Ballyconneely, Co. Galway

i

A stony stretch. Grey boulders
Half-buried in furze and heather,
Purple and gold – Connemara's
Old bones dressed in colours
Out of a royal past.

Inshore the sea is marbled
And veined with foam. The Twelve Pins
Like thunderclouds hewn from rock
Or gods in a cloudy fable
Loom through an overcast.

The roofless dwellings have grown
Back to the earth they were raised from,
And tune with those primordial
Outcrops of grey stone
Among the furze and the heather.

Where man is dispossessed
Silence fills up his place
Fast as a racing tide.
Little survives of our West
But stone and the moody weather.

ii

Taciturn rocks, the whisht of the Atlantic
The sea-thrift mute above a corpse-white strand
Pray silence for those vanished generations
Who toiled on a hard sea, a harsher land.

Not all the bards harping on ancient wrong
Were half as eloquent as the silence here
Which amplifies the ghostly lamentations
And draws a hundred-year-old footfall near.

Preyed on by gombeen men, expropriated
By absentee landlords, driven overseas
Or to mass-burial pits in the great famines,
They left a waste which tourists may call peace.

The living plod to Mass, or gather seaweed
For pigmy fields hacked out from heath and furze –
No eye to spare for the charmed tourist's view,
No ear to heed the plaint of ancestors.

Winds have rubbed salt into the ruinous homes
Where turf-fires glowed once: waves and seagulls keen
Those mortal wounds. The landscape's an heroic
Skeleton time's beaked agents have picked clean.

Land

The boundary stone,
The balk, fence or hedge
Says on one side 'I own',
On the other 'I acknowledge'.

The small farmer carved
His children rations.
He died. The heart was halved,
Quartered, fragmented, apportioned:

To the sons, a share
Of what he'd clung to
By nature, plod and care –
His land, his antique land-hunger.

Many years he ruled,
Many a year sons
Followed him to oat-field,
Pasture, bog, down shaded boreens.

Turf, milk, harvest – he
Grew from earth also
His own identity
Firmed by the seasons' come-and-go.

Now at last the sons,
Captive though long-fledged,
Own what they envied once –
Right men, the neighbours acknowledge.

Kilmainham Jail: Easter Sunday, 1966

Sunbursts over this execution yard
    Mitigate high, harsh walls. A lowly
Black cross marks the deaths we are here to honour,
    Relieved by an Easter lily.
Wearing the nineteen-sixteen medal, a few
    Veterans and white-haired women recall
The Post Office, Clanwilliam House, the College of
                         Surgeons,
    Jacob's factory – all
Those desperate strongholds caught in a crossfire
    Between the English guns
And Dublin's withering incredulity.
    Against the wall where once
Connolly, strapped to a chair, was shot, a platform
    Holds movie cameras. They sight
On the guard of honour beneath the tricolor,
    An officer with a horseman's light
And quiet hands, and now the old President
    Who, soldierly still in bearing,
Steps out to lay a wreath under the plaque.
    As then, no grandiose words, no cheering –

Only a pause in the splatter of Dublin talk,
    A whisper of phantom volleys.

How could they know, those men in the sunless cells,
What would flower from their blood and England's follies?
Their dreams, coming full circle, had punctured upon
The violence that gave them breath and cut them loose.
They bargained on death: death came to keep the bargain.
Pious postcards of men dying in spruce
Green uniforms, angels beckoning them aloft,
Only cheapen their cause. Today they are hailed
As martyrs; but then they bore the ridiculed shame of
Mountebanks in a tragedy which has failed.
And they were neither the one nor the other – simply
Devoted men who, though the odds were stacked
Against them, believed their country's age-old plight
And the moment gave no option but to act.
Now the leaders, each in his sweating cell,
The future a blind wall and the unwinking
Eyes of firing-squad rifles, pass their time
In letters home, in prayer. Maybe they are thinking
Of Mount Street, the blazing rooftops, the Post Office,
Wrapping that glory round them against the cold
Shadow of death. Who knows the pull and recoil of
A doomed heart?

                They are gone as a tale that is told,
The fourteen men. Let them be more than a legend:
Ghost-voices of Kilmainham, claim your due –
This is not yet the Ireland we fought for.
You living, make our Easter dreams come true.

Remembering Con Markievicz*

Child running wild in woods of Lissadell:
Young lady from the Big House, seen
In a flowered dress, gathering wild flowers: Ascendancy
                                                        queen
Of hunts, house-parties, practical jokes – who could
                                                        foretell
(*Oh fiery shade, impetuous bone*)
Where all was regular, self-sufficient, gay
Their lovely hoyden lost in a nation's heroine?
Laughterless now the sweet demesne,
And the gaunt house looks blank on Sligo Bay
A nest decayed, an eagle flown.

The Paris studio, your playboy Count
Were not enough, nor Castle splendour
And fame of horsemanship. You were the tinder
Waiting a match, a runner tuned for the pistol's sound,
Impatient shade, long-suffering bone.
In a Balally cottage you found a store
Of Sinn Fein papers. You read – maybe the old sheets can
                                                        while
The time. The flash lights up a whole
Ireland which you have never known before,
A nest betrayed, its eagles gone.

The road to Connolly and Stephen's Green
Showed clear. The great heart which defied
Irish prejudice, English snipers, died
A little not to have shared a grave with the fourteen.
Oh fiery shade, intransigent bone!
And when the Treaty emptied the British jails,

---

* Markievicz: pronounced Markievitch.

A haggard woman returned and Dublin went wild to greet
her.
But still it was not enough: an iota
Of compromise, she cried, and the Cause fails.
Nest disarrayed, eagles undone.

Fanatic, bad actress, figure of fun –
She was called each. Ever she dreamed,
Fought, suffered for a losing side, it seemed
(The side which always at last is seen to have won),
Oh fiery shade and unvexed bone.
Remember a heart impulsive, gay and tender,
Still to an ideal Ireland and its real poor alive.
When she died in a pauper bed, in love
All the poor of Dublin rose to lament her
A nest is made, an eagle flown.

Lament for Michael Collins

Bicycling around Dublin with the ruddy, anonymous face
Of a rural bank clerk, a price-tag on his head,
While a pack of Auxiliaries, informers, Castle spies,
Nosing through snug and lodging, bayed
For the quarry that came and went like a shadow beneath
its nose –

That was the Big Fellow, the schoolboy Pimpernel.
Toujours l'audace, steel nerves and narrow shaves,
He loved to wrestle with comrades, he blubbered when
they fell.
Homeric heroes thus behaved:
He kept the form. But there's much more of the tale to tell.

With traitor and trigger-happy Tan he settled accounts.
	A martinet for balancing books, he slated
Unready reckoners, looked for no bonuses from chance,
		The risks he took being calculated
As a guerilla leader and an adept of finance.

They brought a Treaty. Now came the need to coax or drag
	His countrymen to some assured foothold
On the future out of their bitter and atavistic bog.
		Split was the nation he would build
And all to do again when the Civil War broke.

Fanaticism and muddle, Ireland wore down his heart
	Long before the ambush in County Cork,
Long before a random, maybe a treacherous shot
		Stopped it for ever. Do we talk
Of best-forgotten things and an elusive shade?

This country boy grown into a General's uniform,
	Gauntleted hands clasped in determination:
Tempestuous, moody man with the lashing tongue and the
						warm
		Sunbursts of laughter – dare a nation
Forget the genius who rode through storm on storm

To give it birth? You flying columns of ragtag cloud
	Stream from the west and weep over the grave
Of him who once dynamic as a powerhouse stood.
		For Ireland all he was he gave –
Energy, vision, last of all the great heart's blood.

Ass in Retirement

Ass
orbits
a firm stake:
each circle round
the last one is stamped
slow and unmomentous
like a tree-trunk's annual rings.

He does not fancy himself as a tragedian,
a circumference mystic or a treadmill hero,
nor takes he pride in his grey humility.
He is just one more Irish ass
eating his way round the clock,
keeping pace with his own appetite.

Put out to grass, given a yard more rope
each week, he takes time off from what's under his nose
Only to bray at rain-clouds over the distant bog;
relishes asinine freedom – having to bear
no topple of hay, nor cleeves crammed with turf;
ignorant that he'll come in time

to the longest tether's end,
then strangle or accept
that stake. Either way
on the endless
grass one day
he'll drop
dead.

Beauty Show, Clifden, Co. Galway

They're come to town from each dot on the compass,
                                                    they're
Wild as tinkers and groomed to an eyelash,
And light of foot as a champion featherweight
Prance on the top of the morning.

They walk the ring, so glossy and delicate
Each you'd think was a porcelain masterpiece
Come to life at the touch of a raindrop,
Tossing its mane and its halter.

The shy, the bold, the demure and the whinnier,
Grey, black, piebald, roans, palominos
Parade their charms for the tweedy, the quite un-
Susceptible hearts of the judges.

Now and again at the flick of an instinct,
As if they'd take off like a fieldful of rooks, they will
Fidget and fret for the pasture they know, and
The devil take all this competing.

The light is going, the porter is flowing,
The field a ruin of paper and straw.
Step neatly home now, unprized or rosetted,
You proud Connemara ponies.

Harebells over Mannin Bay

Half moon of moon-pale sand.
Sea stirs in midnight blue.
Looking across to the Twelve Pins
The singular harebells stand.

The sky's all azure. Eye
To eye with them upon
Cropped grass, I note the harebells give
Faint echoes of the sky.

For such a Lilliput host
To pit their colours against
Peacock of sea and mountain seems
Impertinence at least.

These summer commonplaces,
Seen close enough, confound
A league of brilliant waves, and dance
On the grave mountain faces.

Harebells, keep your arresting
Pose by the strand. I like
These gestures of the ephemeral
Against the everlasting.

At Old Head, Co. Mayo

In a fisherman's hat and a macintosh
He potters along the hotel drive;
Croagh Patrick* is far beyond him now the locust
Has stripped his years of green.
Midges like clouds of memory nag
The drooped head. Fish are rising
Under his hat. He stops against the view.

All is a brushwork vision, a wash
Of new-laid colour. They come alive –
Fuchsia, grass, rock. The mist, which had unfocused
Mountain and bay, is clean
Forgot, and gone the lumpish sag
Of cloud epitomizing
Our ennui. Storms have blown the sky to blue.

He stops, but less to admire the view
Than to catch breath maybe. Pure gold,
Emerald, violet, ultramarine are blazing
From earth and sea: out there
Croagh Patrick stands uncapped for him.
The old man, shuffling by,
Recalls a rod lost, a dead girl's caress.

Can youthful ecstasies renew
Themselves in blood that has blown so cold?
Nature's more merciful: gently unloosing
His hold upon each care
And human tie, her fingers dim
All lights which held his eye,
And ease him on the last lap to nothingness.

* Croagh Patrick: the Holy Mountain.
Croagh: pronounced cro'.

Sailing from Cleggan

Never will I forget it –
Beating out through Cleggan Bay
Towards Inishbofin, how
The shadow lay between us,
An invisible shadow
All but severing us lay
Athwart the Galway hooker.

Sea-room won, turning to port
Round Rossadillisk Point I
Slacken the sheet. Atlantic
Breeze abeam, ahead sun's eye
Opening, we skirt past reefs
And islands – Friar, Cruagh,
Orney, Eeshal, Inishturk.

Porpoises cartwheeling through
Inshore water, boom creaking,
Spray asperging; and sunlight
Transforming to a lime-green
Laughter the lipcurling of
Each morose wave as they burst
On reefs fanged for a shipwreck.

Miracle sun, dispelling
That worst shadow! Salt and sun,
Our wounds' cautery! And how,
Havened, healed, oh lightened of
The shadow, we stepped ashore
On to our recaptured love –
Never could I forget it.

Ballintubber Abbey, Co. Mayo*

'The Abbey that refused to die'

At the head of Lough Carra the royal abbey stands
Huge as two tithe-barns: much immortal grain
In its safe keeping, you might say, is stored.
Masons and carpenters have roofed and floored
That shell wherein a church not built with hands
For seven hundred and fifty years had grown.

I dare not quite say we were led here, driving
Through drifts of clobbering rainstorm (my own natal
Ballintubber is half Ireland away).
Yet, greeted by those walls of peregrine grey,
It felt like something more than the mere arriving
Of two sight-seers. Call it a destination.

Founded (1216) by Cathal O'Conor,
King of Connacht, the holy place was sacked by
Cromwellian louts, starved by the Penal Laws;
Yet all these troubled years, without a pause,
The Mass upheld God's glory, to the honour
Of Irishmen. So much for guidebook fact.

*   *   *

A seventeenth century crucifix, austere
Stonework will take the eye: the heart conceives
In the pure light from wall to whitewashed wall
An unseen presence, formed by the faith of all
The dead who age to age had worshipped here,
Kneeling on grass along the roofless nave.

---

* We had gone to this remote place as sightseers. To our astonishment, the priest recognized CDL, and immediately asked him to write a poem which could be sold to raise funds for the Abbey.

And what is faith? The man who walks a high wire,
Eyes fixed ahead, believing that strong nets
Are spread below – the Hands which will sustain
Each fall and nerve him to climb up again.
Surefoot or stumbler, veteran or tiro,
It could be we are all God's acrobats.

Broaden the high wire now into a bridge
Where Christian men still meet over the fell
Abyss, and walk together: they should cling
Brothers in faith, not wranglers arguing
Each step and slip of the way. Such true religion
Renew this abbey of St Patrick's well!

Up-end the bridge. It makes a ladder now
Between mankind and the timeless, limitless Presence,
Angels ascending or descending it
On His quick errands. See this ladder's foot
Firm-planted here, where men murmur and bow
Like the Lough Carra reed-beds in obeisance.

An Ancestor

Seen once on a family tree, now lost,
Jane Eyre, of Eyrescourt, County Galway.
All I get from the name is a passionate
Prudish lady, crossed
In love, then happy-ended. Jane,
My Jane – while a boy called Patrick Prunty
Dug potatoes in County Down –
Lived upon her demesne.

No governess, an heiress she.
Well, knowing nothing of her – not even
The road to razed or shuttered Eyrescourt –
Like Charlotte I am free
To create a Jane. I give her a score
Of rowdy brothers and sisters, a hunting
Father, a gossipy mother, routs,
Flirtings and flames galore.

Pedigree mares, harp, scandal, new
Recipes fill the hours. I see her
Flitting towards an unclouded future
Down a damp avenue.
Were she alive, I know what would please
Her still – the traditional Anglo-Irish
Pastime of playing hide-and-seek
Among their family trees.

Goldsmith outside Trinity

There he stands, my ancestor, back turned
On Trinity, with his friend Edmund Burke
And others of the Anglo-Irish genius –
Poet, naturalist, historian, hack.

The statue glosses over his uncouth figure,
The pock-marked face, the clownish tongue and mien:
It can say nothing of his unstaunchable charity,
But does full justice to the lack of chin.

Little esteemed by the grave and grey-faced college,
He fiddled his way through Europe, was enrolled
Among the London literates: a deserted
Village brought forth a citizen of the world.

His period and the Anglo-Irish reticence
Kept sentiment unsicklied and unfurred:
Good sense, plain style, a moralist could distinguish
Fine shades from the ignoble to the absurd.

Dublin they flew, the wild geese of Irish culture.
They fly it still: the curdled elegance,
The dirt, the cod, new hucksters, old heroics,
Look better viewed from a remoter stance.

Here from his shadow I note the buses grumbling
On to Rathmines, Stillorgan, Terenure –
Names he'd have known – and think of the arterial
Through-way between us. I would like to be sure

Long-distance genes do more than merely connect us.
But I, a provincial too, an expatriate son
Of Ireland, have nothing of that compulsive gambler,
Nothing of the inspired simpleton.

Yet, as if to an heirloom given a child and long
Unvalued, I at last have returned to him
With gratefuller recognition, get from his shadow
A wordless welcome, a sense of being brought home.

The Whispering Roots

Roots are for holding on, and holding dear.
Mine, like a child's milk teeth, came gently away
From Ireland at the close of my second year.
Is it second childhood now – that I overhear
Them whisper across a lifetime as if from yesterday?

We have had blood enough and talk of blood,
These sixty years. Exiles are two a penny
And race a rancid word; a meaningless word
For the Anglo-Irish: a flighty cuckoo brood
Foisted on alien nests, they knew much pride and many

Falls. But still my roots go whispering on
Like rain on a soft day. Whatever lies
Beneath their cadence I could not disown:
An Irish stranger's voice, its tang and tone,
Recalls a family language I thrill to recognize.

All the melodious places only seen
On a schoolboy's map – Kinsale, Meath, Connemara:
Writers – Swift, Berkeley, Goldsmith, Sheridan:
Fighters, from Vinegar Hill to Stephen's Green:
The Sidhe*, saints, scholars, rakes of Mallow, kings of
                                        Tara: –

Were background music to my ignorant youth.
Now on a rising wind louder it swells
From the lonely hills of Laois. What can a birth-
Place mean, its features comely or uncouth,
To a long-rootless man? Yet still the place compels.

We Anglo-Irish and the memory of us
Are thinning out. Bad landlords some, some good,
But never of a land rightfully ours,
We hunted, fished, swore by our ancestors,
Till we were ripped like parasite growth from native wood.

And still the land compels me; not ancestral
Ghosts, nor regret for childhood's fabled charms,

* Sidhe: pronounced She.
People of the faery mound (found in Irish mythology and W. B. Yeats).

675

But a rare peacefulness, consoling, festal,
As if the old religion we oppressed all
Those years folded the stray within a father's arms.

The modern age has passed this island by
And it's the peace of death her revenants find?
Harsh Dublin wit, peasant vivacity
Are here to give your shallow claims the lie.
Perhaps in such soil only the heart's long roots will bind –

Even, transplanted, quiveringly respond
To their first parent earth. Here God is taken
For granted, time like a well-tutored hound
Brought to man's heel, and ghosting underground
Something flows to the exile from what has been forsaken.

In age, body swept on, mind crawls upstream
Toward the source; not thinking to find there
Visions or fairy gold – what old men dream
Is pure restatement of the original theme,
A sense of rootedness, a source held near and dear.

PART TWO

Some Beautiful Morning

'One can't tell whether there won't be a tide to catch,
some beautiful morning.'

T. H. WHITE

Yes, for the young these expectations charm
There are sealed sailing-orders; but they dream
A cabined breath into the favouring breeze
Kisses a moveless hull alive, will bear
It on to some landfall, no matter where –
The Golden Gate or the Hesperides.

Anchored, they feel the ground-swell of an ocean
Stirring their topmasts with the old illusion
That a horizon can be reached. In pride
Unregimentable as a cross-sea
Lightly they float on pure expectancy.
Some morning now we sail upon the tide.

Wharves, cranes, the lighthouse in a sleep-haze glide
Past them, the landmark spires of home recede,
Glittering waves look like a diadem.
The winds are willing, and the deep is ours
Who chose the very time to weigh the bowers.
How could they know it was the tide caught them?

*   *   *

Older, they wake one dawn and are appalled,
Rusting in estuary or safely shoaled,
By the impression made on those deep waters.
What most sustained has left a residue
Of cartons, peelings, all such galley spew,
And great loves shrunk to half-submerged french letters.

677

Sometimes they doubt if ever they left this harbour.
Squalls, calms, the withering wake, frayed ropes and
                                              dapper
Refits have thinned back to a dream, dispersed
Like a Spice Island's breath. Who largely tramped
The oceans, to a rotting hulk they're cramped –
Nothing to show for this long toil but waste.

It will come soon – one more spring tide to lift
Us off; the lighthouse and the spire shall drift
Vaguely astern, while distant hammering dies on
The ear. Fortunate they who now can read
Their sailing orders as a firm *God-speed*,
This voyage reaches you beyond the horizon.

A Skull Picked Clean

Blank walls, dead grates, obliterated pages –
Vacancy filled up the house.
Nothing remains of the outward shows,
The inner rages.

Picture collection, trophies, library –
All that entranced, endorsed, enslaved –
With gimcrack ornaments have achieved
Nonentity.

How can I even know what it held most
                                    precious,
Its meaning lost, its love consumed?
Silence now where the cool brain hummed:
Where fire was, ashes.

How neatly those rough-tongued removal men
Have done the job. This useless key
They left us when they had earned their pay –
A skull, picked clean.

All Souls' Night

A hairy ghost, sent packing or appeased
    By dances, drums, and troughs of gore.
    A suave but fleshless ancestor
Honoured with fireworks at the birthday feast.

Safe in a harped and houried paradise:
    Pitchforked to some exemplary hell:
    Trooping through fields of asphodel:
Returned to nature's stock in a new guise –

For the cool corpse, impassive in its shroud,
    Such goings-on we have conceived.
    Born to injustice we believed
That underground or above the parting cloud

Pure justice reigns . . . Seraphs may bear a wreath
    Past the unseeing mourner: he
    In euphemism and ceremony
Buries awhile the body of his own death.

         *   *   *

All Souls' Night. Soon closing time will clear
A space for silence, last cars climb towards Kent
Throbbing like wind-torn snatches of lament.
Où sont des morts les phrases familières?

679

And where the dead? Like sun-warmed stones they keep
A little while their touch upon the living,
Remind us of their giving and forgiving,
Then, their fingers loosening, they sleep.

All that uneloquent congress of the shade
Speak through our truisms only, or they're crass
And mutinous like children in disgrace:
In clear or code no signal is relayed.

Who can know death, till he has dared to shave
His own corpse, rubbed his nose in his own noisome
Decay? Oh sweet breath, dancing minds and lissome
Bodies I've met with journeying to the grave!

It's they I want beside me – lovers, friends,
Prospective ghosts; not wind-blown atomies,
Dismantled bones, dissolving memories.
Tonight, a tingle of life at the nerve-ends.

*   *   *

But I may be the poorer for
    Not admitting souls
Into this human company:
    The dead have nothing else
For entrance-fee. Though bloodless, they
    Are brothers of the blood.
If they persist, how could I bar
    Such a convivial crowd?
Not willy-nilly thistledowns
    I fancy them, but as air
Viewless, dimensionless, pervasive,
    Here there and everywhere.
Born with souls, or soul-makers –
    Who knows? What I'm protesting
Is the idea that, if souls we have,
    They have to be everlasting.

I do not want an eternity
      Of self, rubbed clean or cluttered
With past. But it's unlikely that
      My wishes would be considered.

                    *   *   *

Welcome, all you intangible whose touch,
Impressing my own death upon my heart,
Leaves there a ghost of sweetness, like wood-ash
After the fires are out and the rooms aired.

To linger so, or as a horn that echoes
Out of the lost defiles, the sure defeat,
Heartening a few to courage and acceptance,
Is the short afterlife I'd want of fate.

Come then, dead friends, bringing your waft of wood-
                                        smoke,
Your gift of echoes. Sit by the bedside.
Graceless to ask just what I am invoking,
For this is the official visiting night.

Existences, consoling lies, or phantom
Dolls of tradition, enter into me.
Welcome, invisibles! We have this in common –
Whatever you are, I presently shall be.

Hero and Saint

Sad if no one provoked us any more
      To do the improbable –
Catch a winged horse, muck out a preposterous stable,
      Or even some unsensational chore

Like becoming a saint. Those adversaries knew
    The form, to be sure: small use for one
Who after an hour of effort would throw down
    Cross, shovel or lassoo.

It gave more prestige to each prince of lies
    And his far-fetched ordeal
That an attested hero should just fail
    One little finger's breadth from the prize.

Setting for Heracles and Bellerophon
    Such tasks, they judged it a winning gamble,
Forgetting they lived in a world of myth where all
    Conclusions are foregone.

A saint knows patience alone will see him through
    Ordeals which lure, disfigure, numb:
And this (the heroes proved) can only come
    From a star kept in view.

But he forgoes the confidence, the hallowed
    Air of an antique hero:
He never will see himself but as a zero
    Following a One that gives it value.

Hero imagined himself in the constellations,
    Saint as a numbered grain of wheat.
Nowhere but in aspiring do they meet
    And discipline of patience.

He rose to a trial of wit and sinew, *he*
    To improbable heights of loving.
Both, it seems, might have been good for nothing
    Without a consummate adversary.

Sunday Afternoon

'It was like being a child again, listening and thinking of
something else and hearing the voices – endless, inevitable
and restful, like Sunday afternoon.'

JEAN RHYS

An inch beyond my groping fingertips,
Lurking just round the corner of the eye.
Bouquet from an empty phial. A sensual ellipse
So it eludes – the quicksilver quarry.

I stretch my hands out to the farther shore,
Between, the fog of Lethe: no river – a mere thread
Bars me from the self I would re-explore:
Powerless I am to break it as the dead.

Yet a picture forms. Summer it must be. Sunlight
Fixes deck-chairs and grass in its motionless torrents.
The rest are shadows. I am the real: but I could run
To those familiar shades for reassurance.

Light slithers from leaf to leaf. Gossip of aspens.
Cool voices blow about, sprinkling the lawn.
Bells hum like a windrush chime of bees: a tolling hastens
Long-skirted loiterers to evensong.

Flowers nod themselves to sleep at last. I smell
Roses – or is it an Irish nursemaid's florin scent?
Gold afternoon rounds to a breast . . . Ah well,
A picture came, though not the one I meant.

Make what you can of it, to recompense
For the real thing, the whole thing vanished beyond recall.
Gauge from a few chance-found and cherished fragments
The genius of the lost original.

A Privileged Moment

Released from hospital, only half alive still,
Cautiously feeling the way back into himself,
Propped up in bed like a guy, he presently ventured
A glance at the ornaments on his mantelshelf.

White, Wedgwood blue, dark lilac coloured or ruby –
Things, you could say, which had known their place and
                                                    price,
Gleamed out at him with the urgency of angels
Eager for him to see through their disguise.

Slowly he turned his head. By gust-flung snatches
A shower announced itself on the windowpane:
He saw unquestioning, not even astonished,
Handfuls of diamonds sprung from a dazzling chain.

Gently at last the angels settled back now
Into mere ornaments, the unearthly sheen
And spill of diamond into familiar raindrops,
It was enough. He'd seen what he had seen.

A Picture by Renoir

Two stocky young girls in the foreground stoop
For a ball – red dress, white pinafore.
Toned with the sunburnt grass, two more
Follow in beige. That wayward troupe
Is the butterfly soul of summer.

Beyond them a stripe of azure-blue
Distance fades to the kind of sky
That calls for larks. In the blend of high
Colour and hazy line is a clue
To the heart of childhood summer.

So lively they are, I can all but see
Those halycon girls elude the frame
And fly off the picture, intent on their game
Wherever the ball may go, set free
Into eternal summer.

It does what pictures are meant to do –
Grasp a moment and throw it clear
Beyond the reach of time. Those four
Maidens will play for ever, true
To all our youthful summers.

A Tuscan Villa

(FOR KATHLEEN AND JOHANNES)

We took to your villa on trust and sight unseen
As the journey's dreamed-of height; had guessed it
A jewel framed in silver, nested in May-time green,
How the real thing surpassed it!
From the loggia, mountain ranges are seen renewing
Their mystery in the haze: a wedge
Of hill solid with jostled trees, cypresses queueing
Like travellers on their verge:
And at my feet in a lather of silvery fleece
An olive grove silently breaking.
Only a cuckoo, a child's cry breaks on the sylvan peace
And only to reawaken

The charm of silence. A burbling from the spaces
Up there reminds us that too soon
Bearing a spray of forget-me-not, leaving few traces
Behind, we shall move on.
But wrong it is, yearning to recompose
Feature on feature, petal by petal,
A blurring Paradise, the spectre of a rose.
I think they come too late – all
Gifts but the moment's. If we are quick and catch them,
We shall not grudge to let them fly.
Others will sojourn here: it will enrich them
With a present for ear and eye –
Silence and nightingales; the grace and knowledge
Of friends; acacia, lemon flowers,
Lemony tulips; a vista genial with vine and olive.
Today, be glad it is ours.

Merry-go-round

Here is a gallant merry-go-round.
The children all, entranced or queasy,
Cling to saddlebows, crazily fancy the
Circular tour is a free and easy
Gallop into a world without end.
Now their undulating time is up.
Horses, music slow to a stop.

Time's last inches running out,
A vortex, only guessable
Before by the circus ring of bubbles
Sedately riding, now turns visible –
A hole, an ulcer, a waterspout.
Bubbles twirl faster as closer they come
To the brink of the vacuum.

And my thoughts revolve upon death's
Twisted attraction. As limbs move slower,
Time runs more quickly towards the undoer
Of all. I feel each day devour
My future. Still, to the lattermost breath
Let me rejoice in the world I was lent –
The rainbow bubbles, the dappled mount.

Philosophy Lectures*

He goes about it and about,
By elegant indirections clears a route
To the inmost truth.
Cutting the ground from underneath
Rogue analogies, dialectic tares,
See how he bares
And shames the indulgent, weed-choked soil,
Shaving his field to the strictly meaningful!
Now breathless we
Await, await the epiphany –
A miracle crop to leap from the bald ground.

Not one green shoot, however, is discerned.

Well, watch this reaper-and-binder bumbling round
A shuddered field. Proud sheaves collapse
In narrowing squares. A coarser job, perhaps –
Corn, corn cockle and poppy lie
Corded, inseparable. Now each eye
Fastens on that last stand of corn:
Hares, partridge? – no, surely a unicorn

* The lecturer was Professor Bernard Williams. We were in the audience at the British Academy.

Or phoenix will be harbouring there,
Ripe for revelation. Harvest forgot, I stare
From the field's verge as the last ears fall.

Not even a rabbit emerges. Nothing at all.

Are the two fields identical,
Only the reapers different? Misdirected
Or out of our minds, we expected
A wrong thing – the impossible
Or merely absurd; creatures of fire and fable
Where bread was the intention,
Harvest where harvest was not meant.
Yet in both fields we saw a right end furthered:
Something was gathered.

After an Encaenia

This afternoon the working sparrows, glum
Of plumage, nondescript, flurried, quarrelsome,
Appear as cardinal, kingfisher, hoopoe, bird
Of paradise. They stalk the sward

With gait somnambulous beside their not
So colourful hens, or heart to gorgeous heart
Absently confer together
In tones that do not change to match their feathers

Will no one tell me what they chirp? I'd say
Their minds are very far away
From this cloud-cuckoo lawn, impatient to
Resume the drudgery sparrows pursue.

Scavengers are they? Gathering crumbs,
Nibbling at particles and old conundrums,
Pouncing on orts never observed before,
They justify their stay-at-home exploring.

I like these scrap-collectors: and to see
Their hard-earned plumes worn without vanity
Hints that a scholar's search for evidence
Is selfless as the lives of saints.

Truth, knowledge even, seems too grandiose
A word for the flair and flutterings of those
Whose ambition is no more wide
Than to get, once for all, one small thing right.

Tenure

is never for keeps, never truly assured
(tick on, you geological clocks)
though some things almost have it, or seem to have it.
For example, rocks
in a shivering sea: the castaway who has clawed himself on
to one:
a bull's tenacious horn:
archaic myths: the heroin habit.
Even the sun or a dead man's skull among the cactus
does not quite have it.

I turn now to American university practice.
Tenure there is pronounced 'Shangri-
La': once you have it, however spurious
your fame, not even the angriest
trustees, except for certified madness or moral turpitude,

689

can ever dislodge you. I salute
all those tenurious
professors. But I would not wish to be
one, though the life may be happy and sometimes not inglorious.

Tenure is not for me.
I want to be able to drop out of my head,
or off my rock and swim to another, ringed with a roundelay
of sirens. I should not care to be a dead
man's skull, or a myth, or a junkie:
or the too energetic sun.
Since heaven and earth, we are told, shall pass away
(hell, sneers the blonde, is off already)
I would live each day as if it were my last and first day.

Epitaph for a Drug-Addict

Mourn this young girl. Weep for society
Which gave her little to esteem but kicks.
Impatient of its code, cant, cruelty,
Indifferent, she kicked against all pricks
But the dream-loaded hypodermic's. She
Has now obtained an everlasting fix.

A Marriage Song

FOR ALBERT AND BARBARA*

Midsummer, time of golden views and hazes,
Advance in genial air,
Bring out your best for this charmed pair –
Let fly a flamingo dawn, throw open all your roses,
Crimson the day for them and start the dancing.

June-month fruits, yield up your delicate favours
Entrancing them, and be
Foretastes of ripe felicity:
Peach bloom and orange flower, ravish these happy lovers,
Sweeten the hour for them and start the dancing.

Tune to our joy, grass, breezes, philomels,
Enhancing their bright weather
Of inward blessedness; together
With honeying bees and silver waterfalls of bells
Carol our hopes for them, oh start the dancing.

In well-deep looks of love and soft-as-foam
Glances they plight their troth.
Midsummer stars, be kind to both
Through the warm dark when they shall come into their
                                                            own,
Light your candles for them, start the dance.

* Albert and Barbara Gelpi – friends at Harvard, now at Stanford University.

691

At East Coker

At the far end of a bemusing village
Which has kept losing finding and losing itself
Along the lane, as if to exercise a pilgrim's
Faith, you see it at last. Blocked by a hill
The traffic, if there was any, must swerve aside:
Riding the hilltop, confidently saddled,
A serviceable English church.

Climb on foot now, past white lilac and
The alms-house terrace; beneath yew and cedar
Screening the red-roof blur of Yeovil; through
The peaceable aroma of June grasses,
The churchyard where old Eliots lie. Enter.

A brass on the south wall commemorates
William Dampier, son of this unhorizoned village,
Who thrice circumnavigated the globe, was
First of all Englishmen to explore
The coast of Australia . . . An exact observer
Of all things in Earth, Sea and Air. Another
Exploring man has joined his company.

In the north-west corner, sealed, his ashes are
(Remember him at a party, diffident,
Or masking his fire behind an affable mien):
Above them, today, paeonies glow like bowls of
Wine held up to the blessing light.

Where an inscription bids us pray
For the repose of the soul of T. S. Eliot, poet –
A small fee in return for the new worlds
He opened us. 'Where prayer is valid', yes,
Though mine beats vainly against death's stone front,

And all our temporal tributes only scratch
Graffiti on its monumental silence.

*   *   *

But soon obituary yields
To the real spirit, livelier and more true.
There breathes a sweetness from his honoured stone,
A discipline of long virtue,
As in that farmside chapel among fields
At Little Gidding. We rejoice for one
Whose heart a midsummer's long winter,
Though ashen-skied and droughtful, could not harden
Against the melting of midwinter spring,
When the gate into the rose garden
Opening at last permitted him to enter
Where wise man becomes child, child plays at king.
A presence, playful yet austere,
Courteously stooping, slips into my mind
Like a most elegant allusion clinching
An argument. Eyes attentive, lined
Forehead – 'Thus and thus runs,' he makes it clear,
'The poet's rule. No slackening, no infringing
'Must compromise it.' . . . Now, supplying
Our loss with words of comfort, his kind ghost
Says all that need be said about committedness:
Here in East Coker they have crossed
My heart again – For us there is only the trying
To learn to use words. The rest is not our business.

1970

POSTHUMOUS POEMS

This collection was first published by
John Rundle of The Whittington Press, 1979.

TO
PETER COCHRANE

The Park, Guy's Hospital: Early Morning*

Sleep's doctoring hands withdrawn,
The patient wakes early:
His light-switch can still thrust away
Insinuating dawn.

He sees through his window-square
Fuzzed branches, buildings, grass,
Archway and path chiefly because
He knows that they are there.

But what at first he has seen
As candles searching a darkened
Crypt becomes a hurry of white-capped
Girls to their routine

Of healing. For every nurse –
Though never so devoted –
Death, birth, all the body's dramas
Must be a matter of course.

Only the patient, weak
As a leaf, imagines their voices
A dawn chorus and his own
Experience unique.

*First published in the Guy's Hospital House Magazine in 1970. Drafted in an exercise book bought from the hospital trolley-shop.

The Expulsion: Masaccio*

They stumble in naked grief, as refugees
From a flood or pogrom, dispossessed of all
But a spray of leaf like barbed wire round the loins.
For sight, she has mere sockets gouged and charred
By nightmare, and her mouth is a bottomless pit
Of desolation. Her lord, accomplice, dupe,
Ashamed of his failure, as if he cannot face it
Covers his eyes.
           We know they left behind
A place where fruits and animals were kind
And time no enemy. But did they know their loss
As more than a child's when its habitual toys
Are confiscated for some innocent fault,
Or take the accusing cosmic voice that called
To be the same as their dear old garden god's?
The sword that pickets paradise also goads
Towards self-knowledge. More they shall come to wish
Than brutal comfort of committed flesh.
Masaccio paints us both
A childish tragedy – hunched back, bawling mouth,
And the hour when the animal knew that it must die
And with that stroke put on humanity.

---

*Masaccio's Frescoes in Santa Maria del Carmine, Florence, seen for the first time on a convalescent holiday 1970. The poem was published in a Festschrift for W. H. Auden's 65th birthday in 1972 in a limited edition of 500.

My Méséglise Way

Always, along that path hawthorn and lilac
Hedged a demesne
A bare arm's-length away, yet inaccessible
And coaxing in vain
Like the horizon. It was enough to part
The blossoms – eye could embrace
The glades, parterres, crystal-paned gazebos
Of a superior race.
Fountains play. A small girl walks where fidgety
Branches sieve
The sunlight: her shyness and delicate hauteur show me
Original Eve.

One day there was a hole in the hedge. I crawl
Through it. The prospect blurs,
Then clears again, as unperturbed I accept an
Epiphany in reverse –
A common and garden lawn, a hedge of privet
Not scented bloom:
The privileged scene, the sense of grandeur flown like
A drug-born dream.

Young ones in the dowdy garden happily
Tumble and chase. Cast
Is my skin of shrinking solitude when a girl
Cries 'So you've joined us at last!'

Snowfall on a College Garden

While we slept, these formal gardens
Worked into their disguise. The Warden's
Judas and tulip trees awake
In ermine. Here and there a flake
Of white falls from the painted scene,
Or a dark scowl of evergreen
Glares through the shroud, or a leaf dumps
Its load and the soft burden slumps
Earthward like a fainting girl.
No movement else. The blizzard's whirl
Froze to this cataleptic trance
Where nature sleeps and sleep commands
A transformation. See this bush
Furred and fluffed out like a thrush
Against the cold: snow which could snap
A robust veteran branch, piled up
On the razor edge of a weak spray,
Plumping it out in mimicry
Of white buddleia. Like the Elect
Ghosts of summer resurrect
In snowy robes. Only the twangling
Noise of unseen sparrows wrangling
Tells me that my window-view
Holds the garden I once knew.

Three Little Pictures

Municipal Park

In beds of municipal parks the flowers
Stand to attention, dressed by the right,
Each bed a uniform colour –
Even the seeds were drilled.
How regimental, we think, how bright and dull!
     By such a bed he stands, recalling
     A wild lost darling.

Boat from Ireland

     Children chase round and round and round.
     For them the past is past, the deck
     Another windy playground.
Man, though you tear up your used *vacances*,
Fling the white scraps to the wind,
Seagulls follow above your wake –
A mobile shifting, sliding, dancing.

Roger

So Roger is gone. We had not met
Lately. But the news like a flashbulb whipped
Out of the darkness the voice, the features,
The touch of Lear. I notice that
     Picking off our acquaintance one by one,
     One by one Time prises our fingers loose
     From the edge that overhangs oblivion.

Reflections 1

Horse at a pool's edge drinking its own reflection.
Aircraft sledging its shadow across the desert miles.
Young girl begging a mirror to tell her fortune.
Lost man's cooee echoed from aquiline mountain walls.
Here are duelling-grounds of reality and illusion –
Endless shimmer of foils and counterfoils.

Reflections 2

Says the dream to the sleeper, 'Achieve me'.
Says the wife to the mirror, 'Deceive me'.
Says the heart to the mind, 'Believe me'.
Said the shadow to the sun, 'Don't leave me'.

Poets, uncage the Word!

Poets, uncage the word!
It flies beyond all logic, all horizons,
Beyond the rage of men, the reach of time
Carolling over tombs and seasons.

Freedom's a migrant bird,
Now here, now there is heard its homing call:
You makers, tune our souls till it become
Challenge and need and right for all.

Poets gave men the nerve
To ride the rapids of the treacherous ages,

Revealing virgin landfalls yet to come
After the blind and battering stages.

Freedom's our chosen course
Through killing rocks, wild eddies. Poet seer
Summon a rainbow from the cataract's wrath,
Image the faith by which we steer.

A Christmas Way

How to retrace the bygone track
Over two thousand years
And a desert of shifting landmarks, back
To its divine or mythical source –
It seems we have lost the knack.

Grassed-over is now the pilgrim way
Which men of old could plod
To find a first-born in the hay
And recognise him as the Son of God
Any Christmas Day.

Into more tinselled novelties
The fabulous star has dwindled,
Powerless against man's weaponries
And devilish pride were the arms which dandled
That small prince of peace.

One way's still open. Return to the child
You were on Christmas Eve –
His expectation of marvels piled
Against tomorrow, his pure belief
In a responsive world.

Plus Ultra*

FOR WALTER ALLEN

Let us not call it progress: movement certainly
And under direction, though what directions we move in
Is anyone's guess. . . . It is as if a man
Leapt from one ship to another, and instantly looks round
And the ship he leapt from has dropped below the horizon
Or sunk. But not without trace.

The world we were young in has
Disintegrated; yet scraps of it bob in our wake like flotsam.
Not the great wars, discoveries, revolutions –
They have done their worst, or best, and are accomplished,
As the young I has become an historic figure already
Subject to history's over- and under-simplifications.

No, it's the marginal crises, the magical trivia
Which, against all reason, haunt me.
Finding white heather on a Mayo hillside,
A boy lamenting his toy boat lost on its first voyage,
A girl's first glance – no hint of the bliss and bane that
                                        would follow –
In such small relics my dead world lives on.

Time, that has proved we can survive, puts back
The sirens on their rock, the Cyclops in his cave:
We see their point now we no longer fear them.
Those desperate straits are never the world's end:
There is always more beyond, marvels beyond to draw us,
Movement certainly: perhaps we may call it progress.

* First appeared in *On the Novel* edited by B. S. Benedikz – a present for Walter Allen's
60th birthday.

Recurring Dream

. . . the house being the first problem. Dilapidated,
Or is it only half built? He cannot rightly
See or remember. No question it looks unsightly –
All lath and plaster, pipes, treacherous floors
And baffle walls.

               Before him an assault course
That felt familiar. He infiltrated
The house, wriggling through pipes, circumventing
Holes in the floor, scaling walls; but always
The course gained height. Such was his expertise
He could have done it on his head or blindfold
(Perhaps he did). At least he never failed
To make, or to forget, the happy ending.

For, as he reached it, that bare top storey
Is the highest floor of a luxury hotel
And problem number two. No lift, no stair-well
Visible, and he knows he must get down
To ground level.

             He'd sensed, during his lone
Climb, others doing the course. Quite solitary
The new ordeal – no chambermaid, waiter, guest
To show him the way out. Frantic he raced
From end to end of the floor. A deep staircase
Appeared at last, pointing the right direction,
Down which he flew; but has no recollection
Where or indeed whether one egressed.

Going My Way?

1

Now, when there is less time than ever,
Every day less time,
I do have the greatest need for patience.

Not to be rushed by thawing, cracking ice
Into a hasty figure.

Not to require daffodils before spring
But accept each spring as another golden handshake.

Not to be misled by fatuous fires
Into a sanctuary clemmed and de-consecrated.

Never irked that this line has no fancy
Departure lounge for V.I.P.s.

Least of all to lose faith in the experience,
The mortal experiment
To which at birth I was committed.

2

Those three provincials, the dear sisters whom
Abrupt catastrophe and slow dry-rot,
Gutting their hearts of youth, condemn to what
Cheerless routines and seasons yet may come –
Would you not say that they were better dead
Than haunted by their sweet illusion's ghost,
Love ground down to irritable dust,
The ideal city still unvisited?

708

Not so their curtain speech: 'We must go on,
And we must work. Our sufferings will grow.
Peace and joy for coming generations.'
Was it illusion's desperate last throw?
At least those heroines showed that nothing can
Become the mortal heart like trust and patience.

Hellene: Philhellene*

IN MEMORY OF GEORGE SEFERIS AND C. M. BOWRA

Great poet, friend of my later days, you first
I would honour. Driven from shore to shore
Like Odysseus, everywhere you had nursed
The quivering spark of freedom, your heart's core
Loaded and lit by your country's tragedies,
Her gods and heroes. These inhabited
Your poetry with a timeless, native ease
But they moved there among the living dead
Of recent times, so myth and history
Became one medium, deeply interfused.
        I recall, in London or in Rome, you welcoming me –
Warm growl, the Greek 'my dear' – a spirit used
To catching voices from rock, tree, waves, ports,
And so always a shade preoccupied.
Hearing you were dead, I remembered your *Argonauts*,
How 'one after another the comrades died
With downcast eyes', having become reflections

---

*First published in *Cornhill* (winter 1971–1972). Maurice Bowra had been CDL's tutor
when he read Classics at Wadham College, Oxford. We had last been reunited with our
friend George Seferis – the great Greek poet and Nobel Prizewinner – in Rome in 1968,
before the Colonels confiscated his passport. On principle, Maurice would not now travel
to Greece. It was a sacrifice. On a fiercely hot day, Cecil, himself now mortally ill, had
gone from Greenwich to Oxford to follow Maurice's coffin to the graveside.

And articles of the voyage: as you, whose quest is
One now with theirs. My lasting recollections –
Your grace before necessity, your passion for justice.

And you no less, dear tutor of my young days,
Lover of Greece and poetry, I mourn.
To me you seem then the exorbitant blaze
Of Aegean sun dispelling youth's forlorn
Blurred images; the lucid air; the salt
Of tonic sea on your lips. And you were one
Whom new poetic languages enthralled
(After I'd stumbled through a Greek unseen,
You'd take *The Tower* or *The Waste Land* from a shelf
And read me into strange live mysteries.)
    You taught me most by always being yourself
Those fifty years ago. For ever Greece
Remained your second country, even though
You were self-exiled latterly, touched by the same
Indignation which made that other know
Exile was not for him. Yearly your fame
Grew as administrator, scholar, wit:
But my best memory, the young man whose brilliance
Lit up my sombre skies and kept them lit,
Drawing dead poets into the ageless dance.

I miss these men of genius and good sense,
In a mad world lords of their just enclave,
My future emptier for the one's absence,
So much of my youth laid in the other's grave.
Hellene and Philhellene, both gone this year,
They leave a radiance on the heart, a taste
Of salt and honey on the tongue, a dear
Still-warm encampment in the darkening waste.

Remembering Carrownisky*

The train window trapped fugitive impressions
As we passed, grasped for a moment then sucked away –
Woods, hills, white farms changing shape and position,
A river which wandered, as if not sure of the way,

Into and off the pane. A landscape less
Well-groomed than, say, a Florentine painter's one,
But its cross-rhythmed shagginess soothed me through the
glass
As it ambled past out there in the setting sun.

Then, one Welsh mead turned up with a girl rider –
Light hair, red jersey – cantering her horse.
Momently creatures out of some mythical order
Of being they seemed, to justify and endorse

A distrait mood . . . I recalled you at thirteen
Matched against Irish farmers in a race
On Carrownisky – under the cap your dark mane
Streaming, the red windcheater a far-off blaze;

But most how, before the race began, you rode
Slowly round the circuit of sand to calm
The mare and accustom her to a lawless crowd.
Seeing that, I knew you should come to no harm.

Our nerves too can taste of our children's pure
Confidence and grow calm. My daughter rides back
To me down that railside field – elemental, secure
As an image that time may bury but not unmake.

* A strand on the coast of Co. Mayo where the race was held – also the name of a river.

Children Leaving Home*

Soon you'll be off to meet your full-grown selves,
Freed from my guardianship to sweat out your own life-
                                        sentence.
The house will be emptied of you,
For ever tie in time dissolves;
And you, once close to us like a whisper of blood, in due
Season return, if return you will, as polite acquaintance.

What will you then remember? The lime that crowded
Your bedroom windows, shading the square rose-bed
                                        beneath –
All such everyday sights,
Hours by boredom or wrath enclouded,
Or those which burst like a rocket with red-letter delights
In a holiday sky – picnics, the fair on Blackheath?

I heard you last summer, crossing Ireland by road,
Ask the mother to re-tell episodes out of your past.
You gave them the rapt attention
A ballad-maker's audience owed
To fact caught up in fable. Through memory's dimension
The unlikeliest scene may be immortalised.

Forgive my coldnesses, now past recall,
Angers, injustice, moods contrary, mean or blind;
And best, my dears, forgive
Yourselves, when I am gone, for all
Love-signals you ignored and for the fugitive
Openings you never took into my mind.

*First published posthumously in support of a magazine called *Tagus*.

At that hour what shall I have to bequeath?
A sick world we could not change, a sack of genes
I did not choose, some verse
Long out of fashion, a laurel wreath
Wilted . . . So prematurely our old age inters
Puny triumphs with poignant might-have-beens.

Soon you'll be leaving home, alone to face
Love's treacheries and transports. May these early years
Have shaped you to be whole,
To live unshielded from the rays
Which probe, enlighten and mature the human soul.
Go forth and make the best of it, my dears.

At Lemmons*

FOR JANE, KINGSLEY, COLIN, SARGY
WITH MUCH LOVE

Above my table three magnolia flowers
Utter their silent requiems.
Through the window I see your elms
In labour with the racking storm
Giving it shape in April's shifty airs.

Up there sky boils from a brew of cloud
To blue gleam, sunblast, then darkens again.
No respite is allowed
The watching eye, the natural agony.

Below is the calm a loved house breeds
Where four have come together to dwell

*This was written on his deathbed. Lemmons was the house at Hadley Common, where
CDL died. It was owned then by Elizabeth Jane Howard and Kingsley Amis. EJH's
brother, Colin Howard, the inventor, and the painter, Sargy Mann, also lived there.

713

– Two write, one paints, the fourth invents –
Each pursuing a natural bent
But less through nature's formative travail
Than each in his own humour finding the self he needs.

Round me all is amenity, a bloom of
Magnolia uttering its requiems,
A climate of acceptance. Very well
I accept my weakness with my friends'
Good natures sweetening every day my sick room.

VERS D'OCCASION

Then and Now*

Do you remember those mornings after the blitzes
When the living picked themselves up and went on living –
Living, not on the past, but with an exhilaration
Of purpose, a new neighbourliness of danger?

Such days are here again. Not the bansheeing
Of sirens and the beat of terrible wings
Approaching under a glassy moon. Your enemies
Are nearer home yet, nibbling at Britain's nerve.

Be as you were then, tough and gentle islanders –
Steel in the fibre, charity in the veins –
When few stood on their dignity or lines of demarcation,
And few sat back in the padded cells of profit.

Boiler-room, board-room, backroom boys, we all
Joined hearts to make a life-line through the storm.
No haggling about overtime when the heavy-rescue squads
Dug for dear life under the smouldering ruins.

The young cannot remember this. But they
Are graced with that old selflessness. They see
What's needed; they strip off dismay and dickering,
Eager to rescue our dear life's buried promise.

To work then, islanders, as men and women
Members one of another, looking beyond
Mean rules and rivalries towards the dream you could
Make real, of glory, common wealth, and home.

*The first work of C. Day Lewis since his appointment as Poet Laureate was
commissioned by the *Daily Mail* as part of the "I'm Backing Britain" campaign and
appeared in that paper on January 5th, 1968. The campaign, supported by the *Daily Mail*
and the *Evening News*, began with five typists at a heating and ventilation firm offering
to work an extra half day without pay at the end of 1967. Subsequently some firms
pegged prices for six months and some directors took a cut in their salaries.

Hail, Teesside!*

Old ironmasters and their iron men
With northern fire, grit, enterprise began it
A hundred years ago. Later, we scan it –
Desolate homesteads welded into one,
Hamlets grown up to towns, deep anchorage
Gouged out of sand, wastes blossoming with the fierce
White rose of foundries. So the pioneers
Printed their work on nature's open page.
Their steel made bridges from Sydney to Menai;
Their ships networked the sea. Gain was in view
But inch by inch out of the gain there grew
A greater thing – sense of community.

Bridges are for drawing men together
By closing gaps. Could those rough ghosts return,
They'd find a world of difference, but discern
That here is the same breed of men and weather.
You are bridge-builders still. Only, today
You draw six towns into a visioned O,
Spanning from town to town the ebb and flow
Of destiny. A dream is realised. May
The northern kindliness and northern pride
See, as your forebears would, the future in it.
Here a new span – our lives shall underpin it
And earn fresh honours for our own Teesside.

*The work was specially commissioned by the *Evening Gazette*, Middlesbrough, to
celebrate the coming into being of the new County Borough of Teesside.

Old Vic, 1818–1968*

Curtain up on this dear, honoured scene!
A South-bank Cinderella wears
The crown tonight of all our country's theatres.
The stage where Kean
Enthralled and Baylis wove dazzling tradition
On a shoestring, makes good the vision
Of a hundred and fifty years.

Old Vic, your roof held generations under
A magic spell. And we have known
So many incandescent nights flash past and flown
Away – no wonder,
Where the young dreamed their dreams and learned their trade,
Stars come home to celebrate
Their nursery's renown.

Here everyman once bought for a small price
Audience with Shakespeare, and still gleans
Self-knowledge from the hero's fall, the heroine's
Love-sacrifice.
This stage is all the world; in all our hearts
Rosalind smiles, Iago hates,
Lear howls, Malvolio preens.

Old cockney Vic, with what strange art you bring
Us strollers into one family
That learns through discipline, patience, tears and gaiety
'The play's the thing'.

---

*This was on a special four-page programme for the National Theatre production of "As You Like It" at the Old Vic, in the presence of Princess Marina for the 150th Old Vic anniversary performance on the 14th May, 1968.

You show world theatre, old and new, today –
Man's heights and depths, and what he may
Yet crave, yet come to be.

Feed My Little Ones*

How many children starving, did you say?
A million? Five million? It is sad,
Tragic really. But after all, they are
Thousands of miles away, remote as the Black Death
Or the dying stars. Oh, I do sympathise:
But I could never count much beyond ten –
Tragedy multiplied by millions fades
Into a faceless limbo of statistics
And leaves imagination cold on the outside.
Charity, I say, must begin at home.

Let charity begin at home.
Think of one child, your own or the next-door neighbour's.
Tetter the pretty skin with sores, let the bones show
                                        through it
Like ribs of a stranded wreck. This is your child –
This derelict with the animal breath of famine
Whimpering through his frame. He understands nothing,
Nothing he knows but a mother long sucked dry
Of milk and tears, a father drained of hope.
You are that father, you are that mother.
Your child. Imagine. It is so hard to imagine?

Thousands of miles away, yet still they are next-door
                                        neighbours

*Written for Oxfam by the Poet Laureate to commemorate that organisation's 25th
birthday. Spoken by Dame Sybil Thorndike at the Royal Festival Hall.

Within the giant stride, the magic ring of compassion.
Let one child plead for all, as the Christ-child spoke for all
Innocents bundled away into a bloodless limbo.

This need not be so. Our target is mankind's conscience:
Not by the wringing of hands shall our concern be
measured
But in shelter, seed and ploughshares, that hope may be
reborn.
Put one stranger's child to the breast of your warm
compassion.
Find its father a share in earth, his only birthright.
Sow a few handfuls of seed and give that child its future.

In a Library*

A world of speechless time until man came,
So many years before he found his tongue,
Clumsily groping for the words to name
All he touched, saw, desired and died among.

Language grew slowly as a coral reef
From mind's unfathomable depths. Man learned
To articulate his glory and his grief
Communicate the hope with which he burned.

He sent out words exploring, to survey
Nature's enigmas and the mysteries
Of his own being. Myriads had their day
Before words midwifed the first masterpiece.

*Written to herald 'National Library Week'. It appeared on Monday, March 10th, 1969 in
the *Daily Mirror*.

Song, stylus, print – through them at this far end
Of time we inherit all the fabulous store
Those makers left to praise and comprehend
Our little lives and earth's exhaustless lore.

Here, an array of magic essences –
Phial on phial, shelf on shelf –
Stand the elixirs that each subtle alchemist
Distilled from nature and himself.

The epic grandeur and the lyric grace
The traveller's eye, the lover's ear,
Passion and wisdom breaking through the overcast
To hearten us – they are all here.

Myths, morals, tragic action, comic turn –
Makers show humankind its face
Reveal the naked man under the jewelled robe,
The rare beneath the commonplace.

Their works, greater and less, open our eyes
And hearts to human brotherhood.
A ruling passion gave them birth, and in the love
Of them is every man renewed.

For the Investiture of the Prince of Wales*

Today bells ring, bands play, flags are unfurled,
   Anxieties and feuds lie buried
Under a ceremonial joy. You, sir, inherit
   A weight of history in a changing world,
Its treasured wisdom and its true
   Aspirings the best birthday gift for you.

Coming of age, you come into a land
   Of mountain, pasture, cwm, pithead,
Steelworks. A proud and fiery people, thoroughbred
   For singing, eloquence, rugby football, stand
Beneath Caernarvon's battlements
To greet and take the measure of their prince.

But can they measure his hard task – to be
   Both man and symbol? With the man's
Selfhood the symbol grows in clearer light, or wanes.
   Your mother's grace, your father's gallantry
Go with you now to nerve and cheer you
   Upon the crowded, lonely way before you.

May your integrity silence each tongue
   That sneers or flatters. May this hour
Reach through its pageantry to the deep reservoir
   Whence Britain's heart draws all that is fresh and young.
Over the tuneful land prevails
   One song, one prayer – God bless the Prince of Wales.

*This appeared in the *Guardian* on July 1st, 1969, the day of Prince Charles's investiture
as Prince of Wales by the Queen.

Battle of Britain*

What did we earth-bound make of it? A tangle
Of vapour trails, a vertiginously high
Swarming of midges, at most a fiery angel
Hurled out of heaven, was all we could descry.

How could we know the agony and pride
That scrawled those fading signatures up there,
And the cool expertise of them who died
Or lived through that delirium of the air?

Grounded on history now, we re-enact
Such lives, such deaths. Time, laughing out of court
The newspaper heroics and the faked
Statistics, leaves us only to record

What was, what might have been: fighter and bomber,
The tilting sky, tense moves and counterings;
Those who outlived that legendary summer;
Those who went down, its sunlight on their wings.

And you, unborn then, what will you make of it –
This shadow-play of battles long ago?
Be sure of this: they pushed to the uttermost limit
Their luck, skill, nerve. And they were young like you.

*The film *Battle of Britain* received its premiere on September 16th, 1969. The poem
appeared in the centre pages of the programme.

Keep Faith with Nature*

Animal, fish, fowl
Share with man the lease
And limits of creation.
Heron by the pool,
Tiger through the tree
Lend us images
Of action and contemplation.

Soil that gives man bread,
Flowers that feed his eye
For ages have kept him whole.
Virgin lands visited,
Forest and butterfly,
Berry, well, wave supply
The hunger of body and soul.

Now more than ever we need
True science, lest mankind
Lording it over nature's
Territories, by greed
Or thoughtlessness made blind,
To doom shall have consigned
Itself and all earth's creatures.

* Published by Midnag, Ashington, for the environment.

Beethoven, 1770–1970*

Hero musician, two hundred years
Have passed since you were born,
But still with unimpoverished tone
And themes incomparable you bless our ears.
The genius that ran
Like blood through one full-hearted man
Floods over generations and frontiers.

The royal line of Haydn and Mozart
Forwarding he enriched.
His span of inspiration bridged
Between the classic and romantic art.
Followed new aims, new modes,
But his were the original moulds
And Promethean fire from which they start.

To defy Fate he came and to devour
Life whole – jocose or moody,
Versed in suffering, bound in duty
To the creative daemon's intimate power
Begetting on his mind
Themes luminous but scarce-defined.
What long pains went to each perfected score!

No man before or since tuned music's tongue
To depths of tenderness
Or heights of grandeur like to his.
Deafness, a fog chilling and thickening, clung
About his ears while he

*On December 16th, 1970, during the Royal Philharmonic Society's 1970–71 season, a Beethoven bicentenary concert took place in which his Missa Solemnis was performed by soloists and the New Philharmonia Orchestra and Chorus under Carlo Maria Giulini. On page three of the anniversary programme appeared the tribute to Beethoven.

Climbed on to immortality.
Then, at the end, from absolute silence sprang

The last quartets, his music's apogee.
Hear the adagio
Of the A minor – how life's low
Drudge and drone breaks into ecstasy,
Lark-tongued a violin soaring
On hopes ineffable, aspiring
To its pure essence – love's epiphany.

St. Paul's – Old and New*

A famous photograph comes to mind – your dome
Breasting hurricane waves of smoke and flame
Thirty one years ago.
You who rose up, a phoenix, after one
Fire of London, braved another then –
War's crash and undertow.

Weather, war, traffic, age have weakened you.
High time is it for us now to renew
The fabric of Wren's dream,
Shielding as best we may the solid grace,
And aerial soarings of his masterpiece
From envious, nibbling time.

*On November 8th, 1971, an evening of renaissance entertainment was held at the
Mansion House in the City of London as a tribute to the outgoing Lord Mayor for his
inspiring leadership in the Save St. Paul's appeal. It was attended by the Queen Mother.
As well as renaissance music for voice and instruments there was a poetry recital given
by Jill Balcon which included the poem specially written for the occasion. The poem
appeared in the Daily Telegraph on the morning of the entertainment.

Here was no matter of just making good
A stately pile of stone, lead, glass and wood,
But active piety
Towards them by whose quickness time was outpaced –
Donne, Nelson, Churchill, all who this way passed
To immortality.

No less we honour each mute generation,
Which kept this place alive by their devotion,
Then, as obscurely, died:
Whose worshipping – high ceremonials
And humble prayers alike – upheld St. Paul's,
Our city's, nation's pride.

City and nation, rich and poor who joined
To swell this fund, have passed the halfway point.
Now look we to the hour
Your bells shall utter, peal on jubilant peal,
A song of restoration, and reveal
Wren's vision made secure.

Hymn for Shakespeare's Birthday*

The Word was the beginning,
Spirit's and Reason's sire –
Sent the chartered planets spinning
Down their tracks of fire.
After that fiery birth
What endless aeons throng
Before this green and troubled earth
Can grow to her full song!

The all-creative Word
Surveying earth's huge span
From every maker there preferred
One man to speak for Man –
Gifted with art beyond
The best who'd worn the bays,
Sure pilot still on the profound
Heart's uncharted ways.

This man, whose vision ranged
Life's whole from bliss to woe,
Perceived how love, warped or estranged,
Will bring the highest low.
Today his birthday fell.
But he is born once more
Each time we come beneath his spell
And to his genius soar.

---

*Mr. Sam Wanamaker, as Executive Director of the Globe Playhouse Trust, planned a Gala Birthday Concert in Southwark Cathedral as one of the first among a series of events to be held during the week beginning 23rd April, 1972. He invited a number of distinguished poets and composers to contribute. The Poet Laureate's *Hymn* was set to music by Sir Lennox Berkeley for chorus and organ and was sung by the Exultate Singers. CDL was, by then, too ill to leave his room, so the poem was read by JB.

Another Day*

Through the hand's skill gradually
The head learnt its identity.
The shaping hand was touched and led
By the poem in the head.
Head and hand each went its own
Way, yet in strange unison.
Certainly the pair had set
Out by different routes; and yet
Their destination was the same.

A demon, jealous of the fame
That crowns the hard creative game,
BLEW – and turned back to brutish clay
The breathing replica of Day.
But Day survived and K. contrived
To keep her head and bring Day's head
To life again another day.

* In May 1970 we were staying with the late Kathleen and Johannes Schwarzenberg in their Tuscan villa (celebrated in *The Whispering Roots*). In the Cortile, our hostess was modelling CDL's head in clay, preparatory to casting it. A storm blew up and completely wrecked the head. Undaunted, the sculptor started again from scratch, successfully. The finished head is still there, and she captured completely C.'s expression when composing.

732